'In my hot youth'

BYRON'S LETTERS AND JOURNALS
VOLUME 1
1798–1810

. . . some six or seven good years ago
(Long ere I dreamt of dating from the Brenta)
I was most ready to return a blow,
And would not brook at all this sort of thing
In my hot youth—when George the Third was King.

DON JUAN, 1, 212

BYRON LANDING FROM A BOAT. By George Sanders, 1807

*Reproduced by gracious permission
of Her Majesty the Queen*

'In my hot youth'

BYRON'S LETTERS AND JOURNALS

Edited by
LESLIE A. MARCHAND

*The complete and unexpurgated text of
all the letters available in manuscript and
the full printed version of all others*

VOLUME 1
1798–1810

JOHN MURRAY

CONTENTS

This volume contains all the letters of Byron's early years including those of the first year of his pilgrimage to the East. It ends with his last letter from Constantinople on July 4, 1810, shortly before he departed for Athens. Here are the records of his rapid development from the serious school boy to the facetious youth and the maturing man of extraordinary perceptions and sympathies. By the end of this period he had already written his satire *English Bards and Scotch Reviewers* and the first two cantos of *Childe Harold* (published in 1812).

BYRON'S LETTERS AND JOURNALS

1. THE LETTERS

"I am not a cautious letter-writer and generally say what comes uppermost at the moment", Byron wrote on November 14, 1822, in an unpublished letter probably addressed to Mary Shelley. That in part is why his letters are such a clear mirror of his personality, of its weaknesses as well as its strengths, and why they reflect more accurately than any of the records left by his contemporaries the brilliance and charm and wit of his conversation, universally acknowledged to be extraordinary by those who knew him. Medwin's and Lady Blessington's accounts of his conversation, revealing as they are of the substance of his attitudes and prejudices, fall short of giving the true flavour and piquancy of his frankest letters. And Iris Origo says aptly of Teresa Guiccioli's recollections of his spoken words: ". . . she has no ear for any style but her own. It is possible that Byron's meaning is what she conveys; it is hardly possible that that is how he expressed it!" In the end he must be his own Boswell, and in large measure he succeeds better than Boswell himself (the Boswell of the journals) in exposing the many facets of an engaging egoist, a romantic with a balance of common sense which always brings him back to earth and to an honest recognition of his own frailties and limitations.

It is true that one side of Byron—and an important one—is seen in only occasional glimpses in the letters. There is little of Childe Harold or Manfred. That tortured spirit found expression in his poetry, always the safety valve of his deepest feelings. The letters do run the gamut of his emotions and moods, but always with a lighter touch. If one compares some of the letters he was writing from Italy at the same time that he was composing the last act of *Manfred* and the fourth canto of *Childe Harold*, one will see how successfully Byron could shut off one side of his divided self from the other. In the end we need both the poetry and the letters to see the whole Byron. His epistolary prose is less self-conscious than his verse and therefore a truer and more balanced picture of the man. Its bounding spontaneity is its charm. Byron himself realized, and often insisted, that his *Weltschmerz* poetry was a temporary aberration, "the lava of the imagination whose eruption prevents an earthquake". He wrote to

1

Thomas Moore on July 5, 1821, "I can never get people to understand that poetry is the expression of *excited passion*, and that there is no such thing as a life of passion any more than a continuous earthquake, or an eternal fever. Besides, who would ever *shave* themselves in such a state?"

It is the frankness and humanity of Byron's letters which lifts them above the great bulk of literary correspondence in the nineteenth century. They are sparing in the conscious verbal "prettiness" so common in letters at the time. It is a conversation with intimates rather than a literary exercise which is suggested throughout. Whether he was writing a love letter or an epistle to his banker, he cut through to the matter in hand with an enviable directness. And the cutting instrument was frequently ridicule, "the only *weapon* that the English climate cannot rust", he told Lady Blessington.

His style is familiar and unstrained but not quite colloquial. He eschewed "fine writing", but his letters are full of literary allusions and quotations that stuck in his memory and were often repeated in various contexts, modified to suit the occasion. His favourite sources were Scott and Shakespeare, Sheridan and Goldsmith, and the Restoration and eighteenth-century dramatists, even obscure ones. His preference was not for high-sounding rhetoric but for a catch phrase, or the speech of some minor character which could be twisted for his use. He was fond of such pat phrases as "this tight little island", referring to England, from a song by Dibden, and "Absurd womankind", from Scott's *Antiquary*. It was a shared cultural heritage which had become part of his language; the way in which he used it deprived it of any bookishness.

It is remarkable, considering how rapidly he wrote, seldom crossing out a word, that there is such precision in his diction and scarcely an awkward phrase. His sentences rush on without verbosity to a climax of clarity and emphasis. He spares his reader the conventional fawning flatteries and polite clichés and gets at the meat of his meaning. And that meaning follows through all the rapidly changing moods of a single letter and its inevitable and sometimes contradictory postscript. The mobility, the sincerity of the moment honestly recorded, contributes to the spell of his letters.

He usually shuns picturesque description. When tempted to indulge in it, particularly during his first pilgrimage, in Seville, or "sweet Cadiz", he remembers the gushing travel writers and reins in his Pegasus—"but damn description, it is always disgusting". Occasionally in Greece he allowed himself to paint a vivid scene. In a long letter to his mother he gave a colourful account of his descent into Tepelene in Albania as the sun was setting over Ali Pasha's castle. But more often, to other correspondents, he mingled description with facetiousness as in his exuberant letter to Hodgson from Athens on January 20, 1811: "I am living in the Capuchin Convent, Hymettus before me, the Acropolis behind, the Temple of Jove to my right, the Stadium in front, the town to the left, eh, Sir, there's a situation, there's your picturesque! nothing like that, Sir, in Lunnun, no not even the Mansion House. . . . I wish to be sure I had a few books, one's own works for instance, any damned nonsense on a long Evening".

Byron came nearest to serious description in his first letters from Venice. It was, he said, the "greenest island of my imagination", and he was not disappointed in it. "Venice pleases me as much as I expected—and I expected much", he wrote to Murray shortly after his arrival, "it is one of those places which I know before I see them—and has always haunted me the most after the East.— I like the gloomy gaiety of their gondolas—and the silence of their canals".

He was not unaware of his audience. Such long epistles as the one to John Murray giving details of his affair with Margarita Cogni was no doubt written with an eye to its appreciation by his friends in England and the literary coterie which gathered in the publisher's parlour. But most of his letters directed to his intimate friends, particularly those from Italy, have the ring of the deepest sincerity and are disarmingly self-revealing. These letters, in fact, reflect the freedom he had gained from his exile. They shared the liberating influences which brought *Don Juan* into being. He cast discretion to the winds and wrote exactly as he felt and thought, and his attack upon what he believed to be the hypocrisies of English life, and in fact of all life, overflowed from the poem into the letters, or more likely from the letters into the poem. But with all his ridicule of English society, a fond nostalgia overcame him from time to time. On June 8, 1822, he wrote to Moore: "Do you recollect, in the year of revelry 1814, the pleasantest parties and balls all over London?"

Byron shaped himself easily to his correspondents, for he was sensitively attuned to their interests and personalities. This was nowhere more apparent than in his letters to those friends who, he knew, had little sympathy for his Childe Harold moods. He wrote to Moore on March 10, 1817, asking him to assure Francis Jeffrey that "I . . . am not even *now*, the misanthropical and gloomy gentleman he takes me for, but a facetious companion, well to do with those with whom I am

3

intimate, and as loquacious and laughing as if I were a much cleverer fellow".

Incidentally, the voluminous pages he penned, leisurely or at white heat, to Murray and Moore are among his very best. During his Italian years particularly they were his chief correspondents, and he conversed with them on paper with great naturalness and freedom on subjects public and private, unconstrained by the thought that they might show his letters to others, in fact, sometimes wishing it. It is unfortunate that Moore's text is the only one we have of most of the letters addressed to him, for he bowdlerized them considerably in the printing and the originals have since disappeared. Byron's letters to Murray are almost like an intimate diary, for he bared his politics and his personal life to him with a surprising openness considering their vast differences in political, moral, and literary matters. It is a measure of Murray's devotion to his memory that most of these letters have survived intact.

In writing to Hobhouse and Kinnaird, with less thought of a more extensive audience, he indulged more freely his penchant for Falstaffian exaggeration and a mutually accepted cynical toughness inherited from his Cambridge friends and his associations with the Regency men about town. The Rabelaisian passages, many of which were excised in earlier printed texts, show a side of Byron which was little known in the nineteenth century but which is part of the whole man. It was well understood by his correspondents, for it was a common element in the ordinary conversation of part of the society he had known. It was shocking only when it was recorded in writing. But Byron might have said with Falstaff, whom he paid the compliment of quoting frequently, that his grossness did not engross him but "ascends me into the brain; dries me there all the foolish and dull and crudy vapours which environ it; makes it apprehensive, quick, forgetive, full of nimble, fiery, and delectable shapes; which delivered o'er to the voice, the tongue, which is the birth, becomes excellent wit".

Byron's letters to his half-sister Augusta are full of playful tenderness, and also of great frankness with respect to his "bleeding heart", but he complains of the "megrims and miseries" in her letters and says that he can't determine "whether your disorder is a broken heart or the earache".

To Lady Melbourne, whose sophisticated understanding and tolerance made her his chief confidante, he wrote circumstantial accounts of his love affairs, with a mingling of sincerity and tongue-in-cheek cynicism. He confessed to her both his passion for and his disillusion-

4

ment with Lady Caroline Lamb: "I do not mean to deny my attachment—it *was*—and it is not". And he wrote of his future wife, Annabella Milbanke, whom he dubbed the "Princess of Parallelograms" because of her interest in mathematics: "Her proceedings are quite rectangular, or rather we are two parallel lines prolonged to infinity side by side but never to meet". At another time he wrote of her as "a very superior woman a little encumbered with Virtue". And after Annabella's rejection of his proposal through Lady Melbourne, he wrote: "I congratulate A. & myself on our mutual escape.—That would have been but a *cold* collation, & I prefer hot suppers".

Nothing is more amusing in all of Byron's letters than his running account to Lady Melbourne of his unconsummated affair with Lady Francis Webster, in which for a time Platonism was "in some peril". After all his waggishness, he had some difficulty in convincing his confidante that he was serious in the affair, though he had told her "I cannot exist without some object of love". ". . . you really *wrong* me too", he wrote, "if you do not suppose that I would sacrifice everything for Ph [Francis Webster]—I hate sentiment—& in consequence my epistolary levity—makes you believe me as hollow & heartless as my letters are light".

To Annabella Milbanke in the year before his engagement he wrote with an uncensored candour that must have shocked her at the same time that it piqued her interest, since she had already decided that she was destined to reform the wicked Lord Byron, who, she wrote in her diary, "has not resolution (without aid) to adopt a new course of conduct and feelings". Despite his disclaimers he may have been more annoyed and hurt by her rejection than he pretended to Lady Melbourne. At any rate he adopted a devil-may-care attitude toward her sensitivities far different from his usual mode of adapting himself to his correspondents. He wrote: "The great object of life is Sensation—to feel that we exist—even though in pain—it is this 'craving void' which drives us to Gaming—to Battle—to Travel—to intemperate but keenly felt pursuits of every description whose principal attraction is the agitation inseparable from their accomplishment".

But once he had proposed again and been accepted, his whole attitude changed. He told Lady Melbourne: "you very much mistake me if you think I am lukewarm upon it . . . if I think she likes me—I shall be exactly what she pleases—it is her fault if she don't govern me properly—for never was anybody more easily managed". And to Annabella herself he wrote: "I will read what books you please—hear what arguments you please. . . . You shall be 'my Guide—

5

Philosopher and friend' my whole heart is yours. . . ." But it was his mind that was engaged and not much his heart, at least at this period.

Byron's humour in his letters springs mainly from his easy perception of the absurdity of the pretensions of human beings in the face of their own weaknesses, and he did not except himself from the general indictment. He confessed, "we are all selfish & I no more trust myself than others with a good motive". Often the humour turns upon the simple statement of a truth that conventional politeness would have covered up. And some of his best humour seems muted or casual. Of the Wedderburn Webster househould he said: "The place is very well, and quiet, and *the children only scream in a low voice*". Of the cadaverous Samuel Rogers' portrait he remarked it was "a likeness to the *death*". His humour is sometimes ribald, and not the less clever for that, as in the last (only recently printed) stanzas of his epistolary verses beginning, "My dear Mr. Murray,/ You're in a damned hurry,/ To set up this ultimate canto." Oftener it arises from his habit of giving an ironical or cynical ending to a serious statement, in the same way that he deflated sentiment in the final couplet of a stanza of *Don Juan*. Speaking of the third canto of *Childe Harold*, he told Moore: "I am glad you like it; it is a fine indistinct piece of poetical desolation, and my favourite. I was half mad during the time of its composition, between metaphysics, mountains, lakes, love unextinguishable, thoughts unutterable, and the nightmare of my own delinquencies. I should, many a good day, have blown my brains out, but for the recollection that it would have given pleasure to my mother-in-law; and, even *then*, if I could have been certain to haunt her. . . ."

He seldom indulged in wit for wit's sake. It was closely tied to some conviction or prejudice, keenly felt and enforced with irony or exaggeration. He wrote to his sister, "I hear you have been increasing his Majesty's Subjects, which in these times of War & tribulation is really patriotic, notwithstanding Malthus tells us that were it not for Battle, Murder, & Sudden death, we should be overstocked, I think we have latterly had a redundance of these national benefits, & therefore I give you all credit for your matronly behaviour".

He was more than half serious in his dislike of squalling children. Fortunately Augusta knew he was fond of her own and could take his banter in good part. "I don't know what Scrope Davies meant by telling you I liked Children, I abominate the sight of them so much that I have always had the greatest respect for the character of *Herod*."

He developed a style of outrageousness in his letters to Lady Melbourne to the point where even she sometimes could not tell whether he was serious. "As to Annabella," he wrote, "she requires time & all the cardinal virtues, & in the interim I am a little verging towards one who demands neither, & saves me besides the trouble of marrying by being married already. . . . I only wish she did not swallow so much supper, chicken wings—sweetbreads,—custards—peaches & *Port* wine—a woman should never be seen eating or drinking unless it be *lobster sallad & Champagne. . . ."*

Byron's letters are filled with arresting phrases and sentences pregnant with grains of truth encased in wit and hyperbole. It must be said in passing that he was not averse to repeating for different correspondents the clever phrases he had bestowed on others, a not uncommon habit of witty people. Even Coleridge was said to have repeated his brilliant and supposedly spontaneous gems of wisdom in various companies.

Byron's witticisms must be read with some knowledge of his personality and character and his customary modes of expression. He confessed to Moore: "my turn of mind is so given to taking things in the absurd point of view, that it breaks out in spite of me every now and then". There is such a temptation to quote Byron's *bons mots* that the quality of his ordinary serious communication tends to be neglected.

Nowhere has there been more misunderstanding than in the interpretation of Byron's remarks on women, love, and marriage. It is difficult now in this age of freedom of expression in such matters to comprehend how shocking *Don Juan* was to the Romantics of his own time and to the Victorians because he dared to remind them that love and sex were sometimes funny or ridiculous, particularly in their hypocritical manifestations. And many of the innuendoes in *Don Juan* are more explicit and less delicately stated in the letters.

One must recognize in Byron a tendency to boast of his love affairs, or at least to write lightly of them, perhaps a natural concomitant of his deep-seated insecurity resulting from his lameness, a feeling that he must demonstrate his physical capabilities despite his handicap, in the same way and for the same reasons that he vaunted his swimming exploits. One may smile at his boyish boasting to his friend the Rev. John Becher of his first London excesses: "I have this moment received a prescription from Pearson, not for any *complaint*, but from *debility*, and literally *too much Love*. . . . In fact, my blue eyed Caroline, who is only sixteen, has been lately so *charming*, that though we are both in perfect health, we are at present commanded to *repose*, being nearly worn out.—" But it may seem a less attractive aspect of his character

7

when in his maturity he writes with seeming callousness and cynicism to Hoppner of the details of his liaison with the Countess Guicciolo. Yet there is evidence in both instances that his levity was not the true measure of his feelings, but only his habitual mode of avoiding the expression of sentiment in his letters.

Even when he was deeply involved, he could see the humorous aspects of passion. This was true not only in his accounts of his affair with Lady Frances Webster: "We have progressively improved into a less spiritual species of tenderness—but the seal is not yet fixed though the wax is preparing for the impression". Of the black-eyed Marianna Segati, wife of a "Merchant of Venice", with whom he confessed he was in "fathomless love", he could write lightly, "we are one of the happiest—unlawful couples on this side of the Alps", and again, "her great merit is in finding out mine—there is nothing so amiable as discernment". He could write as amusingly of Margarita Cogni, that "gentle tigress" with a fine figure, "fit to breed gladiators from". But he could also be flippant in writing of Teresa Guiccioli, with whom he had fallen desperately and sincerely in love. He described her as "fair as Sunrise—and warm as Noon", and added with a slightly cynical appraisal of the ease of his conquest: "we had but ten days—to manage all our little matters in beginning middle and end, & we managed them—and I have done my duty with the proper consummation. . . ." And after he had become more at ease in his role as *Cavalier Servente*, he wrote to her: "I kiss you more often than I have ever kissed you—and this (if Memory does not deceive me) should be a fine number of times, counting from the beginning". And shortly after that he wrote a sentimental love letter in her copy of Mme. de Staël's *Corinne*: "you will recognize the hand-writing of him who passionately loved you, and you will divine that, over a book which was yours, he could only think of love. In that word, beautiful in all languages, but most so in yours,—*Amor mio*—is comprised my existence here and hereafter. . . ." In which of these statements do we find the real Lord Byron? Undoubtedly in all.

He assured Kinnaird that he had given up miscellaneous harlotry and now confined himself "to the strictest adultery". And replying to a letter from Hoppner telling him of a fantastic story of his abduction of the Countess, he said: "I should like to know *who* has been carried off—except poor dear *me*—I have been more ravished myself than anybody since the Trojan war. . . ." There was more than a grain of truth in that, for after *Childe Harold* had made him famous, he was pursued by dozens of women, many of them quite unknown to him.

8

To a Swiss girl who asked to see him, he wrote: "Excepting your compliments (which are only excusable because you don't know me) you write like a clever woman for which reason I hope you *look* as *un*like one as possible—I never knew but one of your country—M^e. de Stael—and she is frightful as a precipice. . . . If you will become acquainted with me—I will promise not to make love to you unless you like it. . . ."

He emphasized again and again that he was not the traditional Don Juan. ". . . when they give me a character for 'Art'", he wrote to Lady Melbourne, "it is surely most mistaken—no one was ever more heedless". As to his being a heartless pursuer of women, after he had "spared" Lady Frances Webster, he assured Lady Melbourne: "I do detest every thing which is not perfectly mutual. . . . she had so much more dread of the D—l than gratitude for his kindness—and I am not yet sufficiently in his good graces to indulge my own passions at the certain misery of another".

What he had to regret most was his kindness to women who forced their attention on him. He had once told Lady Melbourne: "I could love any thing on earth that appeared to wish it". That amiable weakness brought him many troubles. The most noteworthy example was his unfortunate and unwanted affair with Claire Clairmont, whose persistence in the end forced him, against his nature and his wishes, to be cruel. "I never loved nor pretended to love her", he confided to Kinnaird, "but a man is a man—& if a girl of eighteen comes prancing to you at all hours—there is but one way—the suite of all this is that she was with *child*—& returned to England to assist in peopling that desolate island. . . . This comes of 'putting it about' (as Jackson calls it) & be damned to it—& thus people come into the world".

From time to time he tried to steel himself against his weakness. The conflict is apparent in his later letters from Italy. He wrote to Hobhouse in 1819: "I feel & feel it bitterly—that a man should not consume his life at the side and on the bosom of a woman . . . this Cicisbean existence is to be condemned". And when he was being urged by Teresa to follow her to Pisa, Byron wrote to Moore: "It is awful work, this love, and prevents all a man's projects of good or glory". But he fought against his love and his kindness in vain, and he confessed to Augusta in 1821: ". . . without being so *furiously* in love as at first, I am more attached to her [Teresa]—than I thought it possible to be to any woman after three years. . . ."

Byron was not an unbiased portrayer of character, but his sketches of individuals are sharply drawn, even when they are caustic and un-

9

fair. ". . . everything that confirms or extends one's observations on life & character delights me, even when I don't know people", he wrote to Lady Melbourne. His portraits were frequently sparked by some irritant or absurdity in the character. His exasperation with his valet Fletcher's inability to cope with foreign situations came to a climax during his first visit to Greece, when he sent him home and wrote to his mother: "Besides the perpetual lamentations after beef and beer, the stupid bigoted contempt for every thing foreign, and insurmountable incapacity of acquiring even a few words of any language, rendered him, like all other English servants, an incumbrance". He described with relish the absurd character of Wedderburn Webster, who asked Byron to accompany him and his wife to a tragedy "to see his *wife cry!*" and who boasted of his wife's doting on him at the moment when he was on the verge of being cuckolded.

Byron could be wickedly cutting in his comments on the literary figures who had offended him, either in person or by their writing. He said that "Southey should have been a Parish-clerk, and Wordsworth a man-midwife". His quarrel with Southey reached its peak when he learned that the older poet had said that he and Shelley "had formed a League of Incest" in Switzerland. "He lied like a rascal", he wrote to Hobhouse, "for they *were not sisters*". And when word came that his friend Rogers was gossiping about him, he wrote to Murray: ". . . if he values his quiet, let him look to it—in three months I could restore him to the Catacombs". And later: ". . . there is a mean minuteness to his mind & tittle-tattle that I dislike—ever since I *found him out* . . . why don't he go to bed? What does he do travelling?"

Byron was friendly to Leigh Hunt but extremely candid in writing about him to his friends in England. "He is a good man", he told Moore, "with some poetical elements in his chaos; but spoilt by the Christ-Church Hospital and a Sunday newspaper—to say nothing of the Surrey Gaol, which conceited him into a martyr. . . . When I saw *Rimini* in MS. I told him I deemed it good poetry at bottom, disfigured only a by strange style. His answer was, that his style was a system, or *upon system*, or some such cant; and when a man talks of system, his case is hopeless. . . ." Of Hunt's children, who had defaced his walls at the Casa Lanfranchi, quite unrestrained by their parents, he wrote to Mary Shelley: "They are dirtier and more mischievous than Yahoos what they can['t] destroy with their filth they will with their fingers. . . . was there ever such a *kraal* out of the Hottentot country".

Byron had nothing but praise for Shelley, both before and after his death. He wrote to Douglas Kinnaird on June 2, 1821: *"Shelley* is is *truth* itself, and *honour* itself, notwithstanding his out-of-the-way notions about religion". And to Murray after Shelley was drowned, he proclaimed: "You were all brutally mistaken about Shelley who was without exception—the *best* and least selfish man I ever knew—I never knew one who was not a beast in comparison".

He repented the harsh words he had written about Keats after Shelley sent him a copy of *Adonais*: "Had I known that Keats was dead—or that he was alive and so sensitive—I should have omitted some remarks . . . to which I was provoked by his *attack* on *Pope*, and my disapproval of *his own* style of writing".

In Dr. Johnson's phrase, Byron was a good hater, though his friends testified that he was more formidable in correspondence than in person. And yet he was easily reconciled with Jeffrey, whom he had attacked so bitterly in *English Bards and Scotch Reviewers*, when the editor of the *Edinburgh* published a laudatory review of *Childe Harold* and indicated that he had not written the sarcastic review of Byron's early poems. After that Byron would hear no evil spoken of Jeffrey. His annoyance with his friends in England because of their neglect in matters of business and publishing caused him to write blistering reprimands but they never reached the frenzied heights of his Philippics against Brougham or Romilly or Southey.

His quarrels with Murray stemmed from the publisher's failure to answer letters, his carelessness in printing, and his temerity in publishing *Don Juan* and other "dangerous" poems like *Cain*. Seldom in history has a publisher been scolded as Byron belaboured Murray. It was only because Murray knew Byron's foibles and his temperament so well, and because he was genuinely fond of him, that he was able to maintain his friendship after the publishing alliance was broken. The complaints about the printing were not wholly unjustified, and yet Murray had much to contend with. Byron's handwriting was careless and sometimes illegible, at least to the printers, and he more and more refused to read the proofs himself but left them to Murray or Hobhouse, who scarcely had time to go over them carefully. But Byron was always easily mollified. He added a postscript to one of his most heated letters: "I have since the above was written—received yours of the 11th . . . and can't keep resentment—it hath melted my flint".

Byron's business letters are models of directness and are never quite dull. There is an electric energy in these succinct statements that puts the mark of his personality on them. In writing to his attorney and business agent John Hanson he seldom attempted wit. But he enlivened his epistles to his banker friend Douglas Kinnaird, who was both his business manager and literary agent while he was abroad, with some of his most amusing buffooneries. When he first accepted the advice of his friends not to publish *Don Juan*, he wrote with mock indignation: "this acquiescence is some thousands of pounds out of my pocket—the thought of which brings tears to my eyes—I have imbibed such a love for money that I keep some Sequins in a drawer, to count and cry over them once a week. . . ." He joked with Kinnaird about his growing avarice, and he confided: "I always looked to about thirty as the barrier of any real or fierce delight in the passions—and determined to work them out in the younger ore and better veins of the Mine . . . and now the dross is coming—and I loves lucre. . . ."

He had urged Kinnaird to get as much as he could for the manuscripts he had sent. But at the same time he defended his publisher's business instincts. "I believe M[urray] to be a good man with a personal regard for me.—But a bargain is in its very essence a *hostile* transaction. . . . I contend that a bargain even between brethren is a declaration of war. . . . I have no doubt that he would lend or give—freely—what he would refuse for value received in MSS. So do not think too hardly of him."

Unlike Keats and some of the other Romantic poets, Byron did not consistently expound his poetic philosophy in his letters. Yet some attitudes toward poetry are strongly expressed. If they are not wholly consistent, that is partly due to the fact that he spoke from the mood of the moment, and partly because he had a dual concept of poetry: the Popean ideal, on the one hand, of balanced wit and pungent satire, in polished verse that he emulated but never fully achieved; and the Romantic goal, on the other, of "Look in your heart and write" poetry as self-expression, a liberation of the inner feelings. While most of his poetry, indeed some of his best, fell into the second category, it is necessary to understand that in his deepest being he did not completely approve of it. Hence his deprecation of Romantic poetry, his own and others. He wrote to Annabella Milbanke in 1813: "I by no means rank poetry or poets high in the scale of intellect—this may look like affectation—but it is my real opinion". And to Murray in 1819 he wrote: "If one's years can't be better employed than in sweating poesy—a man had better be a ditcher".

His pretence that he could not revise (his manuscripts show that he did make extensive verbal changes) was partly to emphasize his low

12

opinion of the craft, and partly a defence against the demand by Murray and other friends that he refurbish his poems to make them more acceptable to a squeamish British public. "I can never *recast* anything", he wrote, "I am like the Tiger—if I miss the first spring—I go growling back to my jungle again—but if I *do* hit—it is crushing." Devotion to truth was the one thing he clung to as justifying writing, even of the lesser genre: "But I hate things *all fiction*", he wrote to Murray in 1817; "there should always be some foundation of fact for the most airy fabric—and pure invention is but the talent of a liar".

It was only when he found in *Don Juan* a medium of his own, more pliable than his Popean imitations, less restrictive than the single moods of self-expression, that he defended his work with conviction, whether the unconventionality of his most daring attacks on accepted values in the mock-epic, or the political and theological *lèse-majesté* of *The Vision of Judgment*, written "in my finest ferocious Caravaggio style".

His defence of *Don Juan* against the fears of his friends is a recurrent and entertaining subject of his letters from Italy. At first, not knowing how it would be received, he wrote lightly of it, saying that his purpose was to make it "a little quietly facetious upon every thing", and that his only aim was "to giggle and make giggle". But later when he realized its possibilities as a free expression of the truth of life as he saw it, he changed his tone: "D[on] Juan will be known by and bye for what it is intended," he wrote to Murray, "a *Satire* on *abuses* of the present states of Society—and not as an eulogy of vice—it may be now and then voluptuous—I can't help that—Ariosto is worse— Smollett . . . ten times worse—and Fielding no better. No girl will ever be seduced by reading D. J.—no—no—she will go to Little's poems & Rousseau's romans for that—or even to the immaculate De Stael—they will encourage her & not the Don—who laughs at that—and—and—most other things". Of the Countess Guiccioli's objections to the poem, he wrote: "The truth is that *it is* TOO TRUE —and the women hate every thing which strips off the tinsel of *Sentiment*". "You sha'n't make Canticles of my Cantos", he protested. "The poem will please if it is lively—if it is stupid it will fail—but I will have none of your damned cutting & slashing." "Come what may", he wrote again, "I never will flatter the million's canting in any shape. . . ." And when Murray and others urged him to write some "great work" which would better employ his powers, he replied: "you have so many '*divine*' poems—is it nothing to have written a Human one? without any of your worn out machinery".

Byron's opinions of other writers expressed in the letters do not amount to literary criticism, but his pungent and reflective passages on contemporary and older writers display the characteristic bent of his mind. When he was not immediately irritated by provocation or controversy, he could pronounce balanced judgments of some of those whom he attacked most bitterly. Of one he had ridiculed the most he wrote: ". . . there must be many 'fine things' in Wordsworth . . . but there can be no doubt of his powers to do about anything". And he defended Coleridge to Murray: "I won't have you sneer at 'Christabel' —it is a fine wild poem".

Among contemporaries he preferred Scott, Gifford, and Moore, who have "no nonsense—nor affectations . . . as for the rest whom I have known—there was always more or less of the author about them —the pen peeping from behind the ear & the thumbs a little inky or so". Of older writers he generally defended Pope against the field. "I will show you more *imagery* in twenty lines of Pope than in any equal length of quotation in English poesy. . . ." and he proceeded to do so, drawing striking phrases from Pope's lines on Sporus.

It is difficult to generalize about Byron's pronouncements on religion in his letters. Some of them are serious, some are obviously intended to shock or amuse, and some voice an honest incertitude. He had read enough of Hume and the Voltairian sceptics before he left Cambridge to unsettle his faith in the dogmas of the established religion, both Catholic and Protestant, and to make him an agnostic, though he repudiated vehemently the appellation of atheist. It is doubtful that his occasional references to Catholicism as "the best religion" in his letters from Italy were anything more than persiflage to bait his English friends. But both his journals and his letters indicate a growing preoccupation with some of the fundamental problems of religion such as he had wrestled with in his metaphysical dramas, *Manfred, Cain*, and *Heaven and Earth*. But he never completely made up his mind. The most that could be said is that he latterly came to doubt some aspects of his own scepticism.

But in his brash youth he was quite positive. He wrote to Hodgson, who was about to take orders: "I will have nothing to do with your immortality; we are miserable enough in this life, without the absurdity of speculating upon another". And after speaking of "the seventy-two villainous sects who are tearing each other to pieces for the love of the Lord and the hatred of each other", he added: "Talk of Galileeism? Show me the effects—are you better, wiser, kinder by your precepts? I will show you ten Mussulmans shall shame you in all good will

14

towards men, prayer to God, and duty to their neighbours". And when Hodgson came back with "evidences", Byron answered: "As to miracles, I agree with Hume that it is more probable men should *lie* or be *deceived*, than that things out of the course of nature should so happen. . . . And our carcases, which are to rise again, are they worth raising? I hope, if mine is, that I shall have a better *pair of legs* than I have moved on these two-and-twenty years, or I shall be sadly behind in the squeeze into Paradise".

In later years he was more likely to be flippant than serious on the subject. He wrote to Murray in 1817, ". . . when I turn thirty—I will turn devout—I feel a great vocation that way in Catholic churches —and when I hear the Organ." And to Moore: "One certainly has a soul; but how it came to allow itself to be enclosed in a body is more than I can imagine". And yet beneath his levity was an undercurrent of serious concern, as he confessed to Hobhouse about the same time: "I have read a good deal of Voltaire lately. I wish you were with me— for every now and then there is something to kill me with laughing— what I dislike is his extreme inaccuracy. . . . I do not know what to believe—which is the devil—to have no religion at all—all sense & senses are against it—but all belief & some evidence is for it—it is walking in the dark over a rabbit warren or a garden with steel traps & spring guns—for my part I have such a detestation of *some* of the articles of faith—that I would not subscribe to them—if I were as sure as St. Peter *after* the Cock crew".

It is evident that he was attracted by some aspects of Catholicism, its pageantry and its mothering protection of its believers. According to Medwin, Byron once said: "I have often wished I had been born a Catholic. That purgatory of theirs is a comfortable doctrine. . . ." In a letter to Moore, Byron said that Catholicism "is by far the most elegant worship, hardly excepting the Greek mythology. What with incense, pictures, statues, altars, shrines, relics, and the real presence, confession, absolution—there is something sensible to grasp at". But, though he knew that Moore was a Catholic, albeit not a very strict one, he did not suppress his qualifications: "Besides", he added, "it leaves no possibility of doubt, for those who swallow their Deity, really and truly, in transubstantiation, can hardly find anything else otherwise than easy of digestion".

Byron was much taken with some epitaphs in the Certosa Cemetery at Ferrara: "Martini Luigi *Implora pace*", and "Lucrezia Picini Implora eterna quiete". "That was all", he wrote to Hoppner: "but it appears to me that these two and three words comprise and

15

compress all that can be said on the subject—and then in Italian they are absolute Music. They contain doubt—hope—and humility—nothing can be more pathetic than the 'Implora' and the modesty of the request".

Byron's political stance comes out more clearly in his correspondence than does his religious belief. That does not mean that all his political views were consistent, nor that circumstances and personalities did not govern them to a degree. Though he espoused generally Whiggish causes, he found himself considerably left of centre in his maiden speech in the House of Lords on the Frame Bill, embarrassingly so, for he wished to defer to Lord Holland. His humanitarian appeal for sympathy for "the wretched mechanic, who is famished into guilt" was a novelty in that House and brought him more praise from Burdett and other Radicals in the lower House than from the Lords, Tory or Whig. Not being able to compromise his beliefs he had no chance of a successful political career, and he soon tired of the "Parliamentary mummeries" and proclaimed that he had "no intention to 'strut another hour' on that stage".

But the humanitarian impulse governed his political sympathies and associations henceforth and coloured his remarks on political subjects in his letters. He had the eighteenth-century liberal's distrust of the tyranny of governments and of monarchical absolutism, the working of which he saw in the Holy Alliance. He was a defender of the French Revolution, but not of its mob rule. "I can understand and enter into the feelings of Mirabeau and La Fayette—but I have no sympathy with Robespierre—and Marat. . . ." He disapproved of Hobhouse's associates in radical politics in England. ". . . if these sort of awkward butchers are to get the upper hand—*I* for one will declare *off* . . . I know that revolutions are not to be made with rose water, but though some blood may & must be shed on such occasions, there is no reason it should be *clotted*. . . ."

Yet he saw revolution in England as necessary to overthrow the Tory tyranny. "Your infamous government will drive all honest men into the necessity of reversing it—I see nothing left for it— but a republic *now* . . . all history and experience is in its favour even the French—for they butchered thousands of citizens at first, yet *more* were killed in any one of the great battles [those of the wars that brought back the Bourbons] than ever perished by a democratical proscription—America is a Model of force and freedom & moderation with all the coarseness and rudeness of its people."

It was in the hope of freeing Italy from the Imperial tyranny that

Byron joined with the Carbonari in Ravenna, but it is significant that he was drawn into the movement by Count Gamba and others of the aristocratic revolutionaries. It fired his imagination more than any political activity he had participated in during his brief parliamentary experience. He found it the very "poetry of Politics", as he wrote in his diary. The failure of the Italian insurrection left him disappointed (the Italians should return to making operas and macaroni, he said) but not in despair. It was then that he turned his thoughts to the Greeks and their struggle for independence.

Byron's final letters from Greece show a seriousness of purpose in his venture only occasionally enlivened by the warmth of his wit. When writing to the quarrelling Greeks themselves or to the Greek Committee in London, he never wrote despairingly. To his Genoa banker Barry, Byron opened his mind more than to most others: "Of the Greeks I shall say nothing, till I can say something better—except that I am not discouraged. . . . I shall stay out as long as I can—and do all I can for these Greeks—but I cannot exaggerate—they must expect only the truth from me both of and to them".

He wrote patiently but with humour to Bowring, secretary of the Greek Committee: "The Supplies of the Committee are some useful— and all excellent in their kind—but occasionally hardly *practical* enough in the present state of Greece—for instance the Mathematical instruments are thrown away—none of the Greeks know a problem from a poker—we must conquer first—and plan afterwards.—The use of the trumpets too may be doubted—unless Constantinople were Jericho. . . ."

In one of his last letters from Greece Byron told Bowring: "I shall continue to pursue my former plan of stating to the Committee things as they *really* are—I am an enemy to Cant of all kinds—but it will be seen in time—who are or are not the firmest friends of the Greek cause—or who will stick by them the longest—the Lempriere dictionary quotation Gentlemen—or those who neither dissemble their faults not their virtues".

He had written to Hobhouse before going to Greece: "If I go there —I shall do my best to civilize their mode of treating their prisoners— and could I only save a single life—whether Turk of Greek—I should live 'mihi carior'—and I trust not less so to my friends". And it was this humanitarian impulse that governed his last actions when his frustrations bore him down. He wrote rather pathetically to Kinnaird: "after all it is better playing at Nations than gaming at Almacks or Newmarket or in piecing or dinnering".

In the whole range of the correspondence—and it seems hopeless to

give an adequate idea of its variety and scope in so brief a summary—
a personality emerges that is distinct and that scarcely changes signifi-
cantly with the passing of the years, except for the widening of sympathies and a more tolerant view of the world. His major convictions
were formed early, and remained throughout his life.

The fascination of Byron's letters derives from his immense zest for
life, despite his melancholy, which, in fact, was largely siphoned off in
his poetry. He had an irresistible eagerness for exploring the minds
and emotions, both of others and of himself. The letters are filled with
an abundance of epigrammatic reflections that burrow deep into
motives and are sharply phrased: "I begin to find out that nothing
but virtue will do in this damned world;" "my heart always alights
upon the nearest *perch*"; "All men are intrinsical rascals—and I am
only sorry that not being a dog I can't bite them".

This healthy and good-humoured cynicism combined with a general
benevolence toward human frailty, including his own, is a pervading
tone. And perhaps the key to the whole remarkable performance is to
be seen in this declaration, applied to his poetry but equally applicable
to his letters: "I have flattered no ruling powers; I have never concealed a single thought that tempted me". That is why the letters are
truly a self-portrait, and why Byron's literary reputation will at last
rest as much on them as on his poetry.

2. THE JOURNALS

Byron's journals reveal the scope and intensity of his intellectual
curiosity. His interests range from an analysis of his own emotional
state to the affairs of the country, the world, and the universe. Much
less attention is given to self-absorption than is common in most
intimate diaries. The objectivity extends to his own attitudes, ambi-
tions, and weaknesses. The occasional inward look is mingled casually
with more wide-ranging concerns. On December 6, 1813, he wrote:
"This journal is a relief. When I am tired—as I generally am—out
comes this, and down goes every thing. But I can't read it over; and
God knows what contradictions it may contain. If I am sincere with
myself (and I fear one lies more to one's self than to any one else),
every page should confute, refute, and utterly abjure its predecessor".
The next day he recorded: "Awoke, and up an hour before being
called; but dawdled three hours in dressing. When one subtracts from
life infancy (which is vegetation),—sleep, eating, and swilling—
buttoning and unbuttoning—how much remains of downright existence? The summer of a dormouse". At the end of a paragraph of

amused contemplation of the number of mistresses, *"divorced"* and *"divorceable"* ladies, and *"understood* courtesans", outnumbering "the regular mercenaries", he had seen from his box at Covent Garden, he added: "How I delight in observing life as it really is!—and myself, after all, the worst of any. But no matter—I must avoid egotism, which, just now, would be vanity".

But much more space in the journals is devoted to his reading, his interest in other people, and his passionate concern with political and human problems. While writing the 1813–14 journal he was most deeply involved in the torturing conflicts of his relations with his sister Augusta, with Lady Frances Webster, and with Annabella Milbanke, yet there are only hints of this in his diary. But Byron's convictions about the world were never dispassionate, and often his analysis of events and personalities reveals his own perplexities.

After reading a private collection of Burns's letters, he wrote: "They are full of oaths and obscene songs. What an antithetical mind!— tenderness, roughness—delicacy, coarseness—sentiment, sensuality— soaring and grovelling, dirt and deity—all mixed up in that one compound of inspired clay! It seems strange; a true voluptuary will never abandon his mind to the grossness of reality. It is by exalting the earthly, the material, the physique of our pleasures, by veiling these ideas, by forgetting them altogether, or, at least, never naming them hardly to one's self, that we alone can prevent them from disgusting".

At this time Byron was going into Whig society a good deal, and he recorded much amusing gossip about Sheridan, all the Holland House circle, and many others. But it is more than gossip; it is a fresh and generally sympathetic examination of the inner springs of other personalities as they impinged on his own.

He notes: "To Lady Melbourne I write with most pleasure—and her answers, so sensible, so *tactique*—I never met with half her talent. If she had been a few years younger, what a fool she would have made of me, had she thought it worth her while,—and I should have lost a valuable and most agreeable *friend*". Byron was still as much a lion of society as he had been on the publication of *Childe Harold*, but he preferred the conversation of such men as Sheridan to the small talk of the salons. He recorded on March 22, 1814: "Last night, *party* at Lansdowne House. To-night, *party* at Lady Charlotte Greville's— deplorable waste of time, and something of temper. Nothing imparted —nothing acquired—talking without ideas:—if any thing like *thought* in my mind, it was not on the subjects on which we were gabbling. Heigho!—and in this way half London pass what is called life".

19

His political confessions were as frank and as passionate. "I have simplified my politics into an utter detestation of all existing governments. . . . The fact is, riches is power, and poverty is slavery all over the earth, and one sort of establishment is no better nor worse for a *people* than another." In another entry he observed: "After all, even the highest game of crowns and sceptres, what is it? *Vide* Napoleon's last twelvemonth. . . . But men never advance beyond a certain point; and here we are, retrograding, to the dull, stupid old system,—the balance of Europe—poising straws upon kings' noses, instead of wringing them off! . . . To be the first man—not the dictator—not the Sylla, but the Washington or the Aristides—the leader of talent and truth—is next to the Divinity!"

The diary of his Alpine journey with Hobhouse in 1816, kept for his sister, contains some of his most picturesque descriptions of the scenery that furnished the background for *Manfred*, and it reflects the melancholy mood of that drama. From 7000 feet he observed the Jungfrau and its glaciers. "Heard the Avalanches falling every five minutes nearly—as if God was pelting the Devil down from Heaven with snow balls . . . the clouds rose from the opposite valley curling up perpendicular precipices—like the foam of the Ocean of Hell . . .very fine Glacier—like a *frozen hurricane* . . . the whole day as fine in point of weather—as the day on which Paradise was made.—Passed *whole woods of withered pines—all withered*—trunks stripped and barkless—branches lifeless—done by a single winter—their appearance reminded me of me and my family."

The Ravenna diary, written in the early part of 1821, is a record of Byron's daily life and reflections at a time of imminent revolution. His reading, his writing (he composed one poetic drama and planned another while awaiting the uprising), and his thoughts and introspections get more space than do either the plans of the Carbonari or his meetings with the Countess Guiccioli, deeply as he was committed to both.

"January 5, 1821. Rose late—dull and drooping—the weather dripping and dense. Snow on the ground, and sirocco above in the sky, like yesterday. Roads up to the horse's belly, so that riding (at least for pleasure) is not very feasible. Added a postscript to my letter to Murray. Read the conclusion, for the fiftieth time (I have read all W. Scott's novels at least fifty times), of the third series of *Tales of my Landlord*—grand work—Scotch Fielding, as well as great English poet—wonderful man! I long to get drunk with him. . . . Fed the two cats, the hawk, and the tame (but *not tamed*) crow. Read Mitford's

History of Greece—Xenophon's *Retreat of the Ten Thousand.* . . . Hear the carriage—order pistols and great coat, as usual—necessary articles. Weather cold—carriage open, and inhabitants somewhat savage. Fine fellows, though,—good material for a nation. Out of chaos God made a world, and out of high passions comes a people. Clock strikes—going out to make love. Somewhat perilous, but not disagreeable."

From time to time he was exhilarated by the thought of a free Italy, though he had to view it in the light of some of the less than heroic deeds of the revolutionary leaders: "It is no great matter", he wrote after some of the Carbonari put him in peril by depositing their arms in his house unannounced, "supposing that Italy could be liberated, who or what is sacrificed. It is a grand object—the very *poetry* of politics".

But at other times low spirits and depression settled upon him. These were moods that he confined to his journal and that he did not reveal in his letters. On January 25th, three days after his thirty-third birthday, he wrote: "Scrawled this additional page of life's log-book. One day more is over of it and me:—but 'which is best, life or death, the gods only know', as Socrates said to his judges. . . . It has been said that the immortality of the soul is a *grand peut-être*—but still it is a grand one. Every body clings to it—the stupidest, and dullest, and wickedest of human bipeds is still persuaded that he is immortal". And he asked himself a few days later: "Why, at the very height of desire and human pleasure—worldly, social, amorous, ambitious, or even avaricious,—does there mingle a certain sense of doubt and sorrow—a fear of what is to come—a doubt of what *is*—a retrospect to the past, leading to a prognostication of the future? . . . I allow sixteen minutes, though I never counted them, to any given or supposed possession".

Byron's curious journal which he called his "Detached Thoughts", written mostly in the solitude of the Palazzo Guiccioli in Ravenna before he joined Teresa in Pisa in the autumn of 1821, is alternately objective and subjective. Much of it is composed of piquant recollections of his school days and school friends, and of the people he had known during his years of fame in England. There is a crisp freshness, at once a balance and a relish in his assessment of persons and events, and the same beyond-the-tomb carelessness of accepted opinion as in much of *Don Juan*. His nostalgia for England shines through his anecdotes of "Monk" Lewis, of Scrope Davies, of Sheridan, of his experiences at Drury Lane, of his association with the Dandies and with gamblers and wits and men about town.

But there were memories that he could not trust even to a private diary, though he could not refrain from hinting at them. "If I could explain at length the *real* causes which have contributed to increase this perhaps natural temperament of mine, this Melancholy which hath made me a bye-word, nobody would wonder; but it is impossible without doing much mischief. . . . I have written my memoirs, but omitted *all* the really *consequential* and *important* parts, from deference to the dead, to the living, and to those who must be both."

One thing led to another in his recollections. His regret that he had not studied languages more attentively reminded him that he was distracted from his study of Armenian by falling in love (he had written that the lady was "less obdurate than the language"). This in turn evoked the conclusion: ". . . my master, the Padre Pasquale Aucher . . . assured me 'that the terrestrial Paradise had certainly been in Armenia'. I went seeking it—God knows where—did I find it? Umph! Now and then, for a minute or two".

In his speculations on immortality he arrived at some strange but tentative conclusions. They were intellectual rather than religious, cosmic rather than theological. What seemed to make it probable, he felt, was the action of the mind, which was in perpetual exertion, even in sleep. "It acts also so very independent of the body. . . . Now that this should not act separately as well as jointly, who can pronounce? . . . A *material* resurrection seems strange and even absurd, except for purposes of punishment; and all punishment, which is to *revenge* rather than *correct*, must be *morally wrong*. . . . But God help us all! It is at present a sad jar of atoms."

He recalled that he had been inclined to materialism in philosophy, but: "The devil's in it, if, after having had a Soul (as surely the *Mind*, or whatever you call it, *is*) in this world, we must part with it in the next, for an Immortal Materiality. I own my partiality for *Spirit*". One would be tempted to suspect flippancy had this remark been in a letter: "I am always most religious on a sun-shiny day". But he added with apparent seriousness: "The night is also a religious concern; and even more so, when I viewed the Moon and Stars through Herschell's telescope, and saw that they were worlds".

From this he could go on to lively recollections of conversations with Sheridan and George Colman. to his sentimental meeting with Lord Clare on the road to Pisa, to his conversation with a peasant girl in Ravenna who had never heard of the Pope, and to other matters conjured by his nimble mind.

His last journal was written in Cephalonia while he was living in the village of Metaxata waiting for an opportune moment to join forces with the Greeks on the mainland when they ceased their internal strife and were ready to strike a united blow against the Turks. Here he felt that he could be more outspoken about the Greeks than in his letters. "I did not come here", he wrote, "to join a faction but a nation and to deal with honest men and not with speculators and peculators. . . ." But he concluded: "after all one should not despair, though all the foreigners that I have hitherto met with amongst the Greeks are going or gone back disgusted. Whoever goes into Greece at present should do it as Mrs. Fry went into Newgate—not in expectation of meeting with any especial indication of existing probity, but in the hope that time and better treatment will reclaim the present burglarious and larcenous tendencies which have followed this General Gaol delivery".

But his last entry in the journal was a consideration of his resources, financial and personal, for creating a corps among the Suliotes, the bravest of the Greek soldiers, to "keep on foot a respectable clan, or sept, or tribe, or horde, for some time, and, as I have not any motive for so doing but the well-wishing of Greece, I should hope with advantage".

The exuberance, the clear candour of their statement of what came uppermost to his active mind make Byron's journals an excellent supplement to the letters as an almost total exposure of a truly unique personality. "Tout comprendre est tout pardonner?" One who reads deeply and carefully in these letters and journals and has thus come to know his mind and feelings, almost as one knows his own, will find it difficult not to be as tolerant of Byron's foibles and his less amiable qualities—his inconsistencies, his mobility and his volatile temper, even the implacable hatreds which soured and distorted his naturally friendly temperament—as *he* was of those of mankind in general.

EDITORIAL NOTE

PREVIOUS EDITIONS. The last collected edition of Byron's letters occupied six of the thirteen volumes of the Murray edition of Byron's *Works*. There the *Letters and Journals* (1898–1901), edited by R. E. Prothero, contained 1198 letters. Of these, 561 had been printed by Thomas Moore in his *Letters and Journals of Lord Byron: with Notices of His Life* (2 vols., 1830). Nearly half of these letters, and almost all of those addressed to himself, Moore printed with many omissions, and the manuscripts have since disappeared. Prothero was a careful editor, and when he had the manuscripts before him, as he did for about two-thirds of the letters he published, he was generally reliable, though he too bowdlerized in accordance with late Victorian expectations of reticence and propriety. And it is curious that he made silent excisions, whereas Moore generally indicated by asterisks the omission of part of his text.

Another group of 348 letters, mostly to Lady Melbourne, John Cam Hobhouse, and Douglas Kinnaird, were published as *Lord Byron's Correspondence*, edited by John Murray IV (2 vols., 1922). These letters had been in the possession of Lady Dorchester, Hobhouse's daughter, who bequeathed them to John Murray. As editor Murray printed the letters to Lady Melbourne without omissions because "Lord Byron's descendants have expressed a definite wish that they should be published *verbatim et literatim*". But he took great liberties with the letters to Hobhouse and Kinnaird, leaving out all the saltier passages and much else that he thought not worth printing, and all with no indication of the omissions.

These passages were restored in some of these letters in Peter Quennell's *Byron: A Self-Portrait* (2 vols., 1950) and 50 letters, theretofore unpublished, were added. Byron's letters and notes in Italian to the Countess Teresa Guiccioli, 139 in number, were published by the Marchesa Iris Origo in the appendix to her *The Last Attachment* (1949) and an English translation of most of them was given in the text. This brings the number of Byron's letters published up to 1950 in major works to 1735. If we add to this the several hundred published in part or in whole in books and periodicals before that date and since, the total could possibly reach 2500.

The present collected edition will have about 3000 letters, approximately 80% of which will be published from the original manuscripts or from facsimile or photo copies. This will make possible a complete and correct text of hundreds of letters heretofore published with omissions or errors in the text. It is impossible at present to calculate accurately the number of hitherto unpublished letters which will finally be in the edition, for many have been published obscurely, and more are turning up all the time. Of course, there is no such thing as a definitive edition. All that can be expected is one that is as complete as possible. Letters of earlier periods that come to light after the publication of the appropriate volumes will be collected in an appendix in the last volume. Byron's letters are interesting enough and important enough to justify a collected edition which will bring together in one accessible chronological sequence the now scattered ones.

THE JOURNALS. Byron kept five separate journals in the course of his life. The first one he began on November 14, 1813, carried on fairly regularly until December 18th, resumed it on January 16, 1814, and continued intermittently until April 19th. This journal he gave to Thomas Moore, who published it with large omissions, and the manuscript, along with most of the letters to Moore, has since disappeared. The second journal was the one kept during Byron's Alpine tour with Hobhouse. It is dated from September 17 to 29, 1816. He wrote it for his sister, who later permitted Moore to publish extracts from it. Prothero published it entire from the manuscript in the Murray collection. His next attempt at a daily record of his thoughts and feelings was the Ravenna diary, begun January 4, 1821, and continued until February 27th. This too Byron sent to Moore to supplement the Memoirs which he had given him. Moore published it with a number of omissions, and the original has followed the 1813 journal into the limbo of lost manuscripts. Byron's fourth journal, and one of the most interesting, was a record of miscellaneous thoughts and recollections begun on May 1, 1821, as "My Dictionary", but he left off after "Augustus" and "Aberdeen", and resumed it on October 15th as "Detached Thoughts". This he continued as numbered items until November 6th just after his arrival in Pisa, ending with a poem in No. 118. The following year he added only two more paragraphs, breaking off with No. 120 on May 18, 1822. Except for one small but significant omission, Prothero published it complete from the manuscript now at Murray's. His fifth and last was the brief journal written in Cephalonia from September 28 to 30, 1823, and taken up again on December 17th shortly before he left for Missolonghi. It was published by Prothero from the manuscript also in the Murray archives. Thus we must rely on Moore's bowdlerized text for two of the longest and most vivid diaries, those of 1813 and 1821. It is perhaps futile at this point to bemoan the loss of what probably was one of Byron's most interesting journals, the famous Memoirs, which he gave to Moore. These Memoirs, which Moore had sold to Murray for posthumous publication, were burned in the fireplace of Murray's parlour after Byron's death, over the protest of Moore it must be said. But we should be grateful for what we have, for the journals reveal many things that are not in the letters and that add substantially to our knowledge of the inner depths of the man.

FORGERIES. A word should be said about forgeries, many of which have been printed as genuine Byron letters, and some of the forged manuscripts are in libraries and private collections. Anyone who has seen a number of these manuscripts can recognize them immediately from the handwriting, which is like Byron's scrawling hand but too upright and rigid. They are all the work of the nineteenth-century forger of letters and manuscripts of Byron, Shelley, and others. The forger, who called himself De Gibler at times, but mostly went under the assumed name of Major George Gordon Byron, copied subject matter and phrasing from authentic Byron letters, but generally be-betrayed himself by attempting to be too clever in what he thought was a Byronic way. Occasionally Byron indulges in facetious or shocking remarks in his letters; De Gibler piles one on top of another in a strained attempt at cleverness or smartness which is very unlike Byron. More than a hundred of these forgeries are now known. Many of them were published by Henry Schultes Schultess-Young as *The Unpublished Letters of Lord Byron*, London, Bentley, 1872. Many found their way to the manuscript market and are quoted in auction and booksellers' catalogues, and they are still appearing from time to time, though most dealers are now aware of the style and hand of the forger. Theodore G. Ehrsam has told the story of De Gibler and has listed 88 of his fabricated Byron letters in his *Major Byron, The Incredible Career of a Literary Forger*, New York, 1951. I have avoided these, together with additional ones which I have myself seen. And where the evidence has been strong from internal discrepancies of fact and style of the handiwork of the forger, I have not included supposed Byron letters, whether they were in published works (Prothero has several) or quoted in sale catalogues. A list of known or suspected forgeries will be given chronologically in an appendix of each volume, together with the location when it is known.

EDITORIAL PRINCIPLES. With minor exceptions, herein noted, I have tried to reproduce Byron's letters as they were written. The letters are arranged consecutively in chronological order. The name of the addressee is given at the top left in brackets. The source of the text is indicated in the list of letters in the Appendix. If it is a printed text, it is taken from the first printed form of the letter known or presumed to be copied from the original manuscript, or from a more reliable editor, such as Prothero, when he also had access to the manuscript. In this case, as with handwritten or typed copies, or quotations in sale catalogues, the text of this source is given precisely.

When the text is taken from the autograph letter or a photo copy or facsimile of it, the present whereabouts or ownership is given, whether it is in a library or a private collection. When the manuscript is the source, no attempt is made to indicate previous publication, if any. Here I have been faithful to the manuscript with the following exceptions:

1. The place and date of writing is invariably placed at the top right in one line if possible to save space, and to follow Byron's general practice. Fortunately Byron dated most of his letters in this way, but occasionally he put the date at the end. Byron's usual custom of putting no punctuation after the year is followed throughout.

2. Superior letters such as S^r or 30th have been lowered to Sr. and 30th. The & has been retained, but &^{c} has been printed &c.

3. Byron's spelling has been followed (and generally his spelling is good, though not always consistent), and *sic* has been avoided except in a few instances when an inadvertent misspelling might change the meaning or be ambiguous, as for instance when he spells *there* t-h-e-i-r.

4. Although, like many of his contemporaries, Byron was inconsistent and eccentric in his capitalization, I have felt it was better to let him have his way, to preserve the flavour of his personality and his times. With him the capital letter sometimes indicates the importance he gives to a word in a particular context; but in the very next line it might not be capitalized. If clarity has seemed to demand a modification, I have used square brackets to indicate any departure from the manuscript.

5. Obvious slips of the pen crossed out by the writer have been silently omitted. But crossed out words of any significance to the meaning or emphasis are enclosed in angled brackets ⟨ ⟩.

6. Letters undated, or dated with the day of the week only, have been dated, when possible, in square brackets. If the date is conjectural, it is given with a question mark in brackets. The same practice is followed for letters from printed sources. The post mark date is given, to indicate an approximate date, only when the letter itself is undated.

7. The salutation is put on the same line as the text, separated from it by a dash. The complimentary closing, often on several lines in the manuscript, is given in one line if possible. The P.S., wherever it may be written in the manuscript, follows the signature.

8. Byron's punctuation follows no rules of his own or others' making. He used dashes and commas freely, but for no apparent reason, other than possibly for natural pause between phrases, or sometimes for emphasis. He is guilty of the "comma splice", and one can seldom be sure where he intended to end a sentence, or whether he recognized the sentence as a unit of expression. He did at certain intervals place a period and a dash, beginning again with a capital letter. These larger divisions sometimes, though not always, represented what in other writers, particularly in writers of today, correspond to paragraphs. He sometimes used semicolons, but often where we would use commas. Byron himself recognized his lack of knowledge of the logic or the rules of punctuation. He wrote to his publisher John Murray on August 26, 1813: "Do you know anybody who can *stop*— I mean point—commas and so forth, for I am I fear a sad hand at your punctuation". It is not without reason then that most editors, including R. E. Prothero, have imposed sentences and paragraphs on him in line with their interpretation of his intended meaning. It is my feeling, however, that this detracts from the impression of Byronic spontaneity and the onrush of ideas in his letters, without a compensating gain in clarity. In fact, it may often arbitrarily impose a meaning or an emphasis not intended by the writer. I feel that there is less danger of distortion if the reader may see exactly how he punctuated and then determine whether a phrase between commas or dashes belongs to one sentence or another. Byron's punctuation seldom if ever makes the reading difficult or the meaning unclear. In rare instances I have inserted a period, a comma, or a semicolon, but have enclosed it in square brackets to indicate it was mine and not his.

9. Words missing but obvious from the context, such as those lacunae caused by holes in the manuscript, are supplied within square brackets. If they are wholly conjectural, they are followed by a question mark. The same is true of doubtful readings in the manuscript.

Undated letters have been placed within the chronological sequence when from internal or external evidence there are reasonable grounds for a conjectural date. This has seemed more useful than putting them together at the end of the volumes. Where a more precise date cannot be established from the context, these letters are placed at the beginning of the month or year in which they seem most likely to have been written.

ANNOTATION. I have tried to make the footnotes as brief and informative as possible, eschewing, sometimes with reluctance, the leisurely expansiveness of R. E. Prothero, who in his admirable edition of the *Letters and Journals* often gave pages of supplementary biographical information and whole letters *to* Byron, which was possible at a time when book publishing was less expensive, and when the extant and available Byron letters numbered scarcely more than a third of those in the present edition. Needless to say, I have found Prothero's notes of inestimable assistance in the identification of persons and quotations in the letters which he edited, though where possible I have double checked them. And I must say that while I have found some errors, they are rare. With this general acknowledgment I have left the reader to assume that where a source of information in the notes is not given, it comes from Prothero's edition, where additional details may be found.

The footnotes are numbered for each letter. Where the numbers are repeated on a page, the sequence of the letters will make the reference clear.

In an appendix in each volume I have given brief biographical sketches of Byron's principal correspondents first appearing in that volume. These are necessarily very short, and the stress is always on Byron's relations with the subject of the sketch. Identification of less frequent correspondents and other persons mentioned in the letters are given in footnotes as they appear, and the location of these, as well as the biographical sketches in the appendix, will be indicated by italic numbers in the index. Similarly italic indications will refer the reader to the principal biographical notes on persons mentioned in the text of the letters.

With respect to the annotation of literary allusions and quotations in the letters, I have tried to identify all quotations in the text, but have not always been successful in locating Byron's sources in obscure dramas whose phrases, serious or ridiculous, haunted his memory. When I have failed to identify either a quotation or a name, I have frankly said so, instead of letting the reader suppose that I merely passed it by as unimportant or overlooked it. No doubt readers with special knowledge in various fields may be able to enlighten me. If so, I shall try to make amends with notes in later volumes.

I have sometimes omitted the identification of familiar quotations. But since this work will be read on both sides of the Atlantic, I have explained some things that would be perfectly clear to a British reader but not to an American. I trust that English readers will make allowance for this. As Johnson said in the Preface to his edition of Shakespeare: "It is impossible for an expositor not to write too little for some, and too much for others . . . how long soever he may deliberate, [he] will at last explain many lines which the learned will think impossible to be mistaken, and omit many for which the ignorant will want his help. These are censures merely relative, and must be quietly endured".

I have occasionally given cross references, but in the main have left it to the reader to consult the index for names which have been identified in earlier notes.

An index of proper names will be at the end of each volume, and a cumulative general index and a subject index will be in the last volume of the edition.

ACKNOWLEDGMENTS. (Vols. I and II). My deepest debt of gratitude is to John G. Murray, who is as great a Byron enthusiast as his ancestor, Byron's publisher. He has been a most energetic collaborator in the gathering of Byron letters for this edition. Not only has he furnished me with photo copies of all his Byron letters, more than a third of all those extant, but he has also, at much trouble procured copies of many others. His constant enthusiasm and encouragement have lightened my task. I am grateful to the Earl of Lytton, Byron's great great grandson, for permitting me to take xerox copies of his Byron letters. And to Carl H. Pforzheimer, Jr., I am indebted for much kindness and encouragement and for copies of the numerous Byron letters in the Carl H. Pforzheimer Library. A generous grant from the Carl and Lily Pforzheimer Foundation, Inc. enabled me to travel to libraries in America and to gather letters from many public and private sources, and an additional Pforzheimer grant, supplemented by one from the American Philosophical Society, made possible a summer in England to collect miscellaneous letters. A grant from the American Council of Learned Societies assisted me in visiting libraries to do research on the annotation. To John Murray as legal representative of Lord Byron and controller of Byron copyrights I am indebted for permission to publish the letters in this edition, which are still in copyright or have not hitherto been published.

I wish to thank the following libraries and individuals in addition to those mentioned above, for photo copies of and permission to use in these volumes letters in their possession: The Henry E. and Albert A. Berg Collection of the New York Public Library; Bergen University Library (Norway); Bodleian Library, Oxford; Boston Public Library; British Embassy, Athens; British Museum (Department of Manuscripts and Department of Printed Books); British School of Archaeology, Athens; Child Memorial Library, Harvard University; Colorado College Library; Cornell University Library; Mrs. James Edward Fitzgerald; Fitzwilliam Museum, Cambridge; Mr. Richard Gatty; Harrow School Library; Haverford College Library; Houghton Library, Harvard University; Henry E. Huntington Library; the Marquess of Lansdowne; Carolyn Manovill; Manuscript Division, New York Public Library; John S. Mayfield; Mrs. C. Earle Miller; Mr. James Lees-Milne; Pierpont Morgan Library; National Library of Scotland; Newark-on-Trent Museum; Nottingham Public Libraries; University of Pennsylvania Library; Carl H. Pforzheimer Library; Anthony Powell; Princeton University Library; Royal Library, Windsor; Miriam Lutcher Stark Library, University of Texas; Doris Rich Stuart; Syracuse University Library; Robert H. Taylor; Trinity College Library, Cambridge; Beinecke Rare Book and Manuscript Library, Yale University.

Mrs. Doris Langley Moore has generously shared her wide knowledge of Byron with me and has been most helpful in answering questions. Donald H. Reiman, editor of *Shelley and His Circle* for the Pforzheimer Library, has given me much useful information. And Mark Carroll, when he was Director of the Harvard University Press, gave me much sage advice and assisted my project in many ways. For assistance of various kinds I am indebted to the following: Lord Abinger, Thomas L. Ashton, Bernard Blackstone, William H. Bond, C. L. Cline, John Clubbe, Peter Croft, Miss Lucy Edwards, Malcolm Elwin, David V. Erdman, Paul Fussell, Jr., George H. Healey, E. D. H. Johnson, Ernest J. Lovell, Jr., Lady Mander, John S. Mayfield, Jerome J. McGann, Mrs. June Moll, Winifred A. Myers, P. Laurence O'Keeffe, Willis W. Pratt, M. Byron Raizis, Gordon N. Ray, Dr. Theodore Redpath, Hinda Rose, Charles Ryskamp, William St. Clair, T. G. Steffan, Miss M. Veronica Stokes, Paul Sykes, James Thorpe, Keith Walker, Dr. Neda M. Westlake, Daniel Whitten, Freda Mary Wilkins, Carl Woodring, Marjorie G. Wynne.

BYRON CHRONOLOGY

1788 Jan. 22—Born, 16 Holles Street, Cavendish Square, London.

1789 Mother took lodgings in Queen Street, Aberdeen.

1791 Aug. 2—Father died in France.

Mother took flat at 64 Broad Street, Aberdeen.

1794–98—At Aberdeen Grammar School.

1798 May 21—Fifth Lord Byron died. George Gordon Byron became 6th Baron Byron of Rochdale.

Aug.—Accompanied mother to Newstead Abbey, ancestral estate.

1799 Lived with Parkyns family, Nottingham. Tutored by "Dummer" Rogers.

July—Taken to London by John Hanson, Byron's lawyer and business agent.

Sept.—Entered Dr. Glennie's School, Dulwich.

Christmas holidays with Hanson family, Earl's Court, Kensington.

1800 Summer holiday in Nottingham and Newstead. In love with first cousin, Margaret Parker.

1801 April—Entered Harrow.

Summer with mother at Mrs. Massingberd's, 16 Piccadilly, at Hanson's, and at Cheltenham.

1802 Christmas holiday with mother at Bath.

1803 Feb.—Returned to Harrow.

Newstead leased to Lord Grey de Ruthyn.

July 21—Mrs. Byron rented Burgage Manor, Southwell.

July 26—Byron left Harrow for Southwell.

Aug. 2—With Owen Mealey, Newstead steward, at the gatehouse.

Sept.–Nov.—In love with Mary Chaworth, Annesley Hall; refused to return to Harrow.

Nov.–Jan.—With Lord Grey at Newstead.

1804 Jan.—Broke with Lord Grey; back at Harrow.

March 22—Began holiday at Burgage Manor; friendship with Pigots.

April—Back at Harrow.

July 28—Left for Southwell.

Sept.—To Harrow again.

Christmas holidays with Hansons.

1805 Feb.—Returned to Harrow.

April—At Southwell; quarrels with mother.

May—Left for London.

May 8—At Harrow.

Aug. 2—In cricket match with Eton.

Aug. 4—To Southwell.

Sept. 23—To Hanson's in London.

Oct. 24—Took up residence at Trinity College, Cambridge. Friendship with E. N. Long and John Edleston.

Christmas vacation in London, at Mrs. Massingberd's.

1806 Feb.—Borrowed from usurers; dissipation in London.

April—Returned to Trinity.

July—At Southwell; preparing volume of poems.

Aug. 7—Escaped to London after quarrel with mother.

Aug. [20?]—At Little Hampton with E. N. Long.

Sept.—Back at Southwell; engaged in amateur theatricals; trip to Harrogate with John Pigot.

Nov.—*Fugitive Pieces* privately printed.

1807 Jan.—*Poems on Various Occasions*, second volume of poems, privately printed.

April—Severe dieting; preparing poems for publication.

June—*Hours of Idleness* published.

June 27—At Cambridge; farewell to Edleston; made friends with Hobhouse and Matthews.

July 6—At Gordon's Hotel, London.

Oct.—Returned to Trinity; writing satire and other poems; met Davies and Hodgson.

Christmas—Left Cambridge for good.

1808 Jan.—Dorant's Hotel, Albemarle Street, London; acquaintance with Dallas.

Feb.—*Hours of Idleness* ridiculed in *Edinburgh Review*; dissipations in London.

March—*Poems Original and Translated* published.

July–Aug.—At Brighton with Hobhouse, Davies, and others.

Sept.—Took residence at Newstead after departure of Lord Grey.

Oct.–Nov.—Working on satire.

1809 Jan. 19—At Reddish's Hotel, St. James's Street, London.

March 13—Took seat in House of Lords.

March—*English Bards and Scotch Reviewers* published.

April—Party at Newstead; buffoonery with monks' robes and skull cup.

April 25—At Batt's Hotel, Jermyn Street, London.

June 20—Left for Falmouth with Hobhouse.

July 2—Sailed with Hobhouse on the Lisbon packet, *Princess Elizabeth*.

July 7—Arrived in Lisbon.

July 12–16—Visited Cintra.

July 20—Left for Spain.

July 25—Arrived at Seville.

July 29—Arrived at Cadiz.

July 30—Saw bullfight at Puerta Santa Maria.

Aug. 3—Sailed on *Hyperion* frigate.

Aug. 4—Arrived at Gibraltar.

Aug. 16—Sailed for Malta on *Townshend Packet*; John Galt on board.

Aug. 31—Arrived at Malta.

Sept.—In love with Mrs. Spencer Smith.

Sept. 19—Sailed on the brig *Spider* for Greece and Albania.

Sept. 26—Set foot on Greek soil for first time at Patras.

Sept. 29—Landed at Prevesa.

Oct. 1—Left for Janina.

Oct. 5—Arrived in Janina.

Oct. 11—Left for Tepelene to visit Ali Pasha.

Oct. 12—At Zitsa.

Oct. 19—Arrived at Tepelene.

Oct. 23—Left Tepelene.

Oct. 26—Arrived at Janina.

Oct. 31—Began *Childe Harold*.

Nov. 3—Left Janina.

Nov. 8—At Prevesa; near shipwreck in Turkish boat.

Nov. 13—Left Prevesa.

Nov. 20—At Missolonghi.

Nov. 22—Crossed Gulf to Patras.

Dec. 4—Started for Athens.

Dec. 5—At Vostitza.

Dec. 14—Crossed Gulf of Corinth to Salona.

Dec. 15—Saw Delphi.

Dec. 22—At Thebes.

Dec. 25—Arrived at Athens; lodged with widow Macri, mother of "Maid of Athens".

1810 Jan. 23—First trip to Sunium and Marathon.
March 5—Sailed on *Pylades* sloop-of-war.
March 8—Arrived at Smyrna.
March 13—Visited Ephesus.
March 28—Finished second canto of *Childe Harold*.
April 11—Left for Constantinople on *Salsette* frigate.
April 15—Saw plains of Troy.
May 3—Swam the Hellespont.
May 13—First sight of Constantinople.
July 10—At Ambassador's audience with Sultan Mahmoud II.
July 14—Left Constantinople with Ambassador Robert Adair on *Salsette*.
July 17—Debarked at Zea; Hobhouse returned to England.

BYRON'S LETTERS AND JOURNALS

Newstead Abbey
Novr. 8th. 1798

Dear Madam,—My Mamma being unable to write herself desires I will let you know that the potatoes are now ready and you are welcome to them whenever you please—

She begs you will ask Mrs. Parkyns² if she would wish the poney to go round by Nottingham or go home the nearest way as it is now quite well but too small to carry me—

I have sent a young Rabbit which I beg Miss Frances will accept off and which I promised to send before—My Mamma desires her best compliments to you all in which I join—I am

Dear Aunt Yours sincerely
BYRON

I hope you will excuse all blunders as it is the first letter I ever wrote

[TO MRS. CATHERINE GORDON BYRON] *Nottingham*
13th. March, 1799

Dear Mamma,—I am very glad to hear you are well, I am so myself thank God, upon my word I did not expect so long a Letter from you[;] however I will answer it as well as I can. Mrs. Parkyns & the rest are well and are much obliged to you for the present. Mr. Rogers¹ could attend me every night at a separate hour from the Miss Parkyns's, & I am astonished you do not acquiesce in this scheme which

¹ Byron's aunt, his father's sister Charlotte Augusta Byron, married Christopher Parker (1761–1804). Their son succeeded to the baronetcy of his grandfather as Sir Peter Parker in 1811 and was killed in the American War in 1814 (see Byron's "Elegy on the Death of Sir Peter Parker"). Their daughter Margaret, one of Byron's early cousinly loves, also died young (1802) and inspired his "first dash into poetry" (see *Poetry*, I, 5n.; see also "Detached Thoughts", No. 79).

² Mrs. Parkyns may have been a friend or neighbour of Mrs. Parker. Yet there is evidence that there was some relationship by marriage to the Byrons. Moore has this note: "It is said, that the Newstead ghost appeared, also, to Lord Byron's cousin, Miss Fanny Parkins [sic], and that she made a sketch of him from memory". (Moore, I, 577n.) Prothero refers to George Augustus Henry Anne Parkyns, second Baron Rancliffe, as M.P. for Nottingham in 1814 (*LJ*, III 79n.). Byron stayed with the Parkyns family in Nottingham while he was being tutored and while his foot was being doctored by the quack Lavender. The Parkyns girls apparently fell in love with Byron and later wrote him many letters (now in the Murray MSS.). One of them signed herself "Fanny" or "F. Parkyns", probably the Frances he refers to in this letter.

¹ Byron read parts of Virgil and Cicero with "Dummer" Rogers. (See Moore, I, 27; and *Notes and Queries*, 4th series, vol. III, p. 561.)

would keep me in mind of what I have almost entirely forgot, I recommend this to you because if some plan of this kind is not adopted I shall be called or rather branded with the name of a dunce which you know I could never bear. I beg you will consider this plan seriously & I will lend it all the assistance in my power. I Shall be very glad to see the letter you talk of & I have time Just to say I hope every body is well at Newstead

& remain your affectionate son,
BYRON

P.S.—Pray let me know when you are to send in the horses to go to Newstead. May[2] Desires her duty & I also expect an answer By the Miller.

[TO JOHN HANSON]   *[Dulwich, Nov.? 1799]*

Sir—I am not a little disappointed at your stay, for this last week I expected you every hour, but however I beg it as a favour that you will come up soon from Newstead as the Holidays commence in three weeks time. I congratulate you on Capt. Hanson's[1] being appointed commander of the Brazen sloop of war, and I congratulate myself on Lord Portsmouth's[2] marriage hoping his lady when he and I meet next will keep him in a little better order. The manner I knew that Capt. Hanson was appointed Commander of the ship before mentioned was this[.] I saw it in the public paper. And now since you are going to Newstead I beg if you meet Gray[3] send her a packing as fast as possible, and give my compliments to Mrs. Hanson and to all my comrades of the Battalions in and out upon different stations,

and remain your little friend
BYRON

[2] May Gray, Byron's nurse, accompanied him to Nottingham to help care for his foot.

[1] Captain James Hanson, brother of John Hanson solicitor and business agent of the Byrons, was drowned in a storm when his ship the *Brazen* foundered off Newhaven on January 26, 1800.

[2] Byron had lost his temper when the young Earl of Portsmouth pinched his ear at the Hansons where they were both staying. On Nov. 23, 1799, Lord Portsmouth married Miss Norton, sister of Lord Grantley. (See *LJ*, I, 9–10n.)

[3] The dismissal of May Gray resulted from Byron's confessing to Hanson that she had been in the habit of coming to bed with him and indulging in sex play with him. And he complained that when she took up with low companions in Nottingham and had been drinking she beat him. (See Marchand, *Byron: A Biography*, I, 57.)

I forgot to tell you how I was[.] I am at present very well, and my foot goes but indifferently. I cannot perceive any alteration.[4]

[TO GEORGE BYRON[1]] *Dulwich Grove Feby 24th. 1801*

Dear Cousin—Upon my word you have acted a very pretty part in the holidays while I waited to see you, you took care not to come. pray write me when you go to sea I thought you were going to the Cape but I should have been devilish sorry for that as I should not have had the pleasure of seeing you for three years. I suppose you have heard that I am going to leave this damned place[2] at Easter and am going to Harrow a public school with 250 boys at it—I have not seen my cousin's these holidays, nor shan't next either for They behaved devilish blackguard lately I asked them to come to see me however they never made their appearance—Pray write me soon and I remain

your affectionate Cousin
BYRON

[TO MRS. CATHERINE GORDON BYRON] *Harrow on the Hill*
Sunday May 1st. 1803

My Dear Mother—I received your Letter the other day and am happy to hear you are well I hope you will find Newstead in as favourable a state as you can wish. I wish you would write to Sheldrake[1] to tell him to make haste with my Shoes. I am sorry to Say that Mr. Henry Drury[2] has behaved himself to me in a manner I neither *can* nor *will bear*. He has seized now an opportunity of Showing his resentment towards me. Today in church I was talking to a boy who was sitting next me, *that* perhaps was not right, but hear what followed. after church he spoke not a word to me but he took this boy to his

[4] After he went to London, Byron's club foot was examined by Dr. Baillie, and a brace was designed for him, which he neglected to wear. When this letter was written Byron was at Dr. Glennie's school in Dulwich.

[1] Byron's cousin George Anson Byron was born in 1789, the son of a younger brother of Byron's father. After the poet's death he succeeded to the title as the 7th Baron Byron.

[2] Dr. Glennie's "Academy" in Dulwich.

[1] Mr. T. Sheldrake on the recommendation of Dr. Baillie and Dr. Laurie first made a brace and then a special shoe for Byron's lame foot.

[2] Henry Drury, the son of Dr. Joseph Drury, Headmaster of Harrow, was Byron's first tutor at the school, when he entered in 1801, and remained so until the quarrel here described. After he left Harrow Byron became very friendly with Henry Drury and wrote him a number of facetious letters from abroad.

pupil room, where he abused me in a most violent manner, called me *blackguard* said he *would* and *could* have me expelled from the School, & bade me thank his *charity* that *prevented* him, this was the message he sent me, to which I shall return no answer, but submit my case to *you* and those you may think *fit* to *consult*. Is this usage fit for any body[?] had I *stole* or behaved in the most *abominable* way to him his language could not have been more outrageous, what must the boys think of me to hear such a message ordered to be delivered to me by a *master*[?] better let him take away my Life than ruin my *character*. My conscience acquits me of ever *meriting* expulsion at this school, I have been *idle* and I certainly ought not to talk in church, But I have never done a mean action at this school to him or any *one*. If I had done anything so *heinous* why should he allow me to stay at the School, why should he himself be so *criminal* as to overlook faults, which merit the *appellation* of a Blackguard[?] If he had it in his power to have [me] expelled he would long ago have *done* it, as it is, he has done *worse*, if I am treated in this manner, I will not stay at this *school*. I write you that I will not as yet appeal to Dr. Drury,[3] his son's influence is more than mine & *Justice* would be *refused* me. Remember I told you when *I left* you at *Bath* that he would seize every means & opportunity of Revenge, not for leaving him so much as the mortification he suffered Because I begged you to let me leave him. If I had been the Blackguard he talks of, why did he not of his own accord refuse to keep me as his *pupil*[?] you know Dr. Drury's first Letter in it were these words, "My Son & Lord Byron have had some disagreements, but I hope that his future behaviour will render a change of tutors unnecessary." Last time I was here but a short time and though he endeavoured, he could find nothing to abuse me in, amongst other things I forgot to tell you he said he had a great mind [to] expel the boy for speaking to me and that if he ever again spoke to me he would expel him. Let him explain his meaning, he abused me but he neither did nor can mention anything bad of me further than what every Boy else in the School has done[.] I fear him not but let [him] explain his meaning 'tis all I ask. I beg you will write to Dr. Drury to let him know what I have said, he has behaved to me as also Mr. Evans[4] very kindly. If you do not take notice of this I will leave the School myself, but I am sure *you* will not see me *ill treated* better that I

[3] The Rev. Joseph Drury was Headmaster of Harrow from 1784 to 1805. He disciplined Byron with a "silken string", encouraged his bent toward oratory, and in the end captured his respect and affection.

[4] When Byron returned to Harrow in February, 1803, he was assigned to Mr. Evans as tutor and lived in his house.

should suffer anything than this. I believe you will be tired by this time of reading my Letter but If you love me you will now show it. Pray write me immediately I shall ever remain

your affectionate Son
BYRON

P.S.—Hargreaves Hanson desires his love to you & hopes you are very well. I am not in any want of money so will not ask you for any. God Bless, Bless you.

[TO MRS. CATHERINE GORDON BYRON]   *Harrow on the Hill*
June 23rd. 6th. 8th. 30th. 1803

My dear Mother—I am much obliged to you for the money you sent me, I have already wrote to you several *times* about writing to Sheldrake. I have wrote myself to not [any] Purpose, I wish you would write to him or Mr. Hanson to call on him, to tell him to make an instrument for my leg immediately, as I want one, rather, I have been placed in a higher form in this School to day and Dr. Drury and I go on very well, write Soon My Dear Mother

I remain your affectionate Son
BYRON

[TO MRS. CATHERING GORDON BYRON]   [*Sept. 15? 1803*]

My Dear Mother,—I have sent Mealey[1] to Day to you, before William[2] Came, but now I shall write myself, *I promise* you upon my *honour* I will come over *tomorrow* in the *afternoon*, I was not wishing to resist your *Commands*, and really seriously intended, Coming over tomorrow, ever since I received your Last letter, you know as well as I do that it is not your Company I dislike, but the place you reside in. I know it is time to go to Harrow, It will make me *unhappy*, but I will *obey*; I only *desire*, *entreat*, this one day, and on my *honour* I will be over tomorrow, in the evening or afternoon. I am Sorry you disapprove my Companions, who however are the first this county affords, and my

[1] Owen Mealey, steward of Newstead Abbey, the Byron estate. Byron was staying with him while he courted his distant cousin Mary Chaworth at Annesley Hall, with whom he had fallen desperately and hopelessly in love.

[2] William was a servant of Mrs. Byron. He could have been William Fletcher, later Byron's servant.

equals in most respects, but I will be permitted to Chuse for myself, I shall never interfere in yours and I desire you will not molest me in mine; if you Grant me this favour, and allow me this one day unmolested you will eternally oblige your

unhappy Son
BYRON

I shall attempt to offer no excuse as you do not desire one. I only entreat you as Governor, not as a Mother, to allow me this one day. Those that I most Love live in this county, therefore in the name of Mercy I entreat this one day to take leave, and then I will Join you again at Southwell[3] to prepare to go to a place where—I will write no more it would only incense you, adieu, Tomorrow I come.

[TO AUGUSTA BYRON]   *Burgage Manor, March 22d. 1804*

Although, My ever Dear Augusta, I have hitherto appeared remiss in replying to your kind and affectionate letters; yet I hope you will not attribute my neglect to a want of affection, but rather to a shyness naturally inherent to my Disposition. I will now endeavour as amply as lies in my power to repay your kindness, and for the Future I hope you will consider me not only as *a Brother* but as your warmest and most affectionate *Friend*, and if ever Circumstances should require it as your *protector*. Recollect, My Dearest Sister, that you are *the nearest relation* I have in *the world both by the ties of Blood* and *Affection*, If there is anything in which I can serve you; you have only to mention it; Trust to your Brother, and be assured he will never betray your confidence. When You see my Cousin and future Brother George Leigh,[1] tell him that I already consider him as my Friend, for whoever is beloved by you, my amiable Sister, will always be equally Dear to me.—I arrived here today at 2 o'Clock after a fatiguing Journey, I found my Mother perfectly well, She desires to be kindly remembered to you; as She is just now Gone out to an assembly, I have taken the first opportunity to write to you, I hope she will not return immediately; for if she was to take it into her head to peruse my epistle, there is one

[3] A village about twelve miles from Nottingham, where Mrs. Byron had rented a house, Burgage Manor, after Newstead was leased to Lord Grey de Ruthyn.

[1] Col. George Leigh, son of General Charles Leigh, who had married Frances Byron, sister of John Byron, Augusta's father (and Byron's by a different mother), finally married his cousin Augusta on August 17, 1807, after a long delay caused by the objections of his family.

part of it which would produce from her a panegyric on *a friend of yours* not at all agreeable to me, and I fancy, *not particularly delightful to you.* If you see Lord Sidney Osborne[2] I beg you will remember me to him, I fancy he has almost forgot me by this time, for it is rather more than a year Since I had the pleasure of Seeing him.—Also remember me to poor old Murray,[3] tell him we will see that something is to be done for him, for *while I live he shall never be abandoned In his old Age.* Write to me Soon, my Dear Augusta, And do not forget to love me, In the mean time I remain more than words [can] express, your ever sincere, affectionate

Brother and Friend
BYRON

P.S.—Do not forget to Knit the purse you promised me, Adieu my beloved Sister.—

[TO AUGUSTA BYRON] *Southwell March 26th. 1804*

I received your affectionate letter my ever Dear Sister yesterday and I now hasten to comply with your injunction by answering it as soon as possible. Not my Dear Girl that it can be in the least irksome to me to write to you, on the Contrary it will always prove my Greatest pleasure, but I am sorry that I am afraid my correspondence will not prove the most entertaining, for I have nothing that I can relate to you, except my affection for you, which I can never sufficiently express, therefore I should tire you, before I had half satisfied myself. Ah, How unhappy I have hitherto been in being so long separated from so amiable a Sister, but fortune has now sufficiently atoned by discovering to me a relation whom I love, a Friend in whom I can confide. In both these lights my Dear Augusta I shall ever look upon you, and I hope you will never find your Brother unworthy of your affection and Friendship. I am as you may imagine a little dull here, not being on terms of even intimacy with Lord Grey[1] I avoid Newstead, and my

[2] Lord Sidney Godolphin Osborne was the son of the fifth Duke of Leeds, by his second wife Catherine Anguish, whom he had married after divorcing Augusta's mother who had eloped with Captain Byron.

[3] Joseph Murray had been the trusted servant of the fifth ("Wicked") Lord Byron. The poet was always solicitous for his welfare.

[1] In March, 1803, Newstead Abbey was leased by Hanson to Henry Edward, nineteenth Baron Grey de Ruthyn, a young man of 23. He was to have the mansion and park for the years of Byron's minority for £50 a year. He invited Byron to stay with him at Newstead in November 1803 and apparently made some aberrant sexual advances to the boy, which offended and revolted him.

resources of amusement are Books, and writing to my Augusta, which wherever I am, will always constitute my Greatest pleasure, I am not reconciled to Lord Grey, *and I never will*. He was once my *Greatest Friend*, my reasons for ceasing that Friendship are such as I cannot explain, not even to you my Dear Sister (although were they to be made known to any body, you would be the first,) but they will ever remain hidden in my own breast.—They are Good ones however, for although I am *violent* I am not *capricious* in my *attachments*.—My mother disapproves of my quarrelling with him, but if she knew the cause (which she never will know,) She would reproach me no more. He Has forfeited all *title to my esteem*, but I hold him in too much *contempt* ever *to hate him*. My mother desires to be kindly remembered to you. I shall soon be in town to resume my studies at Harrow, I will certainly call upon you in my way up[.] present my respects to Mrs. Harcourt[.]² I am Glad to hear that I am in her Good Graces for I shall always esteem her on account of her behavour to you my Dear Girl. pray tell me If you say [see?] Lord S. Osborne and how he is, what little I know of him I like very much and If we were better acquainted I doubt not I should like him still better. Do not forget to tell me how Murray is. As to your Future prospects my Dear Girl *may they be happy*[.] I am sure you deserve Happiness and if *you* do not meet with it I shall begin to think it is "a bad world we live in." Write to me soon[.] I am impatient to hear from you. God bless you My amiable Augusta, I remain

your ever affectionate Brother and Friend
B<small>YRON</small>

[TO AUGUSTA BYRON]   *Burgage Manor April 2d. 1804*

I received your present, my beloved Augusta, which was very acceptable, not that it will be of any use as a token of remembrance, No, my affection for you will never permit me to forget you. I am afraid my Dear Girl that you will be absent when I am in town[.]¹ I cannot exactly say when I return to Harrow but however it will be in

---

² The wife of General William Harcourt, who succeeded his brother as third Earl Harcourt in 1809. Augusta, after the death of her grandmother, Lady Holdernesse, in 1801, had no proper home, and spent her time alternately with the families of the Duke of Leeds, of Lord Carlisle, and of the Harcourts, either in town or in the country.

¹ Byron was still at Southwell with his mother and was preparing to leave for Harrow. Augusta was then at General Harcourt's in Windsor.

a very short time. I hope you were entertained by Sir Wm. Fawcet's funeral on Saturday,[2] Though I should imagine such spectacles rather calculated to excite Gloomy ideas, But I believe *your motive* was *not quite of so mournful a cast*. You tell me that *you* are tired of London[.] I am rather surprised to hear that for I thought the Gaieties of the Metropolis were particularly pleasing to *young Ladies*.—For my part I detest it, the smoke and the noise feel particularly unpleasant[;] but however it is preferable to this horrid place, where I am oppressed with ennui, and have no amusement of any Kind, except the conversation of my mother which is sometimes very *edifying* but not always very *agreeable*. There are very few books of any Kind that are either instructive or amusing, no society but old parsons and old Maids; I shoot a Good deal, but thank God I have not so far lost my reason as to make shooting my only amusement. There are indeed some of my neighbours whose only pleasures consist in field sports, but in other respects they are only one degree removed from the brute creation. These however I endeavour not to imitate, but I sincerely wish for the company of a few friends about my own age to soften the austerity of the scene, I am an absolute Hermit, in a short time my Gravity which is increased by my solitude will qualify me for an Archbishoprick, I really begin to think that I should become a mitre amazingly well. You tell me to write to you when I have nothing better to do. I am sure writing to you my Dear Sister, must ever form my Greatest pleasure, but especially so, at this time. Your letters and those of one of my Harrow friends form my only resources for driving away *dull care*. For Godsake write me a letter as long as may fill *twenty sheets* of paper, recollect it is my only pleasure. if you won't Give me twenty sheets, at least send me as long an epistle as you can and as soon as possible, there will be time for me to receive one more Letter at Southwell, and as soon as I Get to Harrow I will write to you, excuse my not writing more my Dear Augusta, for I am sure you will be sufficiently tired of reading this complaining narrative[.] God bless you my beloved Sister. Adieu. I remain your sincere and affectionate

Friend and Brother
BYRON

Remember me kindly to Mrs. Harcourt.

[2] The funeral of General Sir William Fawcett, who had had a distinguished military career and was then Governor of Chelsea Hospital, on March 31, 1804, was attended by the Prince Regent and other notables. Byron hints that Augusta's interest in the event would be increased by the fact that her cousin Col. George Leigh, attached to the 10th Dragoons, a regiment favoured by the Prince, had become an equerry of the Prince and was most likely to be in the procession.

Burgage Manor April 9th. 1804

A thousand thanks my dear and Beloved Augusta for your affectionate Letter, and so ready compliance with the request of a peevish and fretful Brother. it acted as a cordial on my drooping spirits and for a while dispelled the Gloom which envelopes me in this uncomfortable place. you see what power your letters have over me, so I hope you will be liberal in your epistolary Consolation.—You will address your next letter to Harrow as I set out from South-well on wednesday, and am sorry that I cannot contrive to be with you, as I must resume my studies at Harrow directly. If I speak in public at all it will not be till the latter end of June or the beginning of July, you are right in your conjecture for I feel not a little nervous in the anticipation *of my Debut* as *an orator*, by the bye, I do not dislike Harrow I find *ways* and *means* to amuse *myself very pleasantly* there, the friend whose correspondence I find so amusing is an old sporting companion of mine, whose recitals of Shooting and Hunting expeditions are amusing to me as having often been his companion in them, and I hope to be so still oftener.—My mother Gives a *party* to night at which the principal *Southwell Belles* will be present, with one of which although I don't as yet know whom I shall so far *honour having never seen* them, I intend to *fall violently* in love, it will serve as an amusement pour passer le temps and it will at least have the charm of novelty to recommend it, then you know in the course of a few weeks I shall be quite au desespoir, shoot myself and Go out of the world with eclat, and my History will furnish materials for a pretty little Romance which shall be entitled and denominated the loves of Lord B. and the cruel and Inconstant Sigismunda Cunegunda Bridgetina &c&c princess of Terra Incognita.—Don't you think that I have a very Good Knack for *novel writing?*—I have Just this minute been called away from writing to you by two Gentlemen who have Given me an invitation to Go over to [Screveton?] a village a few miles off and spend a few days, but however I shall not accept it, so you will continue to address your letters to Harrow as usual, write to me as soon as possible and Give me a long letter, Remember me to Mrs. Harcourt and all who enquire after me. Continue to love me and believe me your truly affectionate

Brother and Friend
BYRON

P.S.—My Mother's love to you, Adieu.

My Dear Mother—I received your letter and was very Glad to
hear that you are well, I am very comfortable here as far as relates to
my Comrades, but, I have got into two or three scrapes with Drury
and the other Masters, which are not very convenient, the other day
as he was reprimanding me, (perhaps very properly) for my mis-
deeds he uttered the following words, "it is not probable that from
your age and situation in the School your Friends will permit you to
remain longer than Summer, but because you are about to leave
Harrow, it is no reason you are to make the house a scene of riot and
Confusion." this and much more said the Doctor, and I am informed
From creditable authority that Dr. Drury, Mr. Evans and Mark
Drury[1] said I was a *Blackguard*, that Mark Drury said so I *know*, but
I am inclined to doubt the authenticity of the report as to the rest,
perhaps it is true perhaps not, but thank God they may call me a
Blackguard, but they can never make me one, if Dr. Drury can bring
one boy or any one else to say that I have committed a dishonourable
action, and to prove it, I am content, but otherwise I am stigmatized
without a cause, and I disdain and despise the malicious efforts of him
and his Brother. His Brother Mark not Henry Drury (whom I will do
the Justice to say has never since last year interfered with me) is
continually reproaching me with the narrowness of my fortune, to
what end I know not[;] his intentions may be Good, but his manner
is disagreeable, I see no reason why I am to be reproached with it.
I have as much money, as many Clothes, and in every respect of
appearance am equal if not superior to most of my schoolfellows,
and if my fortune is narrow, it is my misfortune not my fault.
But however the way to *riches* to *Greatness* lies before me, I can, I will
cut myself a path through the world or perish in the attempt. others
have begun life with nothing and ended Greatly. And shall I who have
a competent if not a large fortune, remain idle, No, I will carve
myself the passage to Grandeur, but never with Dishonour. These
Madam are my intentions, but why this upstart Son of a Button maker
is to reproach me about an estate which however, is far superior to his
own, I know not, but that he should call me a Blackguard, is far worse,
on account of the former I can blame only Hanson (and that officious
Friend Lord Grey de Ruthyn,[2] whom I shall ever consider my most

---

[1] Mark Drury was the brother of Dr. Joseph Drury, the Headmaster.
[2] See March 26, 1804, to Augusta Byron, note 1.

inveterate enemy), it is a mere trifle, but the latter I cannot bear, I have not deserved it, and I will not be insulted with impunity. Mr. Mark Drury rides out with his Son, sees me at a distance on a poney which I hired to go to the bathing place which is too far for me to walk, he calls out, tells his son I am a Blackguard, This son, who is no friend of mine comes home relates the story to his companions, possibly with a few exaggerations, but however the Greatest part was true, and I am to be considered as such a person by my comrades, it shall not be, I will say no more, I only hope you will take this into your consideration and remove me at Summer from a place where I am goaded with insults by those from whom I little deserved it.

I remain your affectionate Son,

BYRON

[TO JOHN HANSON]   [*July 17, 1804*]

Dear Sir—I should be obliged to you if you would be so good as to take a place in the *Edinburgh* Mail for wednesday the 25th of this month, I particularly wish to set of[f] that evening and in that mail for Nottinghamshire because two of my companions have taken places for that Evening to go on the same road in the Edinburgh mail, I hope you will comply with my request, and write to me as soon as possible to inform me if you have secured it, in the mean time desiring to be remembered to Mrs. H. and the rest of the family I remain yours & ct.,

BYRON

P.S.—Pray order the place to be secured immediately lest it should be preengaged.—

[TO ELIZABETH BRIDGET PIGOT] *Burgage Manor, August 29th. 1804*

I received the arms my dear Miss Pigot and am very much obliged to you for the trouble you have taken;[1] it is impossible I should have any fault to find with them. The sight of the drawings gives me great pleasure for a double reason, in the first place they will ornament my books, in the next, they convince me, that *you* have not entirely *forgot* me. I am however sorry that you do not, return sooner, you have

[1] The Byron Arms are thus described in Burke's Peerage: "Arg., three bendlets enhanced gu. Crest—A Mermaid with her comb and mirror all ppr. Supporters—Two horses of a chestnut colour ppr. hoofs or. Motto—Crede Byron."

already been gone an *age*. I perhaps may have taken my departure for London, before you come back, but however I will hope not. Do not overlook my watch ribbon, and purse as I wish to Carry them with me. Your note was given me by Harry[2] at the play, (whither I attended Miss Leacroft[3] and Dr. [Swimmer?])[4] and now I have sat down to answer it before I go to bed. If I am at Southwell when you return, and I sincerely hope you will soon, for I very much regret your absence, I shall be happy to hear you sing my favourite the *Maid of Lodi*; My mother together with myself desire to be affectionately remembered to Mrs. Pigot, and believe me my dear Miss Pigot,

I remain your affectionate Friend
BYRON

P.S.—If you think proper to send any answer to this I shall be extremely happy to receive it. Adieu.—

P.S. 2d.—As you say you are a novice in the art of knitting I hope it don't give you too much trouble? Go on *Slowly* but *surely*. Once more Adieu.

[TO JOHN HANSON]   *Burgage Manor August 30th. 1804*

My dear Sir—I thank you for your frank invitation, and will accept it with the greatest pleasure, if you will appoint a day on which I could be in town and fix the particulars of my journey, I will be there at the very time. I shall bring my Gun with me, and am Glad to hear that you have many birds on your *manor*, we shall no doubt have fine *sport*. Pray answer my epistle immediately, and with best compts. to Mrs. Hanson, and love to Hargreaves and Charles.[1] I remain your sincere friend.

BYRON

P.S.—My mother is well and desires Compts.

[2] Probably Elizabeth's brother Henry.
[3] Julia Leacroft was a Southwell girl who organized some theatricals in which Byron took part. Byron took enough interest in her to encourage her family to think he was going to marry her. When he saw that they were trying to entrap him, he pulled back, narrowly escaping a duel with her brother.
[4] Unidentified.
[1] Byron stayed with the Hansons in London at various periods and was fond of the Hanson children and of Mrs. Hanson, who took a motherly interest in him. There were three Hanson boys, Hargreaves, who was at Harrow while Byron was there, Charles, and Newton, who, after Byron's death, wrote a memoir of him (never published). Two girls, Harriet and Mary Anne, who in 1814 married the Earl of Portsmouth, seem both to have been romantically interested in Byron.

51

My Dear Augusta,—In compliance with your wish as well as gratitude for your affectionate letter, I proceed as soon as possible to answer it; I am glad to hear that *any body* gives a good account of me, but from the quarter you mention, I should imagine it was exaggerated. That you are unhappy my dear Sister makes me so also, were it in my power to relieve your sorrows, you would soon recover your spirits, as it is, I sympathize in your distress, and hope that things will turn out better than you yourself expect. But really after all (pardon me my dear Sister,) I feel a little inclined to laugh at you, for love in my humble opinion, is utter nonsense, a mere jargon of compliments, romance, and deceit; now for my part had I fifty mistresses, I should in the course of a fortnight, forget them all, and if by any chance I ever recollected one, should laugh at it as a dream, and bless my stars, for delivering me from the hands of the little mischievous Blind God. Can't you drive this Cousin[1] of ours out of your pretty little head, (for as to *hearts* I think they are out of the question,) or if you are so far gone, why don't you give old L'Harpagon[2] (I mean the General) the slip, and take a trip to Scotland, you are now pretty near the Borders. Be sure to Remember me to my formal Guardy Lord Carlisle, whose magisterial presence I have not been into for some years, nor have I any ambition to attain so great an honour, as to your favourite Lady Gertrude,[3] I don't remember her, pray is she handsome, I dare say she is, for although they are a *disagreeable, formal, stiff* Generation, yet they have by no means plain *persons*, I remember Lady Cawdor[4] was a sweet pretty woman, pray does your sentimental Gertrude resemble her[?] I have heard that the duchess of Rutland[5] was handsome also, but we will say nothing about her temper, as I hate Scandal. Adieu my pretty Sister, forgive my levity, write Soon, and God Bless you. I remain your

very affectionate Brother
BYRON

[1] Col. George Leigh.

[2] General Charles Leigh's objection to his son's marriage to Augusta was principally that her income was too small, only £350 a year left her by her grandmother Lady Holdernesse. Hence Byron compared the General to the miser in *L'Avare*.

[3] Lady Gertrude Howard, youngest of three daughters of Lord Carlisle, was a particular favourite of Augusta.

[4] Lord Carlisle's eldest daughter, Lady Caroline Isabella Howard, married, in 1789, John, first Lord Cawdor.

[5] The Duchess of Rutland, formerly Lady Elizabeth Howard, was Lord Carlisle's second daughter. She had married Henry, fifth Duke of Rutland in 1799.

P.S.—I left my mother at Southwell, some time since, in a monstrous pet with you for not writing, I am sorry to say the old lady and myself, don't agree like lambs in a meadow, but I believe it is all my own fault, I am rather too fidgety, which my precise mama objects to, we differ, then argue, and to my shame be it spoken fall out a *little*, however after a storm comes a calm; what's become of our aunt the amiable antiquated *Sophia*?[6] is she yet in the land of the living, or does she sing psalms with the *Blessed* in the other world [?] Adieu. I am happy enough and Comfortable here, my friends are not numerous, but select, among them I rank as the principal Lord Delawarr,[7] who is very amiable and my particular friend, do you know the family at all? Lady Delawarr is frequently in town, perhaps you may have seen her, if she resembles her son she is the most amiable woman in Europe. I have plenty of acquaintances, but I reckon them as mere Blanks, Adieu, my dear Augusta,—

[TO AUGUSTA BYRON]   *Friday November 2d. 1804*

This morning my dear Augusta I received your affectionate letter, and it reached me at a time when I wanted consolation, not however of your kind for I am not old enough or Goose enough to be in love, no, my sorrows are of a different nature though more calculated to provoke risibility than excite compassion. You must know Sister of mine, that I am the most unlucky wight in Harrow perhaps in Christendom, and am no sooner out of one scrape than into another. And today, this very morning I had a thundering Jobation from our Good Doctor, which deranged my *nervous system* for at least five minutes. But notwithstanding He and I now and then disagree, yet upon the whole we are very good friends, for there is so much of the Gentleman, so much mildness, and nothing of pedantry in his character, that I cannot help liking him and will remember his instructions with gratitude as long as I live. He leaves Harrow soon,[1] apropos, so do I. His quitting will be a considerable loss to the school. He is the best master we ever

[6] Sophia Maria Byron, sister of Byron's father was born in 1757. She was unmarried. Her mother, Sophia Trevanion Byron wife of the Admiral, was a favourite of Mrs. Piozzi and Dr. Johnson.

[7] George John, fifth Earl Delawarr, like Byron, had succeeded to his title as a boy. He was one of Byron's younger favourites at Harrow. He was the "Euryalus" of Byron's "Childish Recollections", and was lauded in "To George, Earl Delawarr".

[1] The Rev. Joseph Drury, headmaster of Harrow from 1784 to 1805, retired after the Easter holiday. Byron was so attached to him that he led a rebellion against the new headmaster, Dr. Butler, but characteristically repented after he left Harrow and became friendly with him too.

had, and at the same time respected and feared, greatly will he be regretted by all who know him. You tell me you don't know my friend Ld. Delawarr he is considerably younger than me, but the most good tempered, amiable, clever fellow in the universe. To all which he adds the quality (a good one in the eyes of women) of being remarkably handsome, almost too much so for a boy. He is at present very low in the school, not owing to his want of ability, but to his years, I am nearly at the top of it, by the rules of our Seminary he is under my power but he is too goodnatured ever to offend me, and I like him too well ever to exert my authority over him. If you should ever meet, and chance to know him, take notice of him on my account.

You say that you shall write to the Dowager Soon her address is at Southwell, *that* I need hardly inform you. Now Augusta I am going to tell you a secret, perhaps I shall appear undutiful to you, but believe [me] my affection for you is founded on a more firm basis. My mother has lately behaved to me in such an eccentric manner, that so far from feeling the affection of a Son, it is with difficulty I can restrain my dislike. Not that I can complain of want of liberality, no, She always supplies me with as much money, as I can spend, amd more than most boys hope for or desire. But with all this she is so hasty, so impatient, that I dread the approach of the holidays, more than most boys do their return from them. In former days she spoilt me, now she is altered to the contrary, for the most trifling thing, she upbraids me in a most outrageous manner, and all our disputes have been lately heightened by my one with that object of my cordial, deliberate detestation, Lord Grey de Ruthyn.[2] She wishes me to explain my reasons for disliking him, which I will never do, would I do it to any one, be assured you my dear Augusta would be the first who would know them. She also insists on my being reconciled to him, and once she let drop such an odd expression that I was half inclined to believe the dowager was in love with him. But I hope not for he is the most disagreeable person (in my opinion) that exists. He called once during my last vacation, she threatened, stormed, begged, me to make it up, he himself loved me, and wished it, but my reason was so excellent that neither had effect, nor would I speak or stay in the same room, till he took his departure. No doubt this appears odd but was my reason known, which it never will be if I can help it, I should be justified in my conduct. Now if I am to be tormented with her and him in this style I cannot submit to it. You Augusta are the only relation I have who treats me as a friend, ⟨Impart this to⟩ if you too desert me, I

[2] See March 26, 1804, to Augusta Byron, note 1.

have nobody I can love but Delawarr. If it was not for his sake, Harrow would be a desart, and I should dislike staying at it. You desire me to burn your epistles, indeed I cannot do that, but I will take care that They shall be invisible. If you burn any of mine, I shall be *monstrous angry* take care of them till we meet. [Two lines referring to Delawarr crossed out.] Delawarr and myself are in a manner connected,[3] for one of our forefathers in Charles the 1st's time married into their family. Hartington,[4] whom you enquire after, is on very good terms with me, nothing more, he is of a soft milky disposition, and of a happy apathy of temper which defies the softer emotions, and is insensible of ill treatment—so much for him. Don't betray me to the Dowager, I should like to know your Lady Gertrude, as you and her are so great Friends Adieu my pretty Sister, write Soon.

[Signature, etc., cut out.]

[TO AUGUSTA BYRON] *Harrow Saturday 11th. Novr. 1804*

I thought my dear Augusta that your opinion of my *meek mamma* would coincide with mine; Her temper is so so variable, and when inflamed, so furious, that I dread our meeting, not but I dare say, that I am troublesome enough, but I always endeavour to be as dutiful as possible. She is so very strenuous, and so tormenting in her entreaties and commands, with regard to my reconciliation, with that detestable Lord G[rey][1] that I suppose she has a penchant for his Lordship, but I am confident that he does not return it, for he rather dislikes her, than otherwise, at least as far as I can judge. But she has an excellent opinion of her personal attractions, sinks her age a good six years, avers that when I was born she was only eighteen, when you my dear Sister as well as I know that she was of age when she married my father, and that I was not born for three years afterwards, but vanity is the weakness of *your sex*, and these are mere foibles that I have related to you, and provided she never molested me I should look upon them as follies very excusable in a woman. But I am now coming to what must shock you, as much as it does me, when she has occasion

[3] Thomas, third Lord Delawarr's daughter Cecilie, widow of Sir Francis Bindlose, married Sir John Byron, who was created the first Baron Byron of Rochdale in 1643 by Charles I. But since they left no heirs, there was no Delawarr blood in Byron, for the line was carried on by the first Lord Byron's brother Richard who succeeded him.

[4] William Spencer, Marquis of Hartington (1790–1858) succeeded his father as the sixth Duke of Devonshire in 1811.

[1] See March 26, 1804, to Augusta Byron, note 1.

to lecture me (not very seldom you will think no doubt) she does not do it in a manner that commands respect, and in an impressive style. no. did she do that I should amend my faults with pleasure, and dread to offend a kind though just mother. But she flies into a fit of phrenzy upbraids me as if I was the most undutiful wretch in existence, rakes up the ashes of of my *father*, abuses him, says I shall be a true Byrrone, which is the worst epithet she can invent. Am I to call this woman mother? Because by natures law she has authority over me, am I to be trampled upon in this manner? Am I to be goaded with insult, loaded with obloquy, and suffer my feelings to be outraged on the most trivial occasions? I owe her respect as a Son, But I renounce her as a Friend. What an example does she shew me? I hope in God I shall never follow it. I have not told you all nor can I, I respect you as a female, nor although I ought to confide in you as a Sister, will I shock you with the repetition of Scenes, which you may judge of by the Sample I have given you, and which to all but you are buried in oblivion. Would they were so in my mind. I am afraid they never will. And can I, my dear Sister, look up to this mother, with that respect, that affection I ought. Am I to be eternally subjected to her caprice! I hope not, indeed a few short years will emancipate me from the Shackles I now wear, and then perhaps she will govern her passion better than at present. You mistake me, if you think I dislike Lord Carlisle, I respect him, and might like him did I know him better. For him too my mother has an antipathy, why I know not. I am afraid he could be but of little use to me, in separating me from her, which she would oppose with all her might, but I dare say he would assist me if he could, so I take the will for the Deed and am obliged to him exactly the [sic] in the same manner, as if he succeeded in his efforts. I am in great hopes, that at Christmas I shall be with Mr. Hanson during the vacation, I shall do all I can to avoid a visit to my mother wherever she is. It is the first duty of a parent, to impress precepts of obedience in their children, but her method is so violent, so capricious, that the patience of Job, the versatility of a member of the House of Commons could not support it. I revere Dr. Drury much more than I do her, yet he is never violent, never outrageous, I dread offending him, not however through fear, but the respect I bear him, makes me unhappy when I am under his displeasure. My mother's precepts, never convey instruction, never fix upon my mind, to be sure they are calculated, to inculcate obedience, so are chains, and tortures, but though they may restrain for a time the mind revolts from such treatment. Not that Mrs. Byron ever injures my *sacred* person. I am rather too old for that, but her words are of that rough texture, which offend more than personal ill usage. "A talkative woman is like an Adder's tongue,"[2] so says one of the prophets, but which I can't tell, and very likely you don't wish to know, but he was a true one whoever he was. The postage of your letters My dear Augusta don't fall upon me, but if they did it would make no difference, for I am Generally in cash, and should think the trifle I paid for your epistles the best laid out I ever spent in my life. Write Soon. Remember me to Lord Carlisle, and believe me I ever am your affectionate Brother and Friend

BYRON

[TO AUGUSTA BYRON]   *Harrow on the Hill*
                                                           Saturday Novr. 17th. 1804

I am glad to hear, My dear Sister, that you like Castle Howard[1] so well. I have no doubt what you say is true and the Lord C[arlisle] is much more amiable than he has been represented to me, never having been much with him and always hearing him reviled, it was hardly possible I should have conceived a very *great friendship* for his Ldship. My mother you inform me commends my *amiable disposition* and *good understanding*, if she does this to you it is a great deal more than I ever hear myself, for the one or the other is always found fault with, and I am told to copy the *excellent pattern* which I see before me in *herself*. You have got an invitation too, you may accept it if you please, but if you value your own comfort, and like a pleasant situation, I advise you to avoid Southwell.—I thank you My dear Augusta for your readiness to assist me, and will in some manner avail myself of it; I do not however wish to be separated from *her* entirely, but not to be so much with her as I hitherto have been, for I do believe she likes me, she manifests that in many instances, particularly with regard to money, which I never want, and have as much as I desire. But her conduct is so strange, her caprices so impossible to be complied with, her passions so outrageous, that the evil quite overbalances her *agreeable qualities.* Amongst other things I forgot to mention a most *ungovernable appetite* for Scandal, which she never can govern, and employs most of her time abroad, in displaying the faults, and censuring the foibles, of her acquaintance, therefore I do not wonder, that my precious Aunt, comes in for her share of encomiums. This

[2] Unidentified.
[1] Castle Howard was Lord Carlisle's mansion in Yorkshire, where Augusta frequently stayed.

however is nothing to what happens when my conduct admits of animadversion, "then comes the tug of war". My whole family from the conquest are upbraided, myself abused, and I am told that what little accomplishments I possess either in mind or body are derived from her and *her alone*. When I leave Harrow I know not; that depends on her nod, I like it very well. The master Dr. Drury, is the most amiable *clergyman* I ever knew, he unites the Gentleman with the Scholar, without affectation or pedantry, what little I have learnt I owe to him alone, nor is it his fault that it was not more. I shall always remember his instructions with Gratitude, and cherish a hope that it may one day be in my power to repay the numerous obligations, I am under, to him or some of his family.— —Our holidays come on in about a fortnight. I however have not mentioned that to my mother, nor do I intend it, but if I can I shall contrive to evade going to South-well, depend upon it I will not approach her for some time to come, if It is in my power to avoid it, but she must not know, that it is my wish to be absent. I hope you will excuse my sending so short a letter, but the Bell has just rung to summon us together, write Soon, and believe me ever your affectionate

Brother, Byron

I am afraid you will have some difficulty in deciphering my epistles, but *that* I know you will excuse. Adieu. Remember me to Ld. Carlisle.

[TO AUGUSTA BYRON]   *Harrow on the Hill*
                                      Novr. 21st. 1804

My Dearest Augusta,—This morning I received your by no means unwelcome epistle, and thinking it demands an immediate answer, once more take up my pen to employ it in your service. There is no necessity for my mother to know anything of my intentions, till the time approaches, and when it does come, Mr. H[anson] has only to write her a note saying, that as I could not accept the invitation which he gave me last holidays, he imagined I might do it now, to this she surely can make no objections, but if she entertained the slightest idea, of my making any complaint of her very *lenient* treatment, the scene that would ensue beggars all power of description. You may have some little idea of it, from what I have told you, and what you yourself know. I wrote to you the other day, but you make no mention of receiving my letter in yours of the 18th. inst. It is however of little importance, containing merely a recapitulation of circumstances which I have before detailed at full length. To Lord Carlisle make my warmest acknowledgements. I feel more gratitude, than my feelings can well express, I am truly obliged to him for his endeavours, and am perfectly satisfied with your explanation of his reserve, though I was hitherto afraid it might proceed from personal dislike. I have some idea that I leave Harrow these holidays. The Dr. whose character I gave you in my last leaves the mastership at Easter[;] who his successor may be I know not, but he will not be a better I am confident. You inform me that you intend to visit my mother, then you will have an opportunity of seeing what I have described, and hearing a great *deal of Scandal.* She does not trouble me much with epistolary communications, when I do receive them, they are very concise, and much to the purpose. However I will do her the justice to say that she behaves, or rather means well, and is in some respects very kind, though her manners are not the most conciliating. She likewise expresses a great deal of affection for you, but disapproves your marriage, wishes to know my opinion of it, and complains that you are negligent and do not write to her or care about her. How far her opinion of your love for her is well grounded you best know. I again request you will return my sincere thanks to Lord Carlisle, and for the future I shall consider him as more my friend than I have hitherto been taught to think. I have more reasons than one, to wish to avoid going to Notts, for there I should be obliged to associate with Lord G[rey][1] whom I detest, his manners being unlike those of a Gentleman, and the information to be derived from him but little except about shooting, which I do not intend to devote my life to. Besides, I have a particular reason for not liking him. Pray write to me soon. Adieu my Dear Augusta

I remain your affectionate Brother
BYRON

[TO JOHN HANSON]   *Saturday Decr. 1st. 1804*

My Dear Sir—Our vacation commences on the 5th of this month, when I propose to myself the pleasure of spending the holidays at your house, if it is not too great an inconvenience; I tell you fairly, that at Southwell I should have nothing in the world to do, but play at cards, and listen to the edifying conversation of old Maids, two things which do not at all suit my inclinations, in my mother's last letter I

[1] See March 26, 1804, to Augusta Byron, note 1.

find that my poney and pointers are not yet procured, and that Lord Grey[1] is still at Newstead, the former I should be very dull at Such a place as Southwell without; the latter is still more disagreeable to be with, I presume he goes on in the old way, quarrelling with the farmers, and stretching his *Judicial* powers (he being now in the Commission) to the utmost, becoming a torment to himself, and a pest to all around him.—I am Glad you approve of my Gun, feeling myself happy, that it has been tried by so *distinguished* a *Sportsman*. I hope your campaigns against the Partridges and the rest of the feathered tribe, has been attended with no serious consequences; *trifling accidents* such as the loss of a few fingers and a thumb, you *Gentlemen* of the *city* being used to, of course occasion no interruption to your field Sports. Your accommodations I have no doubt I shall be perfectly satisfied with, only do exterminate that *vile Generation* of *Bugs*, which nearly ate me up last time I *sojourned* at your house. After undergoing the purgatory of Harrow *board* and *lodging* for three months, I shall not be *particular*, or exorbitant in my demands. Pray give my best Compliments to Mrs. Hanson, and the now quildriving Hargreaves, till I see you, I remain yours &ct.

BYRON

[TO AUGUSTA BYRON]   *6 Chancery Lane*[1] *Wednesday 30th. Jany. 1805*

I have delayed writing to you so long, My dearest Augusta, from ignorance of your residence, not knowing whether you *graced* Castle Howard, or Kiveton[2] with your *presence*. The instant Mr. H[anson] informed me where you was, I prepared to address you, and you have but just forestalled my intention. And now, I scarcely know what to begin with, I have so many things, to tell you. I wish to God, that we were together, for It is impossible that I can confine all I have got to

1 See March 26, 1804, to Augusta Byron, note 1.
1 This letter is addressed from John Hanson's office, 6 Chancery Lane.
2 Kiveton, near Worksop in Nottinghamshire, was the home of the Duke of Leeds, who, though he had divorced Augusta's mother, Lady Carmarthen, after she eloped with Captain Byron, remained friendly to the orphan of the wife who had deserted him, as did all his family. Augusta, having no home of her own, lived alternately with relatives and friends, the Carlisles, Lady Holdernesse (her grandmother), General Charles and Frances Leigh (her father's sister), to whose son George she became romantically attached. The Duke of Leeds had three children by Augusta's mother before they were divorced, George, Marquis of Carmarthen, Lord Francis Godolphin, and Lady Mary Osborne. To these half-brothers and half-sister Augusta was devoted, and they were fond of her. At Kiveton she was not far from Southwell; hence Byron's suggestion that she might visit his mother.

say in an epistle, without I was to follow your example, and fill eleven pages, as, I was informed by my *proficiency* in *the art of magic*, that you sometimes sent that *number* to *Lady Gertrude*.[3] To begin with an article of *grand importance*, I on Saturday dined with Lord Carlisle, and on further acquaintance I like them all very much. Amongst other circumstances, I heard of your *boldness* as a *Rider*, especially one anecdote about your horse carrying you into the stable *perforce*. I should have admired amazingly, to have seen your progress, provided you met with no accident. I hope you recollect the circumstance, and know what I allude to, else, you may think that I am *soaring* into the *Regions of Romance*. I wish you to corroberate my account in your next, and inform me whether my information was correct. I think your friend Lady G[ertrude] is a sweet girl. If your taste in *love*, is as good as it is in *friendship*, I shall think you a *very discerning little Gentlewoman*. His Lordship too improves upon further acquaintance, Her Ladyship I always liked, but of the Junior part of the family, Frederick[4] is my favourite. I believe with regard to my future destination, that I return to Harrow until June, and then I am off for the university. Could I have found Room there, I was to have gone immediately. I have contrived to pass the holidays with Mr. and Mrs. Hanson, to whom I am greatly obliged for their hospitality. You are now within a day's Journey of my *amiable Mama*. If you wish your spirits *raised* or rather *roused* I would recommend you to pass a week or two with her. However I daresay she would behave very well to *you*, for you do not know her disposition so well as I do. I return you my dear Girl a thousand thanks for hinting to Mr. H[anson] and Lord C[arlisle] my uncomfortable situation. I shall always remember it with gratitude, as a most *essential service*. I rather think that if you were any time with my mother, she would bore you about your marriage which she *disapproves* of, as much for the sake of finding fault as any thing, for that is her favourite amusement. At any rate she would be very inquisitive, for she was always tormenting me about it, and if you told her any thing, she might very possibly divulge it. I therefore advise you, *when you see her* to say nothing or as little about it as you can help. If you make haste, you can answer this *well written* epistle by return of post, for I wish again to hear from you immediately. You need [not] fill *eleven pages*, *nine* will be sufficient, but whether it

[3] Lady Gertrude Howard, daughter of Lord Carlisle, was one of Augusta's closest confidantes.
[4] The Hon. Frederick Howard, third son of Lord Carlisle, was killed at Waterloo. Byron paid tribute to him in *Childe Harold* (Canto III, stanzas 29–30).

contains nine pages or nine lines, it will always be most welcome my beloved Sister to your affectionate Brother and Friend

BYRON

[TO JOHN HANSON] *Saturday March 2d. 1805*

My dear Sir—Your grave lecture (as you are pleased to term it) has afforded me very great pleasure, and as long as you think proper to continue them, they will be thoughtfully accepted by me. It is an old, true, and *trite* saying, that our *real* friends will tell us our faults, as mine stand in need of some correction, I shall always receive your advice with gratitude.

I was sorry to see, that the governors were insensitive to your *superior* merits, and have elected young *Windsor Brick*[1] to the vacant office, however, we will hope that your next essay in the *electioneering way* will be attended with more success.

I hope that the *Lady*[2] you mentioned will not make her first attack upon the Doctor, as inevitably expulsion would be the consequence, if she appeals to me, I shall refer her to you immediately, but I am not sure that there is any immediate danger to be apprehended.

Apologize to Hargreaves for [my] not answering his letter, I shall set about it in a few days, but there is an old Harrow Saying "Seniores priores." Of Course "Pater" must be declined "before Filius." Every thing goes on in the old track at Harrow, we are making a subscription to present Drury with some plate. I wrote my mother for mine and expect it soon. Remember me in the most affectionate manner to Mrs. H. and all the family, and believe me, when I subscribe myself

your most affectionate Friend
BYRON

[TO AUGUSTA BYRON] *Thursday 4th. April 1805*

My dearest Augusta.—You certainly have excellent reasons for complaint against my want of punctuality in our correspondence, but, as it does not proceed from want of affection, but an idle disposition, you will, I hope, accept my excuses. I am afraid however, that when I shall take up my pen, you will not be greatly *edified* or *amused*,

[1] Windsor Brick: unidentified, as is also the office he won in competition with Hanson, who later, however, through the influence of Lord Grenville, was appointed solicitor of the stamp office. (See letter of Oct. 20, 1814, to Lady Melbourne.)

[2] Byron's mother.

especially at present, since, I sit down in very bad spirits, out of humour with myself, and all the world, except *you*.—I left Harrow yesterday, and am now at Mr. Hanson's till Sunday morning, when I depart for Nottinghamshire, to pay a visit to my *mother*, with whom I shall remain for a week or two, when I return to town, and from thence to Harrow, until July, when I take my departure for the university, but which I am as yet undecided. Mr. H[anson] Recommends Cambridge, Ld. Carlisle allows me to chuse for myself, and I must own I prefer Oxford. But, I am not violently bent upon it, and whichever is determined upon, will meet with my concurrence.—This is the outline of my future plans for the next 6 months.—I am Glad that you are Going to pay his *Lordship* a visit, as I shall have an opportunity of seeing you on my return to town, a pleasure, which as I have been long debarred of it, will be doubly felt after so long a separation. My visit to the Dowager does not promise me all the happiness I could wish, however it must be gone through, as it is some time since I have seen her. It shall be as short as possible.—I shall expect to find a letter from you, when I come down, as I wish to know when you go to town, and how long you remain there.—If you stay till The middle of next month, you may have an opportunity of hearing me speak, as the first day of our *Harrow orations* occurs in May.[1] My friend Delawarr (as you observed) danced with the little princess,[2] nor did I in the least *envy* him the honour. I presume you have heard That Dr. Drury leaves Harrow this Easter, and That as a memorial of our Gratitude for his long services, The scholars presented him with plate to the amount of 330 Guineas. I hope you will excuse this *Hypochondriac* epistle as I never was in such low spirits in my life. Adieu my Dearest Sister and believe me your ever affectionate though negligent

Brother, BYRON

[TO HARGREAVES HANSON]   *Burgage Manor Southwell Notts.*
Monday April 15th. [1805]

Dear Hargreaves,—As I have been unable to return to town with your Father, I must request that you will take care of my books and a

[1] Actually the first Speech Day came on June 6. Byron was already preparing for it. He chose to recite the dramatic speech of Zanga over the body of Alonzo, from Young's tragedy *The Revenge*, which was then being played by Kemble to applauding audiences. Byron may have seen the play while he was in London.

[2] The "little princess" was Charlotte of Wales, and the occasion was a "house warming" at Windsor Castle on February 25, 1805. It was a pretentious affair, and according to the *Gentleman's Magazine* (1805, Part I, pp. 262–64) it "cannot have cost less than £50,000".

parcel which I expect from my Taylors, and as I understand you are going to pay Farleigh[1] a visit, I would be obliged to you to leave them under the care of one of the Clerks, or a Servant, who may inform me where to find them;—I shall be in town on Wednesday the 24th at farthest; when I shall not hope to see you, or wish it; not but that I should be glad of your *entertaining* and *loquacious* society; (but as I think you will be more amused at Farleigh;) it would be selfish in me to wish that you should forego the pleasures of contemplating *pigs*, *poultry*, *pork*, *pease*, and *potatoes*, together with other *Rural Delights*, for my company.—Much pleasure may you find in your excursion, and I dare say, when you have exchanged *pleadings* for *ploughshares* and *fleecing Clients* for *feeding flocks*, you will be in no hurry to resume your law functions.[2] Remember me to your father and mother; and the Juniors, and if you should find it convenient to dispatch a note in answer to this epistle, it will afford great pleasure to

yours very sincerely & affectionately,

BYRON

P.S.—It is hardly necessary to inform you, that I am heartily tired of Southwell, for I am at this minute experiencing those delights which I have often recapitulated to you, and which are more entertaining to be *talked* of at a distance, than enjoyed at home; I allude to the eloquence of a *near relation*[3] of mine, which is as remarkable as your *taciturnity*.

[TO HARGREAVES HANSON]   *Burgage Manor, April 20th. 1805*

Dear Hargreaves,—Dr. Butler[1] our new master has thought proper to postpone our meeting till the 8th of May, which obliges me to Delay my return to town for one week, so that instead of Wednesday the 24th I shall not arrive in London until the 1st of May, on which day (If I live) I shall certainly be in town, where I hope to have the pleasure of seeing you. I shall remain with you only a week, as We are

---

[1] Farleigh was the country house of the Hansons in Hampshire.

[2] Hargreaves Hanson had just left Harrow and had become an apprentice in his father's law business. He died in 1811 at the age of 23.

[3] Byron's mother.

[1] The Rev. George Butler succeeded Dr. Drury as Headmaster of Harrow in April, 1805. Byron, out of loyalty to Dr. Drury, supported the candidacy of his brother Mark Drury, and when he lost to Dr. Butler, lampooned the latter as Pomposus in a satire "On a Change of Masters at a Great Public School" and in "Childish Recollections".

all to return to the very Day, on account of the prolongation of our holidays. However, if you shall, previous to that period take a *jaunt* into *Hants*, I beg you will leave my *valuables* &. &. in the care of one of the *Gentlemen* of your office, as that *Razor faced Villain* James,[2] might perhaps take the Liberty of walking off with a Suit. I have heard several times from Tattersall[3] and it is very possible we may see him on my return. I beg you will excuse this short epistle, as my time is at present rather taken up, and Believe me

yours‾very sincerely
BYRON

[TO AUGUSTA BYRON]   *Burgage Manor April 23d. 1805*

My dearest Augusta.—I presume by this time, that you are safely arrived at the Earls,[1] at least I *hope* so; nor shall I feel myself perfectly easy, till I have the pleasure of hearing from yourself of your safety. I myself shall set out for town this day (Tuesday) week, and intend waiting upon you on Thursday at farthest; in the mean time I must console myself as well as I can; and I am sure, no unhappy mortal ever required much more consolation than I do at present.—You as well as myself know the *sweet* and *amiable* temper of a certain personage to whom I am nearly related; of *course*, the pleasure I have enjoyed during my vacation, (although it has been greater than I expected) yet has not been so *superabundant* as to make me wish to stay a day longer than I can avoid. However, notwithstanding the dullness of the place, and certain *unpleasant things* that occur In a family not a hundred miles distant from Southwell, I contrived to pass my time in peace, till to day, when unhappily, In a most inadvertent manner, I said that Southwell was not *peculiarly* to my taste, but however, I merely expressed this in common conversation, without speaking disrespectfully of the *sweet town*; (which between you and I; I wish was swallowed up by an Earthquake, provided my *Eloquent mother* was not in it)[.] No sooner had the unlucky Sentence, which I believe was prompted by my evil Genius, escaped my lips, than I was treated with an Oration in the *ancient style*, which I have often so *pathetically*

2 Probably Byron's servant.

3 John Cecil Tattersall, one of Byron's friends at Harrow, was praised as "Davus" in "Childish Recollections".

1 The Earl of Carlisle's house was in Grosvenor Place.

described to you, unequalled by any thing of *modern* or *antique* date; nay the Philippics against Ld. Melville[2] were nothing to it, one would really Imagine to have heard the *Good Lady*, that I was a most *treasonable Culprit*, but thank St. Peter, after undergoing this *Purgatory* for the last hour, it is at length blown over, & I have sat down under these *pleasing impressions* to address you, so that I am afraid my epistle will not be the most entertaining. I assure you upon my *honour*, jesting apart, I have never been so *scurrilously* and *violently* abused by any person, as by that woman, whom I think, I am to call mother, by that being who gave me birth, to whom I ought to look up with veneration and respect, but whom I am sorry I cannot love or admire. Within one little hour, I have not only [heard] myself, but have heard my *whole family* by the fathers side, *stigmatized* in terms that the *blackest malevolence* would [perhaps] shrink from, and that too in words [you] would be shocked to hear. Such, Augusta, such is my mother; *my mother*. I disclaim her from this time, and although I cannot help treating her with respect, I cannot reverence as I ought to do, that parent who by her outrageous conduct forfeits all title to filial affection. To you Augusta, I must look up, as my nearest relation, to you I must confide what I cannot mention to others, and I am sure you will pity me, but I entreat you to keep this a secret, nor expose that unhappy failing of this woman, which I must bear with patience. I would be very sorry to have it discovered, as I have only one week more, for the present. In the mean time you may write to me with the greatest safety, as she would not open any of my letters, even from you. I entreat then that you will favour me with an answer to this. I hope however to have the pleasure of seeing you on the day appointed, but If you could contrive any way that I may avoid being asked to dinner by Ld. C[arlisle] I would be obliged to you, as I hate strangers. Adieu, my Beloved Sister,

I remain ever yours, Byron

[TO AUGUSTA BYRON] *Burgage Manor, Southwell*
Friday April 25th. 1805

My dearest Augusta.—Thank God, I believe I shall be in town on Wednesday next, and at last relieved from those *agreeable amusements*, I described to you in my last.—I return you and Lady G[ertrude]

---

[2] Reference to the proceedings against Henry Dundas, Viscount Melville, in April, 1805, in the House of Commons, for mishandling of Naval accounts.

many thanks for your *benediction*, nor do I doubt its efficacy as it is bestowed by *two such Angelic beings*; but as I am afraid my *profane blessing* would but expedite your road to *Purgatory*, instead of *Salvation*, you must be content with my best wishes in return, since the *unhallowed adjurations* of a mere mortal would be of no effect.—You say, you are sick of the Installation,[1] and that Ld. C[arlisle] was not present; I however saw his name in the Morning post, as one of the Knights Companions; I indeed expected that *you* would have been present at the Ceremony.—I have seen this young Roscius[2] several times at the hazard of my life, from the *affectionate squeezes* of the surrounding crowd. I think him tolerable in some characters, but by no means equal to the ridiculous praises showered upon him by *John Bull*.[3] I am afraid that my stay in town ceases after the 10th.—I should not continue it so long, as we meet on the 8th at Harrow, But, I remain on purpose to hear our *Sapient* and *noble Legislators* of Both Houses debate on the Catholic Question,[4] as I have no doubt there will be many *nonsensical*, and some *Clever* things said on the occasion.—I am extremely glad that you *sport* an audience Chamber for the Benefit of your *modest* visitors, amongst whom I have *honour* to reckon myself. I shall certainly be most happy again to see you, notwithstanding my *wise* and *Good* mother, (who is at this minute thundering against Somebody or other below in the Dining Room) has interdicted my visiting at his *Lordship's* house, with the threat of her malediction, in case of disobedience, as she says, he has behaved very ill to her; the truth of this I much doubt, nor should the orders of all the mothers (especially such mothers) in the world, prevent me from seeing my Beloved Sister after so long an Absence.—I beg you will forgive this

[1] The installation of seven Knights of the Garter at Windsor on St. George's Day, April 23, 1805, was a long drawn out and tiresome affair, though colourful. Among the seven Knights invested was the Duke of Rutland, Lord Carlisle's son-in-law.

[2] "Young Roscius" was the boy actor William Henry West Betty, who drew such crowds at Covent Garden and Drury Lane that the military had to be called out to keep order.

[3] "Young Roscius" was extravagantly praised in all the journals and was made an idol by the English public.

[4] On May 10, 1805, Lord Grenville moved in the House of Lords for a committee of the whole to consider a petition to relieve the civil, naval, and military disabilities of the Catholics. Byron apparently attended the session. He was already enthusiastic about oratory and speech making, and in the back of his mind was the thought of becoming a Parliamentary orator. His second speech in the House of Lords, after his return from his first voyage abroad, on April 21, 1812, was in support of the Catholic Claims. In 1805, the motion of Grenville was defeated by 178 to 49 on May 14; and a similar motion by Fox in the Commons went down by 336 to 126 on the 15th.

well written epistle, for I write in a great Hurry, and believe me with the greatest impatience again to behold you, your

attached Brother and [Friend,
Byron]⁵

P.S.—By the bye Lady G[ertrude] ought not to complain of your writing a *decent* long letter to me, since I remember your *11 Pages* to her, at which I did not make the least complaint, but submitted like a *meek Lamb* to the [innovation?] of my privileges, for, nobody *ought* to have had so long an epistle but my *most excellent Self.*

[TO JOHN HANSON] *Harrow-on-the-Hill, 11 May, 1805*

Dear Sir,—As you promised to cash my Draft on the Day that I left your house, and as you was only prevented by the Bankers being shut up, I will be very much obliged to you to *give the ready* to this old Girl, Mother Barnard,¹ who will either present herself or send a Messenger, as she demurs on its being not payable till the 25th of June. Believe me, Sir, by doing this you will greatly oblige

Yours very truly,
Byron

[TO AUGUSTA BYRON] *Harrow June 5th. 1805*

My dearest Augusta.—At last you have had a *decent* specimen of the dowagers talents for epistles in the *furioso* style. You are now freed from the *shackles* of her correspondence, and when I revisit her, I shall be bored with long stories of your *ingratitude* & &. She is as I have before declared certainly mad, (to say she was in her senses, would be condemning her as a Criminal,) her conduct is a *happy* compound of derangement and Folly. I had the other day an epistle from her; not a word was mentioned about you, but I had some of the usual *compliments* on my own account, I am now about to answer her letter, though I shall scarcely have patience, to treat her with civility, far less with affection, that was almost over before, and this has given the finishing stroke to *filial,* which now gives way to *fraternal* duty. Believe me, dearest Augusta, not ten thousand *such* mothers, or indeed any mothers, Could induce me to give you up.—No, No, as the dowager says in that rare epistle which now lies before me, "the time has been, but

---

⁵ The signature is cut out in the MS.

¹ Mother Barnard was keeper of the "tuck-shop" catering to Harrow students.

that is past long since" and nothing now Can influence your *pretty sort of a brother*, (bad as he is) to forget that he is your *Brother*. Our first Speech day will be over ere this reaches you, but against the 2d you shall have timely notice.—I am glad to hear your illness is not of a Serious nature, *young Ladies* ought not to throw themselves in to the fidgets about a trifling delay of 9 or 10 years; age brings experience and when you in the flower of youth, between 40 and 50, shall then marry, you will no doubt say that I am a *wise man*, and that the later, one makes one's self miserable, with the matrimonial clog, the better. Adieu, my dearest Augusta, I bestow my *patriarchal blessing* on you and Lady G[ertrude] and remain

[Signature cut out]

[TO JOHN HANSON]   *Harrow on the Hill 27th June 1805*

Dear Sir,—I will be in town on Saturday morning, but it is absolutely necessary for me to return to Harrow on Tuesday or Wednesday, as Thursday is our 2d Speechday, and Butler[1] says he cannot dispense with my absence [presence?] on that Day. I thank for your compliment in the beginning of your letter and with the hope of seeing you and Hargreaves well on Saturday,

I remain yours & &.
BYRON

[TO AUGUSTA BYRON]   *Tuesday July 2d. 1805*

My dearest Augusta.—I am just returned from Cambridge, where I have been to enter myself at Trinity College.—Thursday is our Speechday at Harrow,[1] and as I forgot to remind you of its approach, previous to our first declamation. I have given you *timely* notice this time. If you intend doing me the *honour* of attending, I would recommend you not to come without a Gentleman, as I shall be too much engaged all the morning to take care of you, and I should not imagine you would admire *stalking* about by yourself. You had better be there by 12 o'clock as we begin at 1, and I should like to procure you a good place; Harrow is 11 miles from town, it will just make a *comfortable* morning's drive for you. I don't know how you are to come, but for

1 See April 20, 1805, to Hargreaves Hanson, note 1.
1 On this Speech Day (July 4th) Byron proclaimed a passionate speech from *King Lear* (Lear's address to the storm). Apparently Augusta did not come to hear him.

Godsake bring as few women with you as possible, I would wish you to Write me an answer immediately, that I may know on Thursday morning, whether you will drive over or not, and I will arrange my other engagements accordingly. I *beg Madam* you may make your appearance in one of his Lordships most *dashing* carriages, as our Harrow *etiquette*, admits of nothing but the most *superb* vehicles, on our Grand *Festivals*. In the mean time believe me dearest Augusta your affectionate Brother,

BYRON

[TO JOHN HANSON]   [*July 8, 1805*]

My dear Sir,—I have just received a letter from my Mother in which she talks of coming to Town about the *commencement* of our Holidays. If she does, it will be *impossible* for Me to to call on *my Sister*, previous to my leaving it, and at the same time I cannot conceive what the Deuce she can want at this Season in London. I have written to tell her that my Holidays commence on the 6th of August, but however July the 31st is the proper day. I beg, that if you cannot find some means to keep her in the country, that you at least will connive at this deception which I can palliate, and then I shall be down in the country before she knows where I am. My reasons for this are, that I do *not wish* to be detained in town so uncomfortably as I know I shall be if I remain with her, that *I do wish* to see my sister, and in the next place she can just as well come to town after my return to Notts, as I don't desire to be dragged about according to her Caprice, and there are some other Causes I think unnecessary to be now mentioned. If you will only contrive by settling her Business (if it is in your power) or if that is impossible; not mention any Thing about the day our Holidays commence, of which you can be easily supposed not to be informed. If I repeat, you can by any means prevent this Mother, from executing her purpose, believe me you will

greatly oblige yours truly
BYRON

[TO CHARLES DAVID GORDON[1]]   *Burgage Manor Southwell Notts.*
August 4th. 1805

Although I am greatly afraid, *my* Dearest Gordon, that you will not receive this Epistle till your return from *Abergeldie*, (as your letter

---

[1] Gordon, son of David Gordon of Abergeldie, was one of Byron's younger favourites at Harrow. The Harrow register gives his name as Charles David Gordon. He entered in the winter term, 1803.

states that you leave Ledbury on Thursday next) yet, that it may not be my fault, I have not deferred answering yours a Moment, and, as I have just now concluded my Journey, my first, and, I trust you will believe me when I say, most pleasing occupation will be to write to you. We have played the Eton and were most confoundedly beat,[2] however it was some comfort to me that I got 11 notches the 1st Innings and 7 the 2d. which was more than any of our side, except Brockman and Ipswich,[3] could contrive to hit. After the match we dined [together, and were][4] extremely friendly, not a single [discordant word] was uttered by either party. To be sure, we were most of us *rather* drunk, and went together to the Haymarket Theatre where we kicked up a row, as you may suppose when so many *Harrovians* and *Etonians* met at one place, I was one of seven in a single Hackney Coach, 4 Eton and 3 Harrow fellows, we all got into the same box, the consequence was that such a devil of a noise arose that none of our neighbours could hear a word of the drama, at which, not being *highly delighted*, they began to quarrel with us, and we nearly came to a *battle royal*. How I got home after the play God knows. I hardly recollect, as my brain was so much confused by the heat, the row, and the wine I drank, that I could not remember in the morning how the deuce I found my way to bed. The rain was so incessant in the evening that we could [hardly get our] Jarveys,[5] which was the cause of so many [being stowed into] one. I saw young Twilt, your brother at the match, and saw also an old schoolfellow of mine whom I had not beheld for six years, but, he was not the one whom you were so good as to enquire after for Me, and for which I return you my sincere thanks. I set off last night at eight o'clock for my mothers and am just arrived this afternoon and have not delayed a second in thanking you for so soon fulfilling my request that you would correspond with me. My address at Cambridge will be Trinity College but I shall not go [there] till the 20th of October[;] you may [continue] to direct your letters here; when I go to Hampshire which will not be till you have returned to Harrow, I will send my address previous to my departure from

[2] Byron boasted of his prowess in this game, which was played on August 2, 1805. He was proud that his lameness had not prevented him from acquitting himself well.

[3] W. Brockman and Lord Ipswich.

[4] Here and elsewhere in the MS. some words are missing. They are supplied from *LJ*, I, 69–72. Prothero published it from a copy apparently supplied by Dr. Blümel of Breslau, who owned the MS. before a corner of the first page was broken off.

[5] In English slang, the driver of a hackney coach, and sometimes the coach itself.

my mothers. I agree with you in the hope that we shall continue our correspondence for a long time. I trust *my* dearest Friend that it will only be interrupted by our being some time or other again in the same place or under the same roof, as when I have finished my *Classical labours* and my minority is expired, I shall expect you to be a frequent visitor to Newstead Abbey, my seat in this county, which lies about 12 miles from my mothers house where I now am; There I can show you plenty of hunting, shooting, and fishing, and be assured no one ever will be a more welcome Guest than yourself. Nor is there any one whose correspondence can give me more pleasure, or whose friendship yield me greater delight than yours. Such, dearest Charles, Believe me, will always be the sentiments of

yours most affectionately,
BYRON

[TO AUGUSTA BYRON] *Burgage Manor August 6th. 1805*

Well, my dearest Augusta, here I am, once more situated at my mothers house, which together with its *inmate* is as *agreeable* as ever. I am at this moment vis a vis and Tete a tete with that amiable personage, who is, whilst I am writing, pouring forth compliments against your *ingratitude*, giving me many oblique hints that I ought not to correspond with you, and concluding with an interdiction that if you ever after the expiration of my minority are invited to my residence, *she* will no longer condescend to grace it with her *Imperial* presence. You may figure to yourself, for your amusement, my solemn countenance on the occasion, and the *meek Lamblike* demeanor of her Ladyship, which contrasted with my *saintlike visage*, forms a *striking family painting*, whilst in the background, the portraits of my Great Grandfather and Grandmother suspended in their frames, seem to look with an eye of pity on their *unfortunate descendant*, whose *worth* and *accomplishments* deserve a *milder fate*. I am to remain in this *Garden of Eden* one month. I do not indeed reside at Cambridge till October, but I set out for Hampshire[1] in September where I shall be on a visit till the commencement of the term. In the mean time, Augusta, your *sympathetic* correspondence must be some alleviation to my *sorrows*, which however are too ludicrous for me to regard them very seriously, but they are *really* more *uncomfortable* than *amusing*.—I perceive you

---

[1] Byron was planning to visit the Hansons at their country house in Hampshire before going to Cambridge.

were rather surprised not to see my *consequential* name in the papers amongst the orators of our 2d speechday, but unfortunately some wit who had formerly been at Harrow, suppressed the *merits* of Long, Farrer,[2] and myself, who were always supposed to take the Lead in Harrow eloquence, and by way of a *hoax* thought proper to insert a panegyric on those speakers who were really and truly allowed to have rather disgraced than distinguished themselves, of course for the *wit* of the thing, the best were left out and the worst inserted, which accounts for the *Gothic omission* of my *superior talents*. Perhaps it was done with a view to weaken our vanity, which might be too much raised, by the flattering paragraphs bestowed on our performance the 1st speechday, be that as it may, we were omitted in the account of the 2d to the astonishment of all Harrow. These are *disappointments* we *great men* are liable to, and we must learn to bear them with philosophy, especially when they arise from attempts at wit. I was indeed very ill at that time, and after I had finished my speech was so overcome by the exertion that I was obliged to quit the room. I had caught cold by sleeping in damp sheets which was the cause of my indisposition. However I am now perfectly recovered, and live in hopes of being emancipated from the slavery of Burgage manor, But Believe me Dearest Augusta, whether well or ill

I always am your affect. Brother

BYRON

[TO AUGUSTA BYRON] *Burgage Manor August 10th. 1805*

I have at last succeeded, my dearest Augusta, in pacifying the dowager, and mollifying that *piece* of *flint* which the good Lady denominates her heart. She now has condescended to send you her *love*, although with many comments on the occasion, and many compliments to herself. But to me she still continues to be a torment, and I doubt not would continue so till the end of my life. However this is the last time she ever will have an opportunity, as, when I go to college, I shall employ my vacations either in town; or during the summer I intend making a tour through the Highlands, and to visit the Hebrides with a party of my friends, whom I have engaged for the purpose. This my old preceptor Drury recommended as the most

[2] Edward Noel Long, Byron's contemporary at Harrow, was later one of his closest friends at Cambridge; T. Farrer played in the cricket match against Eton with Byron.

improving way of employing my summer vacation, and I have now an additional reason for following his advice, as I by that means will avoid the society of this woman, whose detestable temper destroys every Idea of domestic comfort. It is a happy thing that she is my mother and not my wife, so that I can rid myself of her when I please, and indeed if she goes on in the style that she has done for this last week that I have been with her, I shall quit her before the month, (I am to drag out in her company) is expired, and place myself any where, rather than remain with such a vixen. As I am to have a very handsome allowance,[1] which does not deprive her of a sixpence, since there is an addition made from my fortune by the Chancellor for the purpose, I shall be perfectly independent of her, and as she has long since trampled upon, and [harrowed] up every affectionate tie, It is my [serious] determination never again to visit, or be upon any friendly terms with her. This I owe to myself, and to my own comfort, as well as Justice to the memory of my nearest relations, who have been most shamefully libelled by this female Tisiphone, a name which your *Ladyship* will recollect to have belonged to one of the Furies.———You need not take the precaution of speaking in so enigmatical a style, in your next, as bad as the woman is, she would not dare to open any letter addressed to me from you, whenever you can find time to write believe me your epistle will be productive of the greatest pleasure, to your

affectionate Brother
BYRON

[TO CHARLES DAVID GORDON]   *Burgage Manor August 14 1805*

Believe me, my dearest Charles, no letter from you can ever be unentertaining or dull, at least to me; on the contrary they will always be productive of the highest pleasure as often as you think proper to gratify me by your correspondence. My answer to your 1st was addressed to Ledbury, and I fear you will not receive it till your return from your tour, which I hope may answer your expectation in every respect; I recollect some years ago passing near Abergeldie in an excursion through the Highlands, it was at that time a most beautiful

---

[1] Hanson had secured from the Court of Chancery £500 a year for Byron's education during his Harrow years. This was paid to Mrs. Byron in quarterly instalments. When he went to Cambridge, she gave up the entire sum to her son, and applied for an allowance for herself of £200, but this was not granted and her pension from the Civil List was reduced to £200.

place. I suppose you will soon have a view of the eternal Snows that surround the top of Lachin y gair,[1] which towers so majestically above the rest of our *Northern Alps*. I still remember with pleasure the admiration which filled my mind, when I first beheld it, and further on the dark frowning mountains which rise near Invercauld, together with the romantic rocks that overshadow Mar Lodge a seat of Lord Fifes, and the cataract of the Dee, which dashes down the declivity with impetuous violence, in the Grounds adjoining to the house. All these I presume you will soon see, so that [it] is unnecessary for me to expatiate further on the subject; I sincerely wish that every happiness may attend you in your progress.————I have given you an account of our match in my epistle to Herefordshire; we unfortunately lost it, I got 11 notches the first innings and 7 the 2d. making 18 in all which was more runs than any of our side (except Ipswich) could make, Brockman also scored 18. After the match we dined together and were very *convivial*, in the evening we proceeded . . .[2]

ever most affectionately yours
BYRON

[TO AUGUSTA BYRON]   *Burgage Manor August 18th* [1805][1]

My dearest Augusta.—I seize this interval of my *amiable* mothers absence this afternoon, again to inform you, or rather to desire to be informed by you, of what is going on. For my own part I can send nothing to amuse you, excepting, a repetition of my complaints against my tormentor whose *diabolical* disposition (pardon me for staining my paper with so harsh a word) seems to increase with age, and to acquire new force with Time. The more I see of her the more my dislike augments, nor can I so entirely conquer the appearance of it, as to prevent her from perceiving my opinion, this so far from calming the Gale, blows it into a *hurricane*, which threatens to destroy every thing, till exhausted by its own violence, it is lulled into a sullen

[1] Byron's romantic feelings about the Highlands and Lachin y Gair (Erse: Lach na Garr) were expressed in his poem called "Lachin y Gair" published in *Hours of Idleness*. When he was seven or eight, his mother took him for a holiday to the valley of the Dee, not far from Abergeldie and within sight of Lachin y Gair.

[2] Here the manuscript ends.

[1] This letter is misdated 1804 in *LJ*, I, 30–31. The year is not given in the letter itself but is written on the cover where someone has crossed it out and written "1804". It is addressed to Augusta at Castle Howard, where she spent the summer of 1805. Byron's attitude toward his mother was quite different in the summer of 1804, when she was writing to Hanson that he was "truly amiable" (August 13, 1804).

torpor, which after a short period, is again roused into fresh and renewed phrenzy, to me most terrible, and to every other Spectator astonishing. She then declares that she plainly sees I hate her, that I am leagued with her bitter enemies viz. Yourself, Ld. C[arlisle][2] and Mr. H[anson] and as I never Dissemble or contradict her we are all *honoured* with a multiplicity of epithets, too *numerous*, and some of them too *gross*, to be repeated. In this society, and in this amusing and instructive manner have I dragged out a weary fortnight, and am condemned to pass another or three weeks as happily as the former. No Captive Negro, or Prisoner of war, ever looked forward to their emancipation, and return to Liberty, with more Joy, and with more lingering expectation, than I do to my escape from [this] maternal bondage, and this accursed place, [which] is the region of dullness itself, and more stupid than the banks of Lethe, though it possesses contrary qualities to the river of oblivion, as the detested scenes I now witness, make me regret the happier ones already passed, and wish their restoration. Such Augusta is the happy life I now lead, such my *amusements*, I wander about hating every thing I behold, and if I remained here a few months longer I should become, what with *envy spleen and all uncharitableness*, a complete *misanthrope*, but notwithstanding this

Believe me Dearest Augusta ever yours & &

BYRON

[TO HARGREAVES HANSON]   *Burgage Manor August 19th. 1805*

My Dear Hargreaves,—You may depend upon my Observance of your Fathers Invitation to Farleigh[1] in September, where I hope we shall be the Cause of much destruction to the feathered Tribe, and great Amusement to Ourselves. The Lancashire Trial[2] comes on very

---

[2] Frederick Howard, fifth Earl of Carlisle (1748–1825) was distantly related to Byron through the marriage in 1742 of his father, the fourth Earl, to the Hon. Isabella Byron, daughter of the fourth Lord Byron and sister to Byron's grandfather. Through the intervention of John Hanson Lord Carlisle agreed in 1799 to act as the young Lord Byron's guardian, consulting with Hanson on his education and using his influence to get Mrs. Byron a provision of £300 from the Civil List. But Mrs. Byron's temper and tantrums soon alienated him, and Byron himself was shy of asking favours of him. Augusta, who was friendly with the Carlisles and lived with them part of the time, tried with not too great success to bring them together.

[1] The Hanson country house near Basingstoke, Hampshire.

[2] The Rochdale property in Lancashire had been added to the Byron estates in the time of Edward I. The leasehold giving colliery rights on the property had been sold illegally by the fifth Lord Byron. Legal proceedings to recover it were carried on by Hanson for years without result. Shortly before Byron died in Greece that

soon, and Mr. Hanson will come down by Nottingham, perhaps, I may then have a Chance of seeing him, at all Events, I shall probably accompany him on his Way back, as I hope his Health is by this Time perfectly reestablished, and will not require a journey to Harrogate.— I shall not as you justly conjecture have any Occasion for my *Chapeau de Bras*, as there is Nobody in the Neighborhood who would be worth the Trouble of wearing it, when I went to their parties. I am uncommonly dull at this place, as you may easily imagine, nor do I think I shall have much Amusement till the Commencement of the Shooting Season, I shall expect (when you next write) an Account of your military preparations to repel the Invader of our Isle,[3] whenever he makes the Attempt. *You* will doubtless acquire *great Glory* on the Occasion, & In Expectation of hearing of your Warlike Exploits,

I remain yours very truly
BYRON

[TO HARGREAVES HANSON]   *Burgage Manor [Aug. 28, 1805]*

My Dear Hargreaves,—I would be obliged to you, if you would write to your father, and enquire what time It will be most convenient for him to receive my visit, and I will come to town immediately to the time appointed and accompany you to the *Rural Shades* and *Fertile Fields* of Hants. You must excuse the laconic style of my epistle as this place is damned dull and I have nothing to relate, but believe me

yours truly
BYRON

[TO HARGREAVES HANSON]   *Southwell Sept. 20th, 1805*

Dear Hanson,—If nothing intervenes to prevent Me, I shall be with You on Tuesday the 24th the Day of your Appointment, when I will join You with Pleasure on our intended Excursion. Till then I have the *honour* to remain,

& & yours
BYRON

part of the property to which legal claim could be established was sold. In the meantime Hanson kept feeding his hope that the legal tangles would be unravelled and that it would be worth great sums.

[3] When Napoleon was threatening an invasion of England, Hargreaves had apparently joined the home guard.

Dear Hargreaves,—I presume your Father has by this Time informed you of our safe arrival here.[1] I can as yet hardly form an opinion in favour or against the College, but as soon as I am settled you shall have an account. I wish you to pack up carefully & send immediately the Remainder of my books, and also my *Stocks* which were left in Chancery Lane *mon Chapeau de Bras* take care of till Winter extends his Icy Reign, and I shall visit the Metropolis. Tell your Father that I am getting in the Furniture he spoke of, but shall defer papering & painting till the Recess. The sooner you execute my *commands* The better. Beware of Mr. *Terry* & Believe me

yours faithfully
BYRON

The bill for Furniture I shall send to Mr. H. your worthy papa according to his *particular Desire*.[2] The Cambridge Coach sets off from the White Horse Fetter Lane.

Dear Sir.—I will be obliged to you to order me down 4 Dozen of Wine, Port—Sherry—Claret, & Madeira, one Dozen of Each; I have got part of my Furniture in, & begin to *admire* a College Life. Yesterday my appearance in the Hall in my State Robes was *Superb*, but uncomfortable to my *Diffidence*. You may order the Saddle & & for Oateater as soon as you please & I will pay for them. I remain Sir

yours truly
BYRON

P.S.—Give Hargreaves a hint to be expeditious in his sending my *valuables* which I begin to want. Your Cook had the Impudence to charge my Servant 15 Shillings for 5 days provision which I think is exorbitant, but I hear that in *Town* it is but reasonable. Pray is it the Custom to allow your Servants 3 & 6 per Diem, in London? I will thank you for Information on the Subject.

[1] Byron had entered himself at Trinity College, Cambridge, on July 1, but he did not take residence until the autumn term began on October 24, 1805.

[2] In addition to his stipend from the Court of Chancery, Byron was allowed certain funds for furniture, and other necessaries for setting up his establishment at the College.

My Dear Augusta—As might be supposed I like a College Life
extremely, especially as I have escaped the Trammels or rather
Fetters of my domestic Tyrant Mrs Byron, who continued to plague
me during my visit in July and September. I am now most pleasantly
situated in *Super*excellent Rooms,[1] flanked on one side by my Tutor,[2]
on the other by an old Fellow, both of whom are rather checks upon
my *vivacity*. I am allowed 500 a year, a Servant and Horse, so Feel as
independent as a German Prince who coins his own Cash, or a Chero-
kee Chief who coins no Cash at all, but enjoys what is more precious,
Liberty. I talk in raptures of that *Goddess* because my amiable Mama
was so despotic. I am afraid the Specimens I have lately given her, of
my Spirit, and determination to submit to no more unreasonable commands, (or the insults which follow a refusal to obey her implicitly
whether right or wrong,) have given high offence, as I had a most
fiery Letter from the *Court* at *Southwell* on Tuesday, because I would
not turn off my Servant, (whom I had not the least reason to distrust,
and who had an excellent Character from his last Master) at her
suggestion from some caprice she had taken into her head.[3] I sent back
to the Epistle which was couched in *elegant* terms a severe answer,
which so nettled her Ladyship, that after reading it she returned it in a
Cover without *deigning* a Syllable in return. The Letter and my
answer you shall behold when you next see me, that you may judge
of the Comparative merits of Each. I shall let her go on in the
Heroics, till she cools, without taking the least notice. Her Behaviour
to me for the last two Years neither merits my respect, nor deserves

[1] The location of Byron's "*Super*excellent" rooms at Trinity is still in dispute.
One early account gave it as in the southeast corner of the Great Court, rooms that
opened on the staircase of the tower. (See *Alma Mater: or, Seven Years at the
University of Cambridge. By a Trinity-Man* [J. M. F. Wright], 1827, I, 165–67.)
Another says that Byron's rooms were on the north side of Nevile's Court, on the
first floor on the west side of the central staircase. But the author adds: "Another
legend places Byron's rooms at the west end of the first floor on the south side of
the same court." These were the rooms pointed out as Byron's when the Countess
Guiccioli visited Cambridge. (See J. W. Clark, *Cambridge, Brief Historical and
Descriptive Notes*, 1870, pp. 138–39.) Keith Walker ("Byron at Trinity", *Trinity
Review*, 1961) discredits Wright and accepts Clark's statement that the rooms
were on the north side of Nevile's Court. Unfortunately Byron did not himself
give the specific location, and so we are left to legend.

[2] His tutor was the Rev. Thomas Jones (1756–1807), who had been something of
a firebrand in his younger days, having taken with ten younger Fellows a successful
stand against laxity in Fellowship elections.

[3] Mrs. Byron was right about the dishonesty of the servant Frank (Francis
Boyce) who was later found to have stolen from his master. Byron reluctantly
had him transported.

my affection. I am comfortable here, and having one of the best allowances in College, go on Gaily, but not extravagantly. I need scarcely inform you that I am not the least obliged to Mrs. B for it, as it comes off of my property, and She refused to fit out a single thing for me from her own pocket,[4] my Furniture is paid for & she has moreover a handsome addition made to her own income, which I do not in the least regret, as I would wish her to be happy, but by *no means* to live with me in *person*. The sweets of her society I have already drunk to the last dregs, I hope we shall meet on more affectionate Terms, or meet no more. But why do I say? *meet*, her temper precludes every idea of happiness, and therefore in future I shall avoid her *hospitable* mansion, though she has the folly to suppose She is to be Mistress of my house when I come of [age]. I must apologize to you for the [dullness?] Of this letter, but to tell you the [truth the effects?] of last nights Claret have no[t gone?][5] out of my head, as I supped with a large party. I suppose that Fool Hanson in his *vulgar Idiom*, by the word Jolly did not mean Fat, but High Spirits, for so far from increasing I have lost one pound in a fortnight as I find by being regularly weighed. Adieu, Dearest Augusta.

[Signature cut out]

[TO HARGREAVES HANSON]   *Trinity Coll. Novr. 12th. 1805*

Dear Hargreaves.—Return my thanks to your Father, for the *expedition* he has used in filling my Cellar; He deserves commendation for the *Attention* he paid to my Request. The Time of Oateaters Journey approaches, I presume he means to repair his Neglect, by punctuality in this Respect, However no *Trinity Ale* will be forthcoming till I have broached the promised *Falernum*. College improves in every thing but Learning, nobody here seems to look into an author ancient or modern if they can avoid it. The Muses poor Devils, are totally neglected, except by a few Musty old *Sophs* and *Fellows*, who however agreeable they may be to *Minerva*, are perfect Antidotes to the *Graces*. Even I (great as is my *inclination* for *Knowledge*) am carried away by the Tide, having only supped at Home twice, since I saw your Father, and have more Engagements on my hands for A Week to come. Still my Tutor & I go on extremely well, and for the 1st three weeks of my Life, I have not involved myself in any Scrape of

4 See Aug. 10, 1805, to Augusta Byron, note 1.
5 The conjectural words in brackets were torn out with the seal.

80

Consequence.—I have news for you, which I bear with *Christian Resignation*, and without any *violent Transports* of *Grief*. My mother, (whose diabolical Temper you well know) has taken it into her *sagacious* head to quarrel with me her *dutiful Son*. She has such a Devil of a Disposition, that she cannot be quiet, though there arc fourscore miles between us, which I wish were lengthened to 400. [The] Cause [is too fri?]volous to require taking up your [time to?] read, or mine to write. At last in answer to a *Furious Epistle*, I returned a *Sarcastick* answer, which so incensed the *Amiable Dowager*, that my Letter was sent back without her deigning a Line in the Cover. When I next see you, you shall behold her Letter and my answer which will amuse you, as they both contain fiery *Philippics*. I must request you will write immediately, that I may be informed when my Servant shall convey Oateater from London, the 20th was the appointed Day, but I wish to hear Farther from your Father. I hope all the Family are in a Convalescent State. I shall see you at Christmas (if I live) as I propose passing the Vacation, which is only a month, in London. Believe me *Mr. Terry*[1]

yours truly
BYRON

[TO JOHN HANSON]   *Trin. Coll. Cambridge Novr. 23d. 1805*

Dear Sir.—Your advice was good but I have not determined whether I shall follow it, this place is the *Devil*, or at least his principal residence, they call it the University, but any other appellation would have suited it much better, for Study is the last pursuit of the Society; the Master[1] eats, drinks, and Sleeps, the Fellows *drink*, *dispute* and *pun*, the *employments* of the under Graduates you will probably conjecture without my description. I sit down to write with a head confused with dissipation, which though I hate, I cannot avoid. I have only supped at home 3 times since my arrival, and my table is constantly covered with invitations, after all I am the most *steady* man in the College, nor have I got into *many* Scrapes, and none of consequence. Whenever you appoint a day my Servant shall come up for

---

[1] The "Mr. Terry" seems to be a private joke of some sort which Byron shared with Hargreaves. See also Oct. 25, 1805, to Hargreaves.

[1] William Lort Mansel was Master of Trinity from 1798 until his death in 1820. He was a wit and was noted for his epigrams. He also had a reputation for being a strict disciplinarian and stood on his dignity to the point that he became the butt of certain undergraduate wits, notably, Byron's friend Charles Skinner Matthews. See Byron's letter of November 19, 1820, to John Murray.

Oateater, and as the Time of paying my bill now approaches the remaining £50 will be very *agreeable*. You need not make any deduction as I shall want most of it, I will settle with you for the Saddle and accoutrements *next* quarter. The Upholsterer's bill will not be sent in yet, as my Rooms are to be papered and painted at Xmas, when I will procure them; No Furniture has been got except what was absolutely necessary, including some decanters and wine Glasses. Your Cook certainly deceived you, as I know my Servant was in Town 5 days, and she stated 4. I have yet had no reason to distrust him, but we will examine the affair when I come to Town, when I intend Lodging at Mrs. Massingberds.[2] My Mother and I have quarrelled, which I bear with the *patience* of a philosopher, custom reconciles one to every thing. In the hope that Mrs. H. and the *Battalion* are in good Health I remain Sir & &

BYRON

[TO JOHN HANSON]   *Trinity College, Cambridge. Novr. 30th. 1805*

Sir—After the contents of your epistle you will probably be less surprised at my answer, than I have been at many points of yours;[1] never was I more astonished than at the perusal, for I confess I expected very different Treatment.—Your *indirect* charge of Dissipation does not affect me, nor do I fear the strictest enquiry into my conduct, neither here nor at *Harrow* have I disgraced myself, the "Metropolis" & the "Cloisters" are alike unconscious of my debauchery, and on the plains of *merry Sherwood*, I have experienced *Misery* alone; in July I visited them for the *last* Time. Mrs. Byron & myself are now totally separated, injured by her, I sought refuge with Strangers,

[2] Elizabeth Massingberd was a widow with a daughter who lived at 16 Piccadilly. In 1802 Mrs. Byron had taken rooms with her, and Byron spent part of the summer there. Thereafter he frequently rented a room from her when he was in London, and later she and her daughter became security for him with usurers. Whether Mrs. Byron knew of her distant relationship with the Byron family is unknown. According to a genealogical table sent by Anthony Powell to John Murray with some copies of Byron's letters to Mrs. Massingberd, she was descended from Gervase Rosel, whose sister Elizabeth married the 2nd Lord Byron. Her maiden name was Elizabeth Waterhouse. In 1794 she married Captain Thomas Massingberd, RN, of Candlesby Hall, Lincolnshire, a friend of Nelson. Anthony Powell is the great grandson of Mrs. Massingberd's sister Anne and hence inherited the family papers.

[1] Byron misunderstood Hanson's statement about the allowance from the Court of Chancery for his furniture. What he had said was that the sum was not yet available, not that Byron would have to pay the bill out of his general allowance. Byron was mollified by Hanson's explanation in his next letter.

too late I see my error, for how was kindness to be expected from *others*, when denied by a *parent*. In you Sir I imagined I had found an Instructor, for your advice I thank you; the Hospitality of yourself & Mrs. H. on many occasions, I shall always gratefully remember, for I am not of opinion, that even prcsent injustice can cancel past obligations. Before I proceed it will be necessary to say a few words concerning Mrs. Byron; you hinted a probability of her appearance at Trinity; the instant I hear of her arrival, I quit Cambridge, though *Rustication* or *Expulsion* be the consequence, many a weary week of *torment* have I passed with her, nor have I forgot the insulting *Epithets* with which, *myself*, my *Sister*, my *Father*, & my *Family* have been repeatedly reviled. To return to you, Sir, though I feel obliged by your hospitality &&; in the present instance, I have been completely deceived. When I came down to College and even previous to that period, I stipulated that not only my Furniture but even my Gowns & Books, should be paid for, that I might set out, free from *Debt*; now, with all the *Sang Froid* of your profession, you tell me, that not only, I shall not be permitted to repair my Rooms (which was at first agreed to) but that I shall not even be indemnified for my present expence. In one word hear my determination. I will *never* pay for them out of my allowance, and the Disgrace will not attach to me, but to *those* by whom I have been deceived. Still, Sir, not even the Shadow of dishonour shall reflect upon *my* name, for I will see that the Bills are discharged, whether by you or not is to me indifferent, so that the men I [emp]loy are not the victims of my Imprudence or your duplicity. I have ordered nothing extravagant, every man in College is allowed to fit up his rooms, mine are secured to me during my residence which will probably be some time, and in rendering them decent, I am more praiseworthy than culpable.— The money I requested was but a secondary consideration, as a *Lawyer* you were not obliged to advance it till due, as a *Friend* the request might have been complied with, when it is required at Xmas, I shall expect the demand will be answered. In the course of my Letter I perhaps have expressed more asperity than I intended, it is my nature to feel warmly, nor shall any consideration of interest or Fear ever deter me from giving vent to my Sentiments when injured whether by a Sovereign or a subject. I remain & &

BYRON

Sir.—In charging you with downright *Duplicity*, I *wronged* You, nor do I hesitate to atone for an Injury which I feel I have committed, or add to my Fault by the vindication of an expression dictated by Resentment; an *expression* which deserves Censure, & demands the Apology I now offer; For I think that Disposition indeed *mean*, which adds obstinacy to Insult, by attempting the Palliation of unguarded Invective, from the mistaken principle, of disdaining the avowal of even *self convicted* Error.—In Regard to the other *declarations* my Sentiments remain *unaltered*, the Event will shew whether my prediction is false, I know Mrs. Byron too well to imagine that She would part with a *Sous*, and if by some *miracle* she was prevailed upon, the *Details* of her *Generosity* in allowing me part of my *own property*, would be continually *thundered* in my ears, or *launched* in the *Lightning* of her *Letters*, so that I had rather encounter the evils of Embarrassment, than lie under an obligation to one, who would continually reproach me with her *Benevolence*, as if her Charity had been extended to a *Stranger* to the Detriment of her own Fortune. Sir, my opinion is perhaps harsh for a Son, but it is Justified by experience, it is confirmed by *Facts*; it was generated by oppression, it has been nourished by Injury. To you Sir I attach no Blame, I am too much indebted to your kindness, to retain my anger for a length of Time, that *kindness* which by a Forcible contrast has taught me to Spurn the *Ties of Blood* unless strengthened by proper and Gentle Treatment. I declare upon my honour that the Horror of entering Mrs. Byron's House has of late years been so implanted in my Soul, that I dreaded the Approach of the vacations as the Harbingers of Misery, my letters to my Sister written during my residence at Southwell would prove my assertion. With my kind Remembrance to Mrs. H. and Hargreaves,

I remain Sir yours truly
BYRON

Madam,—As I shall have occasion to be a few weeks in Town after the 18th of this Month, I would be obliged to You if you would let me [have] two Rooms one for myself, and the other [for] my Servant, a Sitting Room is not required if it is not inconvenient I should prefer

1 See Nov. 23, 1805, to Hanson, note 2.

living with the Family. The Terms I leave entirely to yourself, and as my Servant is on Board wages, the Lodging is all that will be necessary for him. I request the favour of an Answer, whether you can receive me, as I should be unwilling to put you to the least trouble. I have the honour to be

your obedient Humble Servant

BYRON

[TO JOHN HANSON]   *Trin. Coll. Cambridge Decr. 13th. 1805*

Dear Sir.—I return you my thanks for the remaining 50 which came in extremely apropos, & on my Visit to Town about the 19th will give you a regular Receipt.—In your extenuation of Mrs. Byron's conduct, you use as a *plea* that by her being my Mother, greater allowance ought to be made, for those *little* Traits in her Disposition so much more *energetic* than *elegant*. I am afraid (however good your Intention) that you have added to, rather than diminished my Dislike, for independent of the moral obligations she is under to *protect, cherish,* & *instruct* her *offspring* what can be expected of that mans *heart* & understanding, who has continually (from childhood to Maturity) beheld so pernicious an Example? His nearest Relation is the first person he is taught to revere, as his Guide & Instructor, the perversion of Temper before him leads to a corruption of his own, and when that is depraved, Vice quickly becomes habitual. And though timely Severity may sometimes be necessary & Justifiable, a *peevish harassing* System of Torment is by no means commendable, & when now & then interrupted by Ridiculous Indulgence, the only purpose answered, is to soften the Feelings for a Moment, which are soon after to be doubly wounded by the Recal of accustomed Harshness. I will now give this disagreeable subject to the *Winds*. I conclude by observing, that I am the more confirmed in my opinion of the Futility of Natural Ties unless supported not only by Attachment but *affectionate* & *prudent* Behaviour.—Tell Mrs. H. that the predicted alteration in my Manners & Habits has not taken place. I am still the Schoolboy and as great a *Rattle* as ever, and between ourselves, College is not the place to improve either Morals or Income. I am Sir yours truly

BYRON

[TO AUGUSTA BYRON]   *16 Piccadilly Decr. 26th. 1805*

My dearest Augusta.—By the date of my Letter you will perceive that I have taken up my Residence in the metropolis where I presume we shall behold you in the latter end of January. I sincerely hope you will make your appearance at that Time as I have some subjects to discuss with you, which I do not wish to communicate in my Epistle. The Dowager has thought proper to solicit a reconciliation which in some measure I have agreed to; still there is a cooling which I do not feel inclined to *thaw*, as terms of Civility are the only resources against her impertinent and unjust proceedings with which you are already acquainted. Town is not very full and the weather has been so unpropitious that I have not been able to make use of my Horse above twice since my arrival. I hope your everlasting negociation with the Father or your *Intended* is near a conclusion in *some* manner,[1] if you do not hurry a little, you will be verging into the *"Vale* of *Years"* and though you may be blest with Sons and daughters, you will never live to see your *Grandchildren*. When convenient favour me with an Answer and believe me

[Signature cut out]

[TO AUGUSTA BYRON]   *16 Piccadilly Decr. 27th. 1805*

My dear Augusta.—You will doubtless be surprised to see a second epistle so close upon the arrival of the first, (especially as it is not my custom) but the Business I mentioned rather mysteriously in my last compels me again to proceed. But before I disclose it, I must require the most inviolable Secrecy, for if ever I find that it has transpired, all confidence all Friendship between us has concluded. I do not mean this exordium as a threat to induce you to comply with my request but merely (whether you accede or not) to keep it a Secret. And although your compliance would especially oblige me, yet believe me my esteem will not be diminished by your Refusal; nor shall I suffer a complaint to escape. The Affair is briefly thus; like all other young men just let loose, and especially one as I am freed from the worse than bondage of my maternal home, I have been extravagant, and consequently am in want of Money. You will probably now imagine that I am going to apply to you for some. No, if you would offer me thousands, I declare solemnly that I would without hesitation refuse, nor would I accept them were I in danger of Starvation. All I expect or wish is that you will be joint Security with me for a few Hundreds a person (one of the money lending tribe) has offered to advance in case I can bring forward any collateral guarantee that he will not be a loser, the reason of this requisition, is my being a Minor, and might refuse to dis-

[1] See Oct. 25, 1804, to Augusta Byron, note 2.

86

charge a debt contracted in my non age.[1] If I live to the period of my minority expires, you cannot doubt my paying, as I have property to the amount of 100 times the sum I am about to raise, if, as I think rather probable, a pistol or a Fever cuts short the thread of my existence, you will receive half the *Dross* saved since I was ten years old, and can be no great loser by discharging a debt of 7 or £800 from as many thousands. It is far from my Breast, to exact any promise from you that would be detrimental, or tend to lower me in your opinion. If you suppose this leads to either of those consequences, forgive my impertinence and bury it in oblivion. I have many Friends, most of them in the same predicament with myself, to those who are not I am too proud to apply, for I hate obligation, my Relations you know I *detest*, who then is there that I can address on the subject but yourself, to you therefore I appeal, and if I am disappointed, at least let me not be tormented by the advice of Guardians, and let silence rule your Resolution. I know you will think me foolish if not criminal, but tell me so yourself, and do not rehearse my failings to others, no not even to that proud Grandee the Earl whom [sic] whatever his qualities may be, is certainly not amiable, and that Chattering puppy Hanson would make still less allowance for the foibles of a Boy. I am now trying the experiment, whether a woman can retain a secret, let me not be deceived. If you have the least doubt of my integrity, or that you run too great a Risk, do not hesitate in your refusal. Adieu. I expect an answer with impatience, believe me, whether you accede or not,

[Signature cut out]

P.S.—I apologize for the numerous errors probably enveloped in this cover the temper of my mind at present, and the hurry I have written in, must plead for pardon. Adieu.

[TO AUGUSTA BYRON]   *16 Piccadilly*
January 7th. 1805 [sic] [1806]

My dearest Augusta—Your efforts to reanimate my sinking spirits will, I am afraid, fail in their effect, for my melancholy proceeds from a very different cause to that which you assign, as, my nerves were

[1] This was the beginning of Byron's involvement with money-lenders. Augusta was frightened and offered to lend him money. In the end Mrs. Massingberd and her daughter signed as joint guarantors of his loan, and in the next few years they acted as mediators with the usurers until his debts amounted to nine or ten thousand pounds before he left England on his Eastern voyage in 1809.

always of the strongest texture.—I will not however pretend to say I possess that *Gaieté de Coeur* which formerly distinguished me, but as the diminution of it arises from what you could not alleviate, and might possibly be painful, you will excuse the Disclosure. Suffice it to know, that it cannot spring from Indisposition, as my Health was never more firmly established than now, nor from the subject on which I lately wrote, as that is in a promising Train, and even were it otherwise, the Failure would not lead to Despair.—You know me too well to think it is *Love*;[1] & I have had no quarrel or dissention with Friend or enemy, you may therefore be easy, since no unpleasant consequence will be produced from the present *Sombre* cast of my Temper.—I fear the Business will not be concluded before your arrival in Town, when we will settle it together, as by the 20th these *sordid Bloodsuckers*, who have agreed to furnish the Sum, will have drawn up the Bond, Believe me, dearest Sister, it never entered in to my head, that you either could or would propose to antic[ipate] my application to others, by a P[resent from?] yourself, I and I only will be [injured?] by my own extravagance, nor would have wished you to take the least concern, had any other means been open for extrication. As it is, I hope you will excuse my Impertinence, or if you feel an inclination to retreat, do not let affection for me counterbalance prudence.

[Signature cut out]

[TO MRS. CATHERINE GORDON BYRON] *16 Piccadilly*
Feby. 26th. 1806

Dear Mother,—Notwithstanding your *sage* and economical advice I have paid my *Harrow* Debts, as I can better afford to wait for the Money, than the poor Devils who were my Creditors.—I have also discharged my College Bills, amounting to £231—£75 of which I shall trouble Hanson to repay, being for Furniture, and as my allowance is £500 per annum, I do not chuse to lose the overplus as it makes only £125 per Quarter. I happen to have a few hundreds in ready Cash lying by me,[1] so I have paid the accounts, but I find it incon-

---

[1] It seems probable that Byron's melancholy perturbation at the time was caused by his involvement with John Edleston, a choirboy at Trinity Chapel, for whom he had developed "a violent, though *pure* love and passion". See letter, July 5, 1807, to Elizabeth Pigot, and diary of January 12, 1821. It is possible also that his desperate need for money (he never specified what his "extravagances" were) was the result of his giving some financial assistance to Edleston, as he did later, and more openly, to Hodgson and others when he was himself in economic difficulties and had to borrow money. For further details of Byron's relationship with Edleston, see Marchand, *Byron: A Biography*, I, 107–9.

venient to remain at College, not for the Expence, as I could live on my Allowance, (only I am naturally extravagant) however the mode of going on does not suit my constitution, improvement at an English University to a Man of Rank is you know impossible, and the very Idea *ridiculous*. Now I sincerely desire to finish my Education, and having been some Time at Cambridge, the Credit of the University is as much attached to my Name, as if I had pursued my Studies *there* for a Century, but believe me it is nothing more than a Name, which is already acquired; I can now leave it with honour, as I have paid every thing, and wish to pass a couple of Years abroad, where I am certain of employing my Time to far more advantage and at much less expence, than at our English Seminaries. Tis true I cannot enter France, but Germany, and the Courts of Berlin, Vienna, and Petersburg, are still open; I shall lay this Plan before Hanson & Lord C[arlisle] I presume you will all agree, and if you do not, I will if possible get away without your consent, though I should admire it more in the Regular manner and with a Tutor of your furnishing. This is my project, at present I wish *you* to be silent to Hanson, about it, who by the bye, told me he would endeavour to procure your £600 arrears of Income [Tax?],[2] as his Friends are now in possession of the *Treasury*. Let me have your Answer, I intend remaining in Town a month longer, when perhaps I shall bring my Horses and myself down to your residence in that *execrable* Kennel. I hope you have engaged a Man Servant—else it will be impossible for me to visit you, since my Servant must attend chiefly to his horses, at the same Time you must cut an Indifferent Figure with only maids in your habitation,

I remain yours,

BYRON

[1] According to his later statement to Hanson, Byron had seen an advertisement of a money-lender by the name of King in a newspaper and applied to him, and in January 1806, borrowed several hundred pounds from him at ruinous interest. Through him he became acquainted with other usurers who supplied his needs until he went abroad in 1809, at which time he was in debt to the extent of about £10,000. See letter of Jan. 16, 1812, to Hanson.

[2] Mrs. Byron had applied (unsuccessfully) for £200 a year from the Court of Chancery; her pension from the Civil List was reduced to £200 when the grant of £500 a year was made for Byron's education. The meaning is not clear here, but it seems that Hanson was trying to collect arrears of her pension which was paid irregularly. On October 12, 1820, Byron forwarded to Kinnaird some receipts "sent long ago by Messrs. Hanson. It is some money due from Government to my mother, who was (as a limb of the Stuarts) a pensioner." There are indications that Byron intended to delete the word "tax" with an indecipherably deleted word before it.

16 Piccadilly March 3d. 1806

Sir,—I called at your house in Chancery Lane yesterday Evening, as I expected you would have been in Town, but was disappointed; if convenient I should be glad to see you on Wednesday Morning about one o'clock, as I wish for your advice on some Business. On Saturday one of my horses threw me, I was stunned for a short time, but soon recovered, and suffered no material *Injury*, the accident happened on the Harrow Road.—I have paid Jones's Bill amounting to £231.4S.5D. of which I expect to be reimbursed £75 for Furniture, I have got his Banker's receipt, and the account ready for your Inspection. I now owe nothing at Cambridge, but shall not return this Term, as I have been extremely *unwell*, and at the same Time can stay where I am at much less Expence, and *equal improvement*. I wish to consult you on several Subjects, and expect you will pay me a Visit on Wednesday, in the mean Time

I remain yours, &
BYRON

[TO JOHN HANSON] *16 Piccadilly nr. Park Lane*
10th March 1806

Sir,—As in all probability you will not make your Appearance tomorrow, I must disclose by Letter, the Business I intended to have discussed at our Interview. We know each other sufficiently to render Apology unnecessary. I shall therefore without further Prelude proceed to the Subject in Question.—You are not ignorant, that I have lately lived at considerable Expence, to support which my allotted Income by the *sapient* Court of Chancery is inadequate, I confess I have borrowed a trifling Sum,[1] and now wish to raise £500 to discharge some Debts I have contracted, my approaching Quarter will bring me £200 due from my allowance, and if you can procure me the other £300 at a moderate Interest, it will save me 100 per Cent I must pay my *Israelite* for the same *Service*.—You see by this I have an *excellent* Idea of Economy even in Extravagance by being willing to pay as little for my Money as possible; for the Cash must be disbursed *somewhere* or *somehow*, and if you decline (as in prudence I tell you fairly

---

[1] In his letter to Augusta he had mentioned £700 or £800. Whether he was trying to raise more money through Hanson at normal rates of interest to pay off the usurer, or merely to pay additional debts is not clear. Since Hanson did not supply him, he apparently went again to the "Tribe of Levi".

you ought) the *Tribe* of *Levi* will be my *dernier Resort,* however I thought proper to make this Experiment, with very slender hopes of Success indeed, since Recourse to the *Law,* is at best a *desperate* Effort. I have now laid open my Affairs to You, without Disguise, and stated the Facts as they appear, declining all Comments, or the use of any Sophistry to palliate my application, or urge my Request. All I desire is a speedy Answer, whether successful or not believe me yours truly

BYRON

[TO JOHN HANSON]   *16 Piccadilly 25th. March. 1806*

Sir,—Your last Letter, as I expected, contained much Advice, but no Money, I could have excused the former unaccompanied by the Latter, since any one thinks himself capable of giving that, but very few chuse to own themselves competent to the other.—I do not now write to urge a 2d Request, one Denial is sufficient. I only require what is my Right; this is Lady Day, £125 is due for my last Quarter, and £75 for my Expenditure on Furniture at Cambridge, £200 I will trouble you to remit.—The Court of Chancery may perhaps put in Force your threat,[1] I have always understood it formed a Sanction for legal plunderers to protract the Decision of Justice from Year to Year, till weary of Spoil it at Length condescended to give Sentence, but I never yet understood, even its unhallowed hands preyed upon the Orphan it was bound to protect.—Be it so, only let me have your Answer

I remain & &
BYRON

[TO JOHN HANSON]   *16 Piccadilly April 10th. 1806*

Sir,—In a few Days I set off for Cambridge and will trouble you for £200 due to me since Lady Day last as that alone delays my departure.

B—

---

[1] Hanson had warned Byron that the Court of Chancery might cut off his allowance if he did not return to Cambridge.

Trinity College, Cambridge,
May 16th. 1806

Sir,—You cannot be more indignant, at the insolent and unmerited Conduct of Mr. Mortlock,² than those who authorised you to request his permission.—However, we do not yet despair of gaining our Point, and every Effort shall be made to remove the Obstacles, which at present prevent the Execution of our Project.—I Yesterday waited on the Master of this College,³ who having a personal Dispute with the Mayor, declined interfering, but recommended an Application to the Vice Chancellor, whose Authority is Paramount in the University. —I shall communicate this to Ld. Altamont,⁴ and we will endeavour to bend the O[b]stinacy of the *Upstart* Magistrate, who seems to be equally deficient in Justice, and common Civility.—On my arrival in Town which will take place in a few Days, you will see me at Albany Buildings, when we will discuss the Subject further.—Present my Remembrance to the Messrs. Angelo Jr. and believe me, we will yet *humble* this *impertinent Bourgeois.* I remain, Sir

your Obedt. Servt.
BYRON

[TO JOHN HANSON] *Trin. Coll. Cambridge, June 16, 1806*

Dear Sir,—I have received a letter from your Son, in which he justly complains of my want of punctuality as a Correspondent, but as the Detail of a Cambridge Life can be neither amusing or interesting, I have forebore troubling him, or You with an Epistle.—I will be obliged to you to send £125, the amount of my last quarter, which becomes due about this Time, as I have some payments to make previous to my Departure.—With compts to all the Family I

remain Sir yours & &
BYRON

¹ The popular fencing master, from whom Byron took lessons from his Harrow days on, travelled to Cambridge every other week in 1806 to visit his pupils. It was probably through him that Byron met John ("Gentleman") Jackson, the boxing instructor, for they shared rooms at 13 Bond Street.

² Mr. Mortlock: Mayor of Cambridge.

³ William Lort Mansel, Master of Trinity, 1798–1820.

⁴ Peter Howe Browne, Lord Altamont (1788–1845) was at Jesus College, Cambridge. He succeeded his father as second Marquis of Sligo in 1809. He was in Athens while Byron was there in 1810.

Trin. Coll. Camb.
July 8th. 1806

My dear Madam,—Your Letter was as I expected of the dubious Nature, and you acted perfectly right in demanding a decisive Answer. —I am detained in Cambridge by the painting of my Carriage, nor take my departure till Saturday, if therefore you write tomorrow or on Thursday your Epistle will decide this tedious, protracted Affair.— Believe me the obligation I feel is equal, as if success had attended our Endeavours.—I bear the disappointment with philosophy, notwithstanding the Inconvenience the failure will produce.—I shall however expect your answer, though without the most remote Idea of the Business being finally settled.—you know my opinion of your Agent, ever since the last Transaction, nor shall I feel surprised at any thing, after his conduct on that occasion.—[1] Present my best acknowledgments to Miss M[assingberd] and believe me Madam,

yours very sincerely
BYRON

[TO JOHN M. B. PIGOT[1]] *16. Piccadilly August 9th. 1806*

My dear Pigot,—Many thanks for your amusing Narrative of the late proceedings of my *amiable Alecto*, who now begins to feel the Effects of her Folly.—[2] I have just received a *penitential Epistle*, to which apprehensive of pursuit, I have dispatched a moderate Answer, with a *kind* of promise to return in a fortnight, this however *"entre nous"* I never mean to fulfil.—Her *soft warblings* must have delighted her auditors, her *higher* Notes being particularly *musical*, and on a calm moonlight Evening, would be heard to great Advantage.—Had I been present, as a Spectator, nothing would have pleased me more, but to have come forward as one of the "Dramatis personae"—St Dominic defend me from such a Scene!!! Seriously, your Mother has laid me under great obligations, & you with the rest of the family, merit my warmest thanks, for your kind Connivance at my Escape from "Mrs.

---

[1] Mrs. Massingberd was acting as go-between for Byron with the moneylenders (see Dec. 27, 1805, to Augusta Byron, note 1).

[1] John M. B. Pigot, like his sister Elizabeth, was a close friend of Byron at Southwell. Elizabeth was six years and John three years older than Byron. The Pigots lived across the green from Burgage Manor, Mrs. Byron's house, and Byron often escaped there from his mother's tantrums. The whole Pigot family was devoted to him. John was on holiday from his study of medicine at Edinburgh.

[2] After a quarrel with his mother, Byron aided by the Pigots, left for London in the middle of the night.

Byron furiosa".—Oh! for the pen of Ariosto to rehearse in *Epic*, the *scolding* of that *momentous Eve*, or rather let me invoke the Shade of *Dantè* to inspire me, for none but the author of the *"Inferno"* could properly preside over such an Attempt.—But perhaps where the pen might fail, the pencil would succeed; what a group would you form for the Colours of Poussin (who I think, but will not be positive, dealt in the *horrible*)[3] Mrs. B. the principal figure, you cramming your ears with *Cotton*, as the only antidote to total deafness, Mrs. P. in vain endeavouring, to mitigate the wrath, of the *Lioness* robbed of her *whelp*; and last, though not least, Elizabeth & *Wousky*[4] *wonderful* to relate! *both* deprived of their *parts* of *Speech*. & bringing up the Rear in *mute* astonishment. How did Sherard B.[5] receive the Intelligence? how many *puns* did he utter on so *facetious* an Event? in your next inform me on this point, & what excuse you made to Anne Houson.[6] You are probably by this Time tired of decyphering this *hieroglyphical* Letter; like Tony Lumpkin, you will pronounce mine to be a d--n-d up & down *hand*.—All Southwell without doubt is involved in Amazement, apropos, how does my *blue* eyed Nun the fair Julia?[7] is she *"robed in the sable garb of Woe"*.—To her & Bid, with your Sister Bridget[8] & *Wousky*, or any other Ladies of our Acquaintance, I desire to be remembered.—Here I remain at least a week or 10 days, previous to my departure you shall receive my address, but what it will be I have not determined.—My Lodgings must be kept secret from Mrs. B. You may present my *Compts*. & tell her any attempt to pursue me, will fail, as I have taken measures to retreat immediately to Portsmouth, on the first Intimation of her removal from Southwell. You may add I have now proceeded to a friend's house in the Country, there to remain [a] fortnight.—I have now *blotted*, (I cannot [say] written) a complete

[3] Byron was not knowledgeable about painting, and in general cared little for it, except for some lifelike pictures such as those of Giorgione (see *Beppo*, stanzas 11–13).

[4] Wousky was a dog, perhaps belonging to the Pigots.

[5] Probably Sherard Becher, who was perhaps a cousin of the Pigots (Mrs. Pigot was a Becher before she married). In a letter dated Jan. 13, 1807, to John Pigot, Byron referred to "S. Becher". See also October 26, 1807, to Elizabeth Pigot.

[6] A Southwell girl to whom Byron wrote several poems, posthumously published (see *Poetry*, I, 244–47).

[7] Julia Leacroft interested Byron briefly during his stay in Southwell. See Aug. 29, 1804, to Elizabeth Pigot, note 2. The reference to "the blue-eyed Nun" indicates that the flattering poem "Lines written in 'Letters of an Italian Nun and an English Gentleman', by J. J. Rousseau, founded on facts" was addressed to her, as was also the more facetious "To Lesbia" and "To a Lady who Presented the Author a Lock of Hair . . ."

[8] Elizabeth Bridget Pigot.

double Letter, & in Return shall expect, a *monstrous Budget*, without doubt the *Dames* of S. reprobate the pernicious example I have shewn, & tremble lest their *Babes* should disobey their mandate's, & quit in dudgeon, their *Mamma's* on any grievance.—Adieu. when you begin your next, drop the "Lordship" & put "Byron" in its place. believe me

yours & &

BYRON

[TO EDWARD NOEL LONG[1]]   *16 Piccadilly August 9th. 1806*

My dear Long,—You will probably *marvel*, at the Date of this Epistle, conceiving me still at Burgage, with my *agreeable* Relative.— To explain this Revolution, it is necessary to relate that finding *Gam*, worse instead of Better, I took the Liberty of departing in my Carriage & four, without "*Beat of Drum*" in the "Dead of the Night" but as you will possibly imagine, without "*singing out three Times*" to inform the Inhabitants, of my Retreat.—I shall remain in Town, about a week, till renovated with "*Suskins*"[2] & then proceed to the Sea, but what part is indifferent to me, if you will therefore in your answer, mention the Place where you at present *sojourn*, & the Best Hotel, I will join you speedily.—I have some Idea if I find it convenient, of visiting Cambridge for a couple of Days, to pay my Bills, Should I execute this plan, & you feel an Inclination to review our ancient Residence, I shall be happy in your Society, & we will afterwards proceed to the Ocean together.—In my next, you will learn what I have determined, but in the Interim, I shall expect some Intelligence from your prolific pen. I decamped from Notts. in such a Devil of a hurry that my poem's are left in the hands of the printer, and *Gam* [was?] so suspicious of my Intents [that?] my [pistols?] were left behind, and my Clothes brought off in Bundles.—I wait with some Impatience your Answer, doubtless full of Amazement, at my sudden March, of which you shall hear the Detail at length on our Meeting. Adieu believe me

yours & &

BYRON

[1] One of Byron's closest friends at Harrow and Cambridge. He was the son of E. B. Long of Hampton Lodge, Surrey.

[2] A "suskin" or "seskin" was a small coin used in England in the early 15th century, passing for a penny; here, facetiously, money.

My dear *Bridget*,—As I have already troubled your Brother, with more, than he will find pleasure in decyphering, you are the next, to whom I shall assign, the difficult employment, of perusing this 2d. Epistle.—You will perceive from my 1st. that no Idea of *Mrs. B's* arrival had disturbed me, at the Time it was written; *not* so the present, since the appearance of a Note from the *Illustrious Cause* of my sudden *Decampment*, has driven the "natural Ruby from my Cheeks," & completely *blanched* my woebegone Countenance.—This *Gunpowder* Intimation of her arrival (confound her activity!) breathes less of terror & dismay, than you will probably imagine, from the *volcanic* temperament of her *Ladyship*, & concludes with the comfortable Assurance of all *present motion* being prevented, by the Fatigue of her Journey; for which my *Blessings* are due to the *rough* Roads, & restive quadrupeds of his Majesty's highways, & Innkeepers.—As I have not the smallest Inclination to be chaced round the Country, I shall e'en make a merit of necessity, & since like Macbeth, "they've tied me to a Stake, I cannot fly" I shall imitate that *valourous* Tyrant, & "Bearlike fight the Course" all escape being precluded. I can engage now at less disadvantage, having drawn the Enemy from her *Intrenchments*, though like the *prototype*, to whom I have compared myself, with an *excellent* chance of being knocked on the head, however, "lay on Macduff, & d - - n - - d be he who first cries hold, Enough."—I shall remain fixed in Town for at least a Week, & expect to hear from *you*, before its expiration.—I presume the printer has brought to you, the offspring of my *poetic Mania*, remember in the 1st Line to read "*loud* the winds whistle"[1] instead of *round*, which that Blockhead Ridge[2] has inserted by mistake & makes nonsense of the whole Stanza.—Adio! now to encounter my *Hydra*.

yours ever
BYRON

[1] This was in the first poem of his *Fugitive Pieces*, there titled "On Leaving N - - st - - d". When his next privately printed volume, *Poems on Various Occasions*, appeared, the title was "On Leaving Newstead Abbey", and he had changed the phrase to "the hollow winds whistle".

[2] John Ridge, in the nearby town of Newark, was printing *Fugitive Pieces*.

Dear Pigot,—This *astonishing* packet, will doubtless amaze you, but having an idle hour this evening, I wrote the inclosed Stanza's,[1] which I request you to deliver [to] Ridge to be printed *separate* from my other *Compositions*, as you will perceive them to be *improper* for the perusal of Ladies, of course none of the females of your family must see them;[2] I offer 1000 apologies for the trouble I have given you in this and other instances.

Yours truly,

[TO JOHN M. B. PIGOT] *16 Piccadilly, August 16th. 1806*

My dear Pigot,—I cannot exactly say with Caesar "Veni, vidi, Vici," however the most important part of his laconic account of Success, applies to my present Situation; for though Mrs. Byron took the Trouble of *"coming"* & *"seeing"* yet your *humble* Servt. proved the Victor.—After an obstinate Engagement of some hours, in which *we* suffered considerable damage, from the quickness of the enemy's Fire, *they* at length retired in Confusion, leaving behind their *artillery*, field *Equipage*, and some *prisoners*; their defeat is decisive of the *present* Campaign.—To speak more intelligibly, Mrs. B. returns immediately, but I with all my *laurels* proceed to Worthing,[1] on the Sussex Coast, to which place you will address (to be left at the post office) your next Epistle. By the enclosure of a 2d. *jingle* of *Rhyme*, you will probably conceive my *Muse*, to be *vastly prolific*, poor Girl! she is now past *Child bearing*, her inserted production was *brought forth*, a few years ago, & found by accident on Thursday, amongst some old papers; I have recopied it, and adding the proper Date, request it may be printed with the Rest of the *Family*.—I thought your Sentiments, on her last *Bantling*, would coincide with mine, but it was impossible to give it any other *garb*, being *founded* on *Facts*.—My Stay at Worthing will not

[1] The enclosed stanzas were probably those "To Mary" in the privately printed volume *Fugitive Pieces* which Byron was then preparing and which he distributed to friends in November 1806. The erotic images in this poem shocked many of the Southwell people who saw it, and on the objection of the Reverend John Becher that it was "too warmly drawn", Byron called in and destroyed most of the copies. Only four survived, including John Becher's copy.

[2] The MS. has been cut away here. The remainder of the letter and the date are supplied from Moore, I, 72. The post mark is Aug. 11, 1806.

[1] Byron was planning to visit his friend E. N. Long, whose family was spending the summer on the Channel coast at Little Hampton, near Worthing.

exceed 3 Weeks, & you may *possibly* behold me again at Southwell in the middle of September; the conjecture of your Neighbors, with regard to a companion in my Flight, was cursed *absurd* [and?] will fill the girl's head with Ideas, [which?] upon my honour, I never meant to instil.—By the Bye, will you desire Ridge to suspend the printing of my poems, till he hears further from me, as I have determined to give them a new form entirely; this prohibition does not extend to the 2 last pieces, I have sent with my letters to you.—You will excuse the *dull Inanity* of this Epistle, as my Brain is a *chaos* of *absurd* Images, full of Business, preparations, & projects.—I shall expect an answer with impatience, believe me there is nothing at the Moment, could give me greater delight, than your Letter, to yours ever truly

BYRON

[TO JOHN M. B. PIGOT]   *London, August 18th. 1806*

My dear Pigot,—I am just on the point of setting off for Worthing, & write merely to request, you will send that *idle Scoundrel Charles* with my *Horses* immediately, tell him, I am excessively provoked, he has not made his appearance, before, or written to inform me of the Cause of his Delay, particularly as I supplied him with money for his Journey.—On *no* pretext, is he to postpone his *March* one day longer, & if in obedience to the *Caprices* of Mrs. B. (who, I presume is again *spreading Desolation* through her *little Monarchy*,) he thinks proper to disregard my positive orders, I shall not in future, consider him as my Servant.—He must bring the Surgeons Bill with him, which I will discharge immediately on receiving it; nor can I conceive the Reason of his not ere now acquainting Frank,[1] with the State of my *unfortunate Quadrupeds.*— Dear Pigot, forgive this *petulant* Effusion, & attribute it to the *Idle* Conduct of that *precious Rascal*, who instead of obeying my injunctions, is sauntering through the Streets of that *political Pandemonium*, Nottingham. Present my Remembrances to your Family, & the Leacrofts,[2] & believe me

your obliged & &
BYRON

P.S.—I delegate to you, the *unpleasant* Task, of dispatching him on his Journey, Mrs. B's orders to the contrary, are not to be attended

---

[1] See Nov. 6, 1805, to Augusta Byron, note 3.
[2] See Aug. 9, 1806, to John Pigot, note 7.

to; he is to proceed 1st to London, & then to Worthing without Delay. Every thing I have left, must be sent to London, my *Poetics* you will *pack up* for the Same place & not *even* reserve a Copy for yourself & Sister, as I am about to give them an *entire new* form, when they are complete you shall have the *1st Fruits.* Mrs. B. on no account is to *see*, or *touch* them. *Adieu.*

[TO JOHN M. B. PIGOT]   *Little Hampton, August 26th. 1806*

My dear Pigot,—I this morning received your Epistle, which I was obliged to send for to Worthing, whence I have removed to this place, on the Same coast, about 8 miles distant from the former.—You will probably not be less pleased with this Letter when it informs you, that I am £30 000 richer, than I was at our parting, having just received Intelligence from my Lawyer, that a Cause has been gained at Lancaster assizes,[1] which will be worth that Sum, by the Time I come of Age.—Mrs. B. is doubtless acquainted, of this Acquisition, though not apprised of its exact *value*, of which she had better be kept ignorant; for her Behaviour on any sudden piece of favourable Intelligence, is, if possible, more ridiculous than her *detestable* conduct, on the most trifling circumstance of an unpleasant Nature.—You may present my Compts. to her, & say that her Impertinence in detaining my Servant's things, shall only lengthen my Absence, for unless they are immediately dispatched to 16 Piccadilly, together with those which have been so long delayed, belonging to myself, she shall never again behold my *radiant Countenance* illuminating her gloomy Mansion,— And if they are sent I may probably appear in less than 2 years [from?] the [date?] of my present Epistle.—*metrical* Compliment is an ample Reward for my *Strains*, you are one of the few Votaries of Apollo, who unite the Sciences over which that Deity presides.—I wish you to send my poems, to my Lodgings in London immediately, as I have several alterations & some additions to make; *every* Copy must be sent, as I am about to *amend* them, & you shall soon behold them in all their Glory.—I hope you have kept them from that *Upas Tree*, that *Antidote* to the *Arts*, Mrs. B.—"Entre Nous" you may expect to see me *soon.* Adieu yours ever

BYRON

---

[1] This was only another false hope, soon dissipated by further legal tangles; the lawsuit to regain full control of his Rochdale estate went on until near the end of his life.

My dear Madam,—I lose no Time in Informing you, that my Lancashire Cause is *gained*, and is extremely valuable. I shall be in Town in a few days, I have hardly Time to sign myself, your obliged & sincere, &c.&c. Byron. P.S. If my parcels arrive, retain them till my arrival.—Adieu.—

[TO ELIZABETH BRIDGET PIGOT]   *[September? 1806]*

My dear Bridget,—I have only just dismounted from my *Pegasus*, which has prevented me from descending to *plain* prose in an epistle of greater length to your *fair* self. You regretted in a former letter, that my poems were not more extensive; I now for your satisfaction announce that I have nearly doubled them, partly by the discovery of some I conceived to be lost, and partly by some new productions.[1] We shall meet on Wednesday next; till then believe me yours affectionately,

BYRON

P.S.—Your brother John is seized with a poetic mania, and is now rhyming away at the rate of three lines *per hour*—so much for *inspiration*! Adieu!

[TO REV. THOMAS JONES[1]]   *Southwell Oct. 20th. 1806*

Sir/—As I entertain considerable Suspicion, that I have been robbed by one of my Servants,[2] it becomes necessary for his Vindication, or Conviction, & my Satisfaction, that some Drawers in my Rooms at Trin. Coll. should be examined, I have therefore sent a person to take an exact Inventory of the Contents, for the purpose of ascertaining, whether the account given by the Servant, is correct, with Regard to the things which are missing.—I have troubled you on the present occasion, that the Bearer of this may receive no Interruption in his

---

[1] Byron wrote this from Harrogate, where he went on an excursion with John Pigot in September, 1806. While there he saw a beautiful Quaker, who inspired a poem which appeared in *Fugitive Pieces*.

[1] Byron's Trinity College tutor.

[2] Byron's servant Frank (Francis Boyce) was eventually convicted of stealing from his master and was transported. Byron was reluctant to believe him dishonest until he was proved so beyond a doubt. See Marchand, *Byron: A Biography*, I, 120–21n.

search, and that he may be admitted into my Rooms immediately.—
I wrote some Time since, to inform you that your last Bill. £140.
had been paid to [by?] Messers Styan [Stegan?] & Adams.— I have
the honour to remain

your obedient Servt.
BYRON

[TO THE EARL OF CLARE[1]]   *Southwell. Novr. 4th. 1806*

My dearest Clare,—The Date of my Letter will seem rather extraordinary, when in my last, some Months since, I requested you to
address your Answer to Cambridge.—I now shall commence with the
same Request, as I am about to visit College, after having protracted
my Residence here, much longer than was my original Intention.—I
have been principally detained by some private Theatricals, in which I
sustained the first parts,[2] of these I have given a long Account to
Wingfield,[3] who has probably mentioned it, therefore my Recapitulation will be unnecessary.—I am truly sorry your Situation at Harrow is
so uncomfortable, but the prospect of a speedy Liberation, will
reconcile you to it for the present.—

[TO JOHN HANSON]   *Southwell. Decr. 7th. 1806*

Sir/—A Letter to Mrs. Byron has just arrived, which states, from
what "you have *heard* of the Tenor of my Letters" you will not put up
with *Insult*.—I presume, this means (for I will not be positive on what
is rather ambiguously expressed) that some offence to you, has been
conveyed in the above mentioned Epistles.—If you will peruse the
papers in Question, you will discover that the *person* insulted, is not
yourself, or any of your *"Connections."*—On Mr. B[irch]'s[1] Apology,

---

[1] John Fitzgibbon (1792–1851) succeeded his father as second Earl of Clare in
1802. Four years younger than Byron, he was one of those favourites at Harrow
whom Byron said he "spoilt by indulgence". Like Byron's other favourites among
younger boys, he occasionally plagued the poet, with his sensitivities and jealousies,
but Byron maintained an idealized affection for him throughout his life. He appears
as "Lycus" in Byron's "Childish Recollections". (But see Feb. 23, 1807, to Long,
note 6.)
[2] Byron played the role of Penruddock in Cumberland's *Wheel of Fortune* and
Tristram Fickle in Allingham's *Weathercock*.
[3] John Wingfield another of Byron's Harrow favourites, the "Alonzo" of
"Childish Recollections", and subject of a memorial (stanza 91) in the first canto
of *Childe Harold*, joined the Coldstream Guards and died of fever at Coimbra,
May 14, 1811.
[1] J. Birch was Hanson's law partner.

I have expressed my Opinion in a Letter to your Son, if any Misrepresentation has taken place, it must be through those *"Connections"* to whom I am to pay such Deference, & whose *Conduct* to Me, has deserved such *ample Respect*.—I must now beg leave to observe in turn, that I am by no means disposed to bear Insult, & be the Consequences what they may, I will always declare, in plain & explicit Terms, my Grievance, nor will I overlook the slightest Mark of Disrespect, & silently brood over Affronts from a mean & interested dread of Injury to my person, or property.—The former I have strength & Resolution to protect, the Latter is too trifling, by its loss to occasion a moment's Uneasiness.—Though not conversant in the methodical & dilatory arrangements of Law or Business, I know enough of Justice, to direct my Conduct by the principles of Equity, nor can I reconcile the "Insolence of Office" to her Regulations, or forget in an Instant, a poignant Affront.—But enough of this Dispute, you will perceive my Sentiments on the Subject, in my Correspondence with Mr. B[irch] & Mr. H[anson] Junior.—In future to prevent a Repetition of Altercation, I shall advise, but as even then, since Demur may take place, I wish to be informed, if the equitable Court of Chancery, whose paternal Care of their ward, can never be sufficiently commended, have determined, in the great flow of parental Affection, to withold, their beneficent Support, till I return to "alma Mater" ("i e") Cambridge.—Your Information on this point will oblige, as a College Life is neither [conducive?] to any Improvement, or suitable [to my?] Inclination. As to the Reverse of the Rochdale Trial,[2] I received the news of Success without Confidence or Exultation, I now sustain the Loss without Repining.—My Expectations from *Law*, were never very sanguine.

I remain your very obedt. Servt.
BYRON

[TO DR. T. FALKNER[1]]   *Janry. 8th. 1807*

Sir/—The volume of little pieces, which accompanies this,[2] would have been presented before, had I not been apprehensive, that Miss Falkner's Indisposition, might render such Trifles unwelcome.—

---

2 See Aug. 26, 1806, to John Pigot, note 1.
1 Mrs. Byron's landlord at Burgage Manor.
2 Byron's second volume of privately printed poems, *Poems on Various Occasions*, was ready for distribution early in January.

There are some Errors of the Printer, which I have not had Time to correct in the Collection, you have it then, with "all its Imperfections on its head" a heavy weight when joined with the Faults of its Author. —Such "*Juvenilia*," as they can claim no great degree of approbation, I may venture to hope, will also escape the severity of uncalled for, though perhaps *not* undeserved Criticism.—They were written on many, & various Occasions, and are now published merely for the perusal of a friendly Circle. Believe me, Sir, if they afford the slightest amusement, to yourself and the rest of my *social* Readers, I shall have gathered all the "*Bays*" I ever wish to *adorn* the *Head*

of yours very truly,
BYRON

P.S.—I hope Miss F. is in a State of Recovery.

[TO JOHN M. B. PIGOT]   *Southwell, Jany. 13th. 1807*

My dear Pigot,—I ought to begin with *sundry* Apologies, for my own negligence, but the variety of my Avocations, in *prose* & *verse* must plead my Excuse.—With this Epistle you will receive a volume of all my *Juvenilia*,[1] published since your Departure, it is of considerably greater size, than the *Copy* in your possession which I beg you will destroy, as the present is much more complete; that *unlucky* poem to my poor Mary,[2] has been the Cause of some Animadversion from *Ladies in years*. I have not printed it in this Collection in Consequence of my being pronounced, a *most profligate Sinner*, in short a "*young Moore*"[3] by Mrs. S—— your Oxon *friend*.[4]—I believe in general they have been favourably received, & surely the Age of their Author, will preclude *severe* Criticism.—The Adventures of my Life from 16 to 19 & the dissipation into which I have been thrown when in London, have given a *voluptuous Tint* to my Ideas, but the occasions which called forth my *Muse*, would hardly admit any other *Colouring*; this volume however is *vastly* correct, & miraculously *chaste*,—*Apropos*, talking of *Love*, your adorable "*Caroline*"[5] is a complete "*Jilt*" She has *entangled*

1 See Jan. 8, 1807, To Falkner, note 2.
2 The reaction to the erotic poem "To Mary" among his Southwell readers caused Byron to call in and destroy most of the copies of *Fugitive Pieces*. Only four copies are known to have escaped the flames.
3 Byron had read during his Harrow days the erotic poems of Thomas Moore, particularly *The Poetical Works of the late Thomas Little* (1801) which influenced some of the poems in his early volumes.
4 A Southwell lady, unidentified.
5 Several poems in *Fugitive Pieces* and again in *Poems on Various Occasions* were

S. Becher,[6] in her *golden Net*, I suppose for the next 6 Months the north wind, will be impregnated with your *Sighs*, curse her, she is not worth *regretting*, no more of her.—I am in love, also with a Lady of your Acquaintance, & all the *ancient* Gentlewomen of *Southwell*, shake *their heads*, at the *flirtation* of the *fair Anne*[7] with your *humble Servant*. —The other evening at a public *Supper*, the Tongues of *Beldams* were *all* in motion, as the *nymph* & I conversed with rather too much *Vivacity*, moreover she completely *cut* an unlucky *Admirer*, of hers, a *Nottingham Cavalier*, who looked with *wonderful Complacency* & Astonishment, at my *Impudence* in placing myself next his *Dulcinea* to his great *detriment*, & the *Amusement* of the Company.—She is a *beautiful Girl*, & I *love* her, nor do I *despair*, unless some *damned* accident intervenes, *secrecy* on this subject, my dear P. is requested, you will hear more Anon.—If you can find leisure to answer this *farrago* of unconnected Nonsense, you need not doubt, what gratification will accrue from your Reply, to

yours &ct &c
BYRON

[TO CAPTAIN JOHN LEACROFT[1]]   *January 31, 1807*

Sir,—Upon serious reflection on the conversation we last night held, I am concerned to say, that the only effectual method to crush the animadversions of officious malevolence, is by my declining all future intercourse with those whom my acquaintance has unintentionally injured. At the same time I must observe that I do not form this resolution from any resentment at your representation, which was temperate and gentlemanly, but from a thorough conviction that the desirable end can be attained by no other line of conduct.

I beg leave to return my thanks to Mr. and Mrs. Leacroft, for the attention and hospitality I have always experienced, of which I shall ever retain a grateful remembrance.

So much to them; with your permission, I must add a few words for

addressed to "Caroline". Whether this was the same Caroline is not known. Byron seldom gave the true names of the local girls in print.

[6] Probably Sherard Becher. See Aug. 9, 1806, to John Pigot, note 5.

[7] Anne Houson, another of Byron's transient loves in Southwell. He addressed several poems to her which were posthumously published.

[1] The brother of Julia Leacroft, whom Byron courted until the family of the girl took it too seriously. Hobhouse said later that they "winked at an intercourse between him and [one] of the daughters in hopes of entangling him in an unequal marriage". (Marchand, *Byron: A Biography*, I, 124.)

myself. You will be sensible, that a coolness between families, hitherto remarkable for their intimacy, cannot remain unobserved in a town, whose inhabitants are notorious for officious curiosity; that the causes of our separation will be mis-represented I have little doubt; if, therefore, I discover that such misrepresentation does take place, I shall call upon you, to unite with myself in making a serious example of those *men*, be they *who* they may, that dare to cast an aspersion on the character I am sacrificing my own comfort to protect.

If, on the other hand, they imagine, that my conduct is the consequence of intimidation, from my conference with you, I must require a further explanation of what passed between us on the subject, as, however careful I am of your Sister's honour, I am equally tenacious of my own.

I do not wish this to be misconstrued into any desire to quarrel; it is what I shall endeavour to avoid; but, as a young man very lately entered into the world, I feel compelled to state, that I can permit no suspicion to be attached to my name with impunity.

I have the honour to remain,

Your very obedient Servant,
BYRON

[TO CAPTAIN JOHN LEACROFT (*a*)]   *February 4th, 1807*

Sir,—I have just received your note, which conveys all that can be said on the subject. I can easily conceive your feelings must have been irritated in the course of the affair. I am sorry that I have been the unintentional cause of so disagreeable a business. The line of conduct, however painful to myself, which I have adopted, is the only effectual method to prevent the remarks of a *meddling world*. I therefore again take my leave for the last time. I repeat, that, though the intercourse, from which I have derived so many hours of happiness, is for ever interrupted, the remembrance can never be effaced from the bosom of

Your very obedient Servant,
BYRON

[TO CAPTAIN JOHN LEACROFT (*b*)]   *February 4th, 1807*

Sir,—I am concerned to be obliged again to trouble you, as I had hoped that our conversations had terminated amicably. Your good

Father, it seems, has desired otherwise; he has just sent a most *agreeable* epistle, in which I am honoured with the appellations of *unfeeling* and ungrateful. But as the consequences of all this must ultimately fall on you and myself, I merely write this to apprise you that the dispute is not of my seeking, and that, if we must cut each other's throats to please our relations, you will do me the justice to say it is from no *personal* animosity between us, or from any insult on my part, that such *disagreeable* events (for I am not so much enamoured of quarrels as to call them *pleasant*) have arisen.

I remain, yours, etc.,

BYRON

[TO THE EARL OF CLARE]   *Southwell, Notts, February 6th, 1807*

My dearest Clare,—Were I to make all the apologies necessary to atone for my late negligence, you would justly say you had received a petition instead of a letter, as it would be filled with prayers for forgiveness; but instead of this, I will acknowledge my *sins* at once, and I trust to your friendship and generosity rather than to my own excuses.[1] Though my health is not perfectly re-established, I am out of all danger, and have recovered every thing but my spirits, which are subject to depression. You will be astonished to hear I have lately written to Delawarr,[2] for the purpose of explaining (as far as possible without involving some *old friends* of mine in the business) the cause of my behaviour to him during my last residence at Harrow (nearly two years ago), which you will recollect was rather *"en cavalier."* Since that period I have discovered he was treated with injustice, both by those who misrepresented his conduct, and by me in consequence of their suggestions. I have therefore made all the reparation in my power, by apologizing for my mistake, though with very faint hopes of success; indeed I never expected any answer, but desired one for form's sake; *that* has not yet arrived, and most probably never will. However, I have *eased* my own *conscience* by the atonement, which is humiliating enough to one of my disposition; yet I could not have slept satisfied with the reflection of having, *even unintentionally*, injured any individual. I have done all that could be done to repair the injury, and there the affair must end. Whether we renew our intimacy or not is of very trivial consequence.

[1] See Nov. 4, 1806, to Clare, note 1.
[2] See Nov. 2, 1804, to Augusta Byron, note 3; Oct. 25, 1804, to Augusta Byron, note 7.

My time has lately been much occupied with very different pursuits. I have been *transporting* a servant, who cheated me,—[3]rather a disagreeable event: —performing in private theatricals;—publishing a volume of poems (at the request of my friends, for their perusal);—making *love*,—and taking physic. The two last amusements have not had the best effect *in the world*; for my attentions have been divided amongst so many *fair damsels*, and the drugs I swallow are of such variety in their composition, that between Venus and Ætsculapius I am harassed to death. However, I have still leisure to devote some hours to the recollections of past, regretted friendships, and in the interval to take the advantage of the moment, to assure you how much I am, and ever will be, my dearest Clare,

> Yours truly attached and sincere
> BYRON

[TO MRS. JOHN HANSON]   *Southwell, Febry 8th. 1807*

Dear Madam,—Having understood from Mrs. Byron, that Mr. Hanson is in a very indifferent State of health, I have taken the Liberty of addressing you on the Subject.—Though the *Governor*, & *I* have lately not been on the *best* of *Terms*, yet I should be extremely sorry to hear he was in Danger, & I trust *he* & *I* will live to have many more *Squabbles* in *this world*, before we *finally make peace* in the *next*.—If therefore you can favour me with any *salutary* Intelligence of the *aforesaid* Gentleman, believe me nothing will be more acceptable to

> yours very truly
> BYRON

P.S.—Remember me to all the family now in *Garrison*, particularly my old Friend *Harriet*.[1]

[TO [ELIZABETH BRIDGET PIGOT?]]   *Feb. 9th, 1807*

Dear ————I have the pleasure to inform you we have gained the Rochdale cause a 2d time, by which I am £60,000 *plus*.[1]

> Yours ever,
> BYRON

[3] See Oct. 20, 1806, to [Rev. Thomas Jones?], note 2.

[1] For the Hanson family see Aug. 30, 1804, to Hanson, note 1.

[1] Byron was soon to learn that this was a false hope. The legal battle of appeals and reversals went on interminably.

Sir,—I should feel some hesitation, in troubling you again, did I not conceive that part of my Letter has been misunderstood.—It would seem from the tenor of your answer, that I have laid too much Stress on the words *"Rank in Life"* an Idea I would wish to remove, as I should ever hold the man, who assumed a false Consequence from *Title* only, however exalted in the *List* of *Lords*, to be but *very low* in the *Scale* of *human Beings.*—The fact is, I merely copied your *own words* from a former Communication. I certainly do not feel that predilection for Mathematics, which may pervade the Inclinations of men destined for a clerical, or collegiate Life; if I had any *"penchant"* for the army they might be of service, as far as related to Tactics, & if ever I embrace that profession, I shall resume the Study.—But as my Intentions at present are very different, I have adopted a distinct line of Reading, this, you will probably *smile* at, & imagine (as you *very* naturally may) that because I have not pursued my College Studies, I have pursued *none.*—I have certainly no right to be offended at such a Conjecture, nor indeed am I, that it is erroneous, Time will perhaps discover.—The subjects for your present Lectures, are undoubtedly interesting, but the *"Demonstration* of the *Being* of a *God,"* is, (to *me* at least) unnecessary.—To expatiate on his *"attributes"* is superfluous, do we not know them? he who *doubts* them, does not deserve to be instructed.—To *bewilder* myself in the mazes of Metaphysics, is not my object. I do not wish to explore in treatises, what I may read in every work of Nature, particularly as I have observed that the most voluminous writers on the Subject, conclude, as they begin.—You will pardon these observations, which proceed from any thing, but a wish to give offence.—I have other Reasons for not residing at Cambridge, I dislike it; I was originally intended for Oxford,² my Guardians determined otherwise. I quitted the Society of my earliest associates, who are all *"Alumni"* of the latter, to drag on a weary term, at a place, where I had many acquaintances, but few friends. I therefore can never consider *Granta* as my *"Alma Mater"* but rather as a *Nurse* of no very promising appearance, on whom I have been forced, against *her* Inclination, & contrary to mine.—My affection, is in Consequence by no means *filial,* but I cannot refrain from expressing my obligations, to

---

¹ See Nov. 6, 1805, to Augusta Byron, note 2.

² Byron said later (letter of Nov. 19, 1820, to John Murray) that when he first went to Trinity College, he was "wretched at going to Cambridge instead of Oxford (there were no rooms vacant at Christchurch)". One reason was that several of his closest friends at Harrow had gone to Oxford.

many, & especially yourself, for the friendly attentions, with which I have been honored; if any thing could have removed the Impression, these would have done it effectually.—Believe me, Sir, whatever my *general* opinion, may be, to you, [as an?] Individual, I shall ever retain [one or two words torn off with seal] gratitude, which you well merit

from your very obedt. Servt.

BYRON

[TO EDWARD NOEL LONG]   *Southwell, February 23d. 1807*

My dear Long,—*"Odi profanum Vulgas"*[1] give me the approbation of my Friends, & I would resign all the *Bays*, that ever ornamented the *"Sinciput & Occiput"* of Homer; I had already secured the *"vox populi"* in my favour, that is to say, I had obtained the applause of all the County Lords & Squires, more, I believe, on account of my *youth*, than my merits; but the praise of a Friend, particularly a *Harrovian*, is far preferable to the admiration of the *"Turba Quiritium"*[2]—Your opinions on the comparative *deserts* of the pieces coincide with mine, excepting that I consider my last "Newstead" as my *"Chef d'oeuvre"* however No man is a proper Judge of his own productions, & I will admit *you* are most probably in the Right.—It is a Singular Thing, that all my Readers, have selected a different poem as the *best*, from each other, the Girls (in course) prefer, the *amatory*.—Your conjecture on *pug Hoares*[3] claim to Gratitude is correct, *he* & *Tattersall*[4] were the *worthies* who preserved my *pericranium*, but how to introduce *Pug* into a *serious poem*, I knew not, unless I had purloined the Song of *"Ban Ban Ca Caliban"* from Shakespeares Tempest. I am astonished you did not recognize That *Madcap Tattersall*, is *Davus*,[5] Lycus is old De-Bathe,[6] *Euryalus Delawarr*,[7] when I drew the *portrait* of *Cleon*,[8] I wrote

---

[1] "I loathe the vulgar crowd."

[2] "Citizen Mob."

[3] "Pug" was the nickname of one of Byron's classmates at Harrow. Hoare was listed as one of his schoolfellows at Harrow by E. N. Long (MS., Berg Collection, New York Public Library).

[4] John Cecil Tattersall, a close friend at Harrow, once saved Byron from the butt of a "rustic's musket". The incident is recounted in "Childish Recollections", lines 265–86.

[5] In "Childish Recollections".

[6] The name appeared as Clarus in *Poems on Various Occasions*. Both Prothero (*LJ*, I, 116n.) and Coleridge (*Poetry*, I, 98) identify Lycus as the Earl of Clare. Sir James Wynne de Bathe (1792–1828) succeeded his father as the second Baronet in 1808. Joannes (lines 243–64) was Byron's first (poetic) name for Clare, but he later used the same lines to laud Wingfield as Alonzo.

[7] See Oct. 25, 1804, to Augusta Byron, note 7; and Nov. 2, 1804, to Augusta, note 3.

[8] Byron's final tribute in "Childish Recollections" was to E. N. Long as Cleon.

as I *felt*, nor will I give up my Sentiments on *his character*, to your *Insinuations*, you must know, I am far from a *Hypocrite*, & *tolerably* obstinate.—I am very sorry to hear, you have submitted my poor effusions to the perusal of Bankes,[9] you shall have my opinion in the words of Cowper.[10]

> "He who delights in Repartee,
> "Will seldom scruple to make free
> "With Friendship's finest feeling,
> "He'll plant a dagger in your Breast,
> "And tell you 'twas a *special Jest*,
> "By way of *Balm*, for *Healing*.["]

Tell him from me, I would most *certainly* have sent him a Copy, but I knew his *Talents* as a *Critic*, to be so far superior to *mine* as a *Rhymer*, that I would have rather passed the *Ordeal* of an Edinburgh *Review*, than offered my unfortunate "*Juvenilia*" to his Inspection.—He has too much of the *Man*, ever to approve the *flights* of a *Boy*, & I await in trembling Suspense my *Crucifixion* from his *Decree*.—Besides my Stanzas, have a Colouring of Romance, which only my Contemporaries in age & [MS. ends here; page missing?]

P.S.—If possible I will pass through Granta, in March, pray, keep the subject of my "*Cornelian*" a *Secret*.—[11]

[TO WILLIAM BANKES[1]]   *Southwell, March 6th. 1807*

Dear Bankes,—Your Critique is valuable for many Reasons, in the first place, it is the only one, in which Flattery has borne so slight a part, in the *next*, I am *cloyed* with insipid Compliments, & have a better opinion of your Judgement & Ability, than your *Feelings*.— Accept, my most sincere thanks for your kind decision, not less welcome, because totally unexpected.—With regard to a more exact estimate, I need not remind you, how few of the *best poems* in our

In *Hours of Idleness* he published another poem "To Edward Noel Long, Esq." During his first year at Cambridge, Long was Byron's closest friend.

[9] William John Bankes of Kingston Lacy, Dorsetshire, was another of Byron's Trinity College friends. Byron later referred to him as his "collegiate pastor, and master and patron", who "ruled the roast—or rather the *roasting*—and was the father of all mischiefs". (Letter of Nov. 19, 1820, to John Murray.)

[10] William Cowper, "Friendship", lines 91–96. Byron was quoting from the edition of 1803, which varies slightly from the first edition of 1800.

[11] "The Cornelian" was a poem addressed to John Edleston. See *Poetry*, I, 66.

[1] See Feb. 23, 1807, to Long, note 9.

Language, will stand the Test of *minute*, or *verbal* Criticism; it can therefore hardly be expected, the effusions of a Boy (& most of these pieces have been produced at an early period) can derive much merit, either from the Subject, or Composition.—Many of them were written under great Depression of Spirits, & during severe Indisposition, hence the gloomy Turn of the Ideas.—We coincide in opinion that the *"poesies Erotiques*, ["] are the most exceptionable, they were however, grateful to the *Deities*, on whose altars they were offered, more I seek not.—The portrait of Pomposus[2] was drawn at Harrow after a *long Sitting*, this accounts for the Resemblance or rather the *Caricatura*, he is *your* friend, he *never was mine*, for both our sakes, I shall now be silent on this head.—The *Collegiate* Rhymes,[3] are not personal, one of the Notes may appear so, but could not be omitted; I have little doubt they will be deservedly abused, a just punishment, for my unfilial treatment, of so excellent an Alma Mater. I sent you no Copy, lest *we* should be placed in the Situation of *Gil Blas* & the *Archbishop* of *Grenada*;[4] though running some hazard from the experiment. I wished your *verdict* to be unbiased; had my *"Libellus"* been presented previous to your Letter, it would have appeared a species of Bribe to purchase Compliments.—I feel no hesitation in saying, I was more anxious to hear your Critique however severe, than the praises of the *Million.* On the same day I was honoured with the Encomiums of *Mackenzie*[5] the celebrated author of the "Man of Feeling," whether *his* approbation or *yours* elated me most, I cannot decide.—You will receive my *Juvenilia*, at least all yet published, I have a large volume in Manuscript, which may in part appear hereafter, at present I have neither Time, nor Inclination, to prepare it for the Press.—In the Spring I shall return to Trinity, to dismantle my Rooms, & bid you a final Adieu, the *Cam* will not be much increased by my *Tears*, on the occasion.—Your further Remarks, however *Caustic*, or bitter to a palate vitiated with the *Sweets* of *Adulation*, will be of Service; Johnson has shown us that *no poetry* is perfect, but to correct mine would be an Herculean Labour; in fact I never looked beyond the

[2] A caricature of Dr. George Butler, Headmaster of Harrow, in "Childish Recollections".

[3] "Thoughts Suggested by a College Examination", and "Granta: A Medley."

[4] An allusion to an episode in Book VII, Chapter 4, of Le Sage's *Gil Blas.* For his frankness in criticizing the Archbishop's work, Gil Blas was dismissed: "Adieu, monsieur Gil Blas; je vous souhaite toutes sortes de prospérités, avec un peu plus de goût."

[5] Byron sent Henry Mackenzie his *Poems on Various Occasions*, by John Pigot, then studying medicine in Edinburgh. He was eager to get the opinions of the literary world on his verses. See Moore, I, 109n.

Moment of Composition, & published merely at the Request of my Friends.—Notwithstanding so much has been said concerning the "Genus irritabile Vatum" we shall never quarrel on the Subject, poetic fame is by no means the *"acme"* of my Wishes. Adieu

yours ever
BYRON

[TO [WILLIAM J. BANKES]]   [*March, 1807*]

For my own part,[1] I have suffered severely in the Decease of my two greatest Friends,[2] the only Beings, I ever loved (*females* excepted) I am therefore a solitary animal, miserable enough, & so perfectly a Citizen of the World, that whether I pass my days in Great Britain, or Kamchatka, is to me, a matter of perfect Indifference.— — —I cannot evince greater Respect, for your alteration, than by immediately adopting it, this shall be done in the next Edition; I am sorry your Remarks are not more frequent, as I am certain, they would be equally beneficial.—Since my last, I have received two Critical opinions, from Edinburgh, both too flattering for me to detail, one is from Lord Woodhousie [sic],[3] at the head of the Scotch Literati, & a most *voluminous* Writer (his last work is a Life of Ld. Kames) the other from Mackenzie, who sent his decision a second time more at Length, I am not personally acquainted with either of these Gentlemen, nor ever requested their Sentiments on the Subject, their praise is voluntary, & transmitted through the Medium, of a Friend, at whose house, they read the productions.[4]—Contrary to my former Intention, I am now preparing a volume for the Public at large, my amatory pieces will be expunged, & others substituted, in their place; the whole will be considerably enlarged, & appear the latter end of May.[5]—This is a hazardous experiment, but want of better employment, the encouragement I have met with, & my own Vanity, induce me to stand the Test, though not without *sundry palpitations*.—The Book will circulate fast enough in this County, from mere Curiosity, what I prin-[6]

[1] The first two lines of the first page of this fragment have been crossed out.

[2] There is no clue to the identity of the friends who had died early in 1807.

[3] Alexander Fraser Tytler, Lord Woodhouselee, author and Senator of the College of Justice in Scotland. He had been a friend of Robert Burns.

[4] Byron's only known friend in Edinburgh at the time was John Pigot, his Southwell neighbour, then studying medicine in the Scottish capital.

[5] Byron's *Hours of Idleness*, his first *published* volume; *Fugitive Pieces* and *Poems on Various Occasions* were privately printed.

[6] The manuscript ends here at the bottom of the second page.

Dear Sir,—Before I proceed in Reply to the other parts of your
Epistle, allow me to congratulate you on the *accession* of *Dignity* &
firot, which will doubtless accrue, from your official Appointment.—
You was fortunate in obtaining possession, at so critical a period, your
patrons *"exeunt omnes"*[.]¹ I trust they will soon supersede the Cy-
phers their Successors.—The Reestablishment of your health is
another happy event, & though *secondary* in my *Statement*, is by no
means so in my *Wishes*.—As to our *Feuds*, they are purely *official*, the
natural consequence of our relative Situations, but as little connected
with *personal Animosity*, as the *Florid Declarations* of *parliamentary
Demagogues*.—I return you my thanks for your favourable opinion of
my Muse, I have lately been honoured with many very flattering
literary Critiques, from men of high Reputation in the Sciences, particularly Lord Woodhousie [sic], & Henry Mackenzie, both *Scots*, & of
great Eminence as *Authors* themselves, I have received also some most
favourable Testimonies from *Cambridge*, this you will *marvel* at, as indeed I did myself, encouraged by these & several other Encomiums, I
am about to publish a volume at large, this will be very different from
the present, the amatory effusions (not to be wondered at from the
dissipated Life I have lead) will be cut out, & others substituted; I coincide with you in opinion that the *poet* yields to the *Orator*, but as
nothing can be done in the latter Capacity till the expiration of my
minority, the former occupies my present Attention; & both *ancients* &
moderns, have declared, that the 2 pursuits are so nearly similar, as to
require in a great measure the same Talents, & he who excels in the
one, would on application succeed in the other.—Lyttleton, Glover, &
Young (who was a celebrated *Preacher* & a *Bard*) are instances of the
Kind, *Sheridan* & *Fox* also, *these* are *great* names, I may imitate, I can
never equal them.—You speak of the *Charms* of Southwell, the *place* I
abhor, the Fact is I remain here because I can appear no where else,
being *completely done up*, *Wine* & *Women* have *dished* your *humble
Servant*, not a *Sou* to be *had*, all *over*, condemned to exist, (I cannot
say live) at this *Crater* of Dullness, till my *Lease* of *Infancy* expires; to
appear at Cambridge is impossible, no money, even to pay my College
expenses; you will be surprised to hear I am grown *very thin*, however

¹ Hanson's patrons were in the coalition ministry, which was dismissed by George
III in March 1807, when the Tories under the Duke of Portland were called in to
form a government. See Byron's letter of Oct. 20, 1814, to Lady Melbourne:
"Hanson is the Government solicitor of the stamp office—& was put in by Ld.
Grenville."

it is the Fact, so much so, that the people here think I am *going*, I have lost 18 LB in my weight, that is one Stone & 4 pounds since January, this was ascertained last Wednesday, on account of a *Bet* with an Acquaintance, however dont be alarmed, I have taken every means to accomplish the end, by violent exercise, & Fasting, as I found myself too plump.—I shall continue my Exertions, having no other amusement, I wear *seven* Waistcoats, & a great Coat, run & play at Cricket in this Dress, till quite exhausted by excessive perspiration, use the hot Bath daily, eat only a quarter of [a] pound, [of] Butchers meat in 24 hours, no Suppers, or Breakfast, only one meal a Day, drink no malt Liquor, [only?] little Wine, & take physic occasionally, by these means, my *Ribs* display Skin of no great Thickness, & my Clothes, have been taken in nearly *half* a *yard*, do you believe me now? Adieu, remembrance to Spouse & the *Acorns*.

> yours ever
> BYRON

P.S.—Write when you please, I shall be happy to hear from you, address to this *Abode* of *Darkness*, I shall be nowhere else.—

[TO EDWARD NOEL LONG]   *Southwell, Ap. 16th, 1807*

Your Epistle, my dear *Standard Bearer*,[1] augurs not much in favour of your new life, particularly the latter part, where you say your happiest Days are over. I most sincerely hope not. The past has certainly in some parts been pleasant, but I trust will be equalled, if not exceeded by the future. "You hope it is not so with me."

To be plain with Regard to myself. Nature stampt me in the Die of *Indifference*. I consider myself as destined never to be happy, although in some instances fortunate. I am an isolated Being on the Earth, without a Tie to attach me to life, except a few School-fellows, and a *score of females*. Let me but "hear my fame on the winds" and the song of the Bards in my Norman house, I ask no more and don't expect so much. Of Religion I know nothing, at least in its *favour*. We have *fools* in all sects and Impostors in most; why should I believe mysteries no one understands, because written by men who chose to mistake madness for Inspiration, and style themselves *Evangelicals*? However enough on this subject. Your *piety* will be *aghast*, and I wish for no proselytes. This much I will venture to affirm, that all the virtues and

[1] Long had just joined the Guards.

114

pious *Deeds* performed on Earth can never entitle a man to Everlasting happiness in a future State; nor on the other hand[2] can such a Scene as a Seat of eternal punishment exist, it is incompatible with the benign attributes of a Deity to suppose so; I am surrounded here by parsons & Methodists, but, as you will perceive not infected with the *Mania*, I have lived a *Deist*, what I shall die I know not—however come what may, *"ridens moriar"*.—Nothing detains me here, but the publication, which will not be complete till June, about 20 of the present pieces, will be cut out, & a number of new things added, amongst them a complete Episode of Nisus & Euryalus from Virgil, some Odes from Anacreon, & several original Odes, the whole will cover 170 pages, my last production has been a poem in Imitation of Ossian, which I shall not[3] publish, having enough without it. Many of the present poems are enlarged and altered, in short you will behold an "Old friend with a new face." Were I to publish all I have written in Rhyme, I should fill a decent Quarto; however, half is quite enough at present. You shall have *all* when we meet.

I grow thin daily; since the commencement of my System I have lost 23 lbs. in my weight (*i.e.*) 1 st. and 9 lbs. When I began I weighed 14 st. 6 lbs., and on Tuesday I found myself reduced to 12 st. 11 lb. What sayest thou, Ned? do you not envy? I shall still proceed till I arrive at 12 st. and then stop, at least if I am not too fat, but shall always live temperately and take much exercise.

If there is a possibility we shall meet in June. I shall be in Town, before I proceed to Granta, and if the "mountain will not come to Mahomet, Mahomet will go to the mountain." I don't mean, by comparing you to the mountain, to insinuate anything on the Subject of your Size. Xerxes, it is said, formed Mount Athos into the Shape of a Woman; had he lived now, and taken a peep at Chatham,[4] he would have spared himself the trouble and made it unnecessary by finding a *Hill* ready cut to his wishes.

Adieu, dear Mont Blanc, or rather *Mont Rouge*;[5] don't, for Heaven's sake, turn Volcanic, at least roll the Lava of your indignation in any other Channel, and not consume

Your's ever,
BYRON

Write Immediately.

[2] The facsimile page begins with this word.
[3] The facsimile ends here.
[4] Long was stationed at Chatham, one of the chief Naval Arsenals of Britain.
[5] A reference to the red coats of the Guards.

Sir,—My last was an Epistle *"entre nous"*[;] *this* is a *Letter* of *Business*, of course the formalities of *official communication*, must be attended to.—From lying under pecuniary difficulties, I shall draw for the Quarter due the 25th. June, in a short time, you will recollect I was to receive £100 for the expense of Furniture & ct. at Cambridge, I placed in your possession accounts to that amount, of these I have received £70, for which I believe, you have my Receipt, the extra £25, or £30, (though the Bills are long ago discharged from my own purse) I should not have troubled you for, had not my present Situation, rendered even that trifle, of some consequence; I have therefore to request, that my Draft for £150, instead of £125, the simple Quarter, may be honoured, but think it necessary to apprise you previous to its appearance, & indeed to request an *early* answer, as I *had one draft* returned by mistake from your *house*, some months past;—& have no inclination to be placed in a similar Dilemma.—I lent Mrs. B. £60 last year, of this I have never received a *Sou*, & in all probability never shall, I do not mention the circumstance as any Reproach, on that *worthy* & *lamblike Dame*, but merely to shew you how *affairs* stand, 'tis true myself & 2 Servants lodge in the house, but my Horses &ct. & [their ex]pence, are defrayed by your hum[ble Servan]t.—I quit Cambridge in [July] & shall have considerable payments to make at that period, for this purpose I must sell my *Steeds*,—I paid Jones in January £150, £38 to my Stable Keeper, £21 to my wine merchant, £20 to a *Lawyer* for the prosecution of a Scoundrel a late Servant,[1] in short I have done all I can, but am now completely *done* up, your answer will oblige

yours & ct.

BYRON

E—— is a West Indian married to a *Creole*, C—— is Mrs. Musters-*Chaworth*, a former flame; Caroline is her mother in Law; Mary is a Mrs. Cobourne [Cockburn?], & *Cora*, a *Notts*. Girl, her real name is Julia Leacroft, there is a poem addressed to her, under the name of *Lesbia*.[1]

1 See Oct. 20, 1806, to Thomas Jones, note 2.
1 These identifications of the persons mentioned by initials and names in "To Edward Noel Long" (appended as a note to a copy of the poem sent to Long) are a

Tuesday night [April 21? 1807]

My dear Pigot,—I have been dining at Mr. Smiths & am just come home, I have only time to *congratulate you* on your passing this so much dreaded examination—[1]

[April 1807][2]

My dear Pigot,—Allow me to congratulate you on the Success of your first examination, *"courage* mon *ami"*! The Title of *Dr.* will do wonders with the *Damsels.*—I shall most probably be in Essex or London, when you arrive at this *damned place*,[3] where I am detained by the publication of my *Rhymes.* Adieu, believe me

yours very truly
BYRON

P.S.—Since we met, I have reduced myself by violent exercise, *much* physic, & *hot bathing*, from 14 Stone 6 LB. to 12 Stone 7 LB. in all I have lost 27 pounds. Bravo, what say you?—

[Four lines crossed out at bottom of cover]

[TO EDWARD NOEL LONG] *Southwell, May 1, 1807*

. . . I am truly sorry the duties of your profession call you to combat, for what? Can you tell me? The ambition of Despotism or the caprice of men placed by chance in the Situation of Governors, &

little puzzling. They do not exactly fit with the poems in his early volumes, and are perhaps not quite candid. The poem "To E——" in *Fugitive Pieces* was probably addressed to John Edleston, the Cambridge choirboy. See Marchand, *Byron: A Biography*. I, 109n. But in the poem "To Edward Noel Long" Byron says: "E—— is a wife", and he seems to be speaking of *girls* ("nymphs") throughout. In order to veil their identities, Byron changed some of the fictitious names in his poems several times. In none of the extant poems to Mary Chaworth (Musters) is she addressed as "C——". Several ecstatic love poems in the early volumes were addressed to "Caroline", but it seems unlikely that she was Mary Chaworth's mother-in-law. Byron's distant cousin Mary Duff, his earliest childish love, married Robert Cockburn, a wine merchant in Edinburgh and London. News of their marriage sent Byron into convulsions. (See diary of November 26, 1813.) There is little indication, however, that the poems to "Mary" in the early volumes are addressed to her. The only one clearly referring to her is "When I Roved a Young Highlander". With the title "Song" it first appeared in *Poems Original and Translated* (1808). None of the published poems known to be addressed to Julia Leacroft used the name "Cora".

[1] Pigot had just passed his medical examinations at Edinburgh.
[2] "Lord Byron" and "April 1807" are written across the page in another hand.
[3] Byron was still at Southwell, waiting to go to Cambridge.

117

probably inferior to yourself & many more . . . you know . . . I am no *coward*, nor would I shrink from Danger on[1] a proper occasion, indeed Life has too little valuable for me, to make Death horrible; I am not insensible to Glory, & even hope before I am at *Rest*, to see some service in a military Capacity, yet I cannot conquer my repugnance to a Life absolutely & exclusively devoted to Carnage, or bestow any appellation in my Idea applicable to a *mercenary* Soldier, but the *Slave of Blood*.—You will excuse the freedom of my Remarks, I smile again at Sentiments to which you are no Stranger, as you have heard me declare them before, to *very little* purpose; you have entered into a profession with all the ardour hope &c &c of *19* excusable enough at our age, I sincerely hope some one may hear your opinion on the Subject at *50*.——[2]. . . . When you return from the *Field* bring me the *Scalp* of Massena, or the chin of Bonaparte. . . .

[TO EDWARD NOEL LONG]   *Southwell May 14th. 1807*

My dear Long,—The Spirit of Prophecy certainly animated my pen, when I wrote the *presage* of Petty's Downfall, with his disgrace, at Cambridge, in my *"College Examinations."*[1]—I am sorry I cannot repay the Compliments of your *Sire*, by the requested Copy, all my private volumes are gone, however, my publication will be out in June, & if you are in England at that Time, I shall send a Copy for the purpose.—Not above a dozen of the pieces in my private Copies, will appear *"pro Bono publico"* though the volume will be considerably larger, most of the amatory poems, the Cornelian[2] (which *you* & all the Girls, I know not why think my best) will be omitted, I have lately been brushing up my *Intellects* by Translations from the Greek of Anacreon & Medea, of the former only *2* odes, & a Chorus from the Latter, will make their appearance, I am putting the last touches to a Translation of the Episode of Nisus & Euryalus, (in my opinion the best in point of Versification I have ever written) & now bid an eternal Adieu to the Muse, in an Ode expressive of my Intention to relinquish *Poesy* forever, which will conclude my Volume.[3]—I am tired of versi-

[1] The facsimile begins with this word.
[2] The facsimile ends here.
[1] Lord Henry Petty, M.P. for the University of Cambridge, and Chancellor of the Exchequer, lost his seat in 1807. In 1809 he succeeded his brother as Marquis of Lansdowne. See "Thoughts Suggested by a College Examination".
[2] This was the poem to John Edleston, which appeared in the privately printed volumes.
[3] Byron's poem "Farewell to the Muse" was not finally put in the volume and appeared first posthumously in 1832.

fying, & am irrevocably determined to *rhyme* no more, an employment I merely adopted *"pour passer le Temps"* when this work is accomplished, I shall have obtained all the *Eclat* I desire at present, when it shall be said that I published before I was 20; the merit of the contents is of little Consequence, provided they are not absolutely execrable, the novelty of the *Deed* (which though not *unprecedented*, is at least uncommon, particularly amongst *Patricians*) will secure some share of Credit —All my Girls are *off*, as I told you in *Rhyme*,[4] consequently I am *dull*. I *swim* when the Weather permits, lately it has been unpropitious to that Amusement. I envy you so noble a *Bath*, as the *Medway*, a small River not above 8 feet in depth, constitutes my [*Lavarium?*][5] here, I have now lost 2 Stone & a half & weigh 12 Stone at *"your Service"* I shall reduce myself to 11. & there stop; if the Skies & my Health permit, one Month will effect this, with the assistance of a great coat, 8 Waistcoats, flannel Bandages, daily Physic, no Ale, one meal a Day, & the Hot Bath, in truth, I believe you would not recognize *"George Gordon,*['] at least many of my acquaintance, who have seen me since our meeting, have hardly believed their optics, my visage is lengthened, I appear taller, & somewhat *slim*, & "mirabile dictu!!" my Hair once black or rather very dark brown, is turned (I know not how but I presume by perpetual perspiration) to a *light Chesnut*, nearly approaching *yellow*, so that I am metamorphosed not a little. You must write previous to your Embarkation, & I hope you will return safe, from "cutting foreign throats" in company with the *Scum* of the *Earth.*—Is your Brother at Harrow? if he is I shall *tip* the youth,[6] on my visit to the *Blest Spot*, I see no account of their Speeches in the paper though the speechday is past some time, in our *day* it was different, there has been no mention of a single Speechday since *our departure*, last year or the present.—Wingfield[7] is gone to Marlow, Adieu yours ever

BYRON

[TO JOHN HANSON]   *Southwell. May 18th. 1807*

Sir,—I have this day drawn on you for the Sum of £50. 17S. 5D. the Balance due to me by your own acknowledgement in your last

---

4 See "To Edward Noel Long".
5 [Lavarium?]—cold bath.
6 Byron several times tipped Long's younger brother Henry with five pound notes when he visited Harrow.
7 See Nov. 4, 1806, to the Earl of Clare, note 3.

119

Letter, for the expenses incurred at Cambridge for furniture & c. & c. —the Draft is payable at Sight.—— *Mrs. Byron & indeed myself are much astonished that her last 2 letters req.g an immediate answer have met with no reply I remain yrs &c.

BYRON *1

P.S.—Lest you should be in the country I have addressed this to you & Birch, who I suppose will make no demur in your absence, as in that *cursed* Business in Novr. 1806.—

[TO ELIZABETH BRIDGET PIGOT]   *June 11th. 1807*

Dear *Queen Bess,*—*Savage* ought to be *immortal*, though not a *thorough bred Bulldog*, he is the finest puppy I ever saw, & will answer much better, in his great & manifold Kindness, he has *already bitten* my fingers, & disturbed the *gravity* of old Boatswain,[1] who is *grievously discomposed*, I wish to be informed what he *cost*, his *expences* &c. &c. that I may indemnify Mr. G.——[2] my thanks are *all* I can give for the Trouble he has taken, make a *long speech* & conclude it with *1 2 3 4. 5. 6. 7.*[3]—I am out of practice, so *deputize* you as *Legate, ambassador* would not do, in a matter concerning the *Pope*, which I presume this must, as the *whole* turns upon a *Bull.*

yours
BYRON

P.S.—I write in Bed

[TO JOHN HANSON]   *Southwell. June 11th. 1807*

Sir,—I need hardly inform you that on the 25th. of this month, one quarter of my allowance becomes due, this I shall draw for in course.— Mrs. Byron, my mother, is now in Treaty with Mrs. B[yron] of

1 Part of this letter is cut out from the manuscript. The words between the asterisks are not in Byron's hand.

1 Byron's favourite Newfoundland dog. Byron acquired him as a pup. According to the epitaph he wrote for Boatswain's tomb at Newstead, the dog was born in May, 1803, and died in November, 1808.

2 Unidentified. Apparently he had procured the pup for Byron.

3 According to Moore, who probably got his information from Elizabeth Pigot, whenever Byron "was as a loss for something to say, he used always to gabble over '1 2 3 4 5 6 7'". (Moore, I, 110n.)

Nottingham[1] for a sum of money to be lent by the latter to me, for the payment of which the former is to become security till the expiration of my minority, every thing is in a fair way, as far as *promises* go, but the money will hardly be advanced before the latter end of July, at least *I* imagine this will be the Case.—In the first week of July I have *pledged* myself to pay upwards of £350. to enable me to get rid of Cambridge forever, for which purpose I will be obliged to you, if you will advance me two *additional* Quarters, £250, or in all including the *legal advance*, £375.—For this I am willing to pay lawful Interest, during the Time you are out of the money, the *Security* is doubtless unexceptionable as you are the *Trustee*, & the payment is in your own hands, if the *ancient Gentlewoman*, of Nottingham keeps her word, you shall certainly be repaid immediately, but in case of any demur on her part, as my Income passes through your hands solely, I cannot deprive you of your *right*, even if so inclined.—I shall add little more, as I trust my *proposal* is *plain* enough, nor shall I expatiate on the dilemma, into which I shall be plunged by your Refusal, I must however request an immediate answer.—My Situation here is not very pleasant, or very *novel*, as a year has been nearly consumed in retirement, to this I am reconciled for another year, with the exception of a few days I must pass at Cambridge, to settle my affairs, if you come down, & I am told by Mealey[2] your presence is necessary at Newstead, I shall be happy to see you, though my Spirits are not *above par*.—I am become [fearfully?] *thin*, but my Health is unimpaired,

yours ever
BYRON

[TO EDWARD NOEL LONG] *Trinity College, June 29th. 1807*

My dear Long,—I have been here two days, & find very few of my old acquaintances, except Erskine,[1] Campbell,[2] Hobhouse[3] &c. &c. none of them knew me at first my figure & visage are of such *preter-natural*

[1] The Hon. Mrs. George Byron, the poet's great aunt. She was the widow of the Hon. George Byron, younger brother of Byron's grandfather, Admiral John Byron.
[2] Owen Mealey was the steward at Newstead Abbey.
[1] Two Erskine brothers, Henry David and Thomas, were schoolfellows of Byron at Harrow, and both went to Trinity College, Cambridge. The first became a clergyman, and the second a barrister.
[2] Augustus Campbell had been at Harrow with Byron, but left in 1803 and later went to Trinity College where he got a B.A. in 1807. In later years he was Rector of Liverpool.
[3] For a biographical sketch of Hobhouse see Appendix.

Longitude, I was obliged to tell your ancient *Hospes* Litchfield[4] my *name* & sorry am I to say I lose daily *weight "nolens* volens" I have lost 2 LB since Saturday, & am barely 11 stone by Litchfields *machine* with all my *Clothes, heavy shoes, gaiters* &c. &c—Edleston[5] called on me last night, & told me he saw me in Trinity walks twice, & *knew* me not, till pointed out to him, by his Brother or Cousin, I think he is much grown & rather improved, I shall be in town on Saturday, as I have not determined what Hotel to reside in, I cannot give you my positive address, but if you will call at 16 Piccadilly,[6] my old Lodgings, I will leave word, where I am to be met with, I wish you to answer this immediately, that I may know *when, where,* & *how* we are to meet, or if we are to *meet* at *all,* with the permission of your *Commander.*

yours ever
BYRON

P.S.—Pray what the Devil did you do with my *smaller Lamp?* Smith[7] has only the large one, & there was another, tell me if you have seen it, because I shall *indict* Mrs. Whitaker,[8] if it is not discovered.—

[TO ELIZABETH BRIDGET PIGOT]   *Cambridge. June 30th. 1807*

My dear *Elizabeth,*—"Better late than never Pal"[1] is a saying of which you know the origin, & as it is applicable on the present occasion, you will excuse its conspicuous place in the front of my Epistle. I am almost *superannuated* here, my old friends (with the exception of a very few) *all* departed, & I am preparing to follow them, but remain till monday to be present at *3 Oratorios,* 2 Concerts, a *fair,* a *boxing match,* & a *Ball.*—I find I am not only *thinner,* but *taller* by an Inch since my last visit, I was obliged to tell every body my

4 Litchfield was an inn-keeper in Cambridge.
5 John Edleston, the Trinity choirboy, to whom Byron had become attached during his first residence at Cambridge.
6 The address of Mrs. Elizabeth Massingberd with whom Byron frequently took rooms when in London.
7 Possibly Abel Smith, son of S. Smith, Woodhall Park, Hertford. Smith entered Harrow in 1800 and left in 1805, and afterward went to Trinity College, Cambridge. He was M.P. for Herts., 1835–47.
8 Mrs. Whitaker may have been the housekeeper.
1 The farce *Better Late than Never,* attributed to Peter Andrews, had first been played at Drury Lane on October 17, 1790, and apparently it was still popular. Byron may have seen it, for he went to the theatre frequently when he was in London.

name, nobody having the least recollection of my *visage,* or person.—
Even the *Hero* of my *Cornelian*[2] (Who is now sitting *vis a vis,* reading
a volume of my *poetics*) passed me in Trinity walks without recog-
nizing me in the least, & was thunderstruck at the alteration, which
had taken place in my Countenance &c. &c.—Some say I look *better,*
others *worse,* but all agree I am *thinner,* more I do not require.—I
have lost 2 LB in my weight since I left your *cursed, detestable & ab-
horred* abode of *Scandal, antiquated virginity,* & universal *Infamy,*
where excepting yourself & John Becher,[3] I care not if the whole Race
were consigned to the *Pit* of *Acheron,* which I would visit in person,
rather than contaminate my *sandals* with the polluted Dust of *Southwell.*—*Seriously* (unless obliged by the *emptiness* of my purse to revisit
Mr. B) you will see me no more, on monday I depart for London, &
quit Cambridge forever, with little regret, because our *Set* are
vanished, & my *musical protegé* above mentioned, has left the Choir, &
is to be stationed in a mercantile house of considerable eminence in the
Metropolis. You may have heard me observe he is exactly to an
hour, 2 years younger than myself, I found him grown considerably, &
as you will suppose, very glad to see his former *patron.*—He is nearly
my height, very thin, very fair complexion, dark eyes, & light locks,
my opinion of his mind, you already know, I hope I shall never have
reason to change it.—Every Body here conceives me to be an *Invalid,*
the University at present is very gay from the *fêtes* of divers kinds, I
supped out last night, but *eat* (or ate) nothing, sipped a bottle of Claret,
went to bed at 2, & rose at 8. I have commenced early rising, & find it
agrees with me, the master & the *fellows* all very *polite,* but look a
little *askance,* dont much admire *lampoons,* truth always disagreeable.
—Write & tell me how the Inhabitants of your *menagerie go on,* & if
my publication *goes off* well, do the *Quadrupeds growl,* apropos how is
Boatswain & *Bran,*[4] alas! my Bulldog[5] is deceased, *"Flesh both of cur
& man is grass"*——Address your answer to Cambridge, if I am gone
it will be forwarded, sad news just arrived, Russians beat,[6] a bad set,
eat nothing but oil, consequently must melt before a *hard fire.*—I get
awkward in my academic habiliments, for want of practice, got up in a

[2] Byron had written a poem, "The Cornelian", to the choirboy John Edleston,
which was printed in *Fugitive Pieces.* See Jan. 7 [1806], to Augusta Byron, note 1.

[3] The Rev. John Becher was Byron's friend and literary adviser at Southwell.
His objection to the poem "To Mary" as "too warmly drawn" caused Byron to
suppress *Fugitive Pieces.*

[4] Boatswain was Byron's Newfoundland dog and Bran was another dog, whether
his or the Pigots' is not clear.

[5] Byron's bulldog pup Savage. See June 11, 1807, to Elizabeth Pigot.

[6] The Russians were beaten at the battle of Friedland, June 15, 1807.

Window to hear the Oratorio at St. Mary's, popped down in the middle of the *Messiah*, tore a *woeful rent* in the Back of my best black Silk gown, & damaged an *egregious pair* of Breeches, mem.—never tumble from a church window, during Service.—Adieu, dear Bess, do not remember me to any one, to *forget*, & be forgotten by the people of S.— is all I *aspire* to, too contemptible for hatred, & totally insignificant I leave them to their fate, & think of the tedious *dream* I past there, as a *Blank* in my life, when men without religion are priests, & women without principle, are compelled to drag on a weary form of *involuntary chastity*, what *can* be said? *nothing*—so here ends my *chapter*.—

[Signature torn out]

[TO ELIZABETH BRIDGET PIGOT]   *Trin. Coll. Camb. July 5th. 1807*

My dear *Eliza*,—Since my last letter I have determined to reside *another year* at *Granta* as my Rooms &c. &c. are finished in *great Style*, several old friends *come up* again, & many *new* acquaintances made, consequently my Inclination leads me *forward*, & I shall return to College in October if still *alive*. My life here has been one continued *routine* of Dissipation, out at different places every day, engaged to more *dinners* &c. &c. than my *stay* would permit me to *fulfil*, at this moment I write with a *bottle* of *Claret* in my *Head*, & *tears* in my *eyes*, for I have just parted from "my *Corneilan*"[1] who spent the evening with me; as it was our last Interview, I postponed my engagements to devote the hours of the *Sabbath* to friendship, Edleston & I have separated for the present, & my mind is a *Chaos* of *hope* & *Sorrow*.— Tomorrow I set out for London, you will address your answer to "*Gordon's Hotel*" *Albemarle Street*, where I *sojourn*, during my visit to the *Metropolis*.—I rejoice to hear you are interested in my "protegè", he has been my *almost constant* associate since October 1805, when I entered Trinity College; his *voice* first attracted my notice, his *countenance* fixed it, & his *manners* attached me to him forever, he departs for a *mercantile house* in *Town*, in October, & we shall probably not meet, till the expiration of my minority, when I shall leave to his *decision*, either *entering* as a *Partner* through my Interest, or residing with me altogether. Of course he *would* in his present *frame* of mind prefer the *latter*, but he may alter his opinion previous to that period, however he shall have his choice, I certainly *love* him more than any human being, & neither *time* or Distance have had the least effect on

[1] See June 30, 1807, to Elizabeth Pigot, note 2.

my (in general) changeable Disposition.—In short, We shall put *Lady E. Butler, & Miss Ponsonby*[2] to the *Blush, Pylades & Orestes* out of countenance, & want nothing but a *Catastrophe* like *Nisus* & *Euryalus*,[3] to give *Jonathan* & *David* the *"go by"*.—He certainly is perhaps more *attached* to *me*, than even I am in *return*, during the whole of my residence at *Cambridge*, we met every day summer & Winter, without passing *one tiresome moment*, & separated *each time* with increasing Reluctance. I hope you will *one day* see *us* together, he is the only *being* I *esteem*, though I *like many*.—The Marquis of *Tavistock*[4] was down the other day, I supped with him at his *Tutor's*, entirely a *whig party*, the opposition *muster* very *strong* here, & Lord Hartington,[5] the Duke of Leinster,[6] &c. &c. are to join us in October, so every thing will be *splendid*.—The *Music* is all over at present, met with another *"accidency"*, upset a *Butter Boat* in the *lap* of a *lady*, looked very *blue, spectators* grinned, *"curse em"* apropos, sorry to say, been *drunk* every day, & not quite *sober yet*, however touch no meat, nothing but fish, soup & vegetables, consequently does me no harm, sad dogs all the *Cantabs*, mem, *we mean* to reform next January.—This place is a *Monotony* of *endless variety, like it*, hate Southwell, full of old maids, how is Anne Becher?[7] wants a husband, *men scarce*, wont *bite*, mem—tell Anne to fish more cautiously or the *Gudgeons* will be off; catch nothing but *Roach* & *Dace*.—Write soon, has Ridge[8] sold well? or do the Ancients demur? what Ladies have bought? all disappointed I dare say nothing *indecent* in the present publication, ⟨sorry for it⟩ *bad* set at Southwell, no *faces* & dont ever *"mean* well".—Saw a Girl at St.

[2] Lady Eleanor Butler, sister of the seventeenth Earl of Ormonde, and Sarah Ponsonby, cousin of the Earl of Bessborough, lived together for fifty years (1779–1829) in the Vale of Llangollen. They dressed as men, but their sexual ambivalence was generally regarded as an amiable eccentricity. Their fame spread widely and they were visited by many famous people.

[3] Byron was fond of the classical stories of male friendships. He published in *Hours of Idleness* his paraphrase of the story of Nisus and Euralus from the 9th book of the *Æneid*.

[4] The Marquis of Tavistock was later a fellow member of the Cambridge Whig Club with Byron.

[5] William Spencer, Marquis of Hartington (1790–1858), succeeded his father as sixth Duke of Devonshire in 1811. His sister, Georgiana Dorothy, had married Lord Carlisle's eldest son in 1801.

[6] The third Duke of Leinster, born in 1791, was a contemporary of Byron at Cambridge.

[7] Anne Becher may have been a sister of the Rev. John Becher, and she may have been a cousin of Elizabeth Pigot, whose mother was a daughter of Richard Turner Becher of Southwell. For the Pigot family relationships see Willis W. Pratt, *Byron at Southwell*, pp. 11–12.

[8] John Ridge in the neighbouring town of Newark printed Byron's early poems.

Mary's[9] the Image of Anne Houson,[10] thought it was her, all in the wrong, the Lady stared, so did I, I blushed, so did *not* the Lady, sad thing, wish women, had *more modesty.*—Talking of women brings my *terrier Fanny*[11] into my head[;] how is she? very well I thank you.— Got a Headach, must go to bed, up early in the morning to travel, my "protegé" breakfasts with me, parting spoils my appetite, excepting from Southwell, mem—*I hate Southwell,*

yours ever
BYRON

[TO ELIZABETH BRIDGET PIGOT]   *Gordon's Hotel, July 13th. 1807*

My dear *Elisabat,*—You write most excellent epistles, a fig for other correspondents, with their nonsensical apologies for *"knowing nought about it,"* you send me a delightful Budget, *beginning* with *Anne Becher,*[1] & *ending* with *Crim con.* nothing could be more natural, the moment I saw *her* name in the commencement, I anticipated the *result.*— —I am here in a perpetual vortex of dissipation (very pleasant for all that) & strange to tell get thinner, being now below 11 stone considerably, stay in Town a *month,* perhaps 6 weeks, trip into Essex, & then as a favour *irradiate* Southwell for *3 days* with the light of my Countenance, but nothing shall ever make me *reside* there again, I positively return to Cambridge in October, we are to be uncommonly gay, or in truth, I should *cut* the University.—An extraordinary circumstance occurred to me at Cambridge, a Girl so very like Anne Houson[2] made her appearance, that nothing but the most *minute Inspection* could have undeceived me, I wish I had asked if *she* ever was at [Hockerton?].—What the Devil, would Ridge have? is not 50 in a fortnight before the Advertisements a sufficient sale, I hear many of the London Booksellers have them, & Crosby[3] has sent Copies to the principal watering places. Are they *liked* or *not* in Southwell? how does John Becher[4] go on? & Sherard[5] on his receiving the *"Coup de grace"*

[9] St. Mary's the Great, the Cambridge University Church.

[10] A Southwell girl to whom Byron addressed some of his early poems.

[11] Byron was a lover of all breeds of dogs, though he seemed to be fondest of the Newfoundland and the bulldog.

[1] See July 5, 1807, to Elizabeth Pigot, note 7.

[2] See July 5, 1807, to Elizabeth Pigot, note 10.

[3] Ben Crosby was the London bookseller who was agent for John Ridge of Newark. Ridge sent him a consignment of Byron's *Hours of Idleness* for sale in the capital and the provinces.

[4] The Rev. John Thomas Becher, of a family related to the Pigots, was vicar of Rumpton and of Midsomer Norton, and later prebendary and then Vicar-general of Southwell Minster. See Aug. 10, 1806, to John Pigot.

[5] Sherard Becher. See Aug. 9, 1806, to John Pigot, note 5.

from Miss *"Twizzle"*.—I wish Boatswain[6] had *swallowed* Damon, how is Bran? by the immortal Gods! Bran ought to be a *Count* of the *Holy Roman Empire.*—So, Miss Harriet's[7] *Invalid* is recovered, & declines matrimony. Alas! Alas! Ah! Ah! Good lack! Oh! Oh!—Are the Leacrofts[8] returned? will the *Burtonians bite,* or do they dread Thalaba.[9]—What is become of the "Talents" are they disjoined, or in close alliance.—You perceive questions innumerable? & I expect answers to *all.* The Intelligence of London cannot be interesting to you who *have rusticated* all your life, the annals of Routs, Riots, Balls & Boxing matches, Dowagers & demireps, Cards & Crim-con, Parliamentary Discussion, Political Details, Masquerades, Mechanics, Argyle Street Institution & Aquatic races, Love & Lotteries, Brookes's & Buonaparte, Exhibitions of pictures with Drapery, & *women without*; Statues with more *decent dresses,* than their *originals,* Opera-singers & Orators, Wine, Women, Wax works, & Weathercocks, cannot accord with your *insulated* Ideas, of Decorum & other *silly expressions,* not inserted in our *Vocabulary.*— Oh Southwell, Southwell, how I rejoice to have left thee, & how I curse the heavy hours I have dragged along for so many months, amongst the *Mohawks* who inhabit your *Kraals.*— However one thing I do not regret, which is having *pared* off a sufficient quantity of flesh, to enable me to slip into an *"Eelskin"* & vie with the *slim* Beau's of modern times, though I am sorry to say, it seems to be the mode amongst *Gentlemen,* to grow *fat,* & I am told, I am at least 14 LB below the *Fashion.*—However I *decrease* instead of enlarging, which is extraordinary as *violent* exercise in London is impracticable, but I attribute the *phenomenon* to our *Evening squeezes,* at public & private parties.—I heard from Ridge this morning (the 14th, my letter was begun yesterday) he says the poems go on as well as can be *wished,* the 75 sent to *Town,* are circulated, & a demand for *50* more, complied with, the day he dated his Epistle, though the Advertisements are not yet half published.—Adieu

yours ever
BYRON

[6] See June 11, 1807, to Elizabeth Pigot, note 1.
[7] Harriet Maltby, to whom Byron addressed two poems, one "To Harriet" (posthumously published, *Poetry,* I, 263) and "To Marion" in *Hours of Idleness.*
[8] See Jan. 31, 1807, to Capt. John Leacroft, note 1.
[9] There is no clue to the local reference to the Burtonians, but Thalaba was the righteous hero of Southey's poem of that name.

Ld. Byron's Compts to Mr. Hanson, if there is any mistake in the form of the Draft, Mr. H. must thank himself, as Ld. B. particularly inquired if a stamp was necessary of Mr. H. Hanson, & the reply was in the affirmative, *Mr Hannibal Higgins*[1] has [*descended?*] to endorse the Draft, which removes every *obstacle*, it is very extraordinary, that Ld. B. never can receive his *stipend*, without as much trouble, as might suffice to *pay* the *German Legion 5* years *arrears*; Chancery Lane also being some little distance from Ld. B's residence, Ld. B. would esteem it a favour if his servants could be detained something less than an Hour, as Ld. B. has at present full employment for both, in another quarter.—

Sir,—Your proposal to make Mrs. Byron my *Treasurer* is very kind, but does not meet with my approbation. Mrs. Byron has already made more *free* with my *funds* than suits my convenience, & I do not [propose] to expose her to the danger of Temptation. Things will therefore stand as they are, the Remedy would be worse than the disease, I wish you would order your drafts payable to *me* & not to Mrs. B.— this is worse than *Hannibal Higgins*,[1] who the Devil could suppose, that any Body would have mistaken him for a *real Personage*, & what earthly consequence could it be whether the Blank in the draft was filled up with, *Wilkins, Tomkyns, Simkins, Wiggins, Spriggins, Jiggins,* or *Higgins*, if I had put in *James Johnson* you would not have demurred, & only object to Hannibal Higgins? particularly after his *respectable* Endorsement; as to Business I make [no pre-]tensions to a Knowledge of any thing [but] a Greek Grammar or a Racing Calendar, but if the *Quintessence* of information on that head, consists in unnecessary & unpleasant delays, explanations, rebuffs, retorts, repartees, & recriminations, the House of H— & B—[2] stands preeminent in the profession, as from the Bottom of his soul testifies

yours &c.
BYRON

P.S.—Will you dine with me on Sunday Tete a Tete at 6 o clock, I

---

[1] Byron had written a draft on Hanson for his quarterly allowance under a facetious name, and Hanson warned him that it was illegal and that he might get into trouble.

[1] See July 20, 1807, to Hanson (*a*), note 1.

[2] The law firm of Hanson and Birch.

should be happy to see you before, but my engagements will not permit me, on wednesday I go to the House, I shall have Hargreaves[3] & his Brother on some day after you, I dont like to annoy children with the *formal* faces of *legal* Papa's.—

[TO [BEN CROSBY (*a*)]]   *July 21st. 1807*

Sir,—I have sent you a critique on Wordsworth's poems, for "Literary Recreations,"[1] insert or not as you please, or rather the editors. Of course they must alter or expunge what they disapprove. If it is not deemed worthy of publication, you need not trouble yourself to return the manuscript, but commit it to the flames. In a day or two I will send you a manuscript poem for the same work.

                                                            &c. &c.
                                                            BYRON

[TO BEN CROSBY (*b*)]   *July 21st. 1807*

Sir,—I have sent according to my promise some Stanzas for "Literary Recreations"[1] the Insertion I leave to the option of the Editors, they have never appeared before, I should wish to know, whether they are admitted, or not, & when the work will appear, as I am desirous of a Copy

                                                            &c. &c.
                                                            BYRON

P.S.—Send your answer when *convenient.*

[TO THE EARL OF CLARE[1]]   [*August, 1807?*]

There is little or no doubt a few years, or months, will render us as politely indifferent to each other as if we had never passed a portion of our time together.

[3] Hanson's son.
[1] Byron's review of Wordsworth's *Poems,* 2 vols., 1807, appeared in *Monthly Literary Recreations* for July. Crosby, the London bookseller who, as agent for Ridge, was handling the sale of Byron's *Hours of Idleness,* published the periodical. The editor, whom Byron did not know, was Eugenius Roche.
[1] See July 21, 1807, to Crosby (*a*), note 1. *Monthly Literary Recreations* for July, 1807, published Byron's "Stanzas to Jessy", without the author's name. They were never acknowledged by Byron or included in any authorized edition of his works, until collected by E. H. Coleridge (*Poetry,* I, 234–36). The verses seem obviously addressed to John Edleston.
[1] See Nov. 4, 1806, to the Earl of Clare, note 1. This sentence from Byron's letter to Clare was quoted by Clare (see Moore, I, 50).

My dear Elizabeth—London begins to disgorge its contents, town is empty, consequently I can scribble at leisure, as my occupations are less numerous, in a fortnight I shall depart to fulfil a country engagement, but expect 2 Epistles from you previous to that period.—Ridge, you tell me, does not proceed rapidly in Notts, very possible, in Town things wear a most promising aspect, & a *Man* whose works are praised by *Reviewers*, admired by *Duchesses* & sold by every Bookseller of the Metropolis, does not dedicate much consideration to *rustic Readers*.—I have now a Review before me entitled, "Literary Recreations" where my *Bardship* is applauded far beyond my Deserts.[1] I know nothing of the critic, but think *him* a very *discerning gentleman*, & *myself* a *devilish clever fellow*, his critique pleases me particularly because it is of great length, & a proper quantum of censure is administered, just to give an agreeable *relish* to the praise, you know I hate insipid, unqualified common-place compliments, if you would wish to see it, tell Ridge to order the 13th Number of "Literary Recreations" for the last Month. I assure you, I have not the most distant Idea, of the Writer of the article, it is printed in a periodical publication, & though I have written a paper (a Review of Wordsworth) which appears in the same work, I am ignorant of every other person concerned in it, even the Editor, whose name I have not heard.—My Cousin, Lord Alexander Gordon, who resided in the same Hotel, told me his Mother, her *Grace* of *Gordon*,[2] requested he would introduce my *poetical* Lordship, to her *highness*, as she had bought my volume, admired it extremely, in common with the Rest of the fashionable world, & wished to claim her relationship with the Author.—I was unluckily engaged on an excursion for some days afterwards, & as the Duchess was on the eve of departing for Scotland, have postponed my Introduction till the Winter, when I shall favour this Lady, *whose Taste I shall not dispute*, with my *most sublime & edifying conversation*.—She is now in the Highlands, & Alexander, took his departure a few days ago, for the same *blessed* Seat, of *"dark-rolling Winds"*.—[3] Crosby

[1] A laudatory review of *Hours of Idleness* appeared in the July 1807 number of *Monthly Literary Recreations*. Despite his statement that he did not know the editor, etc., Byron was perfectly aware that the review was not impartial, for the bookseller Crosby was puffing his stock in a periodical which he published and controlled.

[2] The Duchess of Gordon (1748–1812), a leader of the Tories, was a famous matchmaker, who succeeded in marrying three of her daughters to Dukes, Manchester, Richmond, and Bedford.

[3] "dark-rolling Winds" is probably a by-product of Byron's imitation of Ossian, "The Death of Calmar and Orla", published in *Hours of Idleness*.

my London publisher, has disposed of his second importation, & has sent to Ridge for a *third* (at least so he says) in every Bookseller's I see my *own name*, & *say nothing*, but enjoy my *fame* in *secret*.—My last Reviewer, kindly requests me to alter my determination of writing no more, and *"as a friend to the cause of Literature"* begs, I will *gratify* the *Public*, with some new *work* "at no very distant period".— Who would not be a Bard? *Elizabeth*, that is to say, if all critics would be so polite, however the others will pay me off I doubt not, for this *gentle* encouragement.—If so, have at 'em, By the Bye, I have written at my Intervals of leisure, after 2 in the *Morning*. 380 lines in *blank* verse, of "Bosworth Field,"[4] I have luckily procured Hutton's account,[5] & shall extend the Poem to 8 or 10 Books, & shall have finished in a year, whether it will be published or not must depend on circumstances.—So much for *Egotism*, my *Laurels* have turned my Brain, but the *cooling acids* of forthcoming criticisms, will probably restore me to *Modesty.*— — — —Southwell, I agree with your Brother, is a *damned* place, I have done with it, & shall see it no more, (at least in all probability) excepting yourself, I esteem no one within its precincts, you were my only *rational* companion, & in plain truth I had more respect for you, than the whole *Bevy*, with whose foibles I *amused* myself in compliance with their *prevailing propensities*, you gave yourself more trouble with me & my *manuscripts*, than a thousand *dolls* would have done, believe me, I have not forgotten your good nature, in *this Circle* of *Sin*, & one day I trust shall be able to evince my gratitude.—As for the village *"Lass'es"* of *every description*, my *Gratitude* is also unbounded, to be equalled only by my *contempt*, I saw the *designs* of all *parties*,[6] while they imagined me *every thing* to be *wished*, Adieu

yours very truly

BYRON

P.S.—Remembrance to *Dr. Pigot*.—

[TO ELIZABETH BRIDGET PIGOT]   *London, August 11th. 1807*

Dear Elizabeth,—On Sunday next I set off for the Highlands, a friend of mine accompanies me in my Carriege to Edinburgh, there we shall leave it, & proceed in a *Tandem* (a species of open Carriage)

---

[4] The poem was never finished nor published, and the manuscript is not extant.
[5] William Hutton's *The Battle of Bosworth Field* was published in 1788.
[6] The designs of the Southwell girls, or their families, especially the Leacrofts, to entrap him in marriage.

through the Western passes to Inverary, where we shall purchase *Shelties*, to enable us to view places inaccessible to *vehicular Conveyances*, on the Coast, we shall hire a vessel, & visit the most remarkable of the Hebrides, & if we have time & favourable weather mean to sail as far as Iceland only 300 miles from the Northern extremity of Caledonia, to peep at *Hecla*, this last Intention you will keep a secret, as my nice *Mamma* would imagine I was on a *voyage* of *Discovery*, & raise the accustomed *maternal "Warhoop."*[1]—Last week I swam in the Thames from Lambeth through the 2 Bridges Westminster & Blackfriars, a distance including the different turns & tacks made on the way, of 3 miles!! you see I am in excellent training in case of a *squall* at Sea.—I mean to collect all the Erse traditions, poems, & & c. & translate, or expand the subjects, to fill a volume, which may appear next Spring, under the Denomination of *"the Highland Harp"* or some title equally *picturesque.* Of Bosworth Field, one Book is finished, another just begun, it will be a work of 3 or four years, & most probably never *concluded.*—What would you say to some Stanzas on Mount *Hecla?* they would be written at least with *Fire.*—How is the Immortal Bran? & the Phoenix of canine Quadrupeds, Boatswain? I have lately purchased a thoroug[h] bred Bulldog worthy to be the Coadjutor of the aforesaid celestials, his name is *Smut!* "bear it ye breezes! on your *balmy* wings".[2]—Write to me before I set off, I conjure you by the 5th Rib of your Grandfather; you say, Ridge goes on well with the Book now, I thought that worthy *Phrygian*, had not done much in the Country, in Town they have been very very successful, Carpenter (Moore's publisher)[3] told me a few days ago they sold all their's immediately, & had several enquiries made since, which from the Book being gone, they could not supply, the Duke of York, the Marchioness of Headfort,[4] the Duchess of Gordon &c &c. were among the Purchasers, & Crosby says the circulation will be still more extensive in the Winter, the Summer Season being very bad for a sale, as most people are absent from London, however they have gone off extremely well altogether.—I shall pass very near you on my Journey, through Newark, but cannot approach, dont tell this to Mrs.

[1] This scheme for visiting the Hebrides, and Iceland, was never executed, for what reason is not clear, perhaps simple lack of funds.

[2] Probably another by-product of his imitation of Ossian. See Aug. 2, 1807, to Elizabeth Pigot, note 3.

[3] Moore's early pseudonymous *The Poetical Works of the Late Thomas Little* (1801) was printed by J. and T. Carpenter, Old Bond Street. Moore's later work was published by Longman.

[4] Mary, daughter of George Quinn, married the first Marquis of Headfort (in the peerage of Ireland).

B. who supposes I travel a different Road.—If you have any Letter, order it to be left at Ridge's shop, where I shall call, or the post office Newark, which you please, on Monday I shall change horses at Newark, about 6 or 8 in the Evening, if your Brother would ride over, I should be devilish glad to see him, he can return the same night, or sup with us, & go home the following Morning, the Kingston arms is my Inn.—Adieu,

yours ever
BYRON

P.S.—Lord Carlisle on receiving my poems, sent before he opened the Book, a tolerably handsome Letter, I have not heard of or from him since, his opinion I neither know nor care about, if he is the least insolent, I shall enroll him with *"Butler"*[5] & the rest of the worthies, he is in Yorkshire poor man! very ill!—He said he had not had time to read the contents, but thought it necessary to acknowledge the Receipt of the volume immediately.—Perhaps the Earl *"bears no Brother near the Throne"* if so, I will make his *sceptre* totter in [his] *hands.*—Adieu!—

[TO THE EARL OF CLARE]   *Cambridge, August 20th. 1807*

My dear Clare,—What apology will be adequate to atone for my offence, I know not, I can only say your Letter's would not have remained so long unnoticed, had I received them, previous to my arrival at this place, after an absence of 10 months, where your kind Epistles were diligently perused.—Here they had waited for 6 months, & from them I received the first Intimation of your departure from Harrow. Since *we* met they tell me I am grown taller, & so much thinner from Illness & violent Exercise, that many who had lived with me in habits of Intimacy, even old *Schoolfellows*, found great difficulty in acknowledging me to be the *same person.*—Indeed I ought to be *thin* for I weigh less by *three Stone*, & *9 pounds*, than I did 6 months ago.—My weight was then *14* stone & 6 LB. it is now *10 Stone 11* LB.!!!—I believe I saw you and your Brother a few weeks since, passing through Bond Street, in a Lady's Carriage, I was *only* a Pedestrian, & escaped your notice.—The Poems you were pleased to mention, have been

⁵ Byron had caricatured Dr. George Butler, the new Headmaster of Harrow, as Pomposus in "Childish Recollections".

published about 6 weeks, my Bookseller tells me he has sold a great number, when we meet, I shall be happy to present a Copy for your Inspection.—The present volume differs very materially from the one printed privately last Winter, several poems published in the former, are withheld from the latter, which however contains many more pieces, original & translated, & is of considerably larger size.— When you answer this (if I can expect so much, after my apparent yet unintentional neglect) address the Reply to Trinity College, where I remain another year, Illness prevented my Residence for the last twelve months.—I have heard 3 times from Delawarr, that is to say, *twice* more often than I expected, or indeed desired, for though I formerly liked him, long absence, & our serious Quarrel entirely destroyed, the seeds of affection, once *deeply* sown, I addressed him merely to explain the mistaken grounds on which we had acted, without (as I plainly told him) any view to a Reconciliation, this produced a Reply, &c. &c. in short the affair was compromised, & we are what the World commonly call Friends, long may we be so, but never so intimate as before, indeed, I shall take care we are not much together, & I doubt not D's Inclinations, are not more *violently* bent, on a renewal of our acquaintance, than my own, all things considered, how should it be otherwise?—I have never seen Harrow since the last day I spent there with your Lordship; next Summer, *we old Harrow men*, will favour the *little* Boys, our Successors with a visit.—I hope this Letter will find you *safe*, I saw in a Morning paper, a long account of Robbery &c. &c. committed on the persons of *sundry Majors, Colonels*, & Esquires, passing from *Lady Clare's* to *Limerick*, from such Banditti, the *Lord* deliver your *carcase* & *Habitation*, you may exclaim with Pope, in his Imitation of Spencer *"Bad Neighborhood I ween."*—I am now setting off, for the Highlands of Scotland, & expect your answer on my Return, to Cambridge, have we any chance of meeting next Winter? I shall pass some time in Town, where you will probably spend your Vacation, present my Remembrance to *Brother Richard*, & believe me dearest Clare,

> yours ever affectly
> BYRON

[TO JOHN HANSON]   *Dorant's Hotel, October 19th. 1807*

Dear Hanson,—I will thank you to disburse the quarter due as soon as possible, for I am at this moment contemplating with a *woeful visage*, one *solitary Guinea, two bad sixpences* and a *shilling*, being *all* the *Cash* at present in possession of

yours very truly
BYRON

[TO ELIZABETH BRIDGET PIGOT]　　　　*Trinity College Cambridge*
October 26th. 1807

My dear Elizabeth,—Fatigued with sitting up till four in the morning for these last two days at Hazard, I take up my pen to enquire how your Highness, & the rest of my female acquaintance at the seat of Archiepiscopal Grandeur *Southwell*, go on.—I know I deserve a scolding for my negligence in not writing more frequently, but racing up & down the Country for these last three months, how was it possible to fulfil the Duties of a Correspondent?—Fixed at last for 6 weeks, I write, as *thin* as ever (not having gained an ounce since my Reduction) & rather in better humour, for after all, *Southwell* was a detestable residence; thank St. Dominic I have done with it, I have been twice within 8 miles of it, but could not prevail on myself to *suffocate* in its heavy atmosphere.—This place is wretched enough, a villainous Chaos of Dice and Drunkenness, nothing but Hazard and Burgundy, Hunting, Mathematics and Newmarket, Riot and Racing, yet it is a Paradise compared with the eternal dullness of Southwell, oh! the misery of doing nothing, but make *Love, enemies,* and *Verses.*— Next January (but this is *entre nous* only, and pray let it be so, or my maternal persecutor will be throwing her Tomahawk at any of my curious projects) I am going to *Sea* for four of [or?] five months, with my Cousin Capt. Bettesworth,[1] who commands the Tartar the finest frigate in the navy. I have seen most scenes, and wish to look at a naval life.—We are going probably to the Mediterranean, or to the West Indies, or to the Devil, and if there is a possibility of taking me to the Latter, Bettesworth will do it, for he has received four and twenty wounds in different places, and at this moment possesses a Letter from the late Ld. Nelson, stating Bettesworth as the only officer of the navy who had more wounds than himself.— — —I have got a new friend, the finest in the world, a *tame Bear,*[2] when I brought him here, they asked me what I meant to do with him, and my reply was "he should

---

[1] George Edmund Byron Bettesworth (1780–1808) was descended from the Trevanions. Byron's grandmother, Sophia Trevanion, was the wife of Admiral Byron. Bettesworth was killed at Bergen in 1808, while in command of the *Tartar*.

[2] Byron later sent the bear to Newstead to join a growing menagerie.

sit for *a Fellowship.*"—*Sherard* will explain the meaning of the sentence if it is ambiguous.[3]—This answer delighted them not,—we have eternal parties here, and this evening a large assortment of *Jockies*, Gamblers, *Boxers, Authors, parsons,* and *poets,* sup with me.— A precious Mixture, but they go on well together, and for me, I am a *spice* of every thing except a Jockey, by the bye, I was dismounted again the other day.— —Thank your Brother in my name, for his Treatise. I have written 214 pages of a novel, one poem of 380 Lines,[4] to be published (without my name) in a few weeks, with notes, 560 Lines of Bosworth Field, and 250 Lines of another poem in rhyme, besides half a dozen smaller pieces, the poem to be published is a Satire, apropos, I have been praised to the Skies in the Critical Review,[5] and abused equally in another publication,[6] so much the Better, they tell me, for the sale of the Book, it keeps up controversy, and prevents it from being forgotten, besides the first men of all ages have had their share, nor do the humblest escape, so I bear it like a philosopher, it is odd enough the two opposite Critiques came out on the same day, and out of five pages of abuse, [my?] Censor only quotes *two lines,* from different poems, in support of his opinion, now the proper way to *cut* up, is to quote long passages, and make them appear absurd, because simple allegation is no proof.—on the other hand, there are seven pages of praise, and more than *my modesty* will allow, said on the subject.—Adieu yours truly

BYRON

P.S.—Write, Write, Write!!!

[3] In a marginal note in his copy of Moore (I, 121), now in the possession of James M. Osborn, E. H. Coleridge has written: "That is, Miss Pigot's brother. Byron's dirty *double entente* has been quoted seriously as a piece of academic wit". But Miss Pigot's brothers were John, Richard, and Henry. Sherard was probably Sherard Becher. See Aug. 9, 1806, to John Pigot, where Byron refers to "Sherard B." and Jan. 13, 1807, to John Pigot, in which he mentions "S. Becher". No slang dictionary has yielded a *double entendre* for the phrase "sit for a fellowship".

[4] The poem to be published was a satire which he then called "British Bards". With additions that brought it to 696 lines, it appeared in 1809 as *English Bards and Scotch Reviewers.*

[5] For September, 1807.

[6] The abuse in *The Satirist* of October, 1807, rankled more than Byron would admit. He struck back at the editor, Hewson Clarke, in the text and in a postscript of the second edition of *English Bards and Scotch Reviewers,* the first edition to which he affixed his name.

Mr. Ridge.—I had not the slightest idea, we should have any occasion to publish a second Edition, for some Time, nor does it appear necessary till the first at least is entirely sold.—I merely suggest this for your own advantage, the *work* is *your property*, & you may dispose of it as you please.—When I was in London, I observed the Booksellers objected to the size, & two or three said, the poems should have been printed in the same size, as Ld. Strangford's & Little's poems, in this opinion I coincide, & with your leave the next Edition shall be printed & *bound* in the same manner, & in the same coloured Boards as Little. I dont admire the yellow *backs*.—We will also alter the Title, simply to "poems" by Ld. Byron &c. &c. & omit the *Latin Motto*, the two others can remain.—The preface we will omit altogether.[1]—The Dedication I will send in Time.[2]—You could not have the second Edition printed in London? could you? if it made no difference to you, I should prefer it, as I could superintend the proofs in person.—I wish the second poem (Stanzas on a view of Harrow) to be omitted. I have some new pieces which may occupy a place in the latter part of the volume.—These I will send when we have decided, *when, where, & how*, we are to publish, a new Edition.—Your Answer will oblige

&c. &

BYRON

P.S.—I do not know whether Mr. J. Becher would like the trouble of correcting the Sheets, however, if you think it probable I will make the Request.—I think our next Edition, should be on *hot press* as the first has gone off well.—

Sir,—I have this day written to Mrs. Byron, to get my allowance discounted at the Southwell Bank, as you of course will not pay till the 25th Decr.—I have generally signed the Drafts myself, but Mrs. Byron will do it instead on the present occasion, as I am not on the spot; this I presume makes no difference, as I have apprised you in Time.—As I have drawn for the full quarter £125, & not deducted

---

[1] The second edition of *Hours of Idleness* was published in 1808 by Ridge with the title *Poems Original and Translated*, which had been part of the sub-title of the earlier volume. The preface, which was to be the occasion of such heavy ridicule by the *Edinburgh Review*, was omitted.

[2] The dedication was to the Earl of Carlisle.

five pounds for Joe Murray's[1] stipend, I now enclose you five pounds, to make up the difference. Your answer will oblige

yours &c.
BYRON

[TO JOHN RIDGE]   *Trin. Coll. Cambridge Novr. 20th. 1807*

Sir,—I am happy to hear every thing goes on so well, & I presume you will soon commence, though I am still of opinion the first Edition had better be entirely sold, before you risk the printing of a second.— As Crosby recommends fine wove Foolscap, let it be used, & I will order a design in London, for a plate, my own portrait would perhaps be best, but as that would take up so long a time completing, we will substitute probably a view of Harrow, or Newstead in its stead. You will omit the poems mentioned below,

Omit
{
Stanza's on a view of Harrow.
To a Quaker.
The first Kiss of Love.
College Examinations
Lines to the Revd. J. T. Becher

To be inserted not exactly in the same places, but in different parts of the volume I will send you five poems never yet published, two of tolerable length, at least much longer than any of the above, which are ordered to be omitted.—Mention in your answer when you would like to receive the manuscripts, that they may be sent, by the bye, I must have the *proofs* of the *Manuscripts*, sent to Cambridge as they occur, the proofs from the finished copy you can manage with Care, if Mr. Becher will assist you, attend to the List of *Errata*, that we may not have a *second Edition* of them also.—The Preface we have done with, perhaps I may send an Advertisement; a dedication shall be forthcoming in due Season. You will send a proof of the first Sheet, for Inspection, & soon too, for I am about to set out for London next week, if I remain there any time I shall apprise you where to send the Manuscript Proofs.—Do you think, the others will be sold before the next are ready, what says Crosby? remember I have advised you not to risk it a second time, & it is not too late to retract.—However you must abide by your own discretion.—

&c. &c.
BYRON

---

[1] The old servant at Newstead, formerly in the employ of the 5th Lord Byron.

P.S.—You will print from the Copy I sent you, with the alterations, pray attend to them, & be careful of mistakes, in my last, I gave you directions concerning the Title page & Mottoes.—

[TO EDWARD NOEL LONG]   [*November 23. 1807 post mark*]

. . . last night in the concert Room, for seizing my Gown, as I past by him.—We have myriads of Harrow men, whom you & I remember, merely as *third Rates*, Waddy [Core?] Platt Sr. Hales, Burrows of [Carbo's?], & other [*venison? vermin?*], these I cut of course, Harting-ton[1] is here, Bridgeman & Lowther out of six Nobles in this College, four are Harrowmen, there is a Whig Club here, of which Tavistock wants me to become a member.[2] As to my poems, I have been reviewed in twenty different publications, in several very favourably indeed, in others harshly. However between good & bad, they get into notice, for my publisher, is printing a second Edition, the first being out.— Pretty fair in four months & a half,

yours very truly
BYRON

[TO JOHN RIDGE]   *Trin. Coll. Camb. Decr. 11th. 1807*

Mr. Ridge,—Omit *"Love's last Adieu"* we shall then have an equal number, as College Examinations are to remain.

&c. &c.
BYRON

[TO JOHN RIDGE]   *Trin. Coll. Camb. Decr. 14th. 1807*

Mr. Ridge,—In printing "College Examinations" after the 58th Line ending *"more than the verse in which the Critic wrote"* insert these four lines.

> Vain as their honours, heavy as their Ale,
> Sad as their wit, and tedious as their tale,
> To friendship dead, though not untaught to feel
> When Self and Church demand a Bigot zeal

[1] The Marquis of Hartington was soon (1811) to become the sixth Duke of Devonshire.
[2] John Cam Hobhouse, in a letter to John Murray in 1820, named the ten members of the Cambridge Whig Club: "Mr. W. Ponsonby, Mr. George O'Callaghan, the Duke of Devonshire, Mr. Dominick Browne, Mr. Henry Pearce, Mr. Kinnaird [Douglas Kinnaird, later Byron's banker and close friend], Lord Tavistock, Lord Ellenborough, Lord Byron, and myself." (*LJ*, IV, 500.)

With eager haste &c. &c.—

and so on, be careful to observe these directions & print the lines in their proper place

&c &c
BYRON

[TO JOHN RIDGE]   *Trinity College Decr. 20th. 1807*

Mr. Ridge,—In the "Stanzas addressed to the Earl of——"[1] the last Stanza except three or four begins thus

> "I think I said twould be your fate
> "To add one Star to regal State
> "May Royal smiles attend you
> "And *if* a noble monarch reign
> "You will not seek his smiles in vain
> *"That Face* will recommend you

Instead of this let the third Line run

> "And *should* a noble &c."

And the 6th Line be

> "If *Worth* can recommend you."

Let the next Stanza which begins

> "Oh! you will triumph &c &c

be altered to

> "Yet since in Danger courts abound
> Where specious Rivals glitter round
> From Snares may Saints preserve you!
> &c &c

The Rest of the Stanza may stand—when the proof is ready send it, as I am now waiting for it.—

&c &c
BYRON

[TO BEN CROSBY]   *Trin. Coll. Cambridge, Decr. 22d. 1807*

Sir,—I feel considerably obliged to you, for the trouble you have taken with the work, which probably owes it's success more to your

---

[1] These stanzas were addressed to the Earl of Clare.

140

endeavours than any merit of its own.—I received the Monthly Review,[1] and Macdiamid's British Statesmen[2] a few days ago.—A Friend of mine of this University,[3] & son of a member of Parliament, has a Satire in imitation of Juvenal ready for the press, but as it is hardly considerable enough to fill a volume, I have consented to publish a poem of mine in conjunction with his, and we wish to know if you will undertake the publication.—The Satire consists of above three hundred Lines, and the Latin is to be printed on the opposite page, there are also notes, but of no great Length.—Mine is of the same nature, but original, and contains above four hundred Lines, with several notes; the subject, the poetry of the present Day.[4]—It must be published (if at all) anonymously, & in such a manner that my name as the author, may never transpire at any future period, as I feel no inclination to give it to the world a second time, particularly so soon after my DeBût.—I believe it is my Coadjutor's first appearance, and he must also *wear* a *mask*, though from a different Reason.—The whole will probably form a larger volume than the "Baviad" and the poems must be mentioned as the work of different Hands, but without the names.— If you have no objection, your answer will oblige

&c &c

BYRON

P.S.—The second Edition of my poems, is to be printed the same size as "Little's poems"[5] and two or more plates will appear among the pages.—The success of the first, on my account, is nothing, but I am rejoiced that Ridge has not lost by the Undertaking.—On my return to Town in the Beginning of January, I will settle any account between us.—

[1] *The Monthly Review; or Literary Journal* for November, 1807, published a generally favourable review of *Hours of Idleness*, saying that Byron's verses "display both ease and strength, both pathos and fire".

[2] Macdiarmid's *Lives of British Statesmen* (1807) was one of the books in Byron's library which was sold at auction by Evans on April 6, 1816.

[3] The friend was John Cam Hobhouse, who finally published his imitation of the eleventh satire of Juvenal in a volume called *Imitations and Translations* (1809), to which Byron contributed nine poems. The publisher was Longman, Hurst, Rees, and Orme.

[4] "British Bards", published in 1809, with additions, as *English Bards and Scotch Reviewers*.

[5] *The Poetical Works of the Late Thomas Little* was published pseudonymously by Thomas Moore in 1801 in a small octavo volume.

[TO JOHN HANSON]   *Trin. Coll. Cambridge, Decr. 23d. 1807*

My dear Sir,—I hope to take my new years day Dinner with you en Famille, tell Hargreaves I will bring his Blackstones with me, & shall have no objection to see my Daniel's rural Sports,[1] if they have not escaped his recollection.—I certainly wish the expiration of my minority, as much as you do, though for a reason more nearly affecting my magisterial person at this moment, namely, the want of twenty pounds, for no spendthrift peer, or unlucky Poet, was ever less indebted to *Cash* than George Gordon, is at present, or is more likely to continue in the same predicament.—My present quarter due on the 25th. was drawn long ago, & I must be obliged to you for the Loan of twenty on my next, to be deducted when the whole becomes tangible, that is, probably some months after it is expended.—Reserve Murray's quarter of course, and I shall have just £100 to receive at Easter, but if the *risk* of my demand is too great, inform me, that I may if possible convert my Title into cash, though I am afraid twenty pounds will be too much to ask as Times go, if I were an Earl now,—but a Barony must fetch ten, perhaps fifteen, and that is something when we have not as many pence. Your answer will oblige

yours very truly
BYRON

P.S.—Remember me to Mrs. H. in particular, and the Family in general.—

[TO JOHN RIDGE]   *Trin. Coll. Cambridge, Decr. 28th. 1807*

Mr. Ridge—Insert the enclosed after "Childish Recollections,"[1] and send the proof.—

&c &c
BYRON

[TO JOHN HANSON]   *Dorant's.—January 6th. 1807 [sic] [1808]*

Dear Sir,—If you could advance the remainder of my quarter due on the 25th March, you would oblige me much.—I have already re-

[1] William Barker Daniel's *Rural Sports* was a periodical published in London from 1801 to 1813.
[1] Byron finally deleted "Childish Recollections" and it did not appear in *Poems Original and Translated*.

ceived twenty, and five to be deducted for Murray, your answer will render a favour on

yours very truly
BYRON

P.S.—[nothing more in manuscript]

[TO JOHN HANSON]   *Dorant's, January 8th. 1807 [sic] [1808]*

Dear Sir,—I am sorry a prior engagement will prevent me the pleasure of dining with you to day.—I will drop in some day next week, in the Evening.— —If you could dispatch the £. S. D. this morning, I should be obliged to you, & I will send or give a Receipt for the whole, when you please.

yours very truly
BYRON

P.S.—My Compts. to Mrs. H. and the whole Corps.—

[TO JOHN RIDGE]   *Dorant's Hotel Albemarle Street.*
January 9th. 1808

Mr. Ridge,—In "Childish Recollections" omit the whole Character of "*Euryalus*,"[1] and insert instead the Lines to "Florio"[2] as a part of the poem, & send me a proof in course,

&c &c
BYRON

P.S.—The first Line of the passage to be omitted begins
    "Shall fair Euryalus, &c. —and ends at
    "toil for more."—omit the *whole*.

[TO JOHN RIDGE]   *Dorant's Hotel Albemarle Street.*
January 12th. 1807 [sic] [1808]

Mr. Ridge,—I understand from some of my friends, that several of the papers are in the habit of publishing extracts from my volume,

[1] Euryalus was intended to represent George John, fifth Earl Delawarr. A quarrel or a fancied slight caused the sudden withdrawal of the passage.
[2] To which of his school friends the lines to "Florio" were intended to apply is not known, and since the poem was finally suppressed, those lines were not published.

particularly the Morning Herald,[1] I cannot say for my own part I have observed this, but I am assured it is so.—The thing is of no consequence to me, except that I dislike it, but it is to you and as publisher you should put a stop to it, the Morning Herald is the paper, of course you cannot address any other, as I am sure I have seen nothing of the Kind in mine.—You will act upon this as you think proper, and proceed with the 2d Edition as you please, I am in no hurry, and I still think *you* were *premature* in undertaking it.

&c. &c.
BYRON

P.S.—Present a Copy of the Antijacobin Review[2] to Mrs. *Byron*——

[TO JOHN HANSON]   *Dorant's Hotel, Albemarle Street,*
January 12th. 1807 [sic] [1808]

My dear Sir,—I will be much obliged to you to pay Mr. Mitchell[1] his Bill of forty four pounds five shillings, as I really cannot do it at present, without expending all my cash, this will make up my next quarter excepting five & a few shillings.—I remain

yours & c
BYRON

[TO HENRY DRURY[1]]   *Dorant's Hotel, January 13th. 1807 [sic] [1808]*

My dear Sir,—Though the Stupidity of my Servants, or the Porter of the House, in not showing you upstairs, (where I should have joined you directly) prevented me the pleasure of seeing you yesterday, I hoped to meet you at some public place in the Evening.—However my Stars decreed otherwise, as they generally do when I have any favour to request of them.—I think you would have been surprised at

---

[1] The *Morning Herald* was a Whig newspaper which had published the *Rolliad*, a brilliant political satire, in 1784.

[2] *The Antijacobin Review and Magazine* for December, 1807, in a brief review of *Hours of Idleness*, said that the poems "exhibit strong proofs of genius, accompanied by a lively but chastened imagination, a classical taste, and a benevolent heart". (Vol. XXVII, pp. 407–8.)

[1] Mitchell was a saddler.

[1] Henry Joseph Drury was the eldest son of Dr. Joseph Drury, Headmaster of Harrow until Byron's last term. As an assistant master at Harrow, Henry Drury found the young Byron obstreperous and they quarrelled, but after Byron left the school they became good friends. Drury married Ann Caroline Tayler, whose sister later married Byron's friend Francis Hodgson.

my figure, for since our last meeting I am reduced four stone in weight, I then weighed 14 Stone 7LB.—and now only *ten stone* and a *half*;—I have disposed of my *superfluities* by means of hard exercise, abstinence, and an occasional complaint which attacks me on every excursion to Town. Should your Harrow engagements allow you to visit Town between this and February, I shall be most happy to see you in Albemarle Street, if I am not so fortunate, I shall endeavour to join you for an afternoon at H[arrow] though I fear your cellar will by no means contribute to my Cure.—As for my worthy preceptor Dr. B[utler]² our encounter would by no means prevent the *mutual endearments* he and I were wont to lavish on each other, we have only spoken once, since my departure from H— in 1805 and then he politely told Tattersall,³ I was not a proper associate for his pupils, this was long before my strictures in verse, but in plain *prose* had I been some years older, I should have held my tongue on his perfections.—But being laid on my back when that Schoolboy thing was written, or rather dictated, expecting to rise no more, my Physician having taken his 16th fee, and I his prescription, I could not quit this earth without leaving a memento of my constant attachment to Butler, in gratitude for his manifold good offices.—I meant to have been down in July, but thinking my appearance immediately after the publication would be construed into an Insult, I directed my steps elsewhere,—besides I heard that some of the Boys had got hold of my Libellus, contrary to my wishes certainly, for though requested by two or three, I never transmitted a single copy till October, when I gave one to a Boy since gone, after repeated importunities.—You will I trust pardon this Egotism,—as you had touched on the subject, I thought some explanation necessary, defence I shall not attempt "Hic murus aheneus esto, Nil conscire sibi"—and *so on*, (as Lord Baltimore said on his trial for a Rape)⁴ I have been so long at Trinity as to forget the conclusion of the Line, but though I cannot finish my quotation, I will my Letter, and entreat you to believe me

gratefully and affectionately yours

BYRON

² Byron had satirized Dr. George Butler, successor to Dr. Joseph Drury as Headmaster of Harrow, as "Pomposus" in his "Childish Recollections", but Henry Drury helped to effect a reconciliation, which was one reason for Byron's suppressing "Childish Recollections" in the second edition of his poems then in preparation.

³ John Cecil Tattersall was the "Davus" of "Childish Recollections".

⁴ After he was acquitted of a charge of rape, Francis Calvert, seventh Lord Baltimore (1731–1771), was reported to have quoted the "Hic murus" from Horace: "Be this your wall of brass, to have no guilty secrets, no wrong-doing that makes you turn pale". (Horace, *Epistolae*, I, i, 60.)

P.S.—I will not levy a tax on your Time, by requiring an answer, lest you say, as Butler said to Tattersall (when I had written his reverence an impudent epistle on the expression before mentioned) viz, "that I wanted to draw him into a correspondence."—

[TO ROBERT CHARLES DALLAS]   *Dorant's Hotel. Albemarle St.*
                                   January 20th. 1808

Sir,—Your Letter was not received till this morning. I presume it was addressed to me in Nott's, where I have not resided since last June, and as the Date is on the 6th. you will excuse the Delay of my answer for the above reason.— — If the little volume[1] you mention has given pleasure in the perusal to the Author of Perceval and Aubrey,[2] I am sufficiently repaid by his praise, though our periodical Censors have been uncommonly lenient, I confess a tribute from a man of acknowledged Genius is still more flattering.—But I am afraid I should forfeit all claim to Candour, if I did not decline such praise as I do not deserve, and this is, I am sorry to say, the case in the present Instance. —The Compositions speak for themselves, and must stand or fall by their own worth or Demerit, *thus far*, I feel highly gratified by your favourable opinion.—But, my pretensions to virtue are unluckily so few, that though I should be happy to merit, I cannot accept your applause in that respect.—One passage in your Letter struck me forcibly; you mention the two Lords Lyttleton[3] in the manner they respectively deserve, and will be surprised to hear the person who is now addressing you, has been frequently compared to the *Latter*.—I know I am injuring myself in your esteem by this avowal, but the circumstance was so remarkable from your observation, that I cannot help relating the fact.—The events of my short life have been of so singular a nature, that though the pride, commonly called honour, has, and I trust ever will prevent me from disgracing my name by a mean or cowardly action, I have been already held up as the votary of Licentiousness, and the Disciple of Infidelity.—How far Justice may have dictated this accusation, I cannot pretend to say, but like the *Gentleman*,[4] to whom my

[1] *Hours of Idleness.*
[2] *Percival, or Nature Vindicated* (1801) and *Aubrey* (1804) are two of Dallas's novels.
[3] In Dallas's letter of January 6, 1808, he had in flattering Byron compared him to George, first Baron Lyttelton (1708–1772), friend of Pope and patron of literature. Byron saw himself as more nearly resembling his son, the profligate Thomas, second Baron Lyttelton (1744–1779), commonly called the wicked Lord Lyttelton.
[4] See *King Lear*, III, iv, 140: "The prince of darkness is a gentleman".

religious friends in the warmth of their Charity have already [de-voted?] me, I am made worse, than I really am.— — —However to quit myself (the worst theme I could pitch upon) and return to my poems, I cannot sufficiently express my thanks, and hope I shall some day have an opportunity of rendering them in person.—A second Edition is now in the press, with some additions and considerable omissions, you will allow me to present you with a Copy.—Our Critical,[5] Monthly,[6] and Antijacobin Reviewers[7] have been very indulgent, but the Eclectic[8] have pronounced a furious Philippic, not against the *Book*, but the *Author*, where you will find all I have mentioned, asserted by a Reverend Divine, who wrote the Critique.—Your name and connection with our family have been long known to me, and I hope your person will be not less so, you will find me an excellent compound of a "Brainless" and a "Stanhope."[9]—I am afraid you will hardly be able to read this, for my hand is almost as bad, as my Character, but you will find me as legibly as possible

your obliged and obedt. Servt.
BYRON

[TO ROBERT CHARLES DALLAS]   *Dorant's. Albemarle St.*
January 21st. 1808

Sir,—Whenever Leisure and Inclination permit me the pleasure of a visit, I shall feel truly gratified in a personal acquaintance with one, whose mind has been long known to me in his Writings.—You are so far correct in your conjecture, that I am a member of the University of Cambridge, where I shall take my degree of A. M. this term, but were Reasoning, Eloquence or Virtue the objects of my search, Granta is not their metropolis, nor is the place of her Situation an "El Dorado" far less an Utopia, the Intellects of her children are as stagnant as her Cam, and their pursuits limited to the Church,—not of Christ, but of the nearest Benefice.—As to my reading, I believe I may aver without

[5] The *Critical Review* of September, 1807, found in *Hours of Idleness* "ample evidence of a correct taste, a warm imagination, and a feeling heart". The reviewer quoted "On Leaving Newstead Abbey" with approval, but concluded that "it is in tenderness and pathos that his real excellence, as a poet, will consist", and his highest praise went to "Childish Recollections".

[6] See Dec. 22, 1807, to Crosby, note 1.

[7] See Jan. 12 [1808], to Ridge, note 2.

[8] The *Eclectic Review* of November, 1807, pronounced Byron's poems "a collection of juvenile pieces, some of very moderate merit, and others of very questionable morality", and then proceeded to castigate the young lord for his "pagan" attitudes.

[9] Characters in Dallas's novel *Perceval*.

hyperbole, it has been tolerably extensive in the historical department, so that few nations exist or have existed with whose records I am not in some degree acquainted from Herodotus down to Gibbon.—Of the Classics I know about as much as most Schoolboys after a Discipline of thirteen years, of the *Law* of the *Land* as much as enables me to keep "within the Statute" (to use the Poacher's vocabulary) I did study "the Spirit of Laws"[1] and the Law of Nations, but when I saw the Latter violated every month, I gave up my attempts at so useless an accomplishment.—Of Geography—I have seen more land on maps than I should wish to traverse on foot, of Mathematics enough to give me the headache without clearing the part affected, of Philosophy Astronomy and Metaphysicks, more than I can comprehend, and of Common Sense, so little, that I mean to leave a Byronian prize at each of our "Alma Matres" for the first Discovery, though I rather fear that of the Longitude will precede it.—I once thought myself a Philosopher and talked nonsense with great Decorum, I defied pain and preached up equanimity, for some time this did very well, for no one was in *pain* for me but my Friends, and none lost their patience but my hearers, at last a fall from my horse convinced me, bodily suffering was an Evil, and the worst of an argument overset my maxims and my temper at the same moment, so I quitted Zeno for Aristippus, and conceive that Pleasure constitutes the "*το Καλον.*"—In Morality I prefer Confucius to the ten Commandments, and Socrates to St. Paul (though the two latter agree in their opinion of marriage) in Religion, I favour the Catholic Emancipation but do not acknowledge the Pope, and I have refused to take the Sacrament because I do not think eating Bread or drinking wine from the hand of an earthly vicar, will make me an Inheritor of Heaven.—I hold virtue in general, or the virtues severally, to be only in the Disposition, each *a feeling* not a principle.—I believe Truth the prime attribute of the Deity, and Death an eternal Sleep, at least of the Body.—You have here a brief compendium of the Sentiments of the *wicked* George Ld. B.—and till I get a new suit you will perceive I am badly cloathed. I remain

yours very truly
BYRON

[TO JOHN HANSON (*a*)]   *Dorant's, January 25th. 1808*

Dear Sir,—Some time ago I gave Mitchell the Sadler a Letter for you, requesting his Bill might be paid from the Balance of the Quarter

[1] In the list that he made of his early reading Byron included Montesquieu (Moore, I, 97).

you obliged me by advancing, if he has received this, you will further oblige me by paying what remains, I believe somewhere about five pounds if so much.—You will confer a favour upon me by the Loan of twenty, I will endeavour to repay it next week, as I have immediate occasion for that Sum, and I should not require it of you, could I obtain it elsewhere.—I am now in my one and twentieth year, and cannot command as many pounds, to Cambridge I cannot go without paying my Bills, and at present I could as soon compass the National Debt, in London I must not remain, nor shall I, when I can procure a trifle to take me out of it, home I have none, and if there was a possibility of getting out of the Country, I would gladly avail myself of it, but even that is denied me, my Debts amount to three thousand three hundred to Jews, eight hundred to Mrs. B[yron] of Nottingham,[1] to Coachmaker, and other Tradesmen, a thousand more, and these must be much increased before they can be lessened.—Such is the prospect before me, which is by no means brightened by ill health, I would have called on you, but I have neither Spirits to enliven myself or others, or Inclination to bring a gloomy face to spoil a groupe of happy ones.—I remain

your obliged and obedt. &c.

BYRON

P.S.—Your answer to the former part will oblige, as I shall be reduced to a most unpleasant Dilemma if it does not arrive.— —

[TO JOHN HANSON (*b*)]   *Dorant's, January 25th. 1808*

Sir,—The picture I have drawn of my Finances is unfortunately a true one, and I find the colours may be heightened but not improved by time.—I have inclosed the receipt, and return my thanks for the Loan, which shall be repaid the first opportunity, in the concluding part of my last I gave you my reasons for not troubling you with my society at present, but when I can either communicate or receive pleasure, I shall not be long absent.

yours &c.

BYRON

P.S.—I have received a Letter from Whitehead,[1] of course you know the contents, and must act as you think proper.—

[1] Mrs. George Byron, widow of the Admiral's younger brother, and Byron's great aunt. To extricate Byron from his debts in 1807 and keep him from going to the usurers, his mother had borrowed £1,000 on her security, £200 from Wylde & Co., bankers of Southwell, and the remainder from Mrs. Byron and the Misses Parkyns.

[1] Head gamekeeper at Newstead.

My dear Long,—I have sent to Mr. Twiddie[1] demanding whether he is the author of the article in question or not, and if he refuses a satisfactory answer, my second Davies has a challenge to Deliver.— — —We shall probably meet near Harrow, as if I fall, I should like "to die where I was [roused?]" and if Mr. Twiddie takes his departure, I shall breakfast with Harry Drury, instead of Pluto.—I am prepared for either event, you and the few of my best beloved friends will sometimes re-call my image, in one case, and in the other, I shall rid the world of a malignant Scoundrel.—I presume I shall share the fate of others in a future state, as God did not make his creatures to perish, or to suffer pain.—If I come off victorious, I shall surrender myself immediately, nor feel any degree of that remorse, which might shake my breast at the Destruction of a being entitled to the respect, or Love of his fellow creatures. However I am now in suspense, perhaps he is not the Libellist, but from the beginning I make up my mind to these events, I shall not send this Letter till Davies returns, and you shall know all.—

four o Clock, Wednesday, afternoon.

half past five.—

Davies is returned, Mr. Twiddie was not at home, but D. is to call tomorrow early in the morning & bring me an answer, you shall hear of the affair as soon as it is settled, to my *Satisfaction*. believe me here and [else?]where, dear Long,

ever yours, most truly and affectionately

BYRON

[Fragment of letter]

. . . Scrope Davies & I are members of the new Cocoa tree club[2] & next week the dice will rattle.—My worldly affairs are not over flourishing, but that is a common case. . . . [on reverse] note addressed to another made me sick, but I was not angry with her or him. Yet if anyone had foretold such a circumstance, I should have been [cut in paper]—I must console myself, . . .

[1] Mr. Twiddie may well have been the person Byron believed to be the author of the pert review that appeared in January in the *Monthly Mirror*, which ended with a reference to "lords' bottoms". See Jan. 25, 1809, to Dallas, note 3.

[1] This was the time that Byron was carousing and gambling with Scrope Davies in London as other letters to Hobhouse indicate.

[2] The Cocoa Tree Club was founded in the mid eighteenth century, but it may have acquired new quarters about this time.

[TO JOHN HANSON]   *Dorant's Hotel, Feb. 1808*

Dear Sir,—I shall be particularly obliged by the loan of one hundred *promised* last night, and for this and other sums lent by you, I shall sign a receipt with great pleasure—I hope this will not find your determination altered by a night's repose, . . .

                                                            [Yours truly,
                                                            BYRON]

[TO JAMES DE BATHE[1]]   *Dorant's Hotel, February 2d. 1808*

My dear De Bathe,—Last night I saw your Father and Brother, the former I have not the pleasure of knowing, but the Latter informed me *you* came to town on *Saturday* and returned *yesterday*.—I have received a pressing Invitation from Henry Drury to pay him a visit, in his Letter he mentions a very old *friend* of yours, who told him he would join my party if I could inform him, on what day I meant to go over.— This friend you will readily conclude to be a Lord *B*.[2] but *not* the one who now addresses you, shall I bring him to you? and insure a welcome for myself which perhaps might not otherwise be the case.—This will not be for a fortnight to come, I am waiting for Long, who is now at Chatham, when he arrives we shall probably drive down and dine with Drury.—I confess Harrow has lost most of its charms for me, I do not know if Delawarr is still there, but with the exception of yourself and the Earl, I shall find myself among strangers, Long has a Brother at Butler's, and all his predilections remain in full force, mine are weakened if not destroyed, and though I can safely say I never knew a friend out of Harrow, I question whether I have one left in it.—You leave Harrow in July[;] may I ask what is your future Destination?—In January *1809* I shall be twenty one, and in the Spring of the same year proceed abroad, not on the usual tour, but a route of a more extensive description, what say you? are you disposed for a view of the Pelo-pennesus? [and a?] voyage through the Archipelago?[3] I am merely in jest with this [proposal to?] you, but very serious with regard [to my?] own Intention, which is fixed on the [Eastern?] *pilgrimage*, unless some political view, [or] accident induce me to postpone it.—Adieu! if you

---

[1] See Feb. 23, 1807, to Long, note 6.
[2] Probably Lord Bective. See Feb. 5, 1808, to E. N. Long, note 5.
[3] This seems to be Byron's first statement of his intention to make a voyage to the Eastern Mediterranean.

have leisure, I shall be happy to hear from you, as I would have been to have *seen* you. believe me

yours very truly
BYRON

[TO JOHN RIDGE]   *Dorant's Hotel, February 3d. 1808*

Mr. Ridge,—In the first page of "Childish Recollections" which you must reprint, place "Childish Recollections, written during Illness" this is indispensable, as I sent you a Latin motto, which I hope is properly printed, which would be *nonsense*, without the latter words ("written during Illness").—Pray attend to the alterations and Corrections, have you done as I directed about the extracts for the advertisements?

&c &c
BYRON

[TO EDWARD NOEL LONG]   *Dorant's February 5th. 1808*

Dear Long,—I met Harry Drury on Thursday, and am to dine with him on Wednesday next, he wishes much to see you, and if my entreaties can add to your inclination they shall not be wanting.—We are to sleep there, and return to town on Thursday, where by the bye a Masquerade takes place in the evening at the Pantheon,[1] Ld. Altamont,[2] & myself, *Grimaldi*,[3] and a large party are going, do for *my* sake, and *your own* sake, and the *sake* of the *Commonwealth* procure leave of Absence, or *take* it.—At all events send me an immediate answer as I keep a seat in my "*Διφρο*"[4] for your *especial* accommodation.—Harry Drury has bored me to ask *Bective*[5] also, which I am afraid I must do, however *we* shall be very *safe*, Davies accompanies us too, but you and I will take our old Seat on the Barouche Rex.—

yours ever
BYRON

[1] The Pantheon, a large building having a dome like the Pantheon of Rome, was opened in London in 1772 as a place of evening entertainment for the nobility and gentry. It was principally used in Byron's time for exhibitions and masquerades. It had entrances on Oxford Street and Poland Street.

[2] Altamont succeeded his father in 1809 as the second Marquis of Sligo.

[3] Joseph Grimaldi (1779–1837), actor and pantomimist.

[4] Travelling chariot.

[5] Lord Bective (Irish Peerage) was listed by E. N. Long as in the Fourth Form at Harrow, when he entered shortly before Byron in 1801. (Long papers, Berg Collection, New York Public Library.)

P.S.—Of course you will go to the Masquerade, I will have a dress or a Domino ready for you.—

Dorant's.—February 7th. 1808

Dear Sir,—As I hope so soon to have the pleasure of seeing you at Harrow, I ought perhaps to apologize for troubling you before the day of our meeting, but something you mentioned at our late Interview has induced me "to *break* in upon your *repose*" and all things considered you will excuse this Letter.—If I do not mistake, you hinted to me, that you had seen the Revd. Dr. Butler, who was graciously disposed to pass an act of grace in my unworthy favour, and to remit the many and repeated denunciations of his wrath against me on former occasions, in short, to consign the past to oblivion, and laugh at the absurdities on both sides of the Question.—So far, so good, I confess to you fairly, reflection will probably cause me to expunge any opinion I may have expressed of Butler in my *funereal* couplets, and as his character had it not been for my interference would have rested among "things unattempted yet in Prose or Rhyme," I am to blame for two reasons, in the first place for permitting Resentment to appear (contrary to the precepts of Philosophy and *Religion*) and in the second place for adhering to the *Truth* without trusting to my own *Imagination* (contrary to the precepts of *poetry*, and the privileges of Parnassus)——I know that during the time I was under his dominion, I gave him cause for offence, I acted like a turbulent Schoolboy as *you* know me always to have been, what then? a man of liberal mind would have passed over the pranks of a Tyro, at least after his departure, but how did Butler proceed? why thus—he not only libelled me in every company he entered, but encouraged a report that I had been *expelled*, this most diabolical falsehood I know from undoubted authority, was if not *sanctioned*. certainly not contradicted by him, he treated me with a degree of *personal* contempt, which nothing but the respect I bear to his Situation would have prevented me from *personally* meeting, and on my afterwards remonstrating with him by Letter, for I dare not trust my temper in conversation with him, he returned not the slightest answer, though I declare upon my honour, the two Letters I addressed to him were couched in terms far more respectful than his conduct deserved, and I do not hesitate to say, any man of a disposition not totally dead to feeling and generosity would have made some atonement for the manner of my reception.—After this detail you will form your own Judgment how far Butler and I can ever meet on any terms, but though I allow in the fullest extent the rashness of my present, and boyishness of my former conduct, I contend that the Behaviour of the Gentleman above mentioned has *before*, but more especially *since* my departure from H[arrow] been systematically mean, supercilious, and inveterate.—

> Believe me yours very faithfully
> BYRON

[TO WILLIAM HARNESS¹] *Dorant's Hotel, Albemarle-street, Feb. 11th, 1808*

My dear Harness,—As I had no opportunity of returning my verbal thanks, I trust you will accept my written acknowledgments for the compliment you were pleased to pay some production of my unlucky muse last November—I am induced to do this not less from the pleasure I feel in the praise of an old schoolfellow, than from justice to you, for I heard the story with some slight variations. Indeed, when we met this morning, Wingfield² had not undeceived me, but he will tell you that I displayed no resentment in mentioning what I had heard, though I was not sorry to discover the truth. Perhaps you hardly recollect some years ago a short, though, for the time, a warm friendship between us? Why it was not of longer duration, I know not. I have still a gift of yours in my possession, that must always prevent me from forgetting it. I also remember being favoured with the perusal of many of your compositions and several other circumstances very pleasant in their day, which I will not force upon your memory, but entreat you to believe me, with much regret at their short continuance, and a hope they are not irrevocable, yours very sincerely, &c.

> BYRON

[TO JOHN RIDGE] *Dorant's Hotel, February 11th. 1808*

Mr. Ridge.—Something has occurred which will make considerable alteration in my new volume.—You must *go back* and *cut out* the whole

¹ William Harness (1790–1869) was the son of J. Harness, M.D., Commissioner of the Transport Board. He came to Harrow in 1802, and elicited Byron's friendship by his lameness. Byron protected him from bullies and encouraged a sentimental attachment after he left Harrow. Harness took a B.A. at Christ Church, Cambridge, and was ordained in 1812. He held various clerical posts, wrote a life of Shakespeare, was a *Quarterly* reviewer, and a lifelong friend of Mary Russell Mitford.

² See Nov. 4, 1806, to the Earl of Clare.

poem of *"Childish Recollections"*.[1] of course you will be surprised at this, and perhaps displeased, but it must be *done*. I cannot help it's detaining you a *month* longer, but there will be enough in the volume without it, and as I am now reconciled to Dr. Butler I cannot allow any Satire to appear, against him, nor can I alter that part relating to him without spoiling the whole.—You will therefore omit the whole poem.—Send me an *immediate* answer to this Letter but *obey* the directions.—It is better my Reputation should suffer as a poet by the omission, than as a man of honour by the Insertion.—

&c &c
BYRON

[TO JOHN RIDGE]   *Dorant's. A. Street,—February 16th. 1808*

Mr. Ridge,—I am sorry it should happen so unluckily for you, but the *Chasm* cannot be filled up by any thing new in my possession, I have sent you one poem in seven Stanza's or 56 Lines,[1]—cut from my manuscript book, but that will do little, you may place it *last* or *where* you please, but I must see a *proof* of it, as well as every *new* piece in the volume.—You must use your own *discretion* about reprinting, & taking poems from the latter part to fill up the vacancy. I care not how they are arranged except for *your* convenience, by the bye, I shall have no *preface* or *advertisement* nothing but the Dedication.—[2]

&c &c
BYRON

P.S.—The Engravings I do not like at all, and shall only *use* one, *the view* of Harrow.

[TO WILLIAM HARNESS]   *Dorant's Hotel Albemarle Street*
February 16th. 1808

My dear Harness,—Again I trouble you, but I would not do so, did I not hope your Sentiments nearly coincided with mine, on the subject, I am about to mention.—We both seem perfectly to recollect with a

[1] The thing that had occurred which caused Byron to suppress "Childish Recollections" was a final reconciliation with Dr. Butler, whom he had lampooned as "Pomposus" in the poem.
[1] The poem of 56 lines was one titled "Stanzas" beginning "I would I were a careless child".
[2] *Poems Original and Translated* was dedicated "To the Honourable Frederick, Earl of Carlisle . . . by His Obliged Ward, and Affectionate Kinsman".

mixture of pleasure, and regret, the hours we once passed together, and I assure you most sincerely they are numbered among the happiest of my brief chronicle of enjoyment.—I am now *getting into years*, that is to say, I was *twenty* a month ago, and another year will send me into the World to run my career of Folly with the Rest.—I was *then* just fourteen, you were almost the first of my Harrow friends, certainly the *first* in my esteem,[1] if not in Date, but an absence from Harrow for some time, shortly after, and new Connections on your side, with the difference in our conduct (an advantage decidedly in your favour) from that turbulent and riotous disposition of mine, which impelled me into every species of mischief;—all these circumstances combined to destroy an Intimacy, which Affection urged me to continue, and Memory compels me to regret.—But there is not a circumstance attending that period, hardly a sentence we exchanged, which is not impressed on my mind at this moment, I need not say more, this assurance only must convince you, had I considered them as trivial, they would have been less indelible.—How well I recollect the perusal of your *"first flights,"* there is another circumstance you do not know, the *first Lines* I ever attempted at Harrow were addressed to *you*, you were to have seen them, but Sinclair[2] had the copy in his possession when we went home, and on our return *we* were *strangers*, they were destroyed, and certainly no great loss, but you will perceive from this circumstance my opinions at an age, when we cannot be Hypocrites.— I have dwelt longer on this theme, than I intended, and I shall now conclude with what I ought to have begun;—we were once friends, nay, we have always been so, for our Separation was the effect of Chance, not of Disposition, I do not know how far our Destinations in life may throw us together, but if opportunity and Inclination allow you to waste a thought on such a hairbrained being as myself, you will find me at least sincere, & not so bigotted to my faults, as to involve others in the Consequence.—Will you sometimes write to me? I do not ask it often, and when we meet, let us be, what we *should* be, and what we *were*. Believe me, my dear William—

yours most truly
BYRON

[1] Several of Byron's younger favourites at Harrow were "first in my esteem" at varying times. Almost all of these friendships were marred by sensitivities and suspected slights.

[2] George Sinclair, son of Sir John Sinclair, was, Byron wrote in his "Detached Thoughts" (No. 89), the "prodigy of our school days", who did some of Byron's exercises, "he was pacific, and I savage; so I fought for him, or thrashed others for him".

My dear Becher,—Just rising from my Bed, having been up till six at a Masquerade, I find your Letter, and in the midst of this dissipated Chaos it is no small pleasure to discover I have some *distant* friends in their Senses, though mine are rather out of repair.—Indeed, I am worse than ever, to give you some idea of my late life, I have this moment received a prescription from Pearson, not for any *complaint* but from *debility*, and literally *too much Love*.—You know my devotion to woman, but indeed Southwell was much mistaken in conceiving my adorations were paid to any Shrine there, no, my Paphian Goddesses are elsewhere, and I have sacrificed at their altar rather too liberally.— In fact, my blue eyed Caroline,[1] who is only sixteen, has been lately so *charming*, that though we are both in perfect health, we are at present commanded to *repose*, being nearly worn out.—So much for Venus, now for Apollo,—I am happy you still retain your predilection, and that the public allow me some share of praise, I am of so much importance, that a most violent attack is preparing for me in the next number of the Edinburgh Review,[2] this I have from the authority of a friend who has seen the proof and manuscript of the Critique, you know the System of the Edinburgh Gentlemen is universal attack, they praise none, and neither the public or the author expects praise from them, it is however something to be noticed, as they profess to pass judgment only on works requiring the public attention.—You will see this when it comes out, it is I understand of the most unmerciful description, but I am aware of it, and I hope *you* will not be hurt by its severity.—Tell *Mrs. Byron* not to be out of humour with them, and to prepare her mind for the greatest hostility on their part, it will do no injury however, and I trust her mind will not be ruffled.—They defeat their object by indiscriminate abuse, and they never praise except the partizans of Ld. Holland & Co.[3]——It is nothing to be abused, when

---

[1] The blue-eyed Caroline has not been identified, but it is probable that some verses he wrote three days before this letter were addressed to her in a tone that shows that Byron's sentiments are not always to be judged by the seeming callousness of his letters. See "Song", *Poetry*, I, 262–63.

[2] The January number of the *Edinburgh Review*, which appeared in late February, contained the cutting and sarcastic review of *Hours of Idleness* by Henry Brougham.

[3] Byron assumed that the *Edinburgh Review* praised only Whigs such as Lord Holland, leader of the Moderate Whigs in the House of Lords. And in fact many of its reviews were politically inspired, just as were those of the Tory *Quarterly Review*. But as a member of the Cambridge Whig Club, Byron felt it unjust that he should be attacked by a Whig periodical. He brought it on himself, however, by the "lordly" tone of his preface, made worse by juvenile and mawkish humility.

Southey, Moore, Lauderdale, Strangford, and Payne Knight share the same fate.—I am sorry, but C— Recollections must be suppressed during this edition, I have altered at your Suggestion the *obnoxious allusions* in the 6th Stanza of my last ode.—And now, Becher I must return my best acknowledgments for the interest you have taken in me and my poetical Bantlings, and I shall ever be proud to show how much I esteem the *advice* and the *Adviser*.—Believe me

most truly yours
BYRON

P.S.—Write soon.

[TO JOHN CAM HOBHOUSE]   *Dorant's, February 27th. 1808*

Dear Hobhouse,—I write to you to explain a foolish circumstance, which has arisen from some words uttered by me before Pearce and Brown,[1] when I was devoured with Chagrin, and almost insane with the fumes of, not "last night's Punch" but that evening's wine.—[In] consequence of a misconception of something on my part, I mentioned an intention of withdrawing my name from the Whig Club,[2] this I hear has been broached, and perhaps in a moment of Intoxication and passion such might be my idea, but *soberly* I have no such design, particularly as I could not abandon my principles, even if I renounced the society with whom I have the honour to be united in sentiments which I never will disavow.—This I beg you will explain to the members as publicly as possible, but should this not be sufficient, and they think proper to erase my name, be it so, I only request that in this case they will recollect, I shall become a *Tory* of *their own making*. I shall expect your answer on this point with some impatience, now a few words on the subject of my own conduct.—I am buried in an abyss of Sensuality, I have renounced *hazard* however, but I am given to Harlots, and live in a state of Concubinage, I am at this moment under a course of restoration by Pearson's prescription, for a debility occasioned by too frequent Connection.—Pearson sayeth, I have done sufficient with[in?] this last ten days, to undermine my Constitution, I hope however all will soon be well.—As an author, I am

[1] Henry Pearce and Dominick Browne were two of the original members of the Cambridge Whig Club. (*LJ*, IV, 500.)

[2] Byron in his cups no doubt gave voice to his indignation at the Whigs in general because he had been attacked in the Whig *Edinburgh Review*, in which he had just seen the review of his poems.

cut to atoms by the E[dinburgh] Review,[3] it is just out, and has completely demolished my little fabric of fame, this is rather scurvy treatment from a Whig Review, but politics and poetry are different things, & I am no adept in either, I therefore submit in Silence.— Scrope Davies is meandering about London feeding upon Leg of Beef Soup, and frequenting the British Forum, he has given up hazard, as also a considerable sum at the same time.—Altamont is a good deal with me, last night at the Opera Masquerade, we supped with seven whores, a *Bawd* and a *Ballet-master*, in Madame Catalani's[4] apartment behind the Scenes, (of course Catalani was *not* there) I have some thoughts of purchasing D'egville's[5] pupils, they would fill a glorious Harem.—I do not write often, but I like to receive letters, when therefore you are disposed to philosophize, no one standeth more in need of precepts of all sorts than

> yours very truly
> BYRON

[TO JOHN CAM HOBHOUSE]   *Dorant's. February 29th. 1808*

Dear Hobhouse,—Upon my *honour* I do not recollect to have spoken of you and any friend of yours in the manner you state, and to the Club itself I am certain I never applied the epithets mentioned, or any terms of disrespect whatever.—As it is however possible I may have spoken of the very extraordinary state of Intoxication in which I have seen you and another, not conceiving it to be a secret as never having been looked upon to make a part of the *mysteries* of the meeting, I cannot altogether deny the charge, though I do deny and disclaim all malice in the statement.—Besides I do not exactly see, how "your sacrifice to the God of Wine" as you classically term it, can possibly involve the interests or reputation of the Club, or by what sophistry my mention of such a circumstance can be tortured into an "*attack* on the society

[3] The criticism that cut Byron to the quick was the critic's ridicule of the vanities in his preface which he thought he had concealed. The reviewer concludes: "We are well off to have got so much from a man of this lord's station, who does not live in a garret, but 'has the sway' of Newstead Abbey."

[4] Madame Angelica Catalani, the popular Italian Opera singer, came to London in 1806, and was then singing at Covent Garden.

[5] James d'Egville (the name he assumed as a ballet and dancing master—his family name was Harvey) had studied dancing with Gaetano Vestris, dancing master at the court of Frederick the Great, and with Gardel, the court teacher of Marie Antoinette. Byron became a familiar of the theatrical and demi-monde people of his circle.

as a Body."—I have never been in the habit of conversing much on the topic, I have never been entrusted with any particular confidence, consequently I can have betrayed no secret, but so far from treating the Club[1] with disrespect, or joining any *"attack"* upon it as a *"Body,"* I have more than once nearly endangered my own safety in it's defence. —As to any thing which passed between yourself and me, I have been cautious in avoiding the subject with all except Davies, I do not know who related it to Blackburne, I have never seen the latter since the event.—To conclude, I have still, and (though I do think there are circumstances which would justify me in a change of conduct) I ever have had a most sincere regard for the society of which I am a member, and if in a moment of Chagrin under the pressure of a *thousand* vexations I intimated an intention of withdrawing, it has constituted the *thousand* and *first* sensation of disquiet, that I have done so.—It is not very probable that I shall again appear at Cambridge till my degree is granted, and *that* is very problematical; my presence will never annoy you at your meetings, but if the continuance of my name upon your record displease the members, let them erase it, I do not wish to be the cause of discord, or spoil your conviviality "with most admired disorder."—Perhaps this is not enough, well! I am most willing to grant any species of satisfaction to any, or all the society, and he who shall avenge them successfully will do me a favour, for I am at present as miserable in mind and Body, as Literary abuse, pecuniary embarrassment, and total enervation can make me.—I have tried every kind of pleasure, and it is "Vanity."—

yours truly
BYRON

[TO JOHN CAM HOBHOUSE]   *Dorant's, March 14th. 1808*

My dear Hobhouse,—The Game is almost up, for these last five days I have been confined to my room, Laudanum is my sole support, and even Pearson wears a woeful visage as he prescribes, however I am now *better* and I trust my hour is not yet arrived.—I began to apprehend a complete Bankruptcy of Constitution, and on disclosing the mode of my Life for these last two years (of which my residence at Cambridge constituted the most sober part) my Chirugeon pronounced another quarter would have settled my earthly accounts, and left the worms but a scanty repast.—I have given up the Casta, but I hope

[1] The Cambridge Whig Club. See Feb. 27, 1808, to Hobhouse.

to live and reestablish Medmenham Abbey,[1] or some similar temple of Venus, of which I shall be Pontifex Maximus.— — — —You have heard of one *nymph*. Rumour has been kind in this respect, for alas! I must confess that *two* are my *property*, one under my own immediate custody, as the other will be also when I am recovered.— Scrope Davies has mounted a pyeballed palfrey, and quitted London, he is a very profane Scoffer and has but narrow ideas of Revelation; Sir Geoffrey[2] I am happy to hear has made you a Socinian, he hath also run up a long Bill with Worgman the Jeweller who seems to have much faith, the Baronet moreover is about to go to Ireland as he says by the way of Sicily, a new half way house, and promises to be an ornament to his profession, as soon as his Mustachios have attained their full growth.—I am now in full contest with the fellows [concerning?] my degree, they hesitate, [what can?] I do? not recede certainly but [push on at?] all hazards.—Our personal squabbles have arisen from the well meaning interference of Tattlers, if we lend our ears to these Gentry, discontent will soon follow.—The Postman is impatient, Adieu

yours very sincerely
BYRON

[TO JOHN CAM HOBHOUSE]   *Dorant's. March 26th. 1808*

Dear Hobhouse,—I have sent Fletcher[1] to Cambridge for various purposes, & he bears this *dispatch* for you.—I am still living with my Dalilah, who has only two faults, unpardonable in a woman,—she can read and write.—Greet in my name the Bilious Birdmore,[2] if you journey this way, I shall be glad to furnish you with Bread and Salt.— The university still chew the Cud of my degree,[3] please God they shall swallow it, though Inflammation be the Consequence.— I am leading a quiet though debauched life

yours very truly
BYRON

[1] Medmenham Abbey, a mansion occupying the site of a 13th-century Cistercian monastery, was occupied in the middle of the eighteenth century by the "Monks of Medmenham" or "Hell-Fire Club", founded by Sir Francis Dashwood. The motto of the Club was "Fay ce que voudras" ("do what you please"). It was notorious for the blasphemous orgies which reputedly took place there. Among the Club's members were Charles Churchill, the poet, and William Whitehead, dramatist and poet laureate. John Wilkes was a guest there.

[2] Unidentified.

[1] William Fletcher, son of a tenant at Newstead, served Byron as valet from this time until the poet's death in Missolonghi.

[2] Scrope Berdmore Davies.

[3] Byron was finally awarded his M.A. degree on July 4, 1808.

Dear Jack,—I shall take your advice, and remain in town till the fights are over, but my *Valet* must proceed to Cambridge for my Plate &c.—I will take the *same* twice over on Belcher's Battle,² but Cropley's³ will surely be the principal combat, I heard nothing on the subject before the delivery of your note, how the Devil should I? confined to the house with my Disorder.—If Sir H. Smith's⁴ expedition takes place after Wednesday, I shall be happy to avail myself of his polite invitation, I am afraid I must not stir before.—At all events make my acknowledgements to the Baronet;—my Compts to your *little* woman,⁵ and believe me, dear Jack

yours very truly
BYRON

[TO THE REV. JOHN BECHER]   *Dorant's, March 28, 1808*

I have lately received a copy of the new edition¹ from Ridge, and it is high time for me to return my best thanks to you for the trouble you have taken in the superintendence. This I do most sincerely, and only regret that Ridge has not seconded you as I could wish,—at least, in the bindings, paper, & c. of the copy he sent to me. Perhaps those for the public may be more respectable in such articles.

You have seen the Edinburgh Review, of course. I regret that Mrs. Byron is so much annoyed. For my own part, these "paper bullets of the brain"² have only taught me to stand fire; and, as I have been lucky enough upon the whole, my repose and appetite are not discomposed.

¹ John ("Gentleman") Jackson was boxing champion of England from 1795 to 1803, when he retired from the ring. His rooms at 13 Bond Street became headquarters for the Pugilistic Club. His activities included fostering boxing matches and teaching "the art of self-defence". His gentlemanly manners and his dandified dress won him his nickname. He shared rooms with Henry Angelo, the fencing-master. Byron took fencing lessons from the one and boxing lessons from the other. He invited Jackson to Cambridge, to Brighton, and to Newstead, and paid tribute to him in a note to *Don Juan* (Canto XI, stanza 19).

² With Jackson's encouragement Byron arranged in April, 1808, a bout between Tom Belcher and the Irish champion Dan Dogherty, whom he backed. Belcher won.

³ On May 10, 1808, Bill Cropley fought Dutch Sam and lost. On that same day Byron accompanied another pugilist to John Sebright's Park in Hertfordshire to see a bout between the champion John Gully and Bob Gregson. (*LJ*, V, 579.)

⁴ Unidentified. Possibly another fight promoter.

⁵ See May 27, 1812, to Clarke.

¹ The second edition of *Hours of Idleness* (with deletions and additions) bore the title *Poems Original and Translated*.

² Benedick in *Much Ado About Nothing* (II, iii, 220).

Pratt, the gleaner, author, poet, & c. & c. addressed a long rhyming epistle to me on the subject, by way of consolation; but it was not well done, so I do not send it, though the name of the man might make it go down. The E[dinburgh] R[eviewer]s have not performed their task well; at least, the literati tell me this, and I think *I* could write a more sarcastic critique on *myself* than any yet published. For instance, instead of the remark,—ill-natured enough, but not keen,—about Macpherson, I (quoad reviewers) could have said, "Alas, this imitation only proves the assertion of Dr. Johnson, that many men, women, and *children*, could have written such poetry as Ossian's."[3]

I am still in or rather near town residing with a nymph, who is now on the sofa vis-a-vis, whilst I am scribbling. . . .[4] I have three females (attendants included) in my custody. They accompany me of course.[5]

I am *thin* and in exercise. During the spring or summer I trust we shall meet. I hear Lord Ruthyn leaves Newstead in April. * * * As soon as he quits it for ever, I wish much you would take a ride over, survey the mansion, and give me your candid opinion on the most advisable mode of proceeding with regard to the *house*. *Entre nous*, I am cursedly dipped; my debts, *every* thing inclusive, will be nine or ten thousand before I am twenty-one. But I have reason to think my property will turn out better than general expectation may conceive. Of Newstead I have little hope or care; but Hanson, my agent, intimated my Lancashire property was worth three Newsteads. I believe we have it hollow; though the defendants are protracting the surrender, if possible, till after my majority, for the purpose of forming some arrangement with me, thinking I shall probably prefer a sum in hand to a reversion. Newstead I may *sell*;—perhaps I will not,—though of that more anon. I will come down in May or June. * * * *

Yours most truly, &c.

[TO WILLIAM HARNESS] *Dorant's, March 29th. 1808*

My dear Harness,—My Valet who has just arrived from Cambridge, brought me your Letter of the 9th. I have not revisited in person my Alma Mater since our last meeting, having been confined to my room

---

[3] A reference to the well-known reply of Dr. Johnson when asked whether any man of the modern age could have written *Ossian*: "Yes, Sir, many men, many women, and many children". (Boswell, 1763.)

[4] This sentence is from the Bangs catalogue, Jan. 24, 1902.

[5] This sentence is quoted in the H. B. Smith sale catalogue, American Art, Anderson Galleries, April 8, 1936.

by Indisposition almost a month.—I hope my dear H. the mighty difference of three years in our ages (which will cut a distinguished figure if ever we double our grand Climacteric) will not be productive of the consequences you predict, it is indeed possible I may quit Granta before you enter it, but it is not probable such an event will make us forget each other, seeing that might have been effected long ago, were it to be accomplished at all.—Our Destinies will be more propitious, or I shall be very angry with mine.—I shall certainly in another year "go into the World" but I would rather go *out* of it with all my sins on my head (and they form a very decent Catalogue) than consent to that separation, you seem to think the inevitable consequence of frequenting the Card tables of Quality Dowagers.—In short, dear H.——if you only retain a slight portion of that regard with which you honoured me some seven years ago, mine will never diminish, but neither Love or Friendship can subsist on one side only.—I believe I am to dine with H. Drury soon, if so, we shall meet, at all events on two, [if] not three Speechdays, I feel assured from my Recollection of you as a boy you will speak well, and I have the vanity to fancy myself a Critic in Elocution, I hope you may, most sincerely, indeed I *know* you will, for in this Country, nothing is to be done at the Bar, Stage, Pulpit, or Senate, without it—Adieu, dear William,

[Signature cut away]

[TO JOHN CAM HOBHOUSE]   *Dorant's. April 15th. 1808*

My dear Hobhouse,—I proceed as usual turning the twenty four hours to the best account, particularly the nocturnal moiety, my Belles would probably differ, were they together, one is *with* me, and the other *for* me—or any body else, I dare say in my absence.—Besides, I amuse myself with the "chere amie" of a French Painter in Pall Mall, a lively Gaul;—and occasionally an Opera Girl from the same Meridian.— I have been well about a fortnight, and I trust shall continue so, but I am sadly meagre, and vigilant. Alas! for the Shepherd and his Lambkin! how cursedly absurd such proceedings appear compared with your chastity, and my Carnality.——I shall be in Cambridge next month to graduate, the first night I went out after my illness I got into a Row and gave a fellow at the theatre, my address and a black eye, after pugilizing with him and his friend, on their refusing to name their place of Residence, they were kicked out into the Piazzas.—I was very weak and languid, but managed to keep these youths at Bay, till a person whom I dont know engaged one, and I then contended singly with the other till the above consequence ensued. Scrope Davies is at Portsmouth, I form one of a very sad set, consisting of Capt. Wallace, Sir Godfrey,[1] Sir B. Graham, and other sensual Sinners, we have kept it up, with the most laudable systematic profligacy. Sir G. is with his regiment at present, to the Sorrow of [his] Confederates.—I have given up *play* altogether.—I saw Mahon[2] last night, he made one of a party of ten at a house of Fornication.—

When do you come to town? I long to see you, Adieu

> yours very truly
> BYRON

[TO AUGUSTA LEIGH]   *Dorant's. April 26th. 1808*

My dear Augusta,—I regret being compelled to trouble you again, but it is necessary I should request you will inform Col. Leigh,[1] if the P[rince]'s consent is not obtained in a few days, it will be of little service to Mr. Wallace,[2] who is ordered to join the 17th in ten days, the Regiment is stationed in the East Indies, and as he has already served there nine years, he is unwilling to return.—I shall feel particularly obliged by Col Leigh's interference, as I think from his influence the Prince's consent might be obtained.—I am not much in the habit of asking favours, or pressing exertion, but on this occasion, my wish to serve Wallace must plead my excuse.—I have been introduced to Julia Byron[3] by Trevannion[4] at the Opera, she is pretty, but I do not admire her, there is too much Byron in her countenance, I hear she is clever, a very great defect in a woman, who becomes conceited in course; altogether I have not much inclination to improve the acquaintance, I have seen my old Friend George,[5] who will prove the best of the family, and will one day be Lord B.—I do not much care how

---

[1] Sir Godfrey Webster. These were all pot-house cronies, whom Byron may have met through Davies.

[2] Unidentified.

[1] Col. George Leigh, Augusta's cousin whom she married in 1807. As Equerry to the Prince of Wales he might be supposed to have some influence.

[2] Captain Wallace is mentioned frequently in Byron's letters. He seems to have been in Scrope Davies' circle of drinking companions and men about town. Byron mentioned him in "Detached Thoughts", No. 21, as "*then* intimate with most of the more dissipated young men of the day".

[3] Julia Byron was the poet's first cousin, sister of George Anson Byron.

[4] The Trevanions were related to Byron through his grandmother, Sophia Trevanion, who married Admiral John Byron.

[5] George Anson Byron succeeded as the seventh Baron Byron on the death of the poet in 1824.

soon.—Pray name my nephew after his uncle, it must be a nephew (I *wont* have a *niece*) I will make him my *heir*, for I shall never marry, unless I am ruined, and then his *inheritance* would not be great. George will have the title and his *laurels*, my property (if any is left in five years time) I can leave to whom I please, and your son shall be the legatee. —Adieu

yours ever
BYRON

[TO MRS. MASSINGBERD]   *May 12th. 1808*

I shall call with Mr. Davies and the rest at five to-day to finish the business.[1] I hope you and Miss M[assingberd] will be at home and disengaged.

B.

[TO WILLIAM HARNESS]   *London, June 4th. 1808*

My dear Harness,—I have particularly to regret the late hour of my arrival on Thursday, which prevented me the pleasure I anticipated in hearing your Lear.[1] However I heard your *Fame*, & congratulate myself on the escape of my *Vanity*, which would have suffered severely, though the pleasure I must experience in any performance of yours would console me under the mortification of Self-Love. I was so unfortunate as not to meet you during the day, or to see you except at a distance in the Dancing Room, but on Monday I dine with H. Drury & take Harrow in my way to the Montem[2] of the Etonians on Tuesday.—I shall make my escape as soon as possible after Dinner, in the hope of seeing you, & in that expectation I shall only add at present how sincerely I am

yours affectly.
BYRON

[1] The business was probably a loan which Mrs. Massingberd was arranging with the money-lenders, whether for Davies, or for Byron with Davies as co-signer is not known.

[1] Harness, as Byron did in 1805, was reciting a passage from *King Lear* for the Harrow Speech Day.

[2] The Montem was an annual spring festival at Eton. The scholars proceeded in fancy dress to "Salt Hill" where they collected money for the benefit of the senior going to King's College, Cambridge, as an Eton Scholar.

[TO HARGREAVES HANSON]   *St. James Street, June 15th. 1808*

Dear Hargreaves,—I leave town tomorrow, so if the Baron of Exchequer cant receive me before two, the Commission must be sent to Brighton[1] as I will wait no longer to please all the courts of Christendom.

yours,
BYRON

[TO HEWSON CLARKE[1]]   *Cambridge, July 3d. 1808*

Sir,—Report universally attributes to your pen, passages in the Satirist of *this*, & *last* month alluding to me [in so?] marked & unjustifiable a manner, that I can no longer delay requiring an explanation.—I shall expect (if you are not the author) an immediate & unequivocal disavowal.—In case this proposal should not meet your approbation, my friend Mr. Hobhouse is instructed how to act.— I remain

your obedt. Servt.
BYRON

[TO MRS. ELIZABETH MASSINGBERD]   *Brighton July 20th 1808*

Dear Madam,—I have parted with Miss Cameron,[1] & I beg she may have her Clothes & the trunk containing them

yours very truly
BYRON

1 Byron spent part of the summer of 1808 at Brighton with Hobhouse, Scrope Davies, and others.

1 Hewson Clarke, a sizar of Emmanuel College, Cambridge, was editor of *The Satirist*. Since the first publication of *Hours of Idleness* he had been sniping at Byron in the pages of that periodical. In May, 1808, Clarke had printed quotations from some of the most caustic reviews of that volume which had appeared in the *Eclectic*, the *Monthly Mirror*, and the *Edinburgh Review*. When in June he followed this up with some taunting verses "Lord B——n to his Bear", Byron flared up and wrote the challenge in this letter. Whether Hobhouse persuaded him not to send it, or whether Byron himself thought better of it when he calmed down, there is no record of an encounter in person. Byron found his revenge in some lines in a second edition of *English Bards and Scotch Reviewers* (973–80), and in a postscript to that edition.

1 The girl Byron had kept at Brompton, and whom he apparently took to Brighton with him. (See Marchand, *Byron: A Biography*. I, 151, 156.)

Brighton. August 7th. 1808

My dear Lord,—I feel considerably obliged by the information your letter has afforded, & shall avail myself of it accordingly, though I had very little doubt that the game was in perfect preservation.—The Boat I shall be happy to purchase on the stipulated terms, but on the subject of the Keeper I cannot yet decide, though your Lordship's recommendation will have considerable weight.—I regret that any person in my service should have acted in the manner you mention, and if I find that you have not been misinformed as to the *delinquencies* of Mealey,¹ I shall most certainly take proper steps; but as you do not specify the particulars, and merely prefer a general charge of misconduct, I should be glad to learn the grounds of your Lordship's complaint.—I beg leave to assure you, that if it does not originate (as it possibly may) in the misrepresentation of some servant (and we know what servants will assert) I will take care he makes such reparation as will be satisfactory.—I cannot conclude without adverting to circumstances, which though now long past, and indeed difficult for me to touch upon, have not yet ceased to be interesting.—Your Lordship must be perfectly aware of the very peculiar reasons that induced me to adopt a line of conduct, which however painful, and painful to me it certainly was, became unavoidable.—² On these I cannot enter at large, nor would the discussion be a pleasing one, while any farther explanation is unnecessary.—at the same time, though from these and other causes, much intercourse between us must entirely cease, I have still so grateful a recollection of many favours you have conferred upon me when a boy, that I shall always be happy, when we do meet, to meet as friends, and endeavour to forget we have been otherwise. If ever you sojourn again in Notts, I hope you will pay Newstead a visit; I shall be there from September till January, for the present month I reside at Brighton. I remain

very sincerely yours
BYRON

¹ Owen Mealey, the overseer at Newstead.
² See March 26, 1804, to Augusta Byron, note 1. Lord Grey's reply to this letter throws a curious light on the strange affair. He professed ignorance of the reason for Byron's coolness. "We parted in 1804 the best of friends, your letters were afterwards most affectionate. . . . You say the break was painful to yourself, I need not say to you who know I have not the power to command my feelings when [deeply?] wounded what my sensations were. . . ." (From the MS. letter in the Meyer Davis Collection, University of Pennsylvania Library.) In the light of Byron's statements to Augusta, hinting at some unspeakable behaviour on the part of Lord Grey, it would seem that he cut the acquaintance without revealing to Grey the extent of his shock at the time.

[TO JOHN HANSON]   *Brighton. August 14th. 1808*

Dear Sir,—I shall be in town on Wednesday, & shall be happy to
see you at Reddish's on Thursday morning, if however it is not convenient for you to call, I will wait on you in Chancery Lane.

yours truly
BYRON

[TO JOHN HANSON]   *Reddish's. August 29th. 1808*

Dear Sir,—As I shall have occasion for some Cash, and I believe my
quarter has been due some time, I will thank you for the sum of two
hundred pounds, which your Son H[argreaves] will be so good as to
bring tomorrow if convenient, believe me

yours very truly
BYRON

P.S.—I hope you are quite *recovered!*— — —

[TO JOHN JACKSON¹]   *Cambridge, October 30, 1803* [*sic*]
                             [*Sept., 1808?*]²

Dear Jack,— My servants, with their usual acuteness, have contrived
to lose my swordstick. Will you get me such another, or as much
better as you like, and keep it till I come to town. I also wish you to
obtain another bottle of that same Lamb's-Conduit-Street remedy, as I
gave the other to a physician to analyze, and I forgot to ask him what
he made of it. Keep that also till we meet, which I hope will be soon,
and believe me ever yours truly,

B

P.S.—I am this far on my way north, and will write to you again on
my arrival.

¹ See March 27, 1808, to Jackson.
² The date as printed must be from a mistaken reading of the manuscript. Byron
was not at Cambridge until 1805, and was not on his way north (to Southwell or
Newstead?) in any October before he went abroad in 1809. The date is most likely
1808, when Byron was closely associated with Jackson at Brighton and elsewhere.
He could have been in Cambridge in late August or early September of that year on
his way north to Newstead, where he was by the 13th, and did not leave again until
after the New Year.

169

[TO JOHN HANSON]   *Newstead Abbey. Sept 13th. 1808*

Dear Sir,—I have now expected you for some time, and am afraid by
your non-arrival, a relapse has taken place.—I wish very much you
would write, that I may proceed *legally* with my waters; I wish much
to let off the lower lake for the purpose of stocking my other ponds
with the fish therein, but am apprehensive of getting into some law
dispute with Robinson, who opposes it, and I wish for your opinion
before I proceed.—It is rather hard not to be able to procure myself
the Contents of my fishponds.—pray send me your advice, & believe
me

                                                    yours very truly
                                                    BYRON

[TO THE REV. JOHN BECHER]   *Newstead Abbey. Notts.*
                                              Septr. 14th. 1808

Dear Becher,—I am much obliged to you for your enquiries and
shall profit by them accordingly.—I am going to get up a play here,
the hall will constitute a most admirable theatre, I have settled the
Dram[atis] pers[onae] and can do without Ladies, as I have some young
friends who will make tolerable substitutes for females, and we only
want three male characters besides Mr. Hobhouse and myself for the
play we have fixed on, which will be the Revenge.[1]—Pray, direct
Nicholson the Carpenter to come over to me immediately, and inform
me what day you will dine and pass the night here, Believe me

                                                    yours ever
                                                    BYRON

[TO JOHN JACKSON]   *N. A. Notts. September 18, 1808*

Dear Jack,—I wish you would inform me what has been done by
Jekyll, at No. 40, Sloane-square, concerning the pony I returned as
unsound.

I have also to request you will call on Louch at Brompton,[1] and inquire what the devil he meant by sending such an insolent letter to me
at Brighton; and at the same time tell him I by no means can comply
with the charge he has made for things pretended to be damaged.

---

[1] Byron had chosen for his Speech Day oration at Harrow on June 6, 1805, the
lament of Zanga over the body of Alonzo in Edward Young's tragedy *The Revenge*.
[1] In the spring of 1808 Byron had taken rooms in Brompton where he kept a Miss
Cameron. (See Marchand, *Byron: A Biography*, I, 151, 156.)

Ambrose behaved most scandalously about the pony. You may tell Jekyll if he does not refund the money, I shall put the affair into my lawyer's hands. Five and twenty guineas is a sound price for a pony, and by ———, if it costs me five hundred pounds, I will make an example of Mr. Jekyll, and that immediately, unless the cash is returned.

Believe me, dear Jack, &c.

[TO JOHN JACKSON]   *N. A. Notts. October 4, 1808*

You will make as good a bargain as possible with this Master Jekyll, if he is not a gentleman. If he is a *gentleman*, inform me, for I shall take very different steps. If he is not, you must get what you can of the money, for I have too much business on hand at present to commence an action. Besides, Ambrose is the man who ought to refund,—but I have done with him. You can settle with L[ouch] out of the balance, and dispose of the bidets, &c. as you best can.

I should be very glad to see you here; but the house is filled with workmen and undergoing a thorough repair. I hope, however, to be more fortunate before many months have elapsed.

If you see Bold Webster,[1] remember me to him, and tell him I have to regret Sydney, who has perished, I fear, in my rabbit warren, for we have seen nothing of him for the last fortnight.

Adieu.—Believe me, &c.

[TO MRS. CATHERINE GORDON BYRON]   *Newstead Abbey. Notts.*
                                          Octr. 7th. 1808

Dear Madam,—I have no beds for the *Hansons* (or any body else at present) the H's sleep at Mansfield.—I do not know that I resemble Jean Jacques Rousseau,[1] I have no ambition to be like so illustrious a madman, but this I know, that I shall live in my own manner, and as much alone as possible, when my rooms are ready, I shall be glad to

---

[1] James Wedderburn Webster, an early friend of Byron, perhaps from his Cambridge days, with whom he continued to be on good terms to the end of his life, though he later flirted with Webster's wife and considered him something of a buffoon.

[1] In his "Detached Thoughts" (begun Oct. 15, 1821) Byron took exception to his mother's statement that he resembled Rousseau, but certainly he himself must have seen some resemblances in the picture he drew of Rousseau in the third canto of *Childe Harold* (stanzas 76–81).

171

see you, at present it would be improper, & uncomfortable to both parties.—You can hardly object to my rendering my mansion habitable, notwithstanding my departure for Persia[2] in March (or May at farthest) since *you* will be the *tenant* till my return, and in case of any accident (for I have already arranged my will to be drawn up the moment I am twenty one) I have taken care you shall have the house & manor for *life*, besides a sufficient income.—So you see my improvements are not entirely selfish;—as I have a friend here, we will go to the Infirmary Ball on the 12th.—we will drink tea with Mrs. Byron[3] at eight o'clock, & expect to see you at the Ball, if that Lady will allow us a couple of Rooms to dress in, we shall be highly obliged, if we are at the Ball by ten or eleven it will be time enough, & we shall return to Newstead about three or four.—Adieu, believe me yours

very truly
Byron

[TO MRS. CATHERINE GORDON BYRON]   *Newstead Abbey. Notts.*
Novr. 2d. 1808

Dear Mother,—If you please we will forget the things you mention, I have no desire to remember them.—When my rooms are finished I shall be happy to see you; as I tell but the truth, you will not suspect me of evasion.—I am furnishing the house more for you than myself, and I shall establish you in it before I sail for India,[1] which I expect to do in March, if nothing particularly obstructive occurs.— —I am now fitting up the *green* drawing room, the red (as a bedroom), and the rooms over as sleeping rooms, they will be soon completed, at least I hope so.—I have paid Barnet 182 pounds his whole Bill, I think a *large* one.—I wish you would inquire of Major Watson[2] (who is an old East Indian) what things will be necessary to provide for my voyage, I have already procured a friend to write to the *Arabic* Professor at Cambridge,[3]—for some information I am anxious to procure.—I can easily get letters from Government to the Ambassadors Consuls &c. and also to the Governors at Calcutta & Madras; I shall place my

---

[2] Byron's plans for travel had expanded from his first stated intention to visit the Greek Archipelago.

[3] Mrs. George Byron, Byron's great aunt, lived in Nottingham.

[1] In his last letter to his mother he had said he planned to go to Persia; now it is India.

[2] A member of the family in Southwell.

[3] The Rev. John Palmer, Fellow of St. John's College, was Adam's Professor of Arabic at Cambridge from 1804 to 1819.

property and my *will* in the hands of Trustees till my return, and I mean to appoint you one.—From Hanson I have heard nothing; when I do, you shall have the particulars.—After all you must own my project is not a bad one, if I do not travel now, I never shall, and all men should, one day or other. I have at present no connections to keep me at home, no wife, or unprovided sisters Brothers &c.—I shall take care of you, and when I return, I may possibly become a politician, a few years knowledge of other countries than our own will not incapacitate me for that part.—If we see no nation but our own, we do not give mankind a fair chance, it is from *experience* not *Books*, we ought to judge of mankind.—There is nothing like inspection, and trusting to our own senses.

yours very truly
BYRON

[TO FRANCIS HODGSON] *Newstead Abbey Notts. Novr. 3d. 1808*

My dear Hodgson,—I expected to have heard ere this the event of your interview with the mysterious Mr. [Hague?], my volunteer correspondent, however as I had no business to trouble you with the adjustment of my concerns with that illustrious Stranger, I have no right to complain of your silence.— —You have of course seen Drury, in all the pleasing palpitations of anticipated Wedlock,[1] well! he has still something to look forward to, and his present extacies are certainly enviable, "peace be with him and with his spirit" and his flesh also; at least just now.— — —Hobhouse and your humble are still here, Hobhouse hunts & c. and I do nothing, we dined the other day with a neighboring Esquire (not Collet of Staines) and regretted your absence, as the Banquet of Staines was scarcely to be compared to our last "feast of Reason"—You know, laughing is the sign of a rational animal, so says Dr. Smollett, I think so too, but unluckily my spirits dont always keep pace with my opinions.—I had not so much scope for risibility the other day as I could have wished, for I was seated near a woman, to whom when a boy I was as much attached as boys generally are, and more than a man should be.[2]

[1] Henry Drury, eldest son of Dr. Joseph Drury, former Headmaster of Harrow, was a close friend of Hodgson and of Byron too. He married on December 20, 1808, Anne Caroline Tayler.

[2] Byron and Hobhouse accepted an invitation to dinner at Annesley Hall, where he saw again his boyhood love, Mary Chaworth, then Mrs. Chaworth-Musters. The visit prompted two poems: "Well! Thou Art Happy" and "To a Lady on Being Asked My Reason for Quitting England in the Spring".

I knew this before I went, and was determined to be valiant, and converse with "sang froid," but instead I forgot my valour and my nonchalance, and never opened my lips even to laugh, far less to speak, & the Lady was almost as absurd as myself, which made both the object of more observation, than if we had conducted ourselves with easy indifference.—You will think all this great nonsense, if you had seen it you would have thought it still more ridiculous.—What fools we! we cry for a plaything, which like children we are never satisfied till we break it open, though like them, we cannot get rid of it, by putting it in the fire.—I have tried for Gifford's epistle to Pindar[3] & the Bookseller says the copies were cut up for *waste paper*, if you can procure me a copy, I shall be much obliged.—Adieu, believe me my dear Sir

yours ever sincerely

BYRON

[TO J. BIRCH[1]]   *Newstead Abbey Notts. Novr. 9th. 1808*

Dear Sir,—To my great surprize I have not heard from Mr. Hanson since his arrival at Rochdale, and as it seems not likely that I shall hear from him for some time, I must address myself to you on the present business.—One quarter (125 £) was due in October, and two hundred pounds being the sum I required, Mr. H. offered me a draft when here, which in expectation of his return in a few days I then declined. I now want it, and beg you will send me the cash forthwith.—I remain

yours &c. &c.

BYRON

[TO JOHN HANSON]   *Newstead Abbey. Notts. Nov. 15th. 1808*

Dear Sir,—The time of your projected return has so long elapsed, and your silence has been so protracted, that I fear some personal accident or illness has prevented you from fulfilling your intentions in both these respects— —As to myself I have no great curiosity in the business or I should have written before, but I shall be glad to hear you & Mrs. H. with your fair companion are well. I remain

yours very truly

BYRON

---

[3] William Gifford's *Epistle to Peter Pindar* (1800) was a satire on John Wolcot, who had written under the pseudonym of Peter Pindar. Byron's admiration for Gifford made him eager for anything Gifford had written. Hodgson's father had been a friend of Gifford.

[1] Birch was Hanson's law partner.

Dear Sir,—I am truly glad to hear your health is reinstated. As for my affairs I am sure you will do your best, and, though I should be glad to get rid of my Lancashire property for an equivalent in money, I shall not take any steps of that nature without good advice and mature consideration.

I am (as I have already told you) going abroad in the spring; for this I have many reasons. In the first place, I wish to study India and Asiatic policy and manners. I am young, tolerably vigorous, abstemious in my way of living; I have no pleasure in fashionable dissipation, and I am determined to take a wider field than is customary with travellers. If I return, my judgment will be more mature, and I shall still be young enough for politics. With regard to expence, travelling through the East is rather inconvenient than expensive: it is not like the tour of Europe, you undergo hardship, but incur little hazard of spending money. If I live here I must have my house in town, a separate house for Mrs. Byron; I must keep horses, etc., etc. When I go abroad I place Mrs. Byron at Newstead (there is one great expence saved), I have no horses to keep. A voyage to India will take me six months, and if I had a dozen attendants cannot cost me five hundred pounds; and you will agree with me that a like term of months in England would lead me into four times that expenditure. I have written to Government for letters and permission of the Company,[1] so you see I am *serious*.

You honour my debts; they amount to perhaps twelve thousand pounds, and I shall require perhaps three or four thousand at setting out, with credit on a Bengal agent. This you must manage for me. If my resources are not adequate to the supply I must *sell*, but *not Newstead*. I will at least transmit that to the next Lord. My debts must be paid, if possible, in February. I shall leave my affairs to the care of *trustees*, of whom, with your acquiescence, I shall *name you* one, Mr. Parker[2] another, and two more, on whom I am not yet determined.

Pray let me hear from you soon. Remember me to Mrs. Hanson, whom I hope to see on her return. Present my best respects to the young lady, and believe me, etc.,

BYRON

[1] The East India Company.
[2] Byron's cousin, Peter Parker, son of his father's sister Charlotte Augusta, who had married Christopher Parker.

My dear Hodgson,—Boatswain is dead! he expired in a state of
madness on the 10th. after suffering much, yet retaining all the gentle-
ness of his nature to the last, never attempting to do the least injury to
any one near him.[1]—I have lost every thing except Old Murray.— —
I sent some game to Drury lately, which I hope escaped the scrutiny
of the mutineers, I trust the letter to Claridge[2] was equally fortunate
(after being put in the post by you at London) as it contained some
cash, which my correspondent notwithstanding the patriotic fervour of
the moment, might not chuse to submit to the inspection of the William
Tells, and Gracchi of the day.—If my songs have produced the *glorious*
effects you mention, I shall be a complete Tyrtaeus,[3] though I am
sorry to say, I resemble that interesting Harper, more in his person
than Poesy.— —I only lament that Drury's conjecture should be more
facetious than well founded, nothing would give me greater glee than
to suppose, it was perfectly correct.—It is singular enough, that
Wingfield and [Kemmis?][4] were both my fags at Harrow, and they
have now obtained that honour to which their master aspired in vain.—
I have written to Government for letters &c.—wont you come and
broach a farewell batch at Xmas? cant you "tice Drury into the voods
and aftervards dewour him" this day twelvemonth, Deo favente, I

---

[1] Moore (I, 154) wrote that in the beginning Byron was "so little aware . . . of
the nature of the malady, that he, more than once, with his bare hand, wiped away
the slaver from the dog's lips during the paroxysms". On the tomb erected in the
Abbey garden the inscription says: "Near this spot are deposited the remains of one
who possessed beauty without vanity, strength without insolence, courage without
ferocity, and all the virtues of man without his vices. This praise, which would be
unmeaning flattery if inscribed over human ashes, is but a just tribute to the memory
of Boatswain, a dog, who was born in *Newfoundland* May 1803 and died at Newstead Nov. 18th 1808." But writing on the 18th, Byron said he died on the 10th.
The figure in the manuscript is a little indistinct, but he would not have said on the
18th (the date of the letter is quite clear) that he died on the "18th," but "today"
or "this morning". It may be that Byron forgot the date before the inscription was
written.
[2] Two Claridge brothers, sons of J. F. Claridge, Sevenoaks, entered Harrow
during Byron's first term. George became a solicitor at Sevenoaks. John Thomas
was probably Byron's particular friend. He later was awarded B.A. and M.A.
degrees at Oxford. He was knighted in 1825 and finally settled in Guernsey, dying
in 1868.
[3] Tyrtaeus was the lame school-master sent by the Athenians to assist the
Lacedaemonians. His poems exercised such an influence on the Spartans that they
composed their dissensions and gained courage for their battles.
[4] The name is not easy to make out in the MS. It is given as Kemmis by Prothero
(*LJ*, III, 171n.). James Kemmis, son of T. Kemmis, Shaen Castle, Killeen, entered
Harrow in the autumn term, 1802.

shall be crossing Mount Causasus.—Is your information of Jefferies's[5] proposal to Southey well authenticated, if so, pray favour both with a few couplets in your satire.—I should be too happy to think Gifford had troubled [one line cut from MS.] could discover if he really wrote the "exposè" in your possession.—My Rhymes on the Bards are forthcoming,—tell Drury he must purchase a copy, I cant afford to give away.—Hobhouse & myself nearly suffocated a person in the Bath yesterday, by way of ascertaining the soundings, I was obliged to jump in, and extricate the Drownee.—Drury will find a letter from me at Harrow, which I hope he will answer, if still at Cambridge, greet him with an embrace, Hobhouse presents all sorts of remembrances to both. But in the words of Gaffer Thumb, "I can no more" believe me dear H. yours

[Signature missing]

[TO THE DUKE OF PORTLAND[1]]   *Newstead Abbey. Notts.*
                                                Nov. 20th. 1808

My Lord,—If, in requesting your Grace (as head of his Majesty's Government) to procure me the permission of the E[ast] I[ndia] Directors, to pass through their settlements, I have been guilty of any informality, I beg leave to apologize; had any other means appeared more correct, or more obvious, I should not have troubled your Grace on the Subject.—Of the success of my application your Grace is the best Judge, "of the *propriety*" allow me to observe, there can be no violation of decorum in a British subject requesting permission to visit any part of the British Dominions.—I have also to assure your Grace, had I not been serious in my intention, I should neither have trespassed on your time, or patience.—I should be sorry, that inconvenience or trouble should arise from any request of mine, and if (as it appears from the tone of your Grace's letter) Both may be the consequence, I shall regret withdrawing for a moment your Grace's attention from much more important concerns.—However, I shall certainly not desist from all proper endeavours to further my design, nor can I conceive that the permission granted "to persons in the E[ast] I[ndia] service" should be witheld from one who neither seeks favour, or expects emolument.—

---

[5] Byron referred to Francis Jeffrey, editor of the *Edinburgh Review*, whom he still thought the reviewer of his *Hours of Idleness* (it was actually Henry Brougham). Jeffrey had proposed, through Scott, that Southey become a contributor to the *Edinburgh Review*. But, though he was tempted by the money, he turned the offer down. Later he became a contributor to the Tory *Quarterly Review*.

[1] Prime Minister in the Tory government from 1807 to 1809.

Were there a possibility at present, of passing through the Ottoman dominions to the Interior of Asia, I should hardly prefer the circuitous route of our own Colonies, the only motive for my request, is the impracticability of proceeding by a more direct Course.

I have the honour to be your Grace's
very obedt. humble Sert.
BYRON

[TO FRANCIS HODGSON]   *Newstead Abbey, Notts: Nov. 27, 1808*

My dear Sir,—Boatswain is to be buried in a vault waiting for myself.[1] I have also written an epitaph, which I would send, were it not for two reasons: one is, that it is too long for a letter; and the other, that I hope you will some day read it on the spot where it will be engraved.

You discomfit me with the intelligence of the real orthodoxy of the "Arch-fiend's" name,[2] but alas! it must stand with me at present; if ever I have an opportunity of correcting, I shall liken him to Geoffrey of Monmouth, a noted liar in his way, and perhaps a more correct prototype than the Carnifex of James II.

I do not think the composition of your poem "a sufficing reason" for not keeping your promise of a Christmas visit. Why not come? I will never disturb you in your moments of inspiration; and if you wish to collect any materials for the *scenery*, Hardwicke (where Mary was confined for several years)[3] is not eight miles distant, and, independent of the interest you must take in it as her vindicator, is a most beautiful and venerable object of curiosity. I shall take it very ill if you do not come; my mansion is improving in comfort, and, when you require solitude, I shall have an apartment devoted to the purpose of receiving your poetical reveries.

I have heard from our Drury; he says little of the Row, which I regret: indeed I would have sacrificed much to have contributed in any way (as a schoolboy) to its consummation; but Butler survives, and

[1] Byron so specified in a will written in 1809 and repeated it in that of 1811. It was omitted from subsequent wills when he had resolved to sell Newstead.

[2] Byron had at first thought that Francis Jeffrey, editor of the *Edinburgh Review*, whom he still believed to be the critic of his poems, spelled his name the same as that of the famous "hanging judge" George Jeffreys of the "Bloody Assizes" of the seventeenth century, who was noted for his brutality.

[3] In Hodgson's poem *Lady Jane Grey*, Queen Mary of England plays a part. Byron apparently thought Hodgson was writing about Mary Queen of Scots.

thirteen boys have been expelled in vain. Davies is not here, but Hobhouse hunts as usual, and your humble servant "drags at each remove a lengthened chain." I have heard from his Grace of Portland on the subject of my expedition; he talks of difficulties; by the gods! if he throws any in my way I will next session ring such a peal in his ears,[4]

> That he shall wish the fiery Dane
> Had rather been his guest again.[5]

You do not tell me if Gifford is really my commentator:[6] it is too good to be true, for I know nothing would gratify my vanity so much as the reality; even the idea is too precious to part with.

I still expect you here; let me have no more excuses. Hobhouse desires his best remembrance. We are now lingering over our evening potations. I have extended my letter further than I ought, and beg you will excuse it; on the opposite page I send you some stanzas I wrote off on being questioned by a former flame on my motives for quitting this country.[7] You are the first reader. Hobhouse hates everything of the kind, therefore I do not show them to him. Adieu!

Believe me yours very sincerely,
BYRON

[TO THE HON. AUGUSTA LEIGH]   *Newstead Abbey Notts.*
Novr. 30th. 1808

My dearest Augusta,—I return you my best thanks for making me an uncle, and forgive the sex this time, but the next *must* be a nephew.[1] —You will be happy to hear my Lancashire property is likely to prove extremely valuable, indeed my pecuniary affairs are altogether far superior to my expectations or any other person's, if I would *sell*, my income would probably be six thousand per annum, but I will not part at least with Newstead, or indeed with the other, which is of a nature to increase in value yearly.—I am living here *alone*, which suits my inclinations better than society of any kind, Mrs. Byron I have shaken off for two years, and I shall not resume her yoke in future, I am afraid my disposition will suffer in your estimation, but I never can forgive

---

[4] Byron was irritated by the curtness of the Duke of Portland's reply to his request for permission to pass through the domains of the East India Company. See Nov. 20, 1808, to the Duke.

[5] *Marmion*, Canto II, stanza 31.

[6] See Nov. 18, 1808, to Hodgson.

[7] See Nov. 3, 1808, to Hodgson, note 2.

[1] Augusta's first child, Georgiana Augusta, was born November 4, 1808.

that woman, or breathe in comfort under the same roof.—I am a very unlucky fellow, for I think I had naturally not a bad heart, but it has been so bent, twisted, and trampled on, that it is now become as hard as a Highlander's heel-piece.—I do not know that much alteration has taken place in my person, except that I am grown much thinner, and somewhat taller! I saw Col. Leigh at Brighton in July, where I should have been glad to have seen you, I only know your husband by sight,— though I am acquainted with many of the tenth.—Indeed my relations are those whom I know the least, and in most instances, I am not very anxious to improve the acquaintance.—I hope you are quite recovered, I shall be in town in January to take my seat, and will call, if convenient let me hear from you before, &

[Signature cut off]

[TO JOHN JACKSON]   *N. A. Notts. December 12, 1808*

My dear Jack,—You will get the greyhound from the owner at any price, and as many more of the same breed (male or female) as you can collect.

Tell D'Egville[1] his dress shall be returned—I am obliged to him for the pattern. I am sorry you should have so much trouble, but I was not aware of the difficulty of procuring the animals in question. I shall have finished part of my mansion in a few weeks, and, if you can pay me a visit at Christmas, I shall be very glad to see you.

Believe me, &c.

[TO THE HON. AUGUSTA LEIGH]   *Newstead Abbey. Notts.—*
Decr. 14th. 1808

My dearest Augusta,—When I stated in my last, that my intercourse with the world had hardened my heart, I did not mean from any matrimonial disappointment, no, I have been guilty of many absurdities, but I hope in God I shall always escape that worst of evils, Marriage. —I have no doubt there are exceptions, and of course include you amongst them, but you will recollect, that *"exceptions only prove the Rule."*—I live here much in my own manner, that is, *alone*, for I could not bear the company of my best friend, above a month; there is such a sameness in mankind upon the whole, and they grow so much more disgusting every day, there were it not for a portion of Ambition, and a

1 See Feb. 27, 1808, to Hobhouse, note 5.

conviction that in times like the present, we ought to perform our respective duties, I should live here all my life, in unvaried Solitude.—I have been visited by all our Nobility & Gentry, but I return no visits.—Joseph Murray is at the head of my household, poor honest fellow! I should be a great Brute, if I had not provided for him in the manner most congenial to his own feelings, and to mine.—I have several horses, and a considerable establishment, but I am not addicted to hunting or shooting, I hate all field sports, though a few years since, I was a tolerable adept in the *polite* arts of Foxhunting, Hawking, Boxing &c. &c.—My library is rather extensive, (and as you perhaps know) I am a mighty Scribbler; I flatter myself I have made some improvements in Newstead, and as I am independent, I am happy, as far as any person unfortunately enough to be born into this world, can be said to be so.—I shall be glad to hear from you when convenient, and beg you to believe me very sincerely yours

BYRON

[TO JOHN HANSON]   *Newstead Abbey, Notts.—Decr. 17th. 1808*

My dear Sir,—I regret the contents of your letter, as I think we shall be thrown on our backs from the delay,[1] I do not know if our best method would not be to compromise if possible, as you know the state of my affairs will not be much bettered by a protracted and possibly unsuccessful litigation.—However I am and have been so much in the dark, during the whole transaction that I am not a competent Judge of the most expedient measures, I suppose it will end in my marrying a *Golden Dolly*[2] or blowing my brains out, it does not much matter which, the Remedies are nearly alike.—I shall be glad to hear from you further on the business, I suppose now it will be still more difficult to

[1] The delay in settling the legal tangle of Rochdale.

[2] Byron's mother eventually came to the conclusion that the only hope for him was to marry a rich woman, which was then a common and respectable practice among the impoverished upper classes. She wrote to Hanson on January 30, 1809, recommending that Byron mend "his fortune in the old and usual way by marrying a Woman with two or three thousand pounds [a year]. I have no doubt of his being a great speaker and a celebrated public character, and *all* that; but that *won't add* to his fortune, but bring on more expenses on him, and there is nothing to be had in this country to make a man rich in his line of life." And on March 4, 1809, she wrote: "I wish to God he would exert himself and retrieve his affairs. He must marry a Woman of *fortune* this spring; love matches is all nonsense. Let him make use of the Talents God has given him. He is an English Peer, and has all the privileges of that situation." (*LJ*, I, 205–6n.)

come to any terms.—Have you seen Mrs. Massingberd, and how have you arranged my Israelitish accounts?—[3]

Pray remember me to Mrs. Hanson, to Harriet, and all the family female & male. believe me also yours very sincerely

BYRON

[TO FRANCIS HODGSON]   *Newstead Abbey, Notts: Dec. 17, 1808*

My dear Hodgson,—I have just received your letter, and one from B. Drury,[1] which I would send, were it not too bulky to despatch within a sheet of paper; but I must impart the contents and consign the answer to your care. In the first place, I cannot address the answer to him, because the epistle is without date or direction; and in the next, the contents are so singular that I can scarce believe my optics, "which are made the fools of the other senses, or else worth all the rest."[2]

A few weeks ago, I wrote to our friend Harry Drury of facetious memory, to request he would prevail on his brother at Eton to receive the son of a citizen of London well known unto me as a pupil;[3] the family having been particularly polite during the short time I was with them, induced me to this application. "Now mark what follows," as somebody or Southey sublimely saith: on this day, the 17th December, arrives an epistle signed B. Drury, containing, not the smallest reference to tuition or *in*tuition, but a *petition* for *Robert Gregson*,[4] of pugilistic notoriety, now in bondage for certain paltry pounds sterling, and liable to take up his everlasting abode in Banco Regis. Had this letter been from any of my *lay* acquaintance, or, in short, from any person but the gentleman whose signature it bears, I should have marvelled not. If Drury is serious I congratulate pugilism on the acquisition of such a patron, and shall be happy to advance any sum necessary for the liberation of the captive Gregson; but I certainly

[3] By this time Byron was in debt to the amount of several thousand pounds to the usurers.

[1] Benjamin Heath Drury (1782–1835), Henry Drury's younger brother, was an assistant master at Eton.

[2] *Macbeth*, the floating dagger speech before Duncan's murder. (Act II, scene i, 45.)

[3] The boy in whose behalf Byron wrote was John Cowell, a tradesman's son, whom he had first met at Brighton during the summer. Cowell later told Moore that Byron first noticed him when he had formed the habit of playing with Byron's dogs.

[4] Bob Gregson (1778–1824) was a pugilist and pub-keeper, whom Byron had met when he was following the prize fights. Byron saw him lose a bout against John Gully on May 10, 1808. (*LJ*, V, 579.)

hope to be certified from you or some reputable housekeeper of the fact, before I write to Drury on the subject. When I say the *fact* I mean of the *letter* being written by *Drury*, not having any doubt as to the authenticity of the statement. The letter is now before me, and I keep it for your perusal. When I hear from you I shall address my answer to him, under *your care*; for as it is now the vacation at Eton, and the letter is without *time* or *place*, I cannot venture to consign my sentiments on so *momentous* a *concern* to chance.

To you, my dear Hodgson, I have not much to say. If you can make it convenient or pleasant to trust yourself here, be assured it will be both to me.

[TO JOHN HANSON]   *Newstead Abbey. Notts. Decr. 23d. 1808*

Dear Sir,—Mr. Chaworth[1] is enclosing an Annesley Tenant, and threatens to shut up the road, to this [Truman?] Hardstaff, and Palethorpe[2] object not only on the Ground of Inconvenience, but seem to think we have a right to a Road, either from precedent or a claim to some part of the forest extending from the Lodge which is ours.—The Late Ld. Byron, certainly claimed and had a road and hung gates, or caused gates to be hung, I know nothing of the matter but beg you will ascertain the truth, and write to Mr. Chaworth or say to me what is to be done.—Pray decide quickly or the Inclosure will take place, and we shall be too late. Believe me

yours truly
BYRON

[TO JOHN HANSON]   *January 3d. 1809*

Dear Sir,—You will see by the enclosed Letter from Mrs. Massingberd the [possibility?] of coming to some arrangement[1] [which?] I doubt, I remain

yours very sincerely
BYRON

1 Mary Chaworth's husband, John Musters, who took the name of Chaworth-Musters after his marriage.
2 Newstead tenants.
1 Concerning arrangements about the annuities Byron had agreed to pay the money-lenders.

[TO JOHN HANSON]   *Newstead Abbey Notts.*
                                 January 5th. 1808 [sic] [1809]

Dear Sir,—I am surprised to have received no answer to my last
two letters, one of which (the second) required a particular reply.—
Tomorrow I shall draw on you for three hundred pounds payable on
the first of *February*, which I hope it will be convenient to honour, as I
shall then be twenty one, and I have several Bills due, which I mean to
pay before I leave the County. I remain

                                            yours very truly
                                            BYRON

P.S.—Present my best remembrances to Mrs. Hanson & the family.—

[TO SCROPE BERDMORE DAVIES¹]   *Newstead Abbey. Notts.*
                                          January 6th. 1809

Sir,—To convince you, if possible, that my animosity is not so
implacable as you seem to conceive, allow me to offer you my very
sincere congratulations on the award of the University in your favour,
and the success of your Essay.²—With regard to the subject of your
last letter, I certainly conceived your request to Wallace³ a piece of ill
timed waggery, more especially as he informed me that you *"had told
him all about me"* (I quote literally) and that he expected *"a deal of
Fun"* in consequence.—Now next to being "patted on the back by Tom
Davies" having my house converted into a temple of "Fun" appears to
be the penultimate of the practical Bathos though I have no objection

¹ Scrope Berdmore Davies (1783–1852) was born at Horsley, Gloucestershire,
and educated at Eton and King's College, Cambridge, where he was admitted as a
Scholar in 1802, and awarded a Fellowship in 1805. He received the Belham
Scholarship (for Eton Scholars at King's) in 1803. Byron met him through
Hobhouse and other friends at Cambridge, and was attracted by his wit and man-of-
the-world attitudes. He had "a quaint dry caustic manner of speaking and an irresistible stammer". (Hodgson, *Memoir* I, 104.) He was at home in the fashionable
society of London, and at the gaming tables, where he won, and lost, huge sums.
Byron called him "one of the cleverest men I ever knew, in conversation". ("Detached Thoughts", No. 26.) Davies borrowed several thousand pounds from
usurers to give Byron before he went abroad in July 1809, which Byron repaid in
1814. Davies was finally ruined by gambling losses and debts and escaped to
Bruges in 1819. He spent his last days in Paris, living on his King's College
Fellowship.
² No information is available on the award or the essay. Few letters of Davies
survive.
³ Wallace was an army officer who had served nine years in the East Indies. He
was a friend of Byron and Davies. See April 26, 1808, to Augusta Leigh, note 2.

to an occasional Sacrifice to Momus, or even deities of a less harmless description.—You have now the whole of my complaint, I confess myself angry, and as I wrote upon the impulse of the moment, I may have said more than the occasion justified.—However I shall say no more, and as there appears to have been a mistake somewhere, I shall be glad to drop it altogether, and pay my personal respects in turn at Batts, after the 19th. when I set out for London.— I remain your very obedt. Servt.

BYRON

[TO JOHN HANSON]   *Newstead Abbey, Notts. January 10th. 1809*

Dear Sir,—A few days ago I wrote to you stating my intention of drawing on the *first* of *February* for three hundred pounds; I now wish to inform you that I shall only draw for *two hundred* and *fifty eight* pounds, but you will oblige me much by paying the *forty guineas over* into the hands of

   "Samuel Viner Esqre.
    "Stone Buildings
     "Lincoln's Inn, on the account of Lady Perceval;[1]

the sum is for my Opera Subscription, as I am one of her Ladyship's subscribers, and the sooner it is paid the more I shall be obliged, as also *her Ladyship* I dare be sworn.— —You will be extremely welcome here and your presence will preserve order in my absence, the tenants are to have a good dinner and plenty of Ale & Punch, and the *Rabble* will have an Ox and two Sheep to tear in pieces, with *Ale,* and *Uproar*.—[2] dear Sir

yours ever sincerely
BYRON

[TO JOHN HANSON]   *Newstead Abbey. Notts. January 15th. 1809*

My dear Sir,—I am much obliged by your kind invitation, but I wish you if possible to be here on the 22d.[1] your presence will be of

[1] Lady Perceval was perhaps the wife of an Irish Peer. There was a Baron Perceval of Burton, Cork (Barony created 1715), and a Perceval of Kanturk, Cork (Viscountcy created 1722/23).

[2] In celebration in his absence of Byron's coming of age.

[1] Byron's birthday which would mark his coming of age. Because of the embarrassing celebration of it by the tenants, he did not wish to be present at Newstead.

great service, every thing is prepared for your reception exactly as if I remained, & I think Hargreaves will be gratified by the appearance of the place, and the *humours* of the *day*.—I shall on the first opportunity pay my respects to your family, and though I will not trespass on your hospitality on the 22d. my obligation is not less for your agreeable offer, which on any other occasion would be immediately accepted, but I wish you much to be present at the festivities, and I hope you will add *Charles* to the party.—Consider as The Courtier says in the tragedy of "Tom Thumb"

> "This is a day your majesties may boast of it
> "And since it never can come o'er, tis fit you
> make the most of it.

I shall take my seat as soon as circumstances will admit,[2] I have not yet chosen my side in politics, nor shall I hastily commit myself with professions, or pledge my support to any man or measures, but though I shall not run headlong into opposition, I will studiously avoid a connection with ministry.—I cannot say that my opinion is strongly in favour of either party, on the one side we have the late underlings of Pitt, possessing all his ill Fortune, without his Talents, this may render their failure more excusable, but will not diminish the public contempt; on the other we have the ill assorted fragments of a worn out minority, Mr. Windham[3] with his Coat *twice* turned, and my Lord Grenville[4] who perhaps has more sense than he can make a good use of;—between the two, and the *Shuttlecock* of both, is Sidmouth[5] and the general *football* Sir F. Burdett,[6] kicked at by all, and owned by none.

---

[2] Byron's taking his seat in the House of Lords was possible only after he presented proofs of his birth and ancestry. He had hoped to avoid those formalities by being presented to the House by his kinsman and guardian Lord Carlisle.

[3] William Windham (1750–1810), a leader of the opposition to Castlereagh, had opposed the war, but in the ministry of "All the Talents" he won the nickname of "Weathercock" by changing face and supporting the war.

[4] William Wyndham Grenville, Baron Grenville (1759–1834) headed the ministry of "All the Talents" in 1806, which abolished the slave trade, but resigned on the Catholic question in 1807.

[5] Henry Addington, first viscount Sidmouth (1757–1844), a friend of Pitt, became first Lord of the Treasury and Chancellor of the Exchequer in 1801. He was later Home Secretary in the Tory government under Lord Liverpool and enforced the harsh measures against the Luddites. He thanked the troops for their part in the "Manchester Massacre".

[6] Sir Francis Burdett (1770–1844) resided in Paris in the first years of the French Revolution. In 1793 he married Miss Sophia Coutts, daughter of Thomas Coutts, the banker. He formed a friendship with Horne Tooke, the radical reformer, and was a leader of reform and of opposition to Tory repressions in Parliament. He sat for Westminster for 30 years, and was jailed several times for his outspokenness.

— — — —I shall stand aloof, speak what I think, but not often, nor too soon, I will preserve my independence, if possible, but if involved with a party, I will take care not to be the *last* or *least* in the Ranks.—As to *patriotism* The word is obsolete, perhaps improperly so, for all men in this country are patriots, knowing that their own existence must stand or fall with the Constitution, yet every body thinks he could alter it for the better, & govern a people, who are in fact easily governed but always claim the privilege of grumbling.—So much for Politics, of which I at present know little, & care less, by and bye, I shall use the Senatorial privilege of talking, and indeed in such times, and in such a crew, it must be difficult to hold one's tongue.— — — — Believe me to be with great Sincerity

yours very affectly
BYRON

[TO JOHN CAM HOBHOUSE]   *Newstead Abbey Notts.*
January 16th. 1808 [sic] [1809]

My dear Hobhouse,—I do not know how the *dens*-descended Davies came to mention his having received a copy of my epistle to you, but I addressed him & you on the same evening, & being much incensed at the account I had received from Wallace,[1] I communicated the contents to the Birdmore [sic], though without any of that malice, wherewith you charge me. I shall leave my card at Batt's, and hope to see you in your progress to the North.—I have lately discovered Scrope's genealogy to be ennobled by a collateral tie with the Beard-more, Chirurgeon and Dentist to Royalty, and that the town of Southwell contains cousins of Scrope, who disowned them, (I grieve to speak it) on visiting that city in my society.—How I found out I will disclose, the first time "we three meet again" but why did he conceal his lineage, "ah my dear H! it was *cruel*, it was *insulting*, it was *unnecessary*."—I have (notwithstanding your kind invitation to Wallace) been alone since the 8th. of December, nothing of moment has occurred since our anniversary row, except that Lucinda[2] is pregnant, and Robert[3] has recovered of the Cowpox, with which it

He was later a friend of Byron and of Hobhouse, who joined him in Parliament as a reform statesman.

[1] See Jan. 6, 1809, to Davies, note 3; April 26, 1808, to Augusta Leigh, note 2.
[2] See Jan. 17, 1809, to Hanson, note 1.
[3] Robert Rushton, son of a Newstead tenant, to whom Byron became attached. He took him along as a page on his first journey abroad, sending him back from Gibraltar.

pleased me to afflict him.—I shall be in London on the 19th. there are to be oxen roasted and Sheep boiled on the 22d. with ale and Uproar for the Mobility, a feast is also providing for the tenantry, for my own part, I shall know as little of the matter as a Corpse of the Funeral solemnized in its honour.— —A letter addressed to Reddish's will find me. I still intend publishing the Bards, but I have altered a good deal of the "Body of the Book," added & interpolated with some excisions, your lines still stand,[4] and in all there will appear 624 lines. —I should like much to see your Essay upon Entrails, is there any honorary token of silver gilt? any Cups or pounds sterling attached to the prize, besides Glory? I expect to see you with a medal suspended from your Button hole, like a Croix de St. Louis.—Fletcher's father[5] is deceased, and has left his son tway Cottages value ten pounds per annum, I know not how it is, but Fletch though only the 3d. Brother, conceives himself entitled to all the estates of the defunct, & I have recommended him to a Lawyer, who I fear will triumph in the spoils of this ancient family.—A Birthday Ode has been addressed to me by a country Schoolmaster,[6] in which I am likened to the Sun, or Sol as he classically saith, the people of Newstead are compared to Laplanders, I am said to be a Baron and a Byron, the truth of which is indisputable, Feronia is again to reign, (she must have some woods to govern first) but it is altogether a very pleasant performance, & the author is as superior to Pye,[7] as George Gordon to George Guelph. To be sure some of the lines are too short, but then to make amends, the Alexandrines have from fifteen to seventeen syllables, so we may call them Alexandrines the great.— — —I shall be glad to hear from you & beg you to believe me

yours very truly
BYRON

[TO JOHN HANSON]   *Newstead Abbey. Notts. January 17th. 1809*

My dear Sir,—I have left a Nottingham Silversmith's Bill for your examination, you will easily perceive several most enormous imposi-

---

[4] Hobhouse's lines were those on William Lisle Bowles which Byron published as part of *English Bards and Scotch Reviewers* in the first edition (lines 246–62), but substituted some of his own when he published with his name on the title page in the second edition.

[5] William Fletcher was Byron's valet.

[6] See Feb. 15, 1809, to Mr. Mayfield.

[7] Henry James Pye, Poet Laureate from 1790 to 1813, was a constant butt of contemporary ridicule. See Byron's lines on Pye in *English Bards and Scotch Reviewers* (lines 100–103), and in *The Vision of Judgment* (stanza 92).

tions in the prices, more particularly a charge of £17. 17s. 0 D.!!! for mounting a cup,— £3. 3S 0 D.!! for a Mustard pot and sundry other articles in the same proportion.—Surely the charges of these persons are not arbitrary, and I request your advice on this occasion, I will never pay the bill in its present state, and I doubt not your opinion will coincide with mine as to the enormity of the attempt to defraud.— In London the articles would have been finished for half the Sum — I shall be at Reddish's in St James Ot. where I shall be glad to see you at the time most convenient to yourself.—You will discharge my Cook, & Laundry Maid, the other two I shall retain to take care of the house, more especially as the youngest is pregnant (I need not tell you by whom) and I cannot have the girl on the parish.[1]—I wish to have some conversation with you on the subject of raising the Newstead rents, which I hear may be done without distressing the tenantry.—I have put my establishment on board wages, except Joe,[2] who must live in Clover for the rest of his days, and I shall reside in town in lodgings, with only my valet, and perhaps a Groom.—Pray ascertain the road which we claim from Chaworth, and believe me

yours very sincerely
BYRON

P.S.—I wish you would see whether Mealey pays the workmen regularly. I have settled [with] him every month, I have been talking about rebuilding the hut, as I understand the [Papilwick?—sic] folks entered an opposition.
I am ever

[TO ROBERT CHARLES DALLAS]   *Reddish's Hotel. St. James's Street.*
January 20th. 1809

Ld Byron presents his Compts. to Mr. Dallas & would be glad if Mr. D. would favour him with a Call on Sunday morning.—

[TO ROBERT CHARLES DALLAS]   *Reddish's Hotel, Jan. 25, 1809*

My dear Sir,—My only reason for not adopting your lines is because they are *your* lines. You will recollect what Lady Wortley

---

[1] Lucy (Byron called her Lucinda in his letter to Hobhouse of January 16, 1809) was the maid, whom Byron provided for with an annuity of £100, later reduced to £50 and the other £50 to go to the child. That she bore him a son is evidenced by a poem he wrote later, "To My Son": "I hail thee, dearest child of love. . . ."

[2] Joe Murray.

Montague [sic] said to Pope: "No touching, for the good will be given to you, and the bad attributed to me." I am determined it shall be all my own, except such alterations as may be absolutely requisite; but I am much obliged by the trouble you have taken and your good opinion.

The couplet on Lord C.[1] may be scratched out, and the following inserted:

> Roscommon! Sheffield! with your spirits fled,
> No future laurels deck a noble head;
> Nor e'en a hackney'd muse will deign to smile
> On minor Byron, or mature Carlisle.

This will answer the purpose of concealment. Now, for some couplets on Mr. Crabbe, which you may place after "Gifford, Sotheby, McNeil:"

> There be who say in these enlightened days,
> That splendid lies are all the poet's praise;
> That strained invention, ever on the wing,
> Alone impels the modern bard to sing,
> 'Tis true that all who rhyme, nay all who write,
> Shrink from that fatal word to genius, trite:
> Yet Truth sometimes will lend her noblest fires,
> And decorate the verse herself inspires:
> This fact in virtue's name let Crabbe attest;
> Though nature's sternest painter, yet the best.

I am sorry to differ with you with regard to the title,[2] but I mean to retain it with this addition: "The ⟨British⟩ English Bards and Scotch Reviewers:"—and, if we call it a *Satire*, it will obviate the objection, as the bards also were Welch: Your title is too humourous,—and as I know a little of Dubois,[3] I wish not to embroil myself with him, though I do not commend his treatment of * * *.

I shall be glad to hear from you, or see you, and beg you to believe me,

Yours, very sincerely,
BYRON

---

[1] Lord Carlisle.

[2] Dallas had suggested the title "The Parish Poor of Parnassus". (Dallas, *Correspondence*, I 29.)

[3] The name, omitted by Dallas, is here supplied from a quotation in a nineteenth-century bookseller's catalogue of Byron's autograph letters. Edward Dubois (1774–1850), a wit and man of letters, was a contributor to the *Morning Chronicle* under the editor Perry. He was also the editor of the *Monthly Mirror*, which reviewed *Hours of Idleness* (January 1808, pp. 28–30) with light-hearted ridicule, and ended: "If this was one of his lordship's *school exercises* at Harrow, and he escaped whipping, they have there . . . an undue respect for lords' bottoms. . . ."

[TO JOHN HANSON]   *Reddish's Hotel February 4th. 1809*

Dear Sir,—I have been thinking of the alteration in my will, & you may *make* the heir at least succeed, but in the event of his demise without issue, the property must go to my Sister's children & the Trevannions, for no Branch of Richard's[1] shall inherit if I can prevent it.—Lucy's annuity may be reduced to fifty pounds, and the other fifty go to the Bastard.[2] All the rest may stand.—I remain yours very truly

                                                          BYRON

[TO ROBERT CHARLES DALLAS]   *February 6th. 1809*

Dear Sir,—I write to correct an orthographical mistake in the name of "Pillings" which ought to be spelt *"Pillans".*[1]—I also wish much you would compare the manuscript and printed copy, for I am certain there must be nearly 650 lines in all instead of 604.—[2] Perhaps the error may be in the enumeration of the lines.—Believe me yours very truly

                                                          BYRON

[TO JOHN HANSON]   *February seventh 1809*

Dear Sir,—Do not part with your Barouch, because I believe I have found a purchaser, pray forward my business with the Chancellor.[1]

                                          Believe me yours truly
                                                          BYRON

1 Richard Byron was a younger brother of Byron's grandfather, Admiral John Byron.

2 See Jan. 17, 1809, to Hanson, note 1.

1 James Pillans (1778–1864), Rector of the High School and Professor of Humanity in the University of Edinburgh, Byron referred to as "paltry Pillans", in *English Bards and Scotch Reviewers* (line 515), probably because he thought him the reviewer of Hodgson's *Translation of Juvenal* in the *Edinburgh Review*, April, 1808.

2 There were 696 lines in the first edition of *English Bards and Scotch Reviewers*.

1 John Scott, Lord Eldon, was Lord Chancellor when Byron took his seat in the House of Lords. Hanson was gathering affidavits to establish Byron's right to his seat.

My dear Sir,—Suppose we have this couplet—

> Though sweet the sound, disdain a borrowed tone
> ⟨And quit⟩ Resign Achaia's Lyre, & strike your own.
>
> *or*
>
> Though soft the Echo, scorn a borrowed tone
> Resign Achaia's Lyre, and strike your own.[1]

So much for your admonitions, but my note of notes, my solitary Pun[2] must not be given up, no rather

> "Let mightiest of all the beasts of chase
> "That roam in woody Caledon[3]

come against me, my annotation must stand. We shall never sell a thousand, then why print so many? Did you receive my yesterdays note? I am troubling you, but I am apprehensive some of the lines are omitted by your young amanuensis, to whom however I am infinitely obliged.—believe me

yours very truly
BYRON

[TO JOHN HANSON] *February eighth. 1809*

Dear Sir,—I am *dunned* from Morn till Twilight, money I must have or quit the country, and if I do not obtain my seat immediately, I shall sail with Ld. Falkland in the Desiree Frigate for Sicily.[1]—I have a considerable sum to pay tomorrow morning and not five pounds in my purse; something must be done, pray favour me with an answer, and permission to draw for a few hundreds; I *will not* sell Newstead, let my *embarrassments* be what they may! but I would willingly relinquish my Rochdale claims to be out of debt.—I remain yours very truly

BYRON

[1] This second couplet was finally printed in *English Bards and Scotch Reviewers* (lines 889–90). Dallas had objected to the rhyme "disown"–"own" in the first draft.

[2] See note to line 1016 of *English Bards and Scotch Reviewers*: "A friend of mine being asked, why his Grace of Portland was likened to an old woman? replied, 'he supposed it was because he was past bearing.'"

[3] Unidentified.

[1] Captain Charles Cary succeeded his brother as the ninth Lord Falkland in 1796. Before he was able to leave with his frigate he was killed in a duel (see March 6, 1809, Byron to his mother).

[TO WILLIAM HARNESS]   *Reddish's Hotel, St. J's St.*
                                              February 10, 1809

. . . I do not know how you and Alma Mater agree, I was but an untoward Child myself, and I believe the good Lady and her Brat were equally rejoiced when I was weaned, and if I obtained her benediction at parting, it was at best equivocal. . . . I am obsolete amongst Harrow men, or I should desire you to present some remembrances . . . but I believe you are the sole Cantab contemporary of
                              your very sincere and affectionate
                                                         BYRON

[TO ROBERT CHARLES DALLAS]   *Feb. 11th, 1809*

I wish you to call, if possible, as I have some alterations to suggest as to the part about Brougham.[1]

                                                              B.

[TO ROBERT CHARLES DALLAS]   *February twelfth 1809*

Dear Sir,—Excuse this trouble, but I have added two lines which are necessary to complete the poetical character of Ld. C[arlisle].

— — — — — — — — — — — — — "in his age
His Scenes alone *had* damned our sinking stage
But Managers for once cried "hold enough"!
Nor drugged their audience with the tragic stuff.[1]

                              Believe me yours very truly
                                                         BYRON

[TO ROBERT CHARLES DALLAS]   *Reddish's Hotel.*
                                              February 15th. 1809

Dear Sir,—I wish you much to call on me about *one*, not later, if convenient, as I have some thirty or forty lines for addition.—Believe me
                              yours very truly
                                                         BYRON

---

[1] Byron referred to "blundering Brougham" in *English Bards and Scotch Reviewers* (line 524) apropos of a review in the *Edinburgh Review* (actually the joint work of Jeffrey and Brougham) of a book by Don Pedro de Cevallos.
[1] *English Bards and Scotch Reviewers*, lines 734–36.

[TO MR. MAYFIELD[1]]   *Reddish's Hotel, St. James's Street,*
                                                    February 15, 1809

I wish to ascertain what progress your pupils have made since my
departure, particularly Robert,[2] as I have some intention of sending
for him in a few weeks. I have to return you my thanks for your
verses and the subsequent *Birthday Ode,* though I regret your Muse
has not selected a better subject.

                                                    I remain, etc.
                                                    BYRON

[TO ROBERT CHARLES DALLAS]   *Feb. 16th, 1809*

Ecce iterum Crispinus![1]—I send you some lines to be placed after
"Gifford, Sotheby, M'Neil."[2] Pray call to-morrow any time before
two, and believe me, &c.

                                                    B.

P.S.—Print soon or I shall overflow with more rhyme.

[TO ROBERT CHARLES DALLAS]   *February 19th. 1809*

My dear Sir,—I enclose some lines to be inserted (the first six.)
after "Lords too are bards["] &c. or rather immediately following
the line—

        "Ah! who would take their titles for their rhymes"

the next four will wind up the panegyric on Lord Carlisle and come
after *"tragic stuff"*[1]
Believe me yours truly   BYRON

---

[1] See January 16, 1809, to Hobhouse.
[2] Robert Rushton.
[1] Juvenal, *Satire IV,* line 1. Lo, Crispin again (I revert to the topic I have
mentioned so often before). St. Crispin was the patron saint of cobblers, and
Byron had invoked him in line 768 of *English Bards* in speaking of Blacket, the
cobbler-poet.
[2] The line following begins: "Why slumbers Gifford?" (line 819).
[1] *English Bards . . .,* lines 736–40. The other lines were finally deleted (see
Poetry, I, 355).

Feb. 22d, 1809

A cut at the opera.—Ecce signum! from last night's observation,[1] and inuendoes against the Society for the Suppression of Vice.[2] The lines will come well in after the couplets concerning Naldi and Catalani.[3]

Yours truly
BYRON

[TO JOHN HANSON] *March 3d. 1809*

Dear Sir,—Send him off as soon as possible[1]

yours
BYRON

[TO MRS. CATHERINE GORDON BYRON] *8 St. Ja's Street.*
Mch. 6th. 1809

Dear Mother,—My last Letter was written under great depression of spirits from poor Falkland's death,[1] who has left without a shilling four children and his wife, I have been endeavouring to assist them, which God knows, I cannot do as I could wish from my own embarrassments & the many claims upon me from other quarters.— —What you say is all very true, come what may! *Newstead* and I *stand* or fall together, I have now lived on the spot, I have fixed my heart upon it, and no pressure present or future, shall induce me to barter the last vestige of our inheritance; I have that Pride within me, which will

---

[1] Byron had apparently seen at the King's Theatre on February 21st, *I Villegiatori Rezzani* in which Naldi and Catalani were the principal singers. This was followed by d'Egville's musical extravaganza, *Don Quichotte, ou les Noces de Gamache*, with Deshayes in the *corps de ballet*. This prompted his attack on the opera and the musical stage in lines 608–31 of *English Bards*.

[2] Lines 631–37.

[3] Lines 612–15.

[1] Byron was urging Hanson to send a clerk to Carhais in Cornwall for affidavits proving the marriage of his grandfather Admiral John Byron to Miss Sophia Trevanion in the private chapel there. Because of this delay, Byron did not take his seat in the House of Lords until March 13, 1809.

[1] Captain Charles John Cary, R.N., ninth Lord Falkland, married in 1803 Miss Anton, daughter of a West India merchant. He was killed in a duel after a drunken quarrel with a Mr. Powell. Byron had become friendly with him as a man about town and a tavern companion. Later he stood godfather to Falkland's posthumous child, and presented £500 to his widow, leaving it in a teacup to avoid embarrassment. (Moore, 1892, ed., p. 77n.)

enable me to support difficulties, I can endure privations, but could I obtain in exchange for Newstead Abbey the first fortune in the country, I would reject the proposition.—Set your mind at ease on that score. Mr. Hanson talks like a man of Business on the subject, I feel like a man of honour, and I will not sell Newstead.—I shall get my seat on the return of the affidavits from Carhais in Cornwall, and will do something in the house soon, I must dash, or it is all over.—My Satire must be kept secret for a *month*, after that you may say what you please on the subject.—Ld. Carlisle has used me so infamously & refused to state any particular of my family to the Chancellor, I have *lashed* him in my *rhymes*, and perhaps his Lordship may regret not being more conciliatory.² — — —They tell me it will have a sale, I hope so for the Bookseller has behaved well as far as publishing well goes.—

Believe me yours truly
BYRON

P.S.—You shall have a mortgage on one of the *farms*.—³

[TO FRANCIS HODGSON]   *8 St. James's Street March sixth 1809*

Dear Hodgson,—"Si vis, fac iterum" I am very sorry to hear of your embarrassments, and if I can be of any service in any way command me, excuse haste I am just come from Harrow where I dined with Drury.

yours truly
BYRON

P.S.—I send a draft as notes are *bulky*¹

² Byron probably believed erroneously that Lord Carlisle withheld information that he might have given about Byron's ancestry which could have smoothed the way for his entry into the House of Lords.

³ His mother had made herself liable for his debt of £1,000 borrowed from Wylde & Co., bankers, of Southwell, and the Misses Parkyns and his great aunt Mrs. George Byron. No mortgage was given, and Mrs. Byron died before the debt was repaid. Mrs. George Byron had contributed £500, Miss E. and F. Parkyns £300, and Wylde the banker £200. (Letter of Mrs. Byron to Hanson, March 15, 1809. Willis W. Pratt, *Byron at Southwell*, p. 106.)

¹ This was apparently the first of Byron's "loans" to Hodgson. Over the next few years he made several more loans intended as gifts and treated as such, usually when he was himself in great financial difficulty.

My dear Harness,—There was no necessity for all the excuses with which your letter teems, if you have time & inclination to write, "for what we receive the Lord make us thankful!" if I do not hear from you, I console myself with the idea that you are much more agreeably employed.—*I send down to you by this post a certain Satire lately published, and in return for three and sixpence expenditure upon it, only beg that if you should guess the author, you will keep his name secret, at least for the present.*—"Dear London" is full of this duke's business,[1] the commons have been at it these last three nights, and are not yet come to a decision, I do not know if the affair will be brought before our house, unless in the shape of an impeachment, if It makes it's appearance in a debatable form, I believe I shall be tempted to say something on the subject.—I am glad to hear you like Cambridge, firstly because to know that you are happy is pleasant to one who wishes you all possible sublunary enjoyment, and in the last place, I admire the novelty of the sentiment.—Alma Mater was to me "injusta Noverca" and the old Beldam only gave me my M. A. degree because she could not avoid it, you know what a farce a noble Cantab must perform.—[2] I am going abroad if possible in the spring, and before I depart, I am collecting the pictures of my most intimate Schoolfellows, I have already a few, and shall want yours or my cabinet will be incomplete.—I have employed one of the first miniature painters of the day to take them, of course at my own expense as I never allow my acquaintance to incur the least expenditure to gratify a whim of mine.—To mention this may seem indelicate, but when I tell you that a friend at first refused to sit, under the idea that he was to disburse on the occasion, you will see that it is necessary to state these preliminaries to prevent the recurrence of any similar mistake.— — I shall see you in town and will carry you to the *Limner*,[3] it will be a tax on your patience for a week, but pray excuse it, as it is possible the resemblance may be the sole trace I shall be able to preserve of our past friendship & present acquaintance.—Just now it seems foolish enough, but in a few years when some of us are dust, and others are

1 Col. Gwyllym Wardle had brought charges of accepting bribes for commissions against the Duke of York and his mistress, Mary Ann Clarke. The inquiry into the charges lasted from January 27 to March 20, 1809, and ended in the duke's resignation as commander-in-chief of the army. Wardle was later made famous by Dickens who brought him into *Pickwick Papers.*
2 Byron took his M.A. degree at Cambridge on July 4, 1808.
3 George Sanders, who painted several portraits and miniatures of Byron, and whom he had engaged to paint miniatures of several of his Harrow friends.

separated by inevitable circumstances, it will be a kind of satisfaction to retrace in these images of the living the idea of our former selves, and to contemplate in the resemblances of the dead, all that remains of judgment, feeling, and a host of passions.—But all this will be dull enough for you and so, good night, to end my chapter or rather homily in an orthodox manner, "as it was in the beginning, is now & ever shall be" believe me my dear H.

yours most affectly.
BYRON

[TO FRANCIS HODGSON] *March 21st. 1809*

Dear Hodgson,—I send you the contents of my last, and only regret that I cannot at present double them,[1] for the sins of my minority have risen up against me in the shape of long Bills.—As to my Satire, I defy the scribblers and had I been fearful of the effects of these "paper Bullets of the Brain to awe a man from the career of his humour" I should have been silent altogether.—
Believe me Dear H. yours truly   BYRON

P.S.—Will you come to Newstead?

[TO WILLIAM BANKES] *Twelve o'clock, Friday night [March, 1809?]*

My dear Bankes,—I have just received your note; believe me I regret most sincerely that I was not fortunate enough to see it before, as I need not repeat to you, that your conversation for half an hour would have been much more agreeable to me than gambling or drinking, or any other fashionable mode of passing an evening abroad or at home.—I really am very sorry that I went out previous to the arrival of your despatch; in future pray let me hear from you before six, and whatever my engagements may be, I will always postpone them.—Believe me, with that deference which I have always from my childhood paid to your *talents*, and with somewhat a better opinion of your heart than I have hitherto entertained,

Yours ever &c.

[1] See March 6, 1809, to Hodgson.

[TO JOHN HANSON]   *Newstead Abbey, April 4th. 1809*

Dear Sir,—I wish to hear if you have procured me a *Mortgage*,[1] as I must settle that Business directly, pray let me know because if not, I shall apply to the first person in any money concern, I have taken the Malta packet for May next.—When will the money be paid out of court?—the Norfolk copyholds sold? I wish to grant you a power of Attorney in my absence.—Believe me

yours truly
BYRON

[TO JOHN HANSON]   *Newstead Abbey. Notts. April 8th. 1809*

Dear Sir,—It is of the utmost consequence I should learn whether you have procured me a mortgage on Newstead, or if not, or if I do not hear from you directly I must raise money on very bad terms next week.—I have taken the Malta Packet for May, and if not ready shall forfeit my passage money and Baggage part of which is sent off.— Pray write

yours truly
BYRON

[TO JAMES WEDDERBURN WEBSTER]   *Newstead Abbey. Notts.*
April 12. 1809

Dear Webster,—I shall be very happy to see you again with or without the immortal Davies, pray come down soon as I am obliged to be in town on the 23d.—Your seal will be very acceptable and no doubt the motto will be classical. I hope your watch is in the custody of [Stracey?] for here it is not.—Believe me Dr. W.

yours very sincerely
BYRON

[TO JOHN HANSON]   *Newstead Abbey. Notts. April 12th. 1809*

Dear Sir,—I am obliged to draw on you for two hundred & sixty four pounds the amount of my stone mason's Bill, fourteen days after date.— —Before that time you will have the Cash out of court, and no

---

[1] Hanson was trying to get a mortgage on Newstead to prevent Byron from borrowing further from the usurers, but he was unsuccessful.

doubt, (at least I hope so) take care of yourself.—It is very singular, I have heard nothing from you on the subject of mortgage, I sail on May 6th and if you do not write directly, I must raise money as I can, of course disadvantageously.—Believe me

yours truly
BYRON

[TO E. B. LONG[1]]　　　　　　*Newstead Abbey Notts. April 14th. 1809*

Sir,—If I possessed any memorial of my late lamented friend,[2] however unwilling I might be to deliver it to any other claimant, on the present occasion I should not hesitate a moment to gratify the feelings of a parent, even at the expence of my own.—But unfortunately I have no token of remembrance in my possession except your son's letters, and my own regret that I have retained no other memorandum, which would still be soothing, though unnecessary.—God knows! his death has been a heavy blow to me, but the expression of my own grief, would be a mockery of yours, I shall therefore be silent.—
I am about to leave England in a few weeks, but shall endeavour to comply with your request, and furnish the inscription before my departure.—At this moment I confess myself unequal to the attempt, if I had been required to write an epitaph on a person totally indifferent to me, I should have succeeded better, but

> "What mourner ever felt poetic fires?
> "Slow flows the verse that real woe inspires.[3]

You shall however have my humble effort to perpetuate Edward's memory before I sail, and with my best respects to Mrs. Long, I beg you to believe me

your sincere & obedt. Servt.
BYRON

[TO JOHN HANSON]　　　　　*Newstead Abbey. Notts. April 16th 1809*

Dear Sir,—If the consequences of my leaving England, were ten times as ruinous as you describe, I have no alternative, there are cir-

---

[1] E. B. Long, the father of Byron's friend Edward Noel Long, lived at Hampton Lodge, Farnham.

[2] Edward Noel Long, Byron's friend at Harrow and Cambridge, had entered the Coldstream Guards. He was drowned early in 1809 on the passage to Lisbon with his regiment when his transport the *St. George* collided with another in the night.

[3] Unidentified.

cumstances which render it absolutely indispensible, and quit the country I must immediately.—[1]

My passage is taken, and the 6th of May will be the day of my departure from Falmouth, I shall be in town on the 22d. of this month, and must raise money on any terms, all I now look forward [to] is this one object, I have nothing further to say on the subject.—I had given the Mason the draft, which I am sorry for, but I trust you will not dishonour it & *me*.—I am pestered to death in country and town, and rather than submit to my present situation, I would abandon every thing, even had I not still stronger motives for urging my departure.— I remain

yours very truly
BYRON

[TO JOHN HANSON]   *Newstead Abbey. April seventeen 1809*

Dear Sir,—The Duke of Portland owes me a thousand pounds,[1] if possible get the principal, as well as the interest which may be due, pray attend to this as I must have cash any way & every way, & the best beginning is to collect what is our own.—

yours sincerely
BYRON

[TO ROBERT CHARLES DALLAS]   *April 25th, 1809*

Dear Sir,—I am just arrived at Batt's Hotel, Jermyn-street, St James's, from Newstead, and shall be very glad to see you when convenient or agreeable. Hobhouse is on his way up to town, full of printing resolution, and proof against criticism.

Believe me, with great sincerity,

Yours truly,
BYRON

[1] What Byron's urgent reasons for leaving England were at this time has never been revealed. In writing to Hanson from Greece he referred to some secret reason for his not wanting to live in England. See Nov. 12, 1809, to Hanson.

[1] The Duke of Portland owed £1,000 to the Byron estate, for which he had given a mortgage on which he had failed to pay the interest for a number of years. (Hanson and Birch accounts, Murray MSS.)

Dear Sir,—I wish to know before I make my final effort elsewhere, if you can or cannot assist me in raising a sum of money on fair and equitable terms and immediately.—I called twice this morning, and beg you will favour me with an answer when convenient. I hope all your family are well, I should like to see them together before my departure.—The court of Chancery it seems will not pay the money, of which indeed I do not know the precise amount;[1] the Duke of Portland will not pay his debt,[2] and with the Rochdale people nothing is done.— My debts are daily increasing, and it is with difficulty I can command a shilling, as soon as possible I shall quit this country, but I wish to do justice to my creditors (though I do not like their importunity,) more particularly to my *securities*, for their annuities must be paid off soon, or the Interest will swallow up every thing, come what may, in every shape, and in any shape I can meet ruin, but I will never sell Newstead, the Abbey and I shall stand or fall together, and were my head as grey and defenseless as the Arch of the Priory, I would abide by this Resolution.—The whole of my wishes are summed up in this, procure me either of my own, or borrowed from others, three thousand pounds, place two in Hammersley's Hands for Letters of credit at Constantinople, if possible sell Rochdale in my absence, pay off these annuities and my debts, and with the little that remains do as you will, but allow me to depart from this cursed country, and I promise to turn *Mussulman* rather than return to it.—

Believe me to be yours truly
BYRON

P.S.—Is my will finished? I should like to sign it, while I have any thing to leave.—[3]

1 The money from the Court of Chancery may have been some arrears from his own allowance or his mother's.

2 See April 17, 1809, to Hanson, note 1.

3 Byron signed this will June 14, 1809, before leaving on his first journey abroad. In it he bequeathed £25 a year for life to Robert Rushton, the page boy whom he took with him as far as Gibraltar. He requested that his library be given to the Earl of Clare, all his lands and property to Hobhouse and Hanson, and £500 a year for life to his mother. He expressed the desire "to be buried in the vault at Newstead Abbey with as little Pomp as possible—No Burial service or Clergyman or any Monument or Inscription of any Kind" except the date of his death and his initials. The monument over his dog was not to be disturbed when he was laid beside it.

[TO JOHN HANSON]   *Batt's Hotel. May 2d. 1809*

Dear Sir,—Have you heard further from his Grace,[1] or the other person from the city, pray make the arrangements as soon as possible, as I positively must go.—I enclose a Letter from the *Beldam.*—[2]

Believe me yrs. very truly
BYRON

[TO THE REV. ROBERT LOWE[1]]   *8 St. James's Street, May 15, 1809*

My dear Sir,—I have just been informed that a report is circulating in Notts of an intention on my part to sell Newstead, which is rather unfortunate, as I have just tied the property up in such a manner as to prevent the practicability, even if my inclination led me to dispose of it. But as such a report may render my tenants uncomfortable, I will feel very much obliged if you will be good enough to contradict the rumour, should it come to your ears, on my authority. I rather conjecture it has arisen from the sale of some copyholds of mine in Norfolk.[2] I sail for Gibraltar in June, and thence to Malta when, of course, you shall have the promised detail. I saw your friend Thornhill last night, who spoke of you as a friend ought to do. Excuse this trouble, and believe me to be, with great sincerity,

Yours affectionately,
BYRON

[TO MRS. CATHERINE GORDON BYRON]   *8 St. James's Street.*
                                             May nineteen 1809

Dear Mother,—I have detected Fletcher in a connection with prostitutes, and of taking to a woman of the town the very boy[1] whom I had committed to his charge, which lad he sent home with a lie in his mouth to screen them both, after the most strict injunctions on my part to watch over his *morals*, & keep him from the *temptations* of this *accursed place.*—I have sent the lad to his father; before this occurrence he was good hearted, honest, and all I could wish him, and would have been so still, but for the machinations of the scoundrel who has not only been guilty of adultery, but of depraving the mind of an innocent stripling, for no other motive, but that which actuates the devil himself,

---

[1] The Duke of Portland. See April 17, 1809, to Hanson.

[2] Mrs. Byron, his mother.

[1] The Rev. Robert Lowe, a resident of Southwell, was a cousin of Elizabeth Pigot.

[2] At Wymondham the wife of the fifth Lord Byron had copyholds which came into the possession of Byron. Hanson sold them while the poet was abroad in 1810.

[1] Robert Rushton. See April 26, 1809, to Hanson, note 3.

namely, to plunge another in equal infamy.— —For his wife's sake he shall have a farm or other provision of some kind, but he quits me the moment I have provided a servant.—I sail on the 16th June.— —Break this business to his wife, who will probably hear it from the boy's relatives in another manner.—Did you ever hear any thing so diabolical? he did not even deny it, for I found the address of the strumpet, written in *his own hand*, which I have sent in a letter to Mealey, pray get the paper from M. and *keep* it *carefully*. I have a reason for it.— —

Pray write soon, & believe me

yrs. ever
BYRON

[TO JOHN HANSON]   *8 St. James's Street London May 23d. 1809*

Dear Sir,—Your quitting town has put me to the greatest inconvenience, it is really hard with some funds to be compelled to drink the dregs of the cup of Poverty in this manner,—I have not five pounds in my possession.—I do hope the money will be procured for I certainly must leave England on the fifth of June, & by every power that directs the lot of man, I will quit England if I have only cash to pay my passage. I have long told you my determination, & beg leave once more to repeat that I cannot be detained any longer.—This is the *third* month, in which the money was to be paid from chancery, if I cannot give security for the sum to be borrowed, this week, I cannot do it six months hence, —in short I have made all my arrangements, and I do request that you will not treat me like a child, but assist me as my Friend, and as quickly as you can without putting yourself to inconvenience.—Pray let me hear from you, on your return to town. I remain

yrs. very truly
BYRON

[TO JOSEPH MURRAY]   *8 St. James's Street, June 6, 1809*

Mr. Murray, the moment you receive this you will set off for London in some of the coaches with Robert,[1] & take care that he conducts himself properly—Be quick.

[TO JOHN HANSON]   *June 19th. 1809*

Sir,—In consequence of the delay, I have been under the necessity

---

[1] Byron had characteristically forgiven Robert Rushton for his peccadillo (see May 19, 1809, to his mother) and had decided to take him along on his voyage.

of giving Thomas[1] an annuity for his bond, and taking up further monies on annuity at seven years purchase to the *tune* of four hundred per annum altogether including T's bond.— — — —For the payment of this half yearly you will deduct from the money of Sawbridge[2] when complete, and be good enough to place three thousand in Hammersley's hands,[3] & let my letters of credit be sent to Falmouth Post office, where I will take care in case of my departure that they shall follow me to Gibraltar or elsewhere.—I am now setting off, and remain

your very obedt. Servt.
BYRON

[TO JOHN HANSON (*a*)]   *Wynn's Hotel. Falmouth June 21st. 1809*

Dear Sir,—As it is probable the Packet will not sail for some days, let my Letters of Credit be sent if possible either to the Post office or to this Inn.—Believe me

yrs. &c.
BYRON

[TO JOHN HANSON (*b*)]   *Falmouth, June 21, 1809*

Sir,—I enclose you two letters, when the six thousand pounds[1] is paid which it ought to have been by this time, at least a considerable part of it, you will deduct the sums for the annuities till Rochdale & Wymondham[2] can be sold.—The Draft which you have dishonoured I left money in your hands to pay for, and if you please to recollect there could probably be a balance though a trifling one in my favour even after the payments; the sum was either two hundred & ninety seven or three hundred & 97 I do not know which, but admitting it to be the smaller sum, it was your duty to have paid ninety seven as I had only given a draft for 200 out of the sum to Messrs Stevens.—

I remain your obedt. Sert.
BYRON

[1] The money-lender from whom Byron had earlier borrowed considerable sums. See letter of Jan. 16, 1812, to Hanson.

[2] Sawbridge, a friend of Hanson's partner Birch, had agreed to lend Byron £6,000, but only £2,000 had been received before Byron left England.

[3] Hammersley was the international banker with agents in Malta and Constantinople.

[1] The Sawbridge loan. See June 19, 1809, to Hanson, note 2.

[2] Hanson finally sold the Wymondham estate in Norfolk for £4,400, but the money was not immediately forthcoming because of a legal technicality concerning the title. (Hanson business letters, Murray MSS.)

Dear Mother,—I am about to sail in a few days, probably before this reaches you; Fletcher begged so hard that I have continued him in my service,[1] if he does not behave well abroad, I will send him back in a *transport*.—I have a German servant[2] who has been with Mr. Wilbraham in Persia before, and was strongly recommended to me by Dr. Butler of Harrow, Robert, and William,[3] they constitute my whole suite.—I have letters in plenty.—You shall hear from me at different ports I touch upon, but you must not be alarmed if my letters miscarry.—The Continent is in a fine state! an Insurrection has broken out at Paris, and the Austrians are beating Buonaparte, the Tyrolese have risen.—There is a picture of me in oil to be sent down to Newstead soon,[4] I wish the Miss Parkyns's had something better to do than carry my miniature to Nottingham to copy.— — —[5] Now they have done it, you may ask them to copy the others, which are greater favourites than my own.— — —As to money matters I am ruined, at least till Rochdale is sold, & if that does not turn out well I shall enter the Austrian or Russian service, perhaps the Turkish, if I like their manners, the world is all before me, and I leave England without regret, and without a wish to revisit any thing it contains, except *yourself*, and your present residence.— — — —
Believe me yours ever sincerely   BYRON

P.S.—Pray tell Mr. Rushton his son is well, and *doing* well, so is Murray, indeed better than I ever saw him, he will be back in about a month, I ought to add leaving Murray to my few regrets, as his age perhaps will prevent my seeing him again; Robert I take with me, I like him, because like myself he seems to be a friendless animal.—

My dear Mathieu,—I take up the pen which our friend has for a moment laid down merely to express a vain wish that you were with us in this delectable region, as I do not think Georgia itself can emulate

---

[1] See May 19, 1809, to his mother.

[2] The German servant's name was Friese. Byron sent him back from Gibraltar.

[3] At Gibraltar Byron sent back all his servants except William Fletcher, who remained with him for the rest of his (Byron's) life.

[4] The painting was by George Sanders.

[5] Byron had stayed with the Parkyns family in Nottingham in 1799. The two Parkyns girls apparently took a romantic interest in him. A number of their letters to him are among the Murray MSS. See Nov. 8, 1798, to Mrs. Parker, note 2.

in capabilities or incitements to the "Plen. and optabil.—Coit."[1] the port of Falmouth & parts adjacent.— —We are surrounded by Hyacinths[2] & other flowers of the most fragrant [na]ture, & I have some intention of culling a handsome Bouquet to compare with the exotics we expect to meet in Asia.—One specimen I shall certainly carry off, but of this hereafter.—Adieu Mathieu!— —

[TO JOHN HANSON]   *Falmouth June 25. 1809*

Sir,—You will be good enough to forward the letters of credit when ready to Falmouth where I will give directions to Messrs Fox & Co the principal house in the port (to whom I have letters from London) that they may be sent to Malta, or Constantinople.—They ought to have arrived by this time; with regard to the servants who applied for characters, I am generally well satisfied with their conduct when in my service, which they were only for a few months, I believe they are sober & honest.— —It was with considerable regret I left town without taking leave of Mrs. Hanson & the family, believe me I wish them all the prosperity & pleasure that may be adequate to their welfare & happiness.— —I have one word to add about Rochdale[;] when it is sold, I wish the purchase money to be applied to the liquidation of my debts of all descriptions, and what overplus there may be (if any) to be laid out in securing annuities for my own life at as many years purchase as it may be lawful & right to obtain; you see I must turn Jew myself at last.— — — —

                    I remain your very obedt. Servt.
                                        BYRON

[1] The Latin abbreviation Byron quoted (with some confusion of cases and genders) in this letter and several times later is a phrase in the *Satyricon* of Petronius (para. 86, sec. 4): *"coitum plenum et optabilem"* ("complete intercourse to one's heart's desire"). In Petronius the narrator tells how he overcame the reluctance of a boy. I am indebted to Professor Gilbert Highet for tracing the quotation.

[2] There is no doubt some understood significance in the innuendoes of this sentence, probably referring to the boy-love common in the East. Hyacinth was a Laconian youth beloved by Apollo. The name had connotations of young male beauty in ancient Greek, but Byron has used it in a context to suggest definite homosexual associations. In a letter of August 23, 1810, from Athens, Byron wrote to Hobhouse: ". . . the Signore Nicolo also laved, but he makes as bad a hand in the water as L'Abbe Hyacinth at Falmouth". This would suggest that he had a particular person in mind, either one who bore that name or to whom he gave it as a nickname.

My dear Drury,—We sail tomorrow in the Lisbon packet having been detained till now by the lack of wind and other necessaries, these being at last procured, by this time tomorrow evening we shall be embarked on the vide vorld of vaters vor all the vorld like Robinson Crusoe.— — — —The Malta vessel not sailing for some weeks we have determined to go by way of Lisbon, and as my servants term it to see "that there *Portingale*" thence to Cadiz and Gibraltar and so on our old route to Malta and Constantinople, if so be that Capt. Kidd our gallant or rather gallows commander understands plain sailing and Mercator, and takes us on our voyage all according to the Chart. — — —Will you tell Dr. Butler that I have taken the treasure of a servant Friese the native of Prussia Proper into my service from his recommendation.— —He has been all among the worshippers of Fire in Persia and has seen Persepolis and all that.—Hobhouse has made woundy preparations for a book at his return, 100 pens two gallons Japan Ink, and several vols best blank is no bad provision for a discerning Public.—I have laid down my pen, but have promised to contribute a chapter on the state of morals, and a further treatise on the same to be entituled "Sodomy simplified or Paederasty proved to be praiseworthy from ancient authors and modern practice."—Hobhouse further hopes to indemnify himself in Turkey for a life of exemplary chastity at home by letting out his "fair bodye" to the whole Divan.— Pray buy his missellingany as the Printer's Devil calls it, I suppose 'tis in print by this time. Providence has interposed in our favour with a fair wind to carry us out of its reach, or he would have hired a Faquir to translate it into the Turcoman Lingo.— —

> "The Cock is crowing
> "I must be going
> "And can no more

> *Ghost of Gaffer Thumb*[1]
> Adieu believe me yours as in duty bound
> BYRON

turn over

P.S.—We have been sadly fleabitten at Falmouth.— —

[1] Byron was quoting from an adaptation by Kane O'Hara of Fielding's burlesque. *The Tragedy of Tragedies: or the Life and Death of Tom Thumb the Great* as played at the Theatre Royal Haymarket, in 1805.

Dear Ellice,—You will think me a very sad dog for not having written a long acknowledgement of what I really feel, viz, a sincere sense of the many favours I have received at your hands concerning my coming Tour.²—But if you knew the hurry I have been in & the natural laziness of my disposition, you would excuse an omission which cannot be attributed to neglect, or ingratitude.—I beg you will now accept my very hearty thanks for the divers troubles you have had on my account, which I am sure no person but yourself would have taken for so worthless an animal, I am afraid I shall never have any opportunity of repaying them, except by a promise that they shall not be repeated.—We are waiting here for a wind & other necessaries, nothing of moment has occurred in the town save castigation of one of the fair sex at a Cart's tail yesterday morn, whose hands had been guilty of "picking & stealing" and whose tongue of "evil speaking" for she stole a Cock, and *damned* the corporation; she was much whipped but exceeding impenitent.—I shall say nothing of Falmouth because I know it, & you dont, a very good reason for being silent as I can say nothing in it's favour, or you hear any thing that would be agreeable.—The Inhabitants both female & male, at least the young ones, are remarkably handsome, and how the devil they came to be so, is the marvel! for the place is apparently not favourable to Beauty.— — — The Claret is good, and Quakers plentiful, so are Herrings salt & fresh, there is a fort called St. Mawes off the harbour, which we were nearly taken up on suspicion of having carried by storm, it is well defended by one able-bodied man of eighty years old, six ancient demi-culverins, that would exceedingly annoy anybody—except an enemy;—and parapet walls which would withstand at least half a dozen kicks of any given grenadier in the kingdom of France.—
Adieu believe me

your obliged & sincere
BYRON

¹ Edward Ellice (1781–1863), of an Aberdeenshire family, was the son of Alexander Ellice, managing director of the Hudson's Bay Company. Edward married the widow of Captain George Bettesworth, Byron's cousin, who was killed off Bergen in 1808. His wife was a daughter of Earl Grey. After serving an apprenticeship in the fur trade in America, Ellice entered politics, and was, like Sir Francis Burdett, a reformer with means to be independent. He was allied with Hobhouse and Burdett in reform politics in the twenties, and played an important part in the passing of the first Reform Bill. From 1818 he was M.P. for Coventry.

² The favours rendered by Ellice to Byron in connection with his tour may have been to assist him to get introductions abroad, or, more probably, to procure him a loan, which he had been trying desperately to get before leaving.

My dear Hodgson,—Before this reaches you, Hobhouse, two officers' wives, three children two waiting maids, ditto subalterns for the troops, three Portuguese esquires, and domestics, in all nineteen souls will have sailed in the Lisbon packet with the noble Capt. Kidd, a gallant commander as ever smuggled an anker of right Nantz.— — We are going to Lisbon first, because the Malta Packet has sailed d'ye see? from Lisbon to Gibraltar, Malta, Constantinople and "all that," as Orator Henley said when he put the Church and "all that" in danger.[1]—This town of Falmouth as you will partly conjecture is no great ways from the sea, it is defended on the seaside by tway castles St. Mawes, & Pendennis, extremely well calculated for annoying every body except an enemy, St. Mawes is garrisoned by an able bodied person of fourscore, a widower, he has the whole command and sole management of six most unmanageable pieces of ordnance admirably adapted for the destruction of Pendennis a like tower of strength on the opposite side of the Channel, we have seen St. Mawes, but Pendennis they will not let us behold, save at a distance, because Hobhouse & I are suspected of having already taken St. Mawes by a Coup de Main.— —The Town contains many Quakers and salt-fish, the oysters have a taste of copper owing to the soil of a mining country, the women (blessed be the Corporation therefore!) are flogged at the cart's tail when they pick and steal, as happened to one of the fair sex yesterday noon, she was pertinacious in her behaviour, and damned the Mayor.—This is all I know of Falmouth, nothing of note occurred in our way down, except that on Hartford Bridge we changed horses at an Inn where the great Apostle of Paederasty Beckford! sojourned for the night, we tried in vain to see the Martyr of prejudice, but could not; what we thought singular, though you perhaps will not, was that Ld. Courtney travelled the same night on the *same road* only one stage *behind* him.— — — — —[2] Hodgson! remember me to the Drury, and remember me to yourself when drunk;—I am not worth a sober thought.—Look to my satire at Cawthorn's Cockspur Street, and look to the Miscellany of the Hobhouse[;] it has pleased Providence to interfere in behalf of a suffering Public by giving him a sprained wrist so that he cannot write, and there is a cessation of inkshed.— —I don't know when I can write again, because it depends on that ex-

[1] In his *Oratory Transactions*, Henley boasted of his system and said he would persevere until he had "put the Church, *and all that*, in danger".

[2] Lord Courtney's attachment to Beckford was apparently common knowledge at the time, as was also Beckford's homosexual proclivities.

perienced navigator Capt. Kidd, and the "stormy winds that—(dont) blow" at this season.— —I leave England without regret, I shall return to it without pleasure.— —I am like Adam the first convict sentenced to transportation, but I have no Eve, and have eaten no apple but what was sour as a crab and thus ends my first Chapter. Adieu yrs ever

BYRON

[TO FRANCIS HODGSON]   *Falmouth Roads—June 30th 1809*

1

Huzza! Hodgson, we are going,
  Our embargo's off at last
Favourable Breezes blowing
  Bend the canvass oer the mast,
From aloft the signal's streaming
  Hark! the farewell gun is fired,
Women screeching, Tars blaspheming,
  Tells us that our time's expired
    Here's a rascal
    Come to task all
Prying from the custom house,
    Trunks unpacking
    Cases cracking
Not a corner for a mouse
Scapes unsearched amid the racket
Ere we sail on board the Packet.—

2

Now our boatmen quit their mooring
  And all hands must ply the oar;
Baggage from the quay is lowering,
  We're impatient—push from shore—
"Have a care! that Case holds liquor
  "Stop the boat—I'm sick—oh Lord!
"Sick Maam! damme, you'll be sicker
  Ere you've been an hour on board
    Thus are screaming
    Men & women

211

Gemmen, Ladies, servants, Jacks,
   Here entangling
   All are wrangling
Stuck together close as wax,
Such the genial noise & racket
Ere we reach the Lisbon Packet,

3

Now we've reached her, lo! the Captain
  Gallant Kidd commands the crew
Passengers *now* their berths are clapt in
  Some to grumble, some to spew,
Heyday! call you that a Cabin?
  Why tis hardly three feet square
Not enough to stow Queen Mab in,
  Who the deuce can harbour there?
    Who Sir? plenty
    Nobles twenty
Did at once my vessel fill
    Did they—Jesus!
    How you squeeze us
  Would to God, they did so still,
Then I'd scape the heat & racket
Of the good ship, Lisbon Packet.

––––––––––––

Note + Erratum—
  For *"gallant"* read *"gallows."*—

4

Fletcher, Murray, Bob, where are you?
  Stretched along the deck like logs
Bear a hand—you jolly tar you!
  Here's a rope's end for the dogs,
Hobhouse muttering fearful curses
  As the hatchway down he rolls
Now his breakfast, now his verses
  Vomits forth & damns our souls,
    Here's a stanza
    On Braganza

Help!—a couplet—no, a cup
  Of warm water,
   What's the matter?
Zounds! my liver's coming up,
I shall not survive the racket
Of this brutal Lisbon Packet.—

5

Now at length we're off for Turkey,
  Lord knows when we shall come back,
Breezes foul, & tempests murkey,
  May unship us in a crack,
But since life at most a jest is
  As Philosophers allow
Still to laugh by far the best is,
  Then laugh on—as I do now,
    Laugh at all things
    Great & small things,
Sick or well, at sea or shore,
    While we're quaffing
    Let's have laughing
Who the Devil cares for more?
Save good wine, & who would lack it?
Even on board the Lisbon Packet.

BYRON

[TO JOHN HANSON]   *Falmouth. June 30th. 1809*

   Sir,—I have to acknowledge the receipt of the letter of credit.—
The Codicil supersedes the necessity of a bond to Mr. Davies[1] who
professes himself merely to be anxious for security in case of my demise,
besides it is for 10000 £ and Mr. D only stands pledged for £6000,
it is true I offered to sign any satisfactory instrument for Mr. Davies,
but I think the codicil sufficient, without a Bond of indemnity which
shifts the responsibility completely, now as there must be a reliance
either on my part upon Mr. D. or on Mr. D's upon me, I see no
reason why it should not stand in its present state, as the annuities

   [1] See Nov. 26, 1810, to Hobhouse, note 4. Though Davies was "pledged for
£6000", he may have given Byron less than that, for £6,300 seems to have
repaid the whole of Byron's debt with interest after several years.

are fully intended to be redeemed the moment the estates are sold. I remain your very obedt. Servt.

BYRON

P.S.—The Packet is getting under weigh & we sail in a few hours, so that no further communications to Falmouth will reach me.—

[TO JOHN HANSON]   *3d.* [*sic*] [*2d.?*] *July 1809*[1]

Dear Sir/—You will see by the enclosed Letter from Mrs. Massingberd the necessity of coming to some arrangement immediately

I remain yr very sincere
BYRON

[TO JOHN HANSON]   *Lisbon. July 13th. 1809*

Sir,—I have been purchasing a few things of the Honble. J. Ward,[1] who as he is proceeding to England prefers a draft on London, you will pay him on demand thirty pounds sterling.— — —I suppose you have by this time arranged the Norfolk sale & the rest of Col. Sawbridge's business.[2]—I proceed to Gibraltar immediately, & on to *Malta* & Constantinople.—I do not suppose I shall want money for some time but in case of accidents, it will be as well to enable Hammersley to make further remittances against next Spring, when I presume Rochdale will be sold.—I hope your family are all well, if you address to me at Malta, a letter will find me or be forwarded.—I have no intention of returning to England, unless compelled so to do. I only regret I did not quit it sooner.— —This country is in a state of

---

1 Since Byron sailed for Lisbon on July 2, 1809, the date of this letter cannot be correct unless it was mailed from Lisbon. It could have been July 3, 1808, or more probably July 2, 1809. Another possibility is January [Jy.?] 3, 1809.

1 John William Ward (1781–1833) afterward first Earl of Dudley and Ward, became a close friend of Byron during the poet's years of fame in London. He was educated at Oriel and Corpus Christi Colleges, Oxford, and afterwards studied with Dugald Stewart. He became Foreign Minister in the Canning administration. Ward first met Byron in Lisbon and "perceived that he was a person of no common mind", but he later boasted that Byron's extraordinary mind "by no means prevented me from cheating him extremely in the sale of some English saddles with which I equipped him at Lisbon". (Dudley, p. 163.)

2 Col. Sawbridge had agreed to lend Byron £6,000, but provided only £2,000 before Byron left England. Hanson later received £4,000 from Sawbridge, put £1,000 with the international bankers Hammersley for Byron's use, and paid annuity debts with the rest. (Hanson business letters, Murray MSS.)

great disorder, but beautiful in itself, the army is in Spain, and a battle is daily expected. I remain

yr. very obedt. Servt.

BYRON

The Draft is dated London, as no stamps are to be had here.— —

[TO FRANCIS HODGSON]   *Lisbon, July 16th, 1809*

Thus far have we pursued our route, and seen all sorts of marvellous sights, palaces, convents, &c.—which, being to be heard in my friend Hobhouse's forthcoming Book of Travels, I shall not anticipate by smuggling any account whatsoever to you in a private and clandestine manner. I must just observe that the village of Cintra in Estramadura is the most beautiful, perhaps in the world. * * *

I am very happy here, because I loves oranges, and talk bad Latin to the monks, who understand it, as it is like their own,—and I goes into society (with my pocket-pistols),[1] and I swims in the Tagus all across at once,[2] and I rides on an ass or a mule, and swears Portuguese, and have got a diarrhœa and bites from the mosquitoes. But what of that? Comfort must not be expected by folks that go a pleasuring. * * *

When the Portuguese are pertinacious, I say, "Carracho!"—the great oath of the grandees, that very well supplies the place of "Damme,"—and, when dissatisfied with my neighbor, I pronounce him "Ambra di merdo." With these two phrases, and a third, "Avra Bouro," which signifieth "Get an ass," I am universally understood to be a person of degree and a master of languages. How merrily we lives that travellers be!—if we had food and raiment. But, in sober sadness, any thing is better than England, and I am infinitely amused with my pilgrimage as far as it has gone.

To-morrow we start to ride post near 400 miles as far as Gibraltar, where we embark for Melita [Malta?] and Byzantium. A letter to Malta will find me, or to be forwarded, if I am absent. Pray embrace

---

[1] In a note to *Childe Harold* (*Poetry*, II, 86) Byron says that his carriage was stopped by some ruffians while he was on his way to the theatre in Lisbon. Hobhouse confirmed this in his diary of July 19, 1809: "Attacked in street by four men".

[2] Only a few days after he arrived in Portugal Byron swam "from old Lisbon to Belem Castle, and having to contend with a tide and counter current, the wind blowing freshly, was but little less than two hours in crossing the river". (Hobhouse, *Journey*, II, 808.) Hobhouse called the feat "a more perilous, but less celebrated passage", than Byron's later swimming of the Hellespont.

the Drury and Dwyer[3] and all the Ephesians[4] you encounter. I am writing with Butler's donative pencil,[5] which makes my bad hand worse. Excuse illegibility. * * *

Hodgson! send me the news, and the deaths and defeats and capital crimes and the misfortunes of one's friends; and let us hear of literary matters, and the controversies and the criticisms. All this will be pleasant—"Suave mari magno," &c.[6] Talking of that, I have been seasick, and sick of the sea. Adieu. Yours faithfully, &c.

[TO FRANCIS HODGSON]   *Gibraltar, August 6, 1809*

I have just arrived at this place after a journey through Portugal, and a part of Spain, of nearly 500 miles. We left Lisbon and travelled on horseback to Seville and Cadiz, and thence in the Hyperion frigate to Gibraltar. The horses are excellent—we rode seventy miles a day. Eggs and wine and hard beds are all the accommodation we found, and, in such torrid weather, quite enough. My health is better than in England. * * *

Seville is a fine town, and the Sierra Morena, part of which we crossed, a very sufficient mountain,—but damn description, it is always disgusting. Cadiz, sweet Cadiz!—it is the first spot in the creation. * * * The beauty of its streets and mansions is only excelled by the loveliness of its inhabitants. For, with all national prejudice, I must confess the women of Cadiz are as far superior to the English women in beauty as the Spaniards are inferior to the English in every quality that dignifies the name of man. * * * Just as I began to know the principal persons of the city, I was obliged to sail.

You will not expect a long letter after my riding so far "on hollow pampered jades of Asia."[1] Talking of Asia puts me in mind of Africa, which is within five miles of my present residence. I am going over before I go on to Constantinople.

---

[3] Unidentified; perhaps a younger master at Harrow.

[4] An Elizabethan slang term meaning boon companions or good fellows. (See *II Henry IV*, II, ii, 136; and *Merry Wives of Windsor*, IV, v, 17.)

[5] Dr. George Butler, Headmaster of Harrow, had presented Byron with a gold pen before his departure. See May 3, 1810, to Drury.

[6] "Suave, mari magno turbantibus aequora ventis. . . ." (Lucretius, *De Rerum Natura*, II, 1.) The full passage in translation reads: "Pleasant it is, when over a great sea the winds trouble the waters, to gaze from shore upon another's great tribulation; not because any man's troubles are a delectable joy, but because to perceive you are free of them yourself is pleasant."

[1] *II Henry IV*, II, iv, 144; see also Marlowe, *Tamburlaine*, IV, iv, 1: "Holla, ye pampered jades of Asia."

* * * Cadiz is a complete Cythera. Many of the grandees who have left Madrid during the troubles reside there, and I do believe it is the prettiest and cleanest town in Europe. London is filthy in the comparison. * * * The Spanish women are all alike, their education the same. The wife of a duke is, in information, as the wife of a peasant, —the wife of a peasant, in manner, equal to a duchess. Certainly, they are fascinating; but their minds have only one idea, and the business of their lives is intrigue. * * *

I have seen Sir John Carr[2] at Seville and Cadiz, and, like Swift's barber, have been down on my knees to beg he would not put me into black and white. Pray remember me to the Drurys and the Davies, and all of that stamp who are yet extant. Send me a letter and news to Malta. My next epistle shall be from Mount Caucasus or Mount Sion. I shall return to Spain before I see England, for I am enamoured of the country. Adieu, and believe me, &c.

[TO JOHN HANSON]   *Gibraltar August 7th. 1809*

Sir,—I have just ridden between four & five hundred miles across the country from Lisbon to Cadiz, and thence by sea to Gibraltar. I shall pursue my voyage the first opportunity. I have been at Seville where the Spanish Government is at present, of course you have by this time received intelligence of the battle near Madrid.—[1] As I rode seventy miles a day during this intense heat, you will conclude I am rather fatigued, though the journey has been pleasant.— —I send you this, as it is probable you may wish to ascertain my movements, a letter addressed to Malta will find me.—Spain is all in arms, and the French have every thing to do over again, the barbarities on both sides are shocking. I passed some French prisoners on the road from Badajoz to Seville, and saw a spy who was condemned to be shot, you will be surprised to hear that the Spanish roads are far superior to the best English Turnpikes, and the horses excellent, eggs & wine always to be had, no meat or milk, but every thing else very fair.— — Cadiz is the prettiest town in Europe, Seville a large & fine city,

---

[2] Sir John Carr (1772–1832) was already noted for his travel books including *The Stranger in France* (1803), and *A Tour of Holland* (1807). He published his *Descriptive Travels in the Southern and Eastern Parts of Spain* in 1811. Byron's name was not mentioned. At the end of the first canto of *Childe Harold* Byron wrote three stanzas ridiculing "Green Erin's Knight and wandering star!" but suppressed them before publication.

[1] In the battle of Talavera, July 27 and 28, 1809, Sir Arthur Wellesley defeated Marshal Victor.

Gibraltar the dirtiest most detestable spot in existence, Lisbon nearly as bad, the Spaniards are far superior to the Portuguese, and the English abroad are very different from their countrymen. Pray inform Mrs. Byron that I am well, tell her I will write from Malta, at present I have not time to write to her as I could wish.—

I remain your very obedt. Sert.

BYRON

[TO MRS. CATHERINE GORDON BYRON] *Gibraltar*

August 11th. 1809

Dear Mother,—I have been so much occupied since my departure from England that till I could address you a little at length, I have forborn writing altogether.—As I have now passed through Portugal & a considerable part of Spain, & have leisure at this place I shall endeavour to give you a short detail of my movements.—We sailed from Falmouth on the 2d. of July, reached Lisbon after a very favourable passage of four days and a half, and took up our abode for a time in that city.—It has been often described without being worthy of description, for, except the view from the Tagus which is beautiful, and some fine churches & convents it contains little but filthy streets & more filthy inhabitants.—To make amends for this the village of Cintra about fifteen miles from the capitol is perhaps in every respect the most delightful in Europe, it contains beauties of every description natural & artificial, Palaces and gardens rising in the midst of rocks, cataracts, and precipices, convents on stupendous heights a distant view of the sea and the Tagus, and besides (though that is a secondary consideration) is remarkable as the scene of Sir H[ew] D[alrymple]'s convention.[1]—It unites in itself all the wildness of the Western Highlands with the verdure of the South of France. Near this place about 10 miles to the right is the palace of Mafra[2] the boast of

[1] The Convention of Cintra (August 30, 1808), which was negotiated by Sir Hew Dalrymple with Junot, the French commander in Portugal, allowed the French to withdraw from the country with their arms and artillery. The Convention, though it bore the name of Cintra, was mainly negotiated near Torres Vedras, and was signed in Lisbon. Yet Hobhouse says in his diary (July 14): "We entered the very room in which the famous Convention was signed, which is in the right wing of the Palace [at Cintra]". In England there was a cry that Junot should have been forced to unconditional surrender, but the generals brought home for questioning were acquitted of blame by a court of inquiry. Byron, who took the opposition Whig view of the War in the Peninsula, wrote three stanzas critical of the Convention for *Childe Harold* (I, 24–26) which he modified before publication, omitting personal references to Dalrymple and others involved.

[2] The huge monastery at Mafra (the facade is over 800 feet in length) was

Portugal, as it might be of any country, in point of magnificence without elegance, there is a convent annexed, the monks who possess large revenues are courteous enough, & understand Latin, so that we had a long conversation, they have a large Library & asked [me?] if the *English* had *any books* in their country.— —I sent my baggage & part of the servants by sea to Gibraltar, and travelled on horseback from Aldea Gallega (the first stage from Lisbon which is only accessible by water) to Seville (one of the most famous cities in Spain where the Government called the Junta is now held) the distance to Seville is nearly four hundred miles & to Cadiz about 90 further towards the Coast.—I had orders from the Government & every possible accommodation on the road, as an English nobleman in an English uniform is a very respectable personage in Spain at present. The horses are remarkably good, and the roads (I assure you upon my honour for you will hardly believe it) very far superior to the best British roads, without the smallest toll or turnpike, you will suppose this when I rode post to Seville in four days, through this parching country in the midst of summer, without fatigue or annoyance.—

Seville is a beautiful town, though the streets are narrow they are clean, we lodged in the house of two Spanish unmarried ladies, who possess *six* houses in Seville, and gave me a curious specimen of Spanish manners.—They are women of character, and the eldest a fine woman, the youngest pretty but not so good a figure as Donna Josepha, the freedom of women which is general here astonished me not a little, and in the course of further observation I find that reserve is not the characteristic of the Spanish belles, who are in general very handsome, with large black eyes, and very fine forms.—The eldest honoured your *unworthy* son with very particular attention, embracing him with great tenderness at parting (I was there but 3 days) after cutting off a lock of his hair, & presenting him with one of her own about three feet in length, which I send, and beg you will retain till my return.[3]— Her last words were "Adio tu hermoso! me gusto mucho" "Adieu, you pretty fellow you please me much."—She offered a share of her apartment which my *virtue* induced me to decline, she laughed and said I had some English "Amante," (lover) and added that she was going to be married to an officer in the Spanish army.—I left Seville and rode on to Cadiz! through a beautiful country, at Xeres where the Sherry we

completed in 1730. It was built lavishly for João V by the architect John Frederic Ludwig of Ratisbon. One of the most striking features is the grisaille rococo library.

[3] The lock of dark hair given Byron by Donna Josepha is still preserved among the Byron relics at John Murray's.

drink is made I met a great merchant a Mr. Gordon of Scotland, who was extremely polite and favoured me with the Inspection of his vaults & cellars, so that I quaffed at the Fountain head.—Cadiz, sweet Cadiz! is the most delightful town I ever beheld, very different from our English cities in every respect except cleanliness (and it is as clean as London) but still beautiful and full of the finest women in Spain, the Cadiz belles being the Lancashire witches of their land.—Just as I was introduced and began to like the grandees I was forced to leave it for this cursed place, but before I return to England I will visit it again.—The night before I left it, I sat in the box at the opera with Admiral Cordova's family,[4] he is the commander whom Ld. St. Vincent defeated in 1797, and has an aged wife and a fine daughter.— — —Signorita Cordova the girl is very pretty in the Spanish style, in my opinion by no means inferior to the English in charms, and certainly superior in fascination.—Long black hair, dark languishing eyes, *clear* olive complexions, and forms more graceful in motion than can be conceived by an Englishman used to the drowsy listless air of his countrywomen, added to the most becoming dress & at the same time the most decent in the world, render a Spanish beauty irresistible. I beg leave to observe that Intrigue here is the business of life, when a woman marries she throws off all restraint, but I believe their conduct is chaste enough before.—If you make a proposal which in England would bring a box on the ear from the meekest of virgins, to a Spanish girl, she thanks you for the honour you intend her, and replies "wait till I am married, & I shall be too happy."—This is literally & strictly true.—Miss C[ordova] & her little brother understood a little French, and after regretting my ignorance of the Spanish she proposed to become my preceptress in that language; I could only reply by a low bow, and express my regret that I quitted Cadiz too soon to permit me to make the progress which would doubtless attend my studies under so charming a directress; I was standing at the back of the box which resembles our opera boxes (the theatre is large and finely decorated, the music admirable) in the manner which Englishmen generally adopt for fear of incommoding the ladies in front, when this fair Spaniard dispossessed an old women (an aunt or a duenna) of her chair, and commanded me to be seated next herself, at a tolerable distance from her mamma.—At the close of the performance I withdrew and was lounging with a party of men in the passage, when

4 Admiral Cordova commanded the Spanish Fleet, defeated February 14, 1797, off Cape St. Vincent, by Sir John Jervis, afterward Earl of St. Vincent. (*LJ*, I, 239n.)

"en passant" the Lady turned round and called me, & I had the honour of attending her to the Admiral's mansion.—I have an invitation on my return to Cadiz which I shall accept, if I repass through the country on my way from Asia.—I have met Sir John Carr Knight errant at Seville & Cadiz, he is a pleasant man.—I like the Spaniards much, you have heard of the battle near Madrid,[5] & in England they will call it a victory, a pretty victory! two hundred officers and 5000 men killed all English, and the French in as great force as ever.—I should have joined the army but we have no time to lose before we get up the Mediterranean & Archipelago,—I am going over to Africa tomorrow, it is only six miles from this Fortress.—My next stage is Cagliari in Sardinia where I shall be presented to his S[ardinian] Majesty, I have a most superb uniform as a court dress, indispensable in travelling.—

August 13th

I have not yet been to Africa, the wind is contrary, but I dined yesterday at Algesiras with Lady Westmoreland [*sic*] where I met General Castanos[6] the celebrated Spanish leader in the late & present war, today I dine with him, he has offered me letters to Tetuan in Barbary for the principal Moors, & I am to have the house for a few days of one of their great men, which was intended for Lady W[estmorland],[7] whose health will not permit her to cross the Straits.—

August 15th

I could not dine with Castanos yesterday, but this afternoon I had that honour, he is pleasant, & for aught I know to the contrary, clever, —I cannot go to Barbary, the Malta packet sails tomorrow & myself in it, Admiral Purvis with whom I dined at Cadiz gave me a passage in a frigate to Gibraltar, but we have no ship of war destined for Malta at present, the Packets sail fast & have good accommodations, you shall hear from me on our route, Joe Murray delivers this, I have sent him & the boy back, pray shew the lad any kindness as he is my great favourite, I would have taken him on ⟨but you *know boys* are not *safe*

---

[5] The battle of Talavera, July 27 and 28, 1809. Sir Arthur Wellesley defeated Marshal Victor at tremendous loss of British soldiers.
[6] General Francisco Janier de Castaños, Duke of Baylen, won a significant victory over the French General Dupont at Baylen in 1808. Dupont, with 20,000 Swiss and German soldiers, marched on Cadiz, but was cut off at Baylen by Castaños with 30,000 Spanish regulars, and capitulated on July 22, 1808.
[7] Jane Saunders married, as his second wife, the 10th Earl of Westmorland. Byron saw her frequently during his years of fame in London. It was at her house that Lady Caroline Lamb first declined to be introduced to Byron because there were too many women about him.

amongst the Turks.—⟩ Say this to his father, who may otherwise think he has behaved ill.—[I hope] This will find you well, believe me yours ever sincerely—

BYRON

P.S.—So Ld. Grey is married to a rustic,[8] well done! if I wed I will bring you home a sultana with half a score cities for a dowry, and reconcile you to an Ottoman daughter in law with a bushel of pearls not larger than ostrich eggs or smaller than Walnuts.— —

[TO JOHN HANSON]   *Gibraltar August 13th. 1809*

Sir,—I have sent Robert Rushton home, because Turkey is in too dangerous a state for boys to enter, & I beg he may still be considered as my servant, so that in case of my death he may be entitled to his legacy.—

I remain yours &c.
BYRON

P.S.—I hope the drafts are paid out of the different monies from Norfolk & Sawbridge

[TO MR. RUSHTON]   *Gibraltar August 14th 1809*

Mr. Rushton,—I have sent Robert home with Mr. Murray, because the country which I am now about to travel through, is in a state which renders it unsafe, particularly for one so young.—I allow [you] to deduct five and twenty pounds a year for his education for three years provided I do not return before that time, & I desire he may be considered as in my service, let every care be taken of him, & let him be sent to school; in case of my death I have provided enough in my will to render him independent.[1]—He has behaved extremely well, & has travelled a great deal for the time of his absence.—Deduct the expense of his education from your rent.—

BYRON

---

8 Lord Grey de Ruthyn married, in 1809, Anna Maria, daughter of William Kelham, of Ryton-upon-Dunsmore, Warwick. Lord Grey died the following year.
1 See April 26, 1809, to Hanson, note 3.

Sir,—It is rather singular you have not addressed any letter to this place since my departure from England; I have crossed Portugal, travelled through the South of Spain, been in Sardinia & Sicily, & on my arrival here fully expected to hear some account of the sale of Wymondham &c.—several packets have touched with dispatches & as it is probable I proceed to Constantinople immediately the disappointment is greater.—I request that whatever money can be spared may be forwarded in letters of credit to Malta, & Constantinople.—If Sawbridge's money is paid, another thousand was to have been advanced to Hammersley by this time, & when convenient I request that remittances may gradually be made, more or less, and next Spring when Rochdale is sold you will forward an account of the overplus after the deductions are made for debts &c.—I do not speak from any present necessity, but I wish to have all that can be spared, remitted, as I shall remain long abroad, provided no accidents occur.—I have sent back all my English servants but one.—You will remember that remittances travel slowly to Constantinople, consequently the earlier they are made the better, letters are sometimes 6 months on their passage.—As to my affairs you must manage them as you best can, I have full confidence in your integrity, but expect & desire no favours, indeed I need not.—Whatever distress I may encounter, I will not sell Newstead, and whether further monies can be advanced or not, I expect at least a letter on the subject, addressed to this place, from whence it will be forwarded to me, wherever I may be.—You have doubtless received my letters through different channels, & I once more beg they may be answered as they relate to Business. Pray present my remembrances to Mrs. Hanson & the family.—I remain

yr. very obedt. Servt.
BYRON

[TO MRS. CATHERINE GORDON BYRON] *Malta Septr. 15th. 1809*

Dear Mother,—Though I have a very short time to spare, being to sail immediately for Greece, I cannot avoid taking an opportunity of telling you that I am well, I have been in Malta a short time & have found the inhabitants hospitable & pleasant.—This letter is committed to the charge of a very extraordinary woman whom you have doubtless heard of, Mrs. Spencer Smith,[1] of whose escape the Marquis de Salvo[2] published a narrative a few years ago, she has since been shipwrecked, and her life has been from its commencement so fertile in remarkable incidents, that in a romance they would appear improbable, She was born at Constantinople, where her father Baron Herbert was Austrian Ambassador, married unhappily yet has never been impeached in point of character, excited the vengeance of Buonaparte by a part in some conspiracy, several times risked her life, & is not yet twenty five.— —She is here on her way to England to join her husband, being obliged to leave Trieste where she was paying a visit to her mother by the approach of the French, & embarks soon in a ship of war, since my arrival here I have had scarcely any other companion, I have found her very pretty, very accomplished, and extremely eccentric.— —Bonaparte is even now so incensed against her that her life would be in some danger if she were taken prisoner a second time.—You have seen Murray and Robert by this time and received my letter, little has happened since that date, I have touched at Cagliari in Sardinia, and at Girgenti in Sicily, and embark tomorrow for Patras from whence I proceed to Yanina where Ali Pacha holds his court, so I shall soon be amongst the Mussulmen.—Adieu believe me with sincerity

yrs. ever
BYRON

[TO CAPTAIN CARY[1]]   *3. Strada di Torni Sept. 18th. 1809*

Sir,—The marked insolence of your behaviour to me the first time I had the honour of meeting you at table, I should have passed over from respect to the General, had I not been informed that you have

---

[1] Byron's best account of his love affair with Mrs. Constance Spencer Smith was given, after the passion had cooled, to Lady Melbourne (letter of September 15, 1812). But there seems little doubt that he was desperately in love with her at the time of his first Malta visit. His poems addressed to her include: "Lines Written in an Album, at Malta", "To Florence", "Stanzas Written in Passing the Ambacian Gulph", and "Stanzas Composed During a Thunder-Storm." The passing of her spell is recorded in "The spell is broke, the charm is flown!" and in the stanzas to "Florence" in *Childe Harold* (II, 30–35).

[2] The Marquis de Salvo gives a lengthy account of his rescue of Mrs. Smith in the dead of night with a rope ladder in his *Travels in the Year 1806, from Italy to England . . . Containing the Particulars of the Liberation of Mrs. Spencer Smith* (1808).

[1] Aide-de-camp to General Oakes, Military Commander in Malta.

since mentioned my name in a public company with comments not to be tolerated, more particularly after the circumstance to which I allude. —I have only just heard this, or I should not have postponed this letter to so late a period.—As the vessel in which I am to embark must sail the first change of wind, the sooner our business is arranged the better. —Tomorrow morning at 6 will be the best hour, at any place you think proper, as I do not know where the officers and *gentlemen* settle these affairs in your Island.—The favour of an immediate answer will oblige[2]

your obedt. Sert.
BYRON

[TO JOHN HANSON] *Prevesa in Albania. Sept. 29th. 1809*

Sir,—I write merely on the old topic, to put you in mind in time to forward what remittances you can, through Hammersley to the same Bankers at Gibraltar, Malta, & Constantinople.—Address your own letters to the latter city to the care of Messrs Barbauld & Co. Bankers. —I am now in Greece where I shall travel some time, & so on to Constantinople.—I am going tomorrow to Yanina the court of Ali Pacha the Turkish Governor of this country.—I was well received at Malta by the Governor &c. who gave me a passage in a ship of war to this port. —We went from Cadiz to Gibraltar in a frigate, and thence to Sardinia, Sicily, & Malta.— —The Consul has gotten me a house here and when I have viewed the ruins of Nicopolis, I shall proceed to Ali Pacha up the interior.—The bay where we now lie was the scene of the famous battle of Actium.—I have seen Ithaca & touched in the Morea at Patras, where I found the Greeks polite & hospitable.—In a few weeks we shall be at Athens, cross the sea to Smyrna & thence to Constantinople is three days journey.—There I expect to hear from you, you are very *remiss.* Remember me to all your family, particularly to Mrs. Hanson, but do not expect to see me soon, I am now above three thousand miles from Chancery Lane.—Above all, remember the remittances, & tell Mrs. Byron you have heard from me, you have doubtless seen Murray & the boy.—

yrs. truly
BYRON

P.S.—You should write two or three letters, *one* may miscarry, two have a better chance.

2 See May 3, 1810, to Drury and note 4.

My dear Mother,—I have now been some time in Turkey: this place is on the coast but I have traversed the interior of the province of Albania on a visit to the Pacha.—I left Malta in the Spider a brig of war on the 21st. of Septr. & arrived in eight days at Prevesa.—I thence have been about 150 miles as far as Tepaleen his highness's country palace where I staid three days.—The name of the Pacha is Ali,[1] & he is considered a man of the first abilities, he governs the whole of Albania (the ancient Illyricum) Epirus, & part of Macedonia, his Son *Velly* Pacha[2] to whom he has given me letters governs the Morea & he has great influence in Egypt, in short he is one of the most powerful men in the Ottoman empire.—When I reached Yanina the capital after a journey of three days over the mountains through a country of the most picturesque beauty, I found that Ali Pacha was with his army in Illyricum besieging Ibraham Pacha in the castle of Berat.—He had heard that an Englishman of rank was in his dominions & had left orders in Yanina with the Commandant to provide a house & supply me with every kind of necessary, *gratis*, & though I have been allowed to make presents to the slaves &c. I have not been permitted to pay for single article of household consumption.—I rode out on the viziers horses & saw the palaces of himself & grandsons, they are splendid but too much ornamented with silk & gold.—I then went over the mountains through Zitza a village with a Greek monastery (where I slept on my return) in the most beautiful Situation (always excepting Cintra in Portugal) I ever beheld.[3]—In nine days I reached Tepaleen,

---

[1] Ali Pasha (Byron regularly spelled it Pacha) (1741–1822) was born at Tepelene in Albania about 75 miles north of Janina, his new capital in the Epirus. When Byron arrived, he had made himself despotic ruler of the whole of what is now modern Greece as far south as the Gulf of Corinth, and of parts of Albania. He had subdued or driven out by treachery the Suliotes, who long defied him, and he used rivals to his advantage, including the French and English in the Ionian Islands. By cunning, treachery, and the use of bandits as soldiers when it suited him, he had raised himself from a petty leader of robber bands to a ruler more powerful in his own domains than the Sultan himself, to whom, as ruler of the Ottoman Empire, he nominally paid tribute and homage. He was short and fat and had a long white beard, and looked benign. But stories of his barbaric cruelty to enemies were well known. Byron used Ali in some measure for a model for Giaffir in *The Bride of Abydos* and for the pirate father of Haidée in *Don Juan*: "the mildest mannered man/That ever scuttled ship or cut a throat".

[2] Veli Pasha, Ali's second son, was master of the Morea (Peloponnesus). Both father and son had a penchant for young boys, and Veli's treachery, cruelty, and lasciviousness exceeded even those of his father.

[3] Byron wrote glowingly of Zitza (Zitsa) in *Childe Harold* (II, 48–52). The monastery, with its magnificent view, still remains, but it is now deserted. On

our Journey was much prolonged by the torrents that had fallen from the mountains & intersected the roads. I shall never forget the singular scene on entering Tepaleen at five in the afternoon as the Sun was going down, it brought to my recollection (with some change of *dress* however) Scott's description of Branksome Castle in his lay, & the feudal system.—The Albanians in their dresses (the most magnificent in the world, consisting of a long *white kilt*, gold worked cloak, crimson velvet gold laced jacket & waistcoat, silver mounted pistols & daggers,) the Tartars with their high caps, the Turks in their vast pelises & turbans, the soldiers & black slaves with the horses, the former stretched in groupes in an immense open gallery in front of the palace, the latter placed in a kind of cloister below it, two hundred steeds ready caparisoned to move in a moment, couriers entering or passing out with dispatches, the kettle drums beating, boys calling the hour from the minaret of the mosque, altogether, with the singular appearance of the building itself, formed a new & delightful spectacle to a stranger.—I was conducted to a very handsome apartment & my health enquired after by the vizier's secretary "a la mode de Turque." —The next day I was introduced to Ali Pacha, I was dressed in a full suit of Staff uniform with a very magnificent sabre &c.— —The Vizier received me in a large room paved with marble, a fountain was playing in the centre, the apartment was surrounded by scarlet Ottomans, he received me *standing*, a wonderful compliment from a Mussulman, & made me sit down on his right hand.—I have a Greek interpreter for general use, but a Physician of Ali's named [Seculario?] who understands Latin acted for me on this occasion.—His first question was why at so early an age I left my country? (the Turks have no idea of travelling for amusement) he then said the English Minister Capt. Leake[4] had told him I was of a great family, & desired his respects to my mother, which I now in the name of Ali Pacha present to you. He said he was certain I was a man of birth because I had small ears, curling hair, & little white hands, and expressed himself pleased with my appearance & garb.—He told me to consider him as a father

the outer wall is a plaque in Greek recording Byron's visit and quoting two lines from *Childe Harold*:

> Monastic Zitza! from thy shady brow,
> Thou small, but favoured spot of holy ground!

[4] William Martin Leake (1777–1860), a Captain in the British army and British Resident at the court of Ali Pasha, residing at Prevesa and Janina, had been in British service of a semi-diplomatic nature in Constantinople, Egypt and European Turkey since 1800. His travel books and topographical studies of the Near East, published later, brought him fame.

whilst I was in Turkey, & said he looked on me as his son.—Indeed he treated me like a child, sending me almonds & sugared sherbet, fruit & sweetmeats 20 times a day.—He begged me to visit him often, and at night when he was more at leisure—I then after coffee & pipes retired for the first time. I saw him thrice afterwards.—It is singular that the Turks who have no heriditary dignities & few great families except the Sultan's pay so much respect to birth, for I found my pedigree more regarded than even my title.—His Highness is 60 years old, very fat & not tall, but with a fine face, light blue eyes & a white beard, his manner is very kind & at the same time he possesses that dignity which I find universal amongst the Turks.— —He has the appearance of any thing but his real character, for he is a remorseless tyrant, guilty of the most horrible cruelties, very brave & so good a general, that they call him the Mahometan Buonaparte.—Napoleon has twice offered to make him King of Epirus, but he prefers the English interest & abhors the French as he himself told me, he is of so much consequence that he is much courted by both, the Albanians being the most warlike subjects of the Sultan, though Ali is only nominally dependent on the Porte. He has been a mighty warrior, but is as barbarous as he is successful, roasting rebels &c. &c.—Bonaparte sent him a snuffbox with his picture[;] he said the snuffbox was very well, but the picture he could excuse, as he neither liked *it* nor the *original*.—His ideas of judging of a man's birth from ears, hands &c. were curious enough.—To me he was indeed a father, giving me letters, guards, & every possible accommodation.—Our next conversations were of war & travelling, politics & England.—He called my Albanian soldier who attends me, and told him to protect me at all hazards.—His name is Viscillie[5] & like all the Albanians he is brave, rigidly honest, & faithful, but they are cruel though not treacherous, & have several vices, but no meannesses.—They are perhaps the most beautiful race in point of countenance in the world, their women are sometimes handsome also, but they are treated like slaves, *beaten* & in short complete beasts of burthen, they plough, dig & sow, I found them carrying wood & actually repairing the highways, the men are

[5] Byron elsewhere spells his name Vascillie and Basili. He was an Albanian soldier assigned to Byron by Ali Pasha as guide and guard. Byron became attached to him and kept him on as a servant until he left Greece in May 1811. In a note to *Childe Harold* he says that Basili, who was an Albanian Christian, "had a great veneration for the church [Greek Orthodox], mixed with the highest contempt of churchmen, whom he cuffed upon occasion in a most heterodox manner. Yet he never passed a church without crossing himself." When his inconsistency was pointed out, he replied: "Our church is holy, our priests are thieves." (*Poetry*, II, 175–76.)

all soldiers, & war & the chase their sole occupations, the women are the labourers, which after all is no great hardship in so delightful a climate, yesterday the 11th. Nov. I bathed in the sea, today It is so hot that I am writing in a shady room of the English Consul's with three doors wide open no fire or even *fireplace* in the house except for culinary purposes.—The Albanians [11 lines crossed out][6] Today I saw the remains of the town of *Actium* near which Anthony lost the world in a small bay where two frigates could hardly manouvre, a broken wall is the sole remnant.—On another part of the gulph stand the ruins of Nicopolis built by Augustus in honour of his victory.— — — Last night I was at a Greek marriage, but this & 1000 things more I have neither time or *space* to describe.—I am going tomorrow with a guard of fifty men to Patras in the Morea, & thence to Athens where I shall winter.—Two days ago I was nearly lost in a Turkish ship of war owing to the ignorance of the captain & crew though the storm was not violent.—Fletcher yelled after his wife, the Greeks called on all the Saints, the Mussulmen on Alla, the Captain burst into tears & ran below deck telling us to call on God, the sails were split, the main-yard shivered, the wind blowing fresh, the night setting in, & all our chance was to make Corfu which is in possession of the French, or (as Fletcher *pathetically* termed it) "a *watery* grave."—I did what I could to console Fletcher but finding him incorrigible wrapped myself up in my Albanian capote (an immense cloak) & lay down on deck to wait the worst, I have learnt to philosophize on my travels, & if I had not, complaint was useless.—Luckily the wind abated & only drove us on the coast of Suli on the main land where we landed & proceeded by the help of the natives to Prevesa again; but I shall not trust Turkish Sailors in future, though the Pacha had ordered one of his own galleots to take me to Patras, I am therefore going as far as Missolonghi by land & there have only to cross a small gulph to get to Patras.—Fletcher's next epistle will be full of marvels, we were one night lost for *nine* hours in the mountains in a *thunder* storm, & since nearly wrecked, in both cases Fletcher was sorely bewildered, from apprehensions of famine & banditti in the first, & drowning in the second instance.—His eyes were a little hurt by the lightning or crying (I dont know which) but are now recovered.—When you write address to me at Mr. *Strané's*[7] English Consul, Patras, Morea.— — —

[6] This deleted passage seems to be an account of a page of Ali Pacha or his son, "who loved an Albanian girl" and there seems to have been a struggle to save her honour from Ali Pasha's son.

[7] Strané had been on the *Spider*, which brought Byron and Hobhouse from Malta

I could tell you I know not how many incidents that I think would amuse you, but they crowd on my mind as much as would swell my paper, & I can neither arrange them in the one, or put them down on the other, except in the greatest confusion & in my usual horrible hand.—I like the Albanians much, they are not all Turks, some tribes are Christians, but their religion makes little difference in their manner or conduct; they are esteemed the best troops in the Turkish service.—I lived on my route two days at once, & three days again in a Barrack at Salora, & never found soldiers so tolerable, though I have been in the garrisons of Gibraltar & Malta & seen Spanish, French, Sicilian & British troops in abundance, I have had nothing stolen, & was always welcome to their provision & milk.—Not a week ago, an Albanian chief (every village has its chief who is called Primate) after helping us out of the Turkish Galley in her distress, feeding us & lodging my suite consisting of Fletcher, a Greek, Two Albanians, a Greek Priest and my companion Mr. Hobhouse, refused any compensation but a written paper stating that I was well received, & when I pressed him to accept a few sequins, "no, he replied, I wish you to love me, not to pay me." These were his words.—It is astonishing how far money goes in this country, while I was in the capital, I had nothing to pay by the vizier's order, but since, though I have generally had sixteen horses & generally 6 or 7 men, the expence has not been *half* as much as staying only 3 weeks in Malta, though Sir A. Ball[8] the governor gave me a house for nothing, & I had only *one servant.*—By the bye I expect Hanson to remit regularly, for I am not about to stay in this province for ever, let him write to me at Mr. Strané's, English Consul, Patras.— —The fact is, the fertility of the plains are wonderful, & specie is scarce, which makes this remarkable cheapness.—I am now going to Athens to study modern Greek which differs much from the ancient though radically similar.—I have no desire to return to England, nor shall I unless compelled by absolute want & Hanson's neglect, but I shall not enter Asia for a year or two as I have much to see in Greece & I may perhaps cross into Africa at least the Ægyptian part.—Fletcher like all Englishmen is very much dissatisfied, though a little reconciled to the Turks by a present of 80 piastres from the

to Patras and Prevesa. Hobhouse described him as "a good kind man very ugly". (Diary, Sept. 26, 1809.)

[8] Admiral Sir Alexander Ball (1757–1809) had fought with Nelson, and was successful in blockading and forcing the capitulation of Malta in 1800. He was knighted for his feat and sent as governor of the island. S. T. Coleridge served as his secretary from May 1804 to October 1805. Ball died in 1809, shortly after Byron's stay at Malta.

vizier, which if you consider every thing & the value of specie here is nearly worth ten guineas English.—He has suffered nothing but from *cold*, heat, & vermin which those who lie in cottages & cross mountains in a wild country must undergo, & of which I have equally partaken with himself, but he is not valiant, & is afraid of robbers & tempests.—I have no one to be remembered to in England, & wish to hear nothing from it but that you are well, & a letter or two on business from Hanson, whom you may tell to write.— —I will write when I can, & beg you to believe me,

yr affect. Son
BYRON

P.S.—I have some very "magnifique" Albanian dresses the only expensive articles in this country they cost 50 guineas each & have so much gold they would cost in England two hundred.[9]—I have been introduced to Hussein Bey,[10] & Mahmout Pacha[11] both little boys grandchildren of Ali at Yanina. They are totally unlike our lads, have painted complexions like rouged dowagers, large black eyes & features perfectly regular. They are the prettiest little animals I ever saw, & are broken into the court ceremonies already, the Turkish salute is a slight inclination of the head with the hand on the breast, intimates always kiss, Mahmout is ten years old & hopes to see me again, we are friends without understanding each other, like many other folks, though from a different cause;—he has given me a letter to his father in the Morea, to whom I have also letters from Ali *Pacha*.—

[TO JOHN HANSON]   *Prevesa. Novr. 12th. 1809*

Sir,—I have just written to Mrs. Byron a long letter, she will inform you of all my late movements if they chance to interest you.—I write to you pursuant to my intention at every possible convenient opportunity to inform you I am alive, & the reason I write frequently is that some letters probably may not reach their destination. I have been travelling in the interior on a visit to the Pacha who received me with great distinction but of this & other matters Mrs. Bn. can inform you,

[9] One of these Albanian dresses, the one which Byron wore when he sat for a portrait to Thomas Phillips, is now in the Museum of Costume, Assembly Rooms, Bath, secured on loan for the Museum by Mrs. Doris Langley Moore from the Rt. Hon. the Marquess of Lansdowne, descendant of Miss Mercer-Elphinstone, to whom Byron gave the costume for a masquerade.
[10] Son of Mouctar Pasha, Ali's oldest son.
[11] Mahmout was the son of Veli Pasha.

I find Turkey better than Spain or Portugal though I was not displeased with them.—I have been nearly wrecked in a Turkish vessel, the Captain gave all up for lost, but the wind changed & saved us.—I have also been lost in the mountains a whole night in a thunder storm, & if these petty adventures afford you any amusement Mrs. B. (if she receives my letter) can give you a full detail.—I am going to pass a year in Greece before I enter Asia, if you write, address to me at Mr. Strané's English Consul Patras, Morea.—I have no wish to return to England, nor shall I do so unless compelled by necessity.—I am now going to Athens to study the modern Greek which differs from the ancient. Now for my affairs,—I have received not a single letter since I left England,—my copyholds I presume are sold, & my debts in some train, what surplus may be of Rochdale, I should wish to convert into annuities for my own life on good security & tolerable interest, or on good mortgages, if nothing remains, sorry as I should be & much as I should regret it Newstead must go for the sake of justice to all parties, & the surplus be disposed of in like manner in annuities or mortgage.—I still wish to preserve it, though I never may see it again, I never will revisit England if I can avoid it, it is possible I may be obliged to do so lest it should be said I left it to avoid the consequences of my Satire, but I will soon satisfy any doubts on that head if necessary & quit it again, for it is no country for me.—Why I say this is best known to myself, you recollect my impatience to leave it, you also know by what I then & still write that it was not to defraud my creditors, I believe you know me well enough to think no motive of personal fear of any kind would induce me to such a measure; it certainly was none of these considerations, but I never will live in England if I can avoid it, *why* must remain a secret,[1] but the farther I proceed the less I regret quitting it. The country I am now in is extremely cheap from the scarcity of specie & great fertility of the lands in the plains.—I expect to hear from you, & as I have already told you to have fresh remittances as there must be funds long ere now, I also expect some account of my affairs & wish to know what you think

[1] The secret reason for Byron's urgency to leave England (see April 16, 1809, to Hanson) and his reluctance to return must remain a mystery. We have his word that it had nothing to do with the importunities of creditors, nor with any fear of those whom he had attacked in his satire. It is tempting to speculate that such dark hints in contrast to his open and boastful avowals of his prowess with "nymphs" in London and his confessions to Hanson of his *faux pas* with the maid Lucy, could suggest that he had a wish to escape his own proclivities toward attachment to boys, or perhaps that he feared a closer connection with the Cambridge choirboy Edleston, who had wanted to live with him in London. But there is no solid evidence of this.

Newstead & Rochdale would fetch at a fair price, and what income would accrue from the produce if laid out in the purchase of annuities for my life, or good mortgages.—I beg to be remembered to Mrs. H. & the family

> & remain yr. obedt. &c.
> BYRON

Sir,—You will probably receive more letters from me than you expect or wish, but I seize the opportunity of every seaport to acquaint you with my movements.—I have written to you from Prevesa, & if you have not received that letter before this, you will soon have it as will Mrs. Byron one from the same place.—I have only one subject to write upon, which is the old one of remittances, if none have been already made I expect some to be forwarded immediately,— The sale of the copyholds & the remainder of the 6000 $£^1$ must have furnished a tolerable floating sum, for my purpose, till the Lancashire business can be arranged & sold, & if that is insufficient, much as I regret it, Newstead must follow the rest, & the produce be laid out either in mortgage or well secured annuities for my own life.—This would secure me after all is paid a good income for my own life at least, but I should be loath to have recourse to such an expedient, however, time must determine that point.—I have no intention or wish to return to your country & necessity alone will compel me to do it.— Mrs. B. can acquaint you with my movements if my last letter has reached her.—If not I will just state I have been travelling in Turkey through Epirus, Albania, Acarnania, Ætolia, & am now in the Morea, on my way to Athens, where I shall winter. I have been on a visit to the Pacha who gave me a guard of forty men through the dangerous defiles of the mountains; I was driven ashore by a gale in a Turkish vessel on the coast of Suli, & proceeded by land after crossing the Ambracian Gulph to Missologia [sic], & by sea to Patras, whence I now write.—Address to me at Mr. Strané's British Consul, Patras, Morea.— —I hope to hear of you through my Bankers at Constantinople or at least from *Hammersley*.—I trust your family prosper, & believe me their well wisher.—I shall expect to hear of marriages, & grandchildren.—I wish you would order the rents of Newstead to be raised, or at least regularly paid.—However I dont wish to oppress the rascals, but I must live "as the saying is".—Pray get rid of Rochdale

---

1 See July 13, 1809, to Hanson, note 2.

as soon as possible, & do not think of my return except from mere necessity, I dislike England, & the farther I go the less [I] regret leaving it.—

I remain yr. obedt. Sert.
BYRON

[TO JOHN HANSON]   *Athens.—March 3d. 1810*

Sir,—I have written often,—in vain, neither letters nor (what is of more importance) further remittances have arrived.— —I have no redress but to write again, & again, a [merry?] task to one, who hates writing as I do.—Letters to Malta or Constantinople if addressed to my Bankers will be forwarded to me, wherever I am.—Remittances ought to have come long ago from my Norfolk copyholds; from the money raised before I left England, from Newstead, or from my Lancashire Sale,—but I say no more,—for it is useless,—I shall however remember your kindness, in hopes one day to repay it, if I am obliged to visit your country once more, which I trust to avoid for some time.—

yr. very obedt. Sert.
BYRON

P.S.—If you write, address to Malta, or Messrs Barbaud Bankers Constantinople as above.—

[TO MRS. CATHERINE GORDON BYRON]   *Smyrna.—March 19th. 1810*

Dear Mother,—I cannot write you a long letter, but as I know you will not be sorry to receive any intelligence of my movements, pray accept what I can give.—I have traversed the greatest part of Greece besides Epirus &c. resided ten weeks at Athens, and am now on the Asiatic side on my way to Constantinople.—I have just returned from viewing the ruins of Ephesus a day's journey from Smyrna.—I presume you have received a long letter I wrote from Albania with an account of my reception by the Pashaw of the Province.—When I arrive at Constantinople I shall determine whether to proceed into Persia, or return, which latter I do not wish if I can avoid it.—But I have no intelligence from Mr. Hanson, and but one letter from yourself.—I shall stand in need of remittances whether I proceed or return.—I have written to him repeatedly that he may not plead ignorance of my situation for neglect.—I can give you no account of any thing for I have not time or opportunity, the frigate sailing immediately.—Indeed the farther I go the more my laziness increases, and my aversion to letter writing becomes more confirmed. I have written to no one but yourself and Mr. Hanson, and these are communications of duty and business rather than of Inclination.—Fletcher is very *much disgusted* with his fatigues, though he has undergone nothing that I have not shared, he is a poor creature, indeed English servants are detestable travellers.—I have besides him two Albanian soldiers and a Greek interpreter,[1] all excellent in their way.—Greece, particularly in the vicinity of Athens, is delightful, cloudless skies, and lovely landscapes. — —But I must reserve all account of my adventures till we meet, I keep no journal, but my friend Hobhouse scribbles incessantly. —Pray take care of Murray and Robert, and tell the boy it is the most fortunate thing for him that he did not accompany me to *Turkey*[.] Consider this as merely a notice of my safety, and believe me

yours &c. &c.
BYRON

P.S.—If you address to Malta, your letters will be forwarded.—

[TO MRS. CATHERINE GORDON BYRON] *Smyrna. April 10th. 1810*

Dear Mother,—Tomorrow, or this evening I sail for Constantinople in the Salsette 36 gun frigate, she returns to England with our Ambassador whom she is going up on purpose to receive.—I have written to you short letters from Athens, Smyrna, & a long one from Albania. I have not yet mustered courage for a second large epistle, and you must not be angry, since I take all opportunities of apprising you of my safety, but even that is an effort, writing is so irksome.—I have been traversing Greece, and Epirus, Illyria &c. &c. and you see by my date have got into Asia, I have made but one excursion lately, to the Ruins of Ephesus.—Malta is the rendezvous of my letters, so address to that Island.—Mr. Hanson has not written, though I wished to hear of the Norfolk sale, the Lancashire Lawsuit, &c.&c.—I am anxiously expecting fresh remittances. I believe you will like Nottinghamshire, at least my share of it.—Pray accept my good wishes in lieu of a long letter and believe me

yours sincerely & affectionately
BYRON

---

[1] The Greek interpreter was Andreas Zantachi, hired in Patras after Byron dismissed his dragoman George, who had cheated him on his way to Albania. Andreas spoke Turkish, Greek, Italian, and bad Latin learned while in a choir in Rome.

Sir,—It has been my custom to write to you from every seaport on my arrival & previous to my departure, and though (Notwithstanding my repeated requests since the moment I arrived *at Lisbon* to the *present day* no answer has been returned) I shall still remind you of my existence.—I have always told you to address to me at Malta whence any letters will be forwarded to me by my correspondents in that Island.—Tomorrow or tonight I sail for Constantinople in the Salsette frigate, which is to return to England with Mr. Adair our Ambassador at the Porte.[1]—I have the honour to be

&c. &c. your obedt. Sert.

BYRON

P.S.—I request to be remembered to Mrs. Hanson & those of the family who favour me with their recollection. I shall always be happy to hear of their welfare.—

[TO MRS. CATHERINE GORDON BYRON]
Salsette Frigate off the Dardanelles April 17th. 1810

Dear Madam,—I write at anchor (on our way to Constantinople) off the Troad which I traversed two days ago, all the remains of Troy are the tombs of her destroyers, amongst which I see that of Antilochus from my cabin window.— —These are huge mounds of earth like the barrows of the Danes in your Island, the marble and granite have long perished.—There are several monuments about 12 miles distant of the Alexandrian Troas which I also examined, but by no means to be compared with the remnants of Athens & Ephesus.—This will be sent in a ship of war bound with dispatches for Malta; in a few days we shall be at Constantinople, barring accidents, I have also written from Smyrna, & shall from time to time transmit short accounts of my movements, but I feel totally unequal to long letters.—Believe me

yours very sincerely

BYRON

P.S.—No accounts from Hanson!!!—Do not complain of short letters, I write to nobody but yourself, and Mr. H.—

---

[1] Sir Robert Adair (1763–1855), friend of Charles James Fox and son of Robert Adair, who had been sergeant-surgeon to George III, was sent to Constantinople in 1806 to open a negotiation for peace with the Porte.

My dear Drury,—When I left England nearly a year ago you requested me to write to you.—I will do so.—I have crossed Portugal, traversed the South of Spain, visited Sardinia, Sicily, Malta, and thence passed into Turkey where I am still wandering.—I first landed in Albania the ancient Epirus where we penetrated as far as Mount Tomerit,[1] excellently treated by the Chief Ali Pacha, and after journeying through Illyria, Chaonia, &ctr, crossed the Gulph of Actium with a guard of 50 Albanians and passed the Achelous in our route through Acarnania and Ætolia.—We stopped a short time in the Morea, crossed the gulph of Lepanto and landed at the foot of Parnassus, saw all that Delphi retains and so on to Thebes and Athens at which last we remained ten weeks.—His majesty's ship Pylades brought us to Smyrna but not before we had topographised Attica including of course Marathon, and the Sunian Promontory.—From Smyrna to the Troad which we visited when at anchor for a fortnight off the Tomb of Antilochus, was our next stage, and now we are in the Dardanelles waiting for a wind to proceed to Constantinople.—This morning I *swam* from *Sestos* to *Abydos*, the immediate distance is not above a mile but the current renders it hazardous, so much so, that I doubt whether Leander's conjugal powers must not have been exhausted in his passage to Paradise.[2]—I attempted it a week ago and failed owing to the North wind and the wonderful rapidity of the tide, though I have been from my childhood a strong swimmer, but this morning being calmer I succeeded and crossed the "broad Hellespont" in an hour and ten minutes.— —Well, my dear Sir, I have left my home and seen part of Africa & Asia and a tolerable portion of Europe.—I have been with Generals, and Admirals, Princes and Pachas, Governors and Ungovernables, but I have not time or paper to expatiate. I wish to let you know that I live with a friendly remembrance of you and a hope to meet you again, and if I do this as shortly as possible, attribute it to any-thing but forgetfulness.—Greece ancient and modern you know too well to require description. Albania indeed I have seen more of than any Englishman (but a Mr. Leake) for it is a country rarely visited from the savage character of the natives, though

[1] Byron described in *Childe Harold* (II, 55) the sun setting behind Mount Tomerit as he descended to Tepelene in Albania.

[2] Leander, according to the Greek legend, swam every night across the Hellespont from Abydos to visit Hero, the priestess of Aphrodite, in Sestos. One night he perished in the crossing, and Hero threw herself into the sea.

abounding in more natural beauties than the classical regions of Greece, which however are still eminently beautiful, particularly Delphi, and Cape Colonna in Attica.—Yet these are nothing to parts of Illyria, and Epirus, where places without a name, and rivers not laid down in maps, may one day when more known be justly esteemed superior subjects for the pencil, and the pen, than the dry ditch of the Ilissus, and the bogs of Bœotia.—The Troad is a fine field for conjecture and Snipe-shooting, and a good sportsman and an ingenious scholar may exercise their feet and faculties to great advantage upon the spot, or if they prefer riding lose their way (as I did) in a cursed quagmire of the Scamander who wriggles about as if the Dardan virgins still offered their wonted tribute. The only vestige of Troy, or her destroyers, are the barrows supposed to contain the carcases of Achilles[,] Antilochus, Ajax &c. but Mt. Ida is still in high feather, though the Shepherds are nowadays not much like Ganymede.—But why should I say more of these things? are they not written in the *Boke* of Gell?[3] and has not Hobby got a journal? I keep none as I have renounced scribbling.—I see not much difference between ourselves & the Turks, save that we have foreskins and they none, that they have long dresses and we short, and that we talk much and they little.—In England the vices in fashion are whoring & drinking, in Turkey, Sodomy & smoking, we prefer a girl and a bottle, they a pipe and pathic.—They are sensible people, Ali Pacha told me he was sure I was a man of rank because I had *small ears* and hands and *curling hair*.—By the bye, I speak the Romaic or Modern Greek tolerably, it does not differ from the ancient dialects so much as you would conceive, but the pronunciation is diametrically opposite, of verse except in rhyme they have no idea.—I like the Greeks, who are plausible rascals, with all the Turkish vices without their courage. —However some are brave and all are beautiful, very much resembling the busts of Alcibiades, the women not quite so handsome.—I can swear in Turkish, but except one horrible oath, and *"pimp"* and "bread" and "water" I have got no great vocabulary in that language.—They are extremely polite to strangers of any rank properly protected, and as I have got 2 servants and two soldiers we get on with great eclât. We have been occasionally in danger of thieves &

---

[3] Sir William Gell had published *The Topography of Troy* in 1804, and *Itinerary in Greece* in 1808. Byron had referred to Gell in *English Bards and Scotch Reviewers*, "Of Dardan tours let Dilettanti tell,/ I leave topography to coxcomb Gell," but having met him before going to press, he changed the phrase to "classic Gell". But after having seen the Troad, Byron changed it again for a fifth edition (never published in his lifetime) to "rapid Gell", and added the note: "Rapid, indeed! He topographised and typographised King Priam's dominions in three days!"

once of shipwreck but always escaped.—At Malta I fell in love with a married woman and challenged an aid du camp of Genl. Oakes[4] (a rude fellow who grinned at something, I never rightly knew what,) but he explained and apologised, and the lady embarked for Cadiz, & so I escaped murder and adultery.—Of Spain I sent some account to our Hodgson, but I have subsequently written to no one save notes to relations and lawyers to keep them out of my premises.—I mean to give up all connection on my return with many of my best friends as I supposed them, and to snarl all my life, but I hope to have one good humoured laugh with you, and to embrace Dwyer and pledge Hodgson, before I commence Cynicism.—Tell Dr. Butler I am now writing with the gold pen he gave me before I left England, which is the reason my scrawl is more unentelligible [sic] than usual.—I have been at Athens and seen plenty of those reeds for scribbling, some of which he refused to bestow upon me because topographer Gell had brought them from Attica.— —But I will not describe, no, you must be satisfied with simple detail till my return, and then we will unfold the floodgates of Colloquoy.—I am in a 36 gun frigate going up to fetch Bob Adair from Constantinople, who will have the honour to carry this letter.— And so Hobby's *boke* is out,[5] with some sentimental singsong of mine own to fill up, and how does it take? eh! and where the devil is the 2d Edition of my Satire with additions? and my name on the title page? and more lines tagged to the end with a new exordium and what not, hot from my anvil before I cleared the Channel?—The Mediterranean and the Atlantic roll between me and Criticism, and the thunders of the Hyberborean Review[6] are deafened by the roar of the Hellespont.— Remember me to Claridge if not translated to College, and present to Hodgson assurances of my high consideration.—Now, you will ask, what shall I do next? and I answer I do not know, I may return in a few months, but I have intents and projects after visiting Constantinople, Hobhouse however will probably be back in September.—On the 2d. of July we have left Albion one year, "oblitus meorum, obliviscendus et illis," I was sick of my own country, and not much prepossessed in favour of any other, but I drag on "my chain" without

---

[4] General Sir Hildebrand Oakes (1754–1822), after serving in the Egyptian campaign with Sir John Moore, was appointed in 1808 to command the troops at Malta with the local rank of Lt. General. After the death of Sir Alexander Ball, the Governor of Malta, he became Civil and Military Commissioner of the island until the arrival of his successor, Sir Thomas Maitland in 1813. The Aide-de-camp who aroused Byron's ire was Captain Cary. (See letter of September 18, 1809, to him.)

[5] Hobhouse's book was *Imitations and Translations* (1809) which contained nine poems by Byron.

[6] The *Edinburgh Review* which had ridiculed *Hours of Idleness*.

"lengthening it at each remove".—I am like the jolly miller caring for nobody and not cared for. All countries are much the same in my eyes, I smoke and stare at mountains, and twirl my mustachios very independently, I miss no comforts, and the Musquïtoes that rack the morbid frame of Hobhouse, have luckily for me little effect on mine because I live more temperately.—I omitted Ephesus in my Catalogue, which I visited during my sojourn at Smyrna,—but the temple has almost perished, and St. Paul need not trouble himself to epistolize the present brood of Ephesians who have converted a large church built entirely of marble into a Mosque, and I dont know that the edifice looks the worse for it.—My paper is full and my ink ebbing, Good Afternoon!—If you address to me at Malta, the letter will be forwarded wherever I may be.—Hobhouse greets you, he pines for his poetry, at least some tidings of it.—I almost forgot to tell you that I am dying for love of three Greek Girls at Athens, sisters, two of whom have promised to accompany me to England, I lived in the same house, Teresa, Mariana, and Kattinka, are the names of these divinities all of them under 15.[7]—your ταπεινοτατοσ δουλοσ[8]

BYRON

[TO FRANCIS HODGSON]
Salsette Frigate.—in the Dardanelles off Abydos. May 5th. 1810

My dear Hodgson,—I am on my way to Constantinople after a turn through Greece, Epirus &c. and part of Asia minor, some particulars of which I have just communicated to our friend & Host H. Drury, with these then I shall not trouble you.—But as you will perhaps be pleased to hear that I am well &c. I take the opportunity of our Ambassador's return to forward the few lines I have now time to dispatch. —We have undergone some inconveniences and incurred partial perils, but no events worthy of commemoration unless you will deem it one that two days ago I swam from Sestos to Abydos.—This with a few alarms from robbers, and some danger of shipwreck in a Turkish Galliot six months ago, a visit to a Pacha, a passion for a married woman at Malta, a challenge to an officer, an attachment to three Greek Girls at Athens, with a great deal of buffoonery and fine prospects, form all that has distinguished my progress since my departure

[7] The Macri sisters, daughters of Byron's Athens landlady, Mrs. Tarsia Macri, widow of a former British Vice-Consul. The youngest, Teresa, then only 12, Byron celebrated in his poem to the "Maid of Athens".
[8] "most humble servant" in Greek.

from Spain.—Hobhouse rhymes and journalizes. I stare and do nothing, unless smoking can be deemed an active amusement.—The Turks take too much care of their women to permit them to be scrutinized, but I have lived a good deal with the Greeks, whose modern dialect I can converse in enough for my purposes.—With the Turks I have also some male acquaintances, female society is out of the question.—I have been very well treated by the Pachas and Governors, and have no complaints to make of any kind. Hobhouse will one day inform you of all our adventures, were I to attempt the recital, neither *my* paper nor *your* patience would hold during the operation.—Nobody, save yourself has written to me since I left England, but indeed I did not request it, I except my relations who write quite as often as I wish—Of Hobhouse's volume I know nothing except that it is out, and of my 2d. Edition I do not even know *that*, and certainly do not at this distance interest myself in the matter.—My friend H. is naturally anxious on the head of his rhymes, which I think will succeed or at least deserve success, but he has not yet acquired the "calm indifference" (as Sir Fretful has it), of *us old* Authors.—I hope you and Bland roll down the stream of Sale, with rapidity, and that you have produced a new poem, and Mrs. H. Drury a new child. Of my return I cannot positively speak, but think it probable Hobhouse will precede me in that respect, we have now been very nearly one year abroad.—I should wish to gaze away another at least in these evergreen climates, but I fear Business, Law business, the worst of employments, will recall me previous to that period if not very quickly.—If so, you shall have due notice, I hope you will find me an altered personage, I do not mean in body, but in manner, for I begin to find out that nothing but virtue will do in this damned world. I am tolerably sick of vice which I have tried in its agreeable varieties, and mean on my return to cut all my dissolute acquaintance, leave off wine and "carnal company", and betake myself to politics and Decorum.—I am very serious and cynical, and a good deal disposed to moralize, but fortunately for you the coming homily is cut off by default of pen, and defection of paper. Good morrow! if you write, address to me at Malta, whence your letters will be forwarded. You need not remember me to anybody but believe me yours with all faith

BYRON

Constantinople, May 15, 1810

P.S.—My dear H.—The date of my postscript will "prate to you of my whereabouts."[1] We anchored between the Seven Towers and the

---

[1] See *Macbeth*, II, i, 58: "The very stones prate of my whereabout".

Seraglio on the 13th, and yesterday settled ashore. The ambassador is laid up; but the secretary[2] does the honours of the palace, and we have a general invitation to his table. In a short time he has his leave of audience, and we accompany him in our uniforms to the Sultan &c. and in a few days I am to visit the Captain Pasha[3] with the commander of our frigate. I have seen enough of their Pashas already; but I wish to have a view of the Sultan, the last of the Ottoman race.[4] Of Constantinople you have Gibbon's description, very correct as far as I have seen. The mosques I shall have a firman to visit. I shall most probably (Deo volente), after a full inspection of Stamboul, bend my course homewards; but this is uncertain. I have seen the most interesting parts, particularly Albania, where few Franks have ever been, and all the most celebrated ruins of Greece and Ionia. Of England I know nothing, hear nothing, and can find no person better informed on the subject than myself. I this moment drink your health in a bumper of hock; Hobhouse fills and empties to the same; do you and Drury pledge us in a pint of any liquid you please—vinegar will bear the nearest resemblance to that which I have just swallowed to your name; but when we meet again the draught shall be mended and the wine also.

Yours ever,

B.

[TO MRS. CATHERINE GORDON BYRON] *Constantinople*
May 18th. 1810

Dear Madam,—I arrived here in an English frigate from Smyrna a few days ago without any events worth mentioning except landing to view the plains of Troy, and afterwards when we were at anchor in the *Dardanelles, swimming* from *Sestos* to *Abydos*, in imitation of Monsieur Leander whose story you no doubt know too well for me to add any thing on the subject except that I crossed the Hellespont without so

2 Stratford Canning, later first Viscount Stratford de Redcliffe (1786–1880) was a first cousin of George Canning, the Minister. He entered the Foreign Office in 1807, and the following year was sent to Constantinople with Robert Adair as first secretary. He took over as temporary head of the Embassy when Adair returned to England in July 1810.

3 On May 18, Byron accompanied Captain Bathurst of the *Salsette* frigate on a formal visit to the Capudan Pasha or Admiral of the Turkish fleet.

4 Sultan Mahmud II had succeeded his brother, dethroned by a revolution, in 1808, in his twenty-fifth year. He was still Sultan when the Greek Revolution broke out, and it was he who in 1824 proclaimed Byron an enemy of the Porte for his assistance to the Greeks.

good a motive for the undertaking.—As I am just going to visit the Capitan Pacha[1] you will excuse the brevity of my letter, when Mr. Adair takes leave I am to see the Sultan & the Mosques &c.

Believe me yrs ever
BYRON

[TO JOHN HANSON] *Constantinople. May 23d. 1810*

Sir,—I wrote to you the other day but another conveyance offering, I shall trouble you once more in hopes of at least extorting a reply.—I shall return to Greece when Mr. Adair takes his leave, I am to accompany him to the Sultan, you will address to Malta whence my letters are forwarded.—I shall probably pass my summer in the Morea, and expect occasional remittances as circumstances may occur, if Mrs. Byron requires any supply, pray let her have it at my expence, and at all events whatever becomes of me, do not allow her to suffer any unpleasant privation.—I believe I mentioned in my last that I had visited the plains of Troy, and swam from Sestos to Abydos in the Dardanelles, any of your classical men (Hargreaves or Charles) will explain the meaning of the last performance and the old story connected with it.—I came up in an English Frigate, but we were detained in the Hellespont ten days for a wind.—Here I am at last, I refer you for descriptions of Constantinople to the various travellers who have scribbled on the subject.—I am anxiously expecting intelligence from your quarter, I suppose you are now at Rochdale.—Present my respects and remembrances to all your family & believe me yours &c. &c.

BYRON

[TO MRS. CATHERINE GORDON BYRON] *Constantinople*
May 24th. 1810

Dear Mother,—I wrote to you very shortly the other day on my arrival here, and as another opportunity avails take up my pen again that the frequency of my letters may atone for their brevity.—Pray did you ever receive a picture of me in oil by *Sanders* in *Vigo Lane* London? (a noted limner,) if not, write for it immediately, it was paid for except the frame (if frame there be) before I left England.—I believe I mentioned to you in my last that my only notable exploit lately, has been swimming from Sestos to Abydos on the 3d. of this month, in

[1] See P.S. dated May 15, 1810, to Hodgson.

243

humble imitation of *Leander* of amorous memory, though I had no *Hero* to receive me on the other shore of the Hellespont.—Of Constantinople you have of course read fifty descriptions by sundry travellers, which are in general so correct that I have nothing to add on the Subject.—When our Ambassador takes his leave I shall accompany him to see the Sultan, and afterwards probably return to Greece, I have heard nothing of Mr. Hanson but one remittance without any letter from that legal gentleman.—If you have occasion for any pecuniary supply, pray use my funds as far as they *go* without reserve, and lest this should not be enough, in my next to Mr. H. I will direct him to advance any sum you may want, leaving it to your discretion how much in the present state of my affairs you may think proper to require.—I have already seen the most interesting parts of Turkey in Europe and Asia Minor, but shall not proceed further till I hear from England, in the mean time I expect occasional supplies according to circumstances, and shall pass my summer amongst my friends the Greeks of the Morea.—You will direct to Malta, whence my letters are forwarded and believe me to be with great sincerity

yrs ever
BYRON

P.S.—Fletcher is well, pray take care of my boy Robert, and the old man Murray.—It is fortunate they returned, neither the youth of the one or age of the other, would have suited the changes of climate and fatigues of travelling.—

[CAPTAIN WALTER BATHURST[1]]   *Pera. May 29th. 1810*

Dear Sir, My only *English* servant proving refractory, I am under the necessity of giving him a "mittamus" to his own Country.—[2]As I do not wish to be entirely without an Englishman I venture to beg of you (if my request is not improper) to permit me to take a youngster from your ship as a substitute.—I should be very sorry to deprive you

---

[1] Walter Bathurst (1764?–1827) was made a Captain in 1798 after serving under Rodney in the West Indies and under Lord St. Vincent at Cadiz. Byron became well acquainted with him during his voyage from Smyrna to Constantinople and his return to Greece on the *Salsette* frigate. Bathurst was killed in 1827 at the battle of Navarino.

[2] Byron had quarrelled with William Fletcher, his valet, and threatened to send him home, but on Fletcher's begging to remain he kept him.

of an able-bodied seaman, but if you would be good enough to allow me one of the lads, you will confer an additional obligation on your already

much obliged and very obedt. Servt.

BYRON

P.S.—I hope you were amused with the ceremony and pleased with your *garment* of yesterday.

[TO JOHN HANSON]   *Constantinople June 15th. 1810*

Sir,—This letter will be delivered by Mr. Hobhouse; I find by Hammersley that it was the sum of £1000 & not £500 as I supposed which was added to my credit last December, but half of this being lodged at Malta & half at Constantinople; I conceive it better in future either to place the entire sum (whatever it may be) with one Banker, or to send me a general credit for the same on both as was the case in my letters of Credit when I left England. I should also have deemed it as well for you to have written at the same time in reply to my repeated requests to that effect.—Perhaps you have done so, but your letters have never reached me, which they would if addressed to Malta. Mr. H[obhouse] will inform you as to my progress, and present my respects to the family. I remain Sir

your very obedt. Servt.

BYRON

[TO HENRY DRURY]   *Constantinople, June 17th, 1810*

Though I wrote to you so recently, I break in upon you again to congratulate you on a child being born, as a letter from Hodgson apprizes me of that event, in which I rejoice.

I am just come from an expedition through the Bosphorus to the Black Sea and the Cyanean Symplegades,[1] up which last I scrambled at as great a risk as ever the Argonauts escaped in their hoy. You remember the beginning of the nurse's dole in the Medea, of which I beg you to take the following translation, done on the summit.

---

[1] These rocks, treacherous to shipping, at the entrance to the Bosporus from the Black Sea, were supposed to be the fabled ones the Argonauts passed on their way to seek the Golden Fleece.

"Oh how I wish that an embargo
Had kept in port the good ship Argo!
Who, still unlaunch'd from Grecian docks,
Had never pass'd the Azure rocks;
But now I fear her trip will be a
Damn'd business for my Miss Medea, &c. &c.["]

as it very nearly was to me;—for, had not this sublime passage been
in my head, I should never have dreamed of ascending the said rocks,
and bruising my carcass in honour of the ancients.

I have now sat on the Cyaneans, swam from Sestos to Abydos (as I
trumpeted in my last), and, after passing through the Morea again,
shall set sail for Santa Maura, and toss myself from the Leucadian promontory;[2]—surviving which operation, I shall probably rejoin you in
England. H[obhouse], who will deliver this, is bound straight for these
parts; and, as he is bursting with his travels, I shall not anticipate his
narratives, but merely beg you not to believe one word he says, but
reserve your ear for me, if you have any desire to be acquainted with
the truth. * * *

I am bound for Athens once more, and thence to the Morea; but my
stay depends so much on my caprice, that I can say nothing of its probable duration. I have been out a year already, and may stay another;
but I am quicksilver, and say nothing positively. We are all very much
occupied doing nothing, at present. We have seen every thing but the
mosques, which we are to view with a firman on Tuesday next. But of
these and other sundries let H[obhouse] relate, with this proviso, that
I am to be referred to for authenticity; and I beg leave to contradict all
those things whereon he lays particular stress. But, if he soars, at any
time, into wit, I give you leave to applaud, because that is necessarily
stolen from his fellow-pilgrim. Tell Davies that H[obhouse] has made
excellent use of his best jokes in many of his majesty's ships of war;
but, add, also, that I always took care to restore them to the right
owner; in consequence of which he (Davies) is no less famous by
water than by land, and reigns unrivalled in the cabin, as in the "Cocoa
Tree."[3]

And Hodgson has been publishing more poesy—I wish he would
send me his "Sir Edgar,"[4] and "Bland's Anthology"[5] to Malta, where

[2] Byron was fascinated by the legend that Sappho ended her life by jumping from
a cliff on a promontory of the island of Lefkas in the Ionian Sea.

[3] The Cocoa Tree was a London Club dating from the days of Queen Anne, of
which Davies and Byron were members.

[4] Hodgson's *Sir Edgar, a Tale* was published in 1810.

[5] The Rev. Robert Bland (1780–1825), a friend of Hodgson and an assistant

they will be forwarded. In my last, which I hope you received, I gave an outline of the ground we have covered. If you have not been overtaken by this dispatch, H[obhouse]'s tongue is at your service. Remember me to Dwyer, who owes me eleven guineas. Tell him to put them in my banker's hands at Gibraltar or Constantinople. I believe he paid them once, but that goes for nothing, as it was an annuity.

I wish you would write. I have heard from Hodgson frequently. Malta is my post-office. I mean to be with you by next Montem.[6] You remember the last,—I hope for such another; but, after having swam across the "broad Hellespont," I disdain Datchett.[7] Good afternoon! I am yours, very sincerely,

BYRON

[TO DOCTOR————[1]]   *June 20th, 1810*

Dear Doctor,—They tell me the wind is too high for our expedition to Seraglio point, & I cannot think of putting your precious life in peril, but I hope to have the pleasure another day & beg you to believe me

yrs. very sincerely
BYRON

[TO ROBERT CHARLES DALLAS]   *Constantinople, June 23d, 1810*

Dear Sir,—I seize the opportunity of Mr. Hobhouse's return to England to write a few lines, in the hope that they will find you well and as happy as philosophers are, and men ought to be. I have since my departure from your country (a year ago) been in Portugal, Spain, Sardinia, Sicily, Malta, all the most interesting parts of Turkey in Europe, and Asia Minor, including Athens, &c. in the former, and the Troad and Ephesus in the latter, and have at last reached my headquarters, the capital. I have, of course, seen some variety, but I shall content myself with stating my only remarkable personal achievement, namely swimming from Sestos to Abydos, which I did on the 3d of May, as we lay at anchor in the Dardanelles, in the Salsette frigate.

master at Harrow while Byron was there, had published a series of translations, by himself and others, from the Greek Anthology in 1806.

[6] See June 4, 1808, to Harness, note 2.

[7] Datchet, a village on the Thames near Windsor, was the place where Byron engaged in a swimming contest after the Montem. (See Moore, I, 228n.)

[1] Unidentified. Perhaps the ship's doctor on the *Salsette* frigate.

You will [perhaps][1] smile at this exploit, but as it made an ancient immortal, I see no reason why a modern may not be permitted to boast of it, particularly as I had no mistress to comfort me at landing, and my labour was even to be its own reward. Mr. Hobhouse, our brother author, will narrate, no doubt, all our adventures, if you seriously incline that way. We have, moreover, been very high up into Albania, the wildest province in Europe, where very few Englishmen have ever been: but I say no more on this head, as my companion will be ready to gratify your inquiries.

I received your letter and request of a prologue at Lisbon, but it was too late; I have ever since been in motion, or I would have prologuized with pleasure. I presume you have had your run by this time. I need not add my good wishes for your drama. If I rightly recollect. you stated something about Murray's publishing my rhymes all together, including my Satire. Upon second thoughts, he had better let them alone; and if they are not begun on, pray suspend the operation till my return. I heard the other day that my Satire was in a third edition; that is but a poor progress, but Cawthorn published too many copies in the first. However, this circumstance will not interrupt my tranquillity beneath the blue skies of Greece, where I return to spend my summer, and perhaps the winter. I am alike distant from praise or censure, which tends to make both very indifferent to me, and so good night to scribbling. Hobhouse's book has been out some time I hear; but more we know not, except in a letter from my friend * * * [Hodgson?], who says the Reviews have attacked it for indecency. I suppose the few stanzas of my writing in the volume have been bedeviled, and indeed they deserve little better. Has your friend Wright[2] galloped on the highway of letters? and what have you done yourself? I thirst for intelligence; if you have nothing better to do some afternoon, remember that Malta is my post office.

I refer you to Mr. Hobhouse for detail, and having now discharged a duty, I will trouble you no more at present, except to state that all climates and nations are equally interesting to me; that mankind are every where despicable in different absurdities; that the farther I proceed from your country the less I regret leaving it, and the only advantage you have over the rest of mankind is the sea, that divides you from your foes; your other superiorities are merely imaginary. I would be a citizen of the world, but I fear some indispensable affairs will soon

[1] This word is in the text as quoted in the Sotheby catalogue, Dec. 2, 1910.
[2] Walter Rodwell Wright, author of *Horae Ionicae*, whom Byron praised in *English Bards and Scotch Reviewers* (lines 877–880).

call me back; and as I left the land without regret, I shall return without pleasure. The only person whom I expected to have grieved took leave of me with a coolness which, had I not known the heart of man, would have surprised me; I should have attributed it to offence, had I ever been guilty in that instance of any thing but affection. But what is all this to you? nothing. Good night!

Believe me, Yours very truly,
BYRON

P.S.—I again repeat my request that you will write to Malta. I expect a world of news, not political, for we have the papers up to May. If you tear one another to pieces for a continuance, I must come back and share the carrion. Have the military murdered any more mechanics? and is the flower of chivalry released? We are not very quiet here, the Russians have drubbed the Mussulmen, but we talk of peace.

[TO MRS. CATHERINE GORDON BYRON]   *Constantinople*
                                               June 28th. 1810

My dear Mother,—I regret to perceive by your last letter, that several of mine have not arrived, particularly a very long one written in November last from Albania, when I was on a visit to the Pacha of that province.—Fletcher has also written to his spouse perpetually.— Mr. Hobhouse who will forward or deliver this and is on his return to England, can inform you of our different movements, but I am very uncertain as to my own return. He will probably be down in Notts some time or other, but Fletcher whom I send back as an Incumbrance, (English servants are sad travellers) will supply his place in the Interim, and describe our travels which have been tolerably extensive.— I have written twice briefly from this capital, from Smyrna, from Athens and other parts of Greece, from Albania, the Pacha of which province desired his respects to my mother, and said he was sure I was a man of high birth because I had *"small ears, curling hair,* and *white hands"*!!! He was very kind to me, begged me to consider him as a father, and gave me a guard of forty soldiers through the forests of Acarnania.—But of this and other circumstances I have written to you at large, and yet hope you will receive my letters.—I remember Mahmout Pacha, the grandson of Ali Pacha at Yanina, (a little fellow of ten years of age, with large black eyes which our ladies would purchase at any price, and those regular features which distinguish the Turks) asked me how I came to travel about so *young*, without any

249

body to take care of me, this question was put by the little man with all the gravity of threescore.—I cannot now write copiously, I have only time to tell you that I have passed many a fatiguing but never a tedious moment, and that all I am afraid of *is*, that I shall contract a Gipsy-like wandering disposition, which will make home tiresome to me, this I am told is very common with men in the habit of peregrination, and indeed I feel it so.—On the third of May I swam from *Sestos* to Abydos, you know the story of Leander, but I had no *Hero* to receive me at landing. —I also passed a fortnight in the Troad, the tombs of Achilles and Æsietes [sic] &c. still exist in large barrows similar to those you have doubtless seen in the North.—The other day I was at Belgrade (a village in these environs) to see the house built on the same site as Lady Mary Wortley's, by the bye, her Ladyship, as far as I can judge, has lied, but not half so much as any other woman would have done in the same situation.—I have been in all the principal Mosques by virtue of a firman, this is a favour rarely permitted to infidels, but the Ambassador's departure obtained it for us. I have been up the Bosphorus into the Black Sea, round the walls of the city, and indeed I know more of it by sight than I do of London.—I hope to amaze you some winter's evening with the details but at present you must excuse me, I am not able to write long letters in *June*.—I return to spend my summer in Greece, I shall not proceed farther into Asia, as I have visited Smyrna, Ephesus, and the Troad.—I write often but you must not be alarmed when you do not receive my letters, consider we have no regular post farther than Malta where I beg you will in future send your letters, & not to this city.—Fletcher is a poor creature, and requires comforts that I can dispense with, he is very sick of his travels, but you must not believe his account of the country, he sighs for Ale, and Idleness, and a wife and the Devil knows what besides.—I have not been disappointed or disgusted, I have lived with the highest and the lowest, I have been for days in a Pacha's palace, and have passed many a night in a cowhouse, and I find the people inoffensive and kind, I have also passed some time with the principal Greeks in the Morea & Livadia, and though inferior to the Turks, they are better than the Spaniards, who in their turn excel the Portuguese. Of Constantinople you will find many correct descriptions in different travels, but Lady Wortley errs strangely when she says "St. Paul's would cut a poor figure by St. Sophia's".[1] I have been in both, surveyed them inside & out atten-

[1] Lady Mary Wortley Montagu had not compared St. Paul's to St. Sophia, but to the mosque of the Sultana Validé (or Queen mother) on the square near the Galata Bridge. It is now known as the Yeni-Cami (New Mosque). It was begun

tively, St. Sophia's is undoubtedly the most interesting from its immense antiquity, and the circumstance of all the Greek Emperors from Justinian having been crowned there, and several murdered at the Altar, besides the Turkish Sultans who attend it regularly, but it is inferior in beauty & size to some of the other Mosques, particularly "Soleyman Etc" and not to be mentioned in the same page with St. P's (I speak like a *cockney*) however, I prefer the Gothic Cathedral of Seville to St. P's, St. Sophia's and any religious building I have ever seen.—The walls of the Seraglio are like the walls of Newstead Gardens only higher, and much in the same *order*, but the ride by the walls of the city on the land side is beautiful, imagine, four miles of immense triple battlements covered with *Ivy*, surmounted with 218 towers, and on the other side of the road Turkish burying grounds (the loveliest spots on earth) full of enormous cypresses, I have seen the ruins of Athens, of Ephesus, and Delphi, I have traversed great part of Turkey and many other parts of Europe and some of Asia, but I never beheld a work of Nature or Art, which yielded an impression like the prospect on each side, from the Seven Towers to the End of the Golden Horn.—Now for England, you have not received my friend Hobhouse's volume of Poesy, it has been published several months, you ought to read it.—I am glad to hear of the progress of E. Bards &c. of course you observed I have made great additions to the new Edition.—Have you received my picture from Sanders in Vigo lane London? it was finished and paid for long before I left England, pray send for it.—You seem to be a mighty reader of magazines, where do you pick up all this intelligence? quotations &c. &c.?—Though I was happy to obtain my seat without Ld. C[arlisle]'s assistance, I had no measures to keep with a man who declined interfering as my relation on that occasion, and I have done with him, though I regret distressing Mrs. Leigh, poor thing! I hope she is happy.—It is my opinion that Mr. Bowman ought to marry Miss Rushton,[2] our first duty is not to do evil, but alas! that is impossible, our next is to repair it, if in our power, the girl is his equal, if she were his inferior a sum of money and provision for the child would be some, though a poor compensation, as it is,

by the widow of Murad III, the mother of Mehmet III, and completed by the mother of Mehmet IV in 1663. What Lady Mary wrote in 1718 was: "That of the Validé, is the largest of all, built entirely of Marble, the most prodigious and I think the most beautiful structure I ever saw . . . (between friends) *St. Paul's Church* would make a pitiful figure near it. . . ." (*Letters*, ed. by Robert Halsband, Vol. I, p. 400. Letter of April 10, 1718, to Lady Bristol.)

[2] Bowman was the son of one of the tenants at Newstead; Miss Rushton was probably a sister of Robert Rushton, Byron's page.

he should marry her. I will have no gay deceivers on my Estate, and I shall not allow my tenants a privilege I do not permit myself, viz— *that*, of debauching each other's daughters.—God knows, I have been guilty of many excesses, but as I have laid down a resolution to reform, and *lately* kept it, I expect this Lothario to follow the example, and begin by restoring this girl to society, or, by the Beard of my Father! he shall hear of it.—Pray, take some notice of Robert, who will miss his master, poor boy, he was very unwilling to return.—I trust you are well & happy, it will be a pleasure to hear from you, believe me

yours ever sincerely
BYRON

P.S.—How is Joe Murray?—

P.S.—July 6th. 1810

Dear M[othe]r,—I open my letter to tell you that Fletcher having petitioned [to] accompany me into the Morea, I have taken him with me contrary to the intention expressed in my letter.—

yours ever
BYRON

[TO JOHN HANSON] *Constantinople. June 30th. 1810*

Sir,—In case of any accident befalling the letter which Mr. Hobhouse has in charge for you, I send a second merely to state that my own return will not take place for some time, and to request you will continue to remit regularly, according to circumstances, but I think it better instead of dividing the sum between two bankers, either to lodge it entire with one, or to send me a *general* letter of credit for the amount, as when I left England.—You will present my best regards to your family & believe me

yours very sincerely
BYRON

P.S.—I shall not return to England for two years at least (from this date) except in case of war.—

[TO JAMES CAWTHORN] *Constantinople July 1st. 1810*

Mr. Cawthorne [sic],—You have paid much *attention* to my desire that you would send a copy of the second Edition of my Satire to

Malta for me; I presume if the sale is successful it is nothing to you hot-press gentry what becomes of the author.—I again request however, that you will attend to my order; though you have not written to give the smallest intimation of it's progress, I have heard through other channels that the work goes on tolerably.—I suppose that my directions have been obeyed with regard to the additions &c. before I left London, and it is said to be in a third Edition,[1] wishing you success & a little more politeness I remain

&c. &c.

BYRON

[TO FRANCIS HODGSON]   *Constantinople, July 4, 1810*

My dear Hodgson,—Twice have I written—once in answer to your last, and a former letter when I arrived here in May. That I may have nothing to reproach myself with, I will write once more—a very superfluous task, seeing that Hobhouse is bound for your parts full of talk and wonderment. My first letter went by an ambassadorial express; my second by the "Black John" lugger; my third will be conveyed by Cam, the miscellanist. I shall begin by telling you, having only told it you twice before, that I swam from Sestos to Abydos. I do this that you may be impressed with proper respect for me, the performer; for I plume myself on this achievement more than I could possibly do on any kind of glory, political, poetical, or rhetorical. Having told you this I will tell you nothing more, because it would be cruel to curtail Cam's narrative, which, by-the-bye, you must not believe till confirmed by me, the eye-witness. I promise myself much pleasure from contradicting the greatest part of it. He has been plaguily pleased by the intelligence contained in your last to me respecting the reviews of his hymns. I refreshed him with that paragraph immediately, together with the tidings of my own third edition, which added to his recreation. But then he has had a letter from a Lincoln's Inn Bencher full of praise of his harpings, and vituperation of the other contributions to his *Missellingany*, which that sagacious person is pleased to say must have been put in as FOILS (horresco referens!); furthermore he adds that Cam "is a genuine pupil of Dryden," concluding with a comparison rather to the disadvantage of Pope . . . I

---

[1] Cawthorn had published four editions of *English Bards and Scotch Reviewers* before Byron returned to England in July 1811. The venture was so profitable that when Byron suppressed the fifth edition before publication, Cawthorn continued putting out spurious and unauthorized editions for a number of years.

have written to Drury by Hobhouse; a letter is also from me on its way to England intended for that matrimonial man.[1] Before it is very long I hope we shall again be together; the moment I set out for England you shall have intelligence, that we may meet as soon as possible. Next week the frigate sails with Adair; I am for Greece, Hobhouse for England. A year together on the 2nd July since we sailed from Falmouth. I have known a hundred instances of men setting out in couples, but not one of a similar return. Aberdeen's party split;[2] several voyagers at present have done the same. I am confident that twelve months of any given individual is perfect ipecacuanha.

The Russians and Turks are at it, and the Sultan in person is soon to head the army. The Captain Pasha cuts off heads every day, and a Frenchman's ears; the last is a serious affair. By-the-bye I like the Pashas in general. Ali Pasha called me his son, desired his compliments to my mother, and said he was sure I was a man of birth, because I had "small ears and curling hair." He is Pasha of Albania six hundred miles off, where I was in October—a fine portly person. His grandson Mahmout, a little fellow ten years old, with large black eyes as big as pigeon's eggs, and all the gravity of sixty, asked me what I did travelling so young without a Lala? (tutor).

Good night, dear H. I have crammed my paper and crave your indulgence. Write to me at Malta.

I am, with all sincerity, yours affectionately,

BYRON

[TO EDWARD ELLICE]   *Constantinople. July 4th. 1810*

My dear Ellice,—I seize the occasion of Mr. Adair's return to convey my congratulations on your marriage, (for I hear you have taken unto yourself a wife) these, though somewhat of the latest, will arrive at a time when you must be more sensible of their value, as having full experience of matrimony and it's concomitant blessings.—Hobhouse is returning, but I am going back to Greece[;] to that loquacious traveller I refer you for all our adventures, but I must beg leave to

[1] Henry Drury.
[2] George Hamilton Gordon, fourth Earl of Aberdeen, in 1802 joined Mr. Drummond, the new British Ambassador to the Porte, and accompanied him to Constantinople. He then set out to explore Greece and Asia Minor. He rediscovered and excavated the Pnyx, and then went on to Smyrna, Ephesus, the Morea, Albania, and Corfu, before returning to England in 1804. He was the founder of the Athenian Society. Byron referred to him in *English Bards and Scotch Reviewers* as "The travelled Thane, Athenian Aberdeen" (line 509). Aberdeen afterward had a long ministerial career, becoming Foreign Secretary and Prime Minister.

mention to you as a feat that I have swum from Sestos to Abydos.—I hear your friend Brougham[1] is in the lower house mouthing at the ministry, notwithstanding my enmity against him and the dogs without faith with whom he is critically connected, I wish him success, you remember he would not believe that *I* had written my pestilent Satire, now that was very cruel and unlike me, for the moment I read his speech, I believed it to be *his* entire from Exordium to Peroration.— My fellow traveller Hobby who is posting to your country full of marvels, has, as you no doubt know, put forth a volume of Poesy, which I do exhort you and all your acquaintance who may be possessed of a dormant half-guinea to purchase, and he himself (when he is worth so much money) will in return buy rhyme at the same rate from any of the said persons who shall please to be poetical. *My* work it seems has frisked through another edition with my name prefixed to it, despite of the advice of all my friends, who were fearful I should be cut off in the flower of my youth by an Insurrection in Grubstreet, now I mean to live a long time in defiance of pens or penknives.—I suppose by this time you have become a bitter politician, I hope in no very long time to be amongst you, but I have one or two little things to adjust in the Morea, before I sail.—We have been in Portugal, Spain, Sardinia, Sicily, Malta, Albania, Greece, Asia Minor, and seen the Troad, Athens, Ephesus and sundry cities with names that would choak you, but I spare you;—I shall not proceed into Persia, as I prophesied in rather too great a hurry, but having satiated my curiosity in this metropolis, quietly repair home, and then—and then—I hope you will be glad to see me, and I will have a speech ready for your spouse, and marry myself seeing I have such excellent encouragement.—Present my humble service to your brethren, and my cousin Trevanion, I am sorry to hear that my Sister Mrs. Leigh is annoyed at my attack on the Earl of C[arlisle][2] though I had motives enough to

[1] Henry Peter Brougham (1778–1868), later Baron Brougham and Vaux, was one of the founders of the *Edinburgh Review*. It was he who wrote the anonymous review of *Hours of Idleness* which so incensed Byron and which he erroneously ascribed to the editor Francis Jeffrey. In 1810 Brougham entered Parliament and became a powerful advocate of reform. He defended Queen Caroline during her trial in 1820, worked for the abolition of slavery and for legal reform. He was one of the founders of London University and of the Society for the Diffusion of Useful Knowledge. When Byron learned later that Brougham had spread evil rumours about him during the Separation proceedings, and that he was the *Edinburgh* reviewer of his poems, he vowed that if he ever came back to England he would challenge Brougham to a duel.

[2] After what he considered a rebuff by his kinsman and guardian, who did not come forward to introduce him in the House of Lords, Byron had changed the flattering lines on Carlisle, when he revised *English Bards and Scotch Reviewers*

justify any measures against that silly old man, had I been aware that she would have laid it to heart, I would have cast my pen and poem both into the flames, and, in good truth (if she knew the feelings of us scribblers) no small sacrifice.—But the mischief is done, Lord forgive me! this it is to have tender hearted she-relations, if I had been lucky enough to be a bastard, I might have abused everybody to my dying-day, and *nobody never* the *worser*.—I have sent no descriptions to you of these parts, because you know the Mackenzies[3] and other vagrant people who have told you all how and about them.—I address this to Brookes's, supposing marriage to have driven you from Park-Street, I have nothing left to wish you but an heir, of whose Papa I remain the obliged and very sincere friend

BYRON

[TO ROBERT ADAIR]   *Pera July 4th. 1810*

Sir,—I regret that your Excellency should have deemed me or my concerns of sufficient importance to give you a thought beyond the moment when they were forced (perhaps unreasonably) on your attention.—On all occasions of this kind one of the parties must be wrong, at present it has fallen to my lot, your authorities (particularly the *German*) are too many for me.[1]—I shall therefore make what atonement I can by cheerfully following not only your excellency "but your servant or your maid your ox or your ass, or any thing that is yours."—I have to apologize for not availing myself of your Excellency['s] kind invitation and hospitable intentions in my favour, but the fact is, that I am never very well adapted for or very happy in society, and I happen at this time from some particular circumstances to be even less so than usual.[2] Your excellency will I

for a second edition, to "No Muse will cheer, with renovating smile,/The paralytic puling of Carlisle."

[3] Alexander Mackenzie published in 1801 *Voyages from Montreal, on the River St. Laurence, through the Continent of North America, to the Frozen and Pacific Oceans; in the Years 1789 and 1793. With a Preliminary Account of the Rise, Progress, and Present State of the Fur Trade of that Country*. With his connection with the fur trade, Ellice undoubtedly knew the book and probably the author.

[1] The Austrian Internuncio, the authority on diplomatic etiquette, assured Byron that the Turks did not acknowledge precedence of rank in the procession. He had been invited to attend the ceremony of the Ambassador's farewell audience with the Sultan.

[2] Byron was depressed at the time by news from England. His financial affairs were in the worst state imaginable. Brothers, the Nottingham upholsterer, had presented his bill for £1,600 for furnishing the rooms at Newstead and threatened an execution. Hanson was desperately trying to placate Byron's creditors, who had

trust attribute my omissions to the *right* cause rather than disrespect in your

truly obliged & very obedient humble servant

BYRON

bills totalling £10,000, and was only able to pay the £3,000 due the usurers. An additional cause of Byron's depression may have been a letter he had received from Hodgson. Hobhouse recorded in his diary on June 6, 1810: "messenger arrived from England—bringing a letter from Hodgson to B— tales spread—the *Edleston* accused of indecency". (Marchand, *Byron: A Biography*, I, 245n.)

Appendix I

LIST OF LETTERS AND SOURCES

VOLUME 1

259

Date	Recipient	Source of Text	Page
		1804 (continued)	
Nov. 17	Augusta Byron	MS. Murray	57
Nov. 21	Augusta Byron	MS. Murray	58
Dec. 1	John Hanson	MS. Murray	59

1805

Date	Recipient	Source of Text	Page
Jan. 30	Augusta Byron	MS. Murray	60
March 2	John Hanson	MS. Murray	62
April 4	Augusta Byron	MS. Murray	62
April 15	Hargreaves Hanson	MS. Murray	63
April 20	Hargreaves Hanson	MS. Murray	64
April 23	Augusta Byron	MS. Murray	65
April 25	Augusta Byron	MS. Murray	66
May 11	John Hanson	Text: *LJ*, I, 65	68
June 5	Augusta Byron	MS. Lytton	68
June 27	John Hanson	MS. Huntington Library	69
July 2	Augusta Byron	MS. Murray	69
[July 8]	John Hanson	MS. Murray	70
Aug. 4	Charles D. Gordon	MS. Harrow Library	70
Aug. 6	Augusta Byron	MS. Murray	72
Aug. 10	Augusta Byron	MS. Murray	73
Aug. 14	Charles D. Gordon	MS. Berg Coll., N.Y. Public Library	74
Aug. 18	Augusta Byron	MS. Murray	75
Aug. 19	Hargreaves Hanson	MS. Murray	76
[Aug. 28]	Hargreaves Hanson	MS. Murray	77
Sept. 20	Hargreaves Hanson	MS. Murray	77
Oct. 25	Hargreaves Hanson	MS. Murray	78
Oct. 26	John Hanson	MS. Murray	78
Nov. 6	Augusta Byron	MS. Lytton	79
Nov. 12	Hargreaves Hanson	MS. Murray	80
Nov. 23	John Hanson	MS. Murray	81
Nov. 30	John Hanson	MS. Murray	82
Dec. 4	John Hanson	MS. Murray	84
Dec. 9	Mrs. Massingberd	MS. Anthony Powell	84
Dec. 13	John Hanson	MS. Murray	85
Dec. 26	Augusta Byron	MS. Lytton	85
Dec. 27	Augusta Byron	MS. Lytton	86

Date	Recipient	Source of Text	Page
		1806	
Jan. 7	Augusta Byron	MS. Lytton	87
Feb. 26	His Mother	MS. Murray	88
March 3	John Hanson	MS. Murray	90
March 10	John Hanson	MS. Murray	90
March 25	John Hanson	MS. Murray	91
April 10	John Hanson	Text: Copy by Newton Hanson, Murray MSS.	91
May 16	Henry Angelo	MS. British Museum (in Grangerized edition of Byron's *Works*, Vol. 38)	92
June 16	John Hanson	MS. British Museum (Eg. 2611)	92
July 8	Mrs. Massingberd	MS. Murray	93
Aug. 9	John Pigot	MS. Nottingham Public Libraries	93
Aug. 9	E. N. Long	MS. Berg Coll., N.Y. Public Library	95
Aug. 10	Elizabeth Pigot	MS. Nottingham Public Libraries	96
Aug. 10	John Pigot	MS. Nottingham Public Libraries	97
Aug. 16	John Pigot	MS. Nottingham Public Libraries	97
Aug. 18	John Pigot	MS. Nottingham Public Libraries	98
Aug. 26	John Pigot	MS. Huntington Library	99
Aug. 26	Mrs. Massingberd	Text: Sotheby Catalogue, June 3, 1929	100
[Sept.?]	Elizabeth Pigot	Text: Moore, I, 76–77	100
Oct. 20	[Rev. Thomas Jones?]	MS. Stark Library, University of Texas	100
Nov. 4	Earl of Clare	MS. Roe-Byron Coll., Newstead Abbey	101
Dec. 7	John Hanson	MS. Murray	101
		1807	
Jan. 8	Dr. T. Falkner	MS. Boston Public Library	102
Jan. 13	John Pigot	MS. Nottingham Public Libraries	103

Date	Recipient	Source of Text	Page
		1807 (continued)	
Jan. 31	Capt. John Leacroft	Text: *LJ*, I, 113–115	104
Feb. 4	Capt. John Leacroft (a)	Text: *LJ*, I, 115	105
Feb. 4	Capt John Leacroft (b)	Text: *LJ*, I, 115–116	105
Feb. 6	Earl of Clare	Text: Moore, I, 82–83	106
Feb. 8	Mrs. John Hanson	MS. Murray	107
Feb. 9	[Elizabeth Pigot?]	Text: Moore, I, 109	107
Feb. 14	Rev. Thomas Jones	MS. Carl H. Pforzheimer Library	108
Feb. 23	E. N. Long	MS. Berg Coll., N.Y. Public Library	109
March 6	William Bankes	MS. Stark Library, University of Texas	110
[March?]	[William Bankes]	MS. Child Memorial Library, Harvard University	112
April 2	John Hanson	MS. Murray	113
April 16	E. N. Long	Text: *LJ*, II, 19–20n; Sotheby Catalogue, Dec. 20, 1937 (Fac. of one page)	114
April 19	John Hanson	MS. Murray	116
April 19	E. N. Long	MS. Carl H. Pforzheimer Library	116
[April 21?]	John Pigot	MS. Nottingham Public Libraries	117
May 1	E. N. Long	Text: Sotheby Catalogue, Dec. 20, 1937 (Fac. of one page)	117
May 14	E. N. Long	MS. Meyer Davis Coll., University of Pennsylvania Library	118
May 18	John Hanson	MS. Murray	119
June 11	Elizabeth Pigot	MS. Nottingham Public Libraries	120
June 11	John Hanson	MS. Murray	120
June 29	E. N. Long	MS. Beinecke Library, Yale University	121
June 30	Elizabeth Pigot	Nottingham Public Libraries	122

Date	Recipient	Source of Text	Page
		1807 (continued)	
July 5	Elizabeth Pigot	MS. Nottingham Public Libraries	124
July 13	Elizabeth Pigot	MS. Nottingham Public Libraries	126
July 20	John Hanson (a)	MS. Murray	128
July 20	John Hanson (b)	MS. Murray	128
July 21	Ben Crosby (a)	Text: Eugenius Roche, *London in a Thousand Years*, 1830, p. vi	129
July 21	Ben Crosby (b)	MS. British Museum (Eg. 2332)	129
[Aug.?]	Earl of Clare	Text: Moore, I, 50	129
Aug. 2	Elizabeth Pigot	MS. Huntington Library	130
Aug. 11	Elizabeth Pigot	MS. Nottingham Public Libraries	131
Aug. 20	Earl of Clare	MS. Beinecke Library, Yale University	133
Oct. 19	John Hanson	MS. British Museum (Eg. 2611)	134
Oct. 26	Elizabeth Pigot	MS. Nottingham Public Libraries	135
Nov. 11	John Ridge	MS. Morgan Library	137
Nov. 13	John Hanson	MS. British Museum (Eg. 2611)	137
Nov. 20	John Ridge	MS. Stark Library, University of Texas	138
[Nov. 23?]	E. N. Long	MS. Houghton Library, Harvard University	139
Dec. 11	John Ridge	MS. Newark-on-Trent Museum	139
Dec. 14	John Ridge	MS. Beinecke Library, Yale University	139
Dec. 20	John Ridge	MS. Stark Library, University of Texas	140
Dec. 22	Ben Crosby	MS. Stark Library, University of Texas	140
Dec. 23	John Hanson	MS. British Museum (Eg. 2611)	142
Dec. 28	John Ridge	MS. Morgan Library	142

Date	Recipient	Source of Text	Page
		1808	
Jan. 6	John Hanson	MS. British Museum (Eg. 2611)	142
Jan. 8	John Hanson	MS. Stark Library, University of Texas	143
Jan. 9	John Ridge	MS. Bodleian Library	143
Jan. 12	John Ridge	MS. Stark Library, University of Texas	143
Jan. 12	John Hanson	MS. British Museum (Eg. 2611)	144
Jan 13.	Henry Drury	MS. Trinity College Library, Cambridge	144
Jan. 20	R. C. Dallas	MS. Stark Library, University of Texas	146
Jan. 21	R. C. Dallas	MS. Berg Coll., N.Y. Public Library	147
Jan. 25	John Hanson (a)	MS. British Museum (Eg. 2611)	148
Jan. 25	John Hanson (b)	MS. British Museum (Eg. 2611)	149
Jan. 28	E. N. Long	MS. Berg Coll., N.Y. Public Library	150
[Feb.?]	[John Cam Hobhouse?]	MS. James Lees-Milne	150
Feb.	John Hanson	Text: Waller Catalogue 111, 1877	151
Feb. 2	James De Bathe	MS. Murray	151
Feb. 3	John Ridge	MS. Robert H. Taylor Coll., Princeton University Library	152
Feb. 5	E. N. Long	MS. Berg Coll., N.Y. Public Library	152
Feb. 7	Henry Drury	MS. Trinity College Library, Cambridge	153
Feb. 11	William Harness	Text: Moore, I, 140	154
Feb. 11	John Ridge	MS. Stark Library, University of Texas	154
Feb. 16	John Ridge	MS. Morgan Library	155
Feb. 16	William Harness	MS. Stark Library, University of Texas	155

Date	Recipient	Source of Text	Page
		1808 (continued)	
Feb. 26	Rev. John Becher	MS. Morgan Library	157
Feb. 27	John Cam Hobhouse	MS. Murray	158
Feb. 29	John Cam Hobhouse	MS. Murray	159
March 14	John Cam Hobhouse	MS. Murray	160
March 26	John Cam Hobhouse	MS. Murray	161
March 27	John Jackson	MS. Carl H. Pforzheimer Library	162
March 28	Rev. John Becher	Text: Moore, I, 145–6; Bangs & Co. Catalogue, Jan. 24, 1902; H. B. Smith sale catalogue, April 8, 1936	162
March 29	William Harness	MS. Stark Library, University of Texas	163
April 15	John Cam Hobhouse	MS. Murray	164
April 26	Augusta Leigh	MS. Lytton	165
May 12	Mrs. Massingberd	Text: Nottingham Mechanics' Institution Catalogue, 1915	166
June 4	William Harness	MS. Stark Library, University of Texas	166
June 15	Hargreaves Hanson	MS. British Museum (Eg. 2611)	167
July 3	Hewson Clarke	MS. Murray	167
July 20	Mrs. Massingberd	MS. Anthony Powell	167
Aug. 7	Lord Grey de Ruthyn	MS. Meyer Davis Coll., University of Pennsylvania Library	168
Aug. 14	John Hanson	MS. British Museum (Eg. 2611)	169
Aug. 29	John Hanson	MS. Morgan Library	169
[Sept.?]	John Jackson	Text: Alfred Bunn, *The Stage: Both Before and Behind the Curtain*, 1840, III, 20	169
Sept. 13	John Hanson	MS. British Museum (Eg. 2611)	170
Sept. 14	Rev. John Becher	MS. Stark Library, University of Texas	170
Sept. 18	John Jackson	Text: Moore, I, 148	170
Oct. 4	John Jackson	Text: Moore, I 149	171

Date	Recipient	Source of Text	Page
		1808 (continued)	
Oct. 7	His Mother	MS. Morgan Library	171
Nov. 2	His Mother	MS. Morgan Library	172
Nov. 3	Francis Hodgson	MS. Facsimile in Garnett and Gosse, *Illustrated Record of English Literature*	173
Nov. 9	J. Birch	MS. British Museum (Eg. 2611)	174
Nov. 15	John Hanson	MS. British Museum (Eg. 2611)	174
Nov. 18	John Hanson	Text: *LJ*, I, 199–200	175
Nov. 18	Francis Hodgson	MS. Murray	176
Nov. 20	Duke of Portland	MS. Murray	177
Nov. 27	Francis Hodgson	Text: Hodgson, *Memoir*, I, 107–109	178
Nov. 30	Augusta Leigh	MS. Lytton	179
Dec. 12	John Jackson	Text: Moore, I, 149	180
Dec. 14	Augusta Leigh	MS. Murray	180
Dec. 17	John Hanson	MS. British Museum (Eg. 2611)	181
Dec. 17	Francis Hodgson	Text: Hodgson, *Memoir*, I, 110–112	182
Dec. 23	John Hanson	MS. British Museum (Eg. 2611)	183
		1809	
Jan. 3	John Hanson	MS. Murray	183
Jan. 5	John Hanson	MS. British Museum (Eg. 2611)	184
Jan. 6	Scrope Berdmore Davies	MS. Murray	184
Jan. 10	John Hanson	MS. Beinecke Library, Yale University	185
Jan. 15	John Hanson	MS. Stark Library, University of Texas	185
Jan. 16	John Cam Hobhouse	MS. Murray	187
Jan. 17	John Hanson	MS. Houghton Library, Harvard University	188
Jan. 20	R. C. Dallas	MS. Stark Library, University of Texas	189

Date	Recipient	Source of Text	Page
		1809 (continued)	
Jan. 25	R. C. Dallas	Text: Dallas, *Correspondence*, I, 32–34	189
Feb. 4	John Hanson	MS. Murray	191
Feb. 6	R. C. Dallas	MS. Berg Coll., N.Y. Public Library	191
Feb. 7	John Hanson	MS. British Museum (Eg. 2611)	191
Feb. 7	R. C. Dallas	MS. Berg Coll., N.Y. Public Library	192
Feb. 8	John Hanson	MS. British Museum (Eg. 2611)	192
Feb. 10	William Harness	Text: Sotheby Catalogue, July 21, 1970	193
Feb. 11	R. C. Dallas	Text: Dallas, *Correspondence*, I, 44	193
Feb. 12	R. C. Dallas	MS. Roe-Byron Coll., Newstead Abbey	193
Feb. 15	R. C. Dallas	MS. Fitzwilliam Museum, Cambridge	193
Feb. 15	Mr. Mayfield	Text: Sotheby Catalogue, July 12, 1921	194
Feb. 16	R. C. Dallas	Text: Dallas, *Correspondence*, I, 46	194
Feb. 19	R. C. Dallas	MS. Robert H. Taylor Coll., Princeton University Library	194
Feb. 22	R. C. Dallas	Text: Dallas, *Correspondence*, I, 47	195
March 3	John Hanson	MS. Murray	195
March 6	His Mother	MS. Berg Coll., N.Y. Public Library	195
March 6	Francis Hodgson	MS. Stark Library, University of Texas	196
March 18	William Harness	MS. Berg Coll., N.Y. Public Library	197
March 21	Francis Hodgson	MS. Stark Library, University of Texas	198
[March?]	William Bankes	Text: Moore, I, 184	198

Date	Recipient	Source of Text	Page
		1809 (continued)	
April 4	John Hanson	MS. British Museum (Eg. 2611)	199
April 8	John Hanson	MS. British Museum (Eg. 2611)	199
April 12	J. Wedderburn Webster	MS. Murray	199
April 12	John Hanson	MS. British Museum (Eg. 2611)	199
April 14	E. B. Long	MS. Berg Coll., N.Y. Public Library	200
April 16	John Hanson	MS. British Museum (Eg. 2611)	200
April 17	John Hanson	MS. British Museum (Eg. 2611)	201
April 25	R. C. Dallas	Text: Dallas, *Correspondence*, I, 57	201
April 26	John Hanson	MS. British Museum (Eg. 2611)	202
May 2	John Hanson	MS. British Museum (Eg. 2611)	203
May 15	Rev. Robert Lowe	Text: *Life and Letters of Viscount Sherbrooke*, I, 46	203
May 19	His Mother	MS. Murray	203
May 23	John Hanson	MS. British Museum (Eg. 2611)	204
June 6	Joseph Murray	Text: Myers & Co. Catalogue, 379, Spring 1954, p. 16	204
June 19	John Hanson	MS. British Museum (Eg. 2611)	204
June 21	John Hanson (a)	MS. Carl H. Pforzheimer Library	205
June 21	John Hanson (b)	MS. British Museum (Eg. 2611)	205
June 22	His Mother	MS. Morgan Library	206
June 22	Charles Skinner Matthews	MS. Hobhouse papers	206
June 25	John Hanson	MS. British Museum (Eg. 2611)	207

Date	Recipient	Source of Text	Page
		1809 (continued)	
June 25	Henry Drury	MS. Beinecke Library, Yale University	208
June 25	Edward Ellice	MS. National Library of Scotland	209
June 25	Francis Hodgson	MS. Beinecke Library, Yale University	210
June 30	Francis Hodgson	MS. Stark Library, University of Texas	211
June 30	John Hanson	MS. Murray	213
July 3 [2?]	John Hanson	Text: Copy in Murray MSS.	214
July 13	John Hanson	MS. British Museum (Eg. 2611)	214
July 16	Francis Hodgson	Text: Moore, I, 193–194	215
Aug. 6	Francis Hodgson	Text: Moore, I, 194–196	216
Aug. 7	John Hanson	MS. British Museum (Eg. 2611)	217
Aug. 11	His Mother	MS. Morgan Library	218
Aug. 13	John Hanson	MS. British Museum (Eg. 2611)	222
Aug. 14	Mr. Rushton	MS. Murray	222
Aug. 31	John Hanson	MS. British Museum (Eg. 2611)	223
Sept. 15	His Mother	MS. Morgan Library	223
Sept. 18	Capt. Cary	MS. Murray	224
Sept. 29	John Hanson	MS. British Museum (Eg. 2611)	225
Nov. 12	His Mother	MS. Morgan Library	226
Nov. 12	John Hanson	MS. British Museum (Eg. 2611)	231
Nov. 24	John Hanson	MS. British Museum (Eg. 2611)	233
		1810	
March 3	John Hanson	MS. British Museum (Eg. 2611)	234
March 19	His Mother	MS. Morgan Library	234
April 10	His Mother	MS. Morgan Library	235
April 10	John Hanson	MS. British Museum (Eg. 2611)	236

Date	Recipient	Source of Text	Page
		1810 (continued)	
April 17	His Mother	MS. Morgan Library	236
May 3	Henry Drury	MS. Trinity College Library, Cambridge	237
May 5–15	Francis Hodgson	MS. Roe-Byron Coll., Newstead Abbey; P. S., Hodgson, *Memoir*, I, 166–167	240
May 18	His Mother	MS. Morgan Library	242
May 23	John Hanson	MS. British Museum (Eg. 2611)	243
May 24	His Mother	MS. Morgan Library	243
May 29	Capt. Walter Bathurst	MS. Carl H. Pforzheimer Library	244
June 15	John Hanson	MS. British Museum (Eg. 2611)	245
June 17	Henry Drury	Text: Moore, I, 227–228	245
June 20	Doctor ———	MS. Carl. H. Pforzheimer Library	247
June 23	R. C. Dallas	Text: Dallas, *Correspondence*, I, 70	247
June 28	His Mother	MS. Morgan Library	249
June 30	John Hanson	MS. British Museum (Eg. 2611)	252
July 1	James Cawthorn	MS. Morgan Library	252
July 4	Francis Hodgson	Text: Hodgson, *Memoir*, I, 168–170	253
July 4	Edward Ellice	MS. National Library of Scotland	254
July 4	Robert Adair	MS. Murray	256

BIBLIOGRAPHY FOR VOLUMES 1 & 2

(*Principal short title or abbreviated references*)

Airlie, Mabell, Countess of: *In Whig Society* . . . London 1921.

Blessington, Marguerite, Countess of: *Lady Blessington's Conversations of Lord Byron*, ed. Ernest J. Lovell, Jr., Princeton, N.J., 1969.

Borst, William A.: *Lord Byron's First Pilgrimage*, New Haven, 1948.

Dallas, R. C.: *Correspondence of Lord Byron with a Friend*, 3 vols., Paris, 1825.

Elwin, Malcolm: *Lord Byron's Wife*, New York, 1963.

Hobhouse, John Cam: *A Journey through Albania and Other Provinces of Turkey in Europe and Asia, to Constantinople, during the Years 1809 and 1810*, 2nd edn., 2 vols. London, 1813.

[Hodgson, Rev. Francis]: *Memoir of the Rev. Francis Hodgson, B.D.*, by his son, the Rev. James T. Hodgson, 2 vols., London, 1878.

[Lamb, Lady Caroline]: *Glenarvon*, 2nd edn., 3 vols., London, 1816.

LJ—The Works of Lord Byron. A New, Revised and Enlarged Edition. Letters and Journals, ed. Rowland E. Prothero, 6 vols., London 1898–1901.

Marchand, Leslie A.: *Byron: A Biography*, 3 vols., New York, 1957.

Medwin, Thomas: *Medwin's Conversations of Lord Byron*. . . . ed. Ernest J. Lovell, Jr., Princeton, N.J., 1966.

Moore, Thomas: *Memoirs, Journal, and Correspondence*, ed. by the Right Hon. Lord John Russell, 2 vols., New York, 1858.

Moore, Thomas: *Letters and Journals of Lord Byron: with Notices of His Life*, 2 vols., London, 1830.

Poetry—The Works of Lord Byron. A New, Revised and Enlarged Edition. Poetry, ed. Ernest Hartley Coleridge, 7 vols., London, 1898–1904.

Pratt, Willis W.: *Byron at Southwell*, Austin, Texas, 1948.

Appendix III

FORGERIES OF BYRON'S LETTERS

March 30, 1807: To E. N. Long. Sotheby Catalogue, Dec. 20, 1937
Oct. 10 [n.y.] [1808?] [dated from Brighton]: To H. Gaspey. Anderson Galleries, Sale 2007
April 26, 1809: To [Dallas?]. MS. Roe-Byron Coll., Newstead Abbey
April 9, 1810: To His Mother. Schultess-Young, p. 94; *LJ*, I, 259
July 1, 1810: To His Mother. Schultess-Young, pp. 102–104; *LJ*, I, 284–285

BIOGRAPHICAL SKETCHES
OF PRINCIPAL CORRESPONDENTS AND PERSONS
FREQUENTLY MENTIONED

Augusta Byron (later Mrs. George Leigh)

Augusta, born in January 1783, was the daughter of Byron's father by his first wife, Amelia d'Arcy, Baroness Conyers in her own right, the divorced wife of Francis, Marquis of Carmarthen (later the fifth Duke of Leeds). Her mother died shortly after she was born and she was raised by her grandmother, Lady Holderness, who died while Augusta was a young girl. Subsequently she divided her time among several relatives and friends. She did not see her half-brother until he went to Harrow, and then only rarely, but from 1804 onward she corresponded with him frequently. She became his confidante in his quarrels with his mother. Their correspondence was interrupted when Byron went abroad (he was aware that she was hurt by his attack on her cousin Lord Carlisle), and was not resumed until she wrote him on the death of his mother in 1811. She had married in 1807 her first cousin, Col. George Leigh, and bore him a numerous family. Byron saw her again in the summer of 1813, when she came to London about the time that Lady Oxford, his latest flame, had gone abroad with her husband. Not having been raised together, they were almost like strangers and yet shared many traits and sympathies. Before the summer ended they had fallen in love and formed a dangerous liaison from which they struggled in vain to extricate themselves. Augusta encouraged Byron to marry, and when he wed Annabella Milbanke she befriended Lady Byron and did all she could to make the marriage a success. At the time of the Byron separation, rumours of incest were spread, and after Byron went abroad she was persecuted by Lady Byron, but she cherished the memory of her brother to the end of her days in 1851.

Mrs. Catherine Gordon Byron

Byron's mother was proud of her descent from the second Earl of Huntly and his wife Princess Annabella Stewart, daughter of James I of Scotland. She was the daughter of George Gordon, the twelfth laird of Gight, and Catherine Innes, his second cousin. Born in 1765, she was twenty when she married Captain John Byron in 1785. She was somewhat awkward and provincial in accent and manner. She had much capacity for affection, but had a violent temper. During his early years Byron was attached to her and she treated him with indulgence, but his increasing embarrassment and annoyance at her flighty temper eroded his respect and caused many quarrels after he had tasted some freedom at school. From his Harrow days onward he avoided her as much as he could and confided in his half-sister Augusta. It is only fair, however, to say that her character and reputation have rested too exclusively on Byron's own letters and on biographers who saw her only from his point of view, as a virago, one moment kissing her son and the next throwing fire tongs at him. Her own letters show her to have been a woman of warm sympathies and good feeling, abundant good sense, and real love and admiration for her son. She was severely tried by his youthful flightiness and extravagance, but she kept a careful watch on his financial interests, initiated a loan to keep him from going to the usurers, and took meticulous care of the Newstead estate in his absence. She had great pride in his accomplishments and confidence in his future greatness.

ROBERT CHARLES DALLAS

Dallas first sought out Byron in 1808 on the basis of a distant relationship (his sister Henrietta Charlotte had married George Anson Byron, the poet's uncle). Dallas was born in Jamaica in 1754 and had held a lucrative post there, but he returned to England and settled down to literary work. When he met Byron he had already published some poetry, a tragedy, and two novels. He soon became a frequent caller and eventually became Byron's literary agent, arranging for the publication of *English Bards* by Cawthorn and later placing the first two cantos of *Childe Harold* with John Murray. Byron gave him the copyrights and considerable sums in addition, having resolved not to take money for himself for his writing. It was a strange friendship. Dallas tried to impose some of his own ideas and phrases on Byron and to modify his sceptical and radical stanzas. Like Hodgson he attempted to convert Byron to Church of England orthodoxy. Byron bore with his fawning flattery, though he considered him "a *damned* nincom. assuredly", as he told Hobhouse in 1813. But he gave Dallas his letters to his mother written during his first voyage to the East, and these Dallas published together with letters of the poet to himself immediately after Byron's death.

John Hanson

Byron's solicitor and business agent had been introduced to Mrs. Byron by an Aberdeenshire friend. From the time (1798) that George Gordon Byron became the 6th Baron, Hanson took over the management of the Newstead and Rochdale estates, arranged for the young lord's education, persuaded Lord Carlisle to become his guardian, procured an allowance for Mrs. Byron, and took a personal interest in his welfare, seeing that he got proper medical attention for his lame foot, and inviting him to spend holidays with the Hanson family, who were devoted to him. Byron too considered Hanson as a friend and trusted his judgment as business manager and adviser. In his maturity, however, he became increasingly impatient with Hanson's delays in the sale of Newstead and in interminable litigation over Rochdale. He nearly came to a break with Hanson when the lawyer let other matters interfere with the preparation and signing of the papers and settlements connected with Byron's marriage. After he went abroad in 1816, Byron put more and more of his business affairs in the hands of his banker friend Douglas Kinnaird. While Byron remained loyal to his boyhood attachment to the Hanson family, he increasingly mistrusted Hanson's judgment when he saw by contrast how much more efficiently Kinnaird managed his business. Hanson was no doubt earnest in his desire to serve Byron, though he profited greatly from that service, his bill on the sale of Newstead having reached the total of £12,000, which he was slow to render an account of in detail. Hanson died in reduced circumstances in 1841.

John Cam Hobhouse

Hobhouse was born in 1786 and was thus two years older than Byron, with whom he first became friendly at Cambridge in 1807. The oldest son of Benjamin Hobhouse, a Whig M.P., who was created a baronet in 1812, John Cam was a liberal Whig who was later (1820) elected to Parliament from Westminster as a Radical or Reform candidate. Byron was first attracted to him because of their common interest in Juvenalian satire. They soon became fast friends and remained so throughout Byron's life. Byron respected Hobhouse's solid qualities and relied on his judgment, but they also shared a turn for the cynical and the facetious. Byron furnished the money for Hobhouse to accompany him on his first journey to the East in 1809. Hobhouse kept a diary and made notes which he used in his *Journey through Albania* . . . (1813). He was with Byron much during his years of fame in London, and his diary gives valuable sidelights on Byron's activities during those years. He was "groomsman" at Byron's wedding, and stuck by him through the ordeal of the separation, being the last to wave goodbye to him at Dover when he went into voluntary exile in 1816. He joined Byron at Geneva in August of that year, accompanied him to Italy, was with him in Venice and later acted as his cicerone in Rome when Byron was gathering impressions which he wove into the fourth canto of *Childe Harold*, for which Hobhouse wrote historical notes. He returned to England in 1818, but corresponded constantly with him. Byron's letters to Hobhouse are among his most candid and revealing. Hobhouse saw his friend for the last time briefly in Pisa in September 1822. He had hoped to join him in Missolonghi. He was profoundly shocked by Byron's death. In his hysterical concern for Byron's posthumous reputation, he was chiefly responsible for the burning of Byron's Memoirs. In 1851 he was created Baron Broughton de Gyfford.

FRANCIS HODGSON

Born in 1781, Hodgson was seven years Byron's senior. He had been educated at Eton and King's College, Cambridge, where he was resident tutor when Byron met him in 1807. He published in that year his *Translation of Juvenal*, a poem for which Byron had a great liking. Byron was then beginning to write his satire *British Bards*. The fact that both were severely handled by the *Edinburgh Review* and that they both composed literary replies drew them together. A further bond was that Hodgson's father had been a friend of William Gifford, whose edition of Juvenal Byron admired, and whose *Baviad* and *Maeviad* were the immediate models for Byron's satire. Byron revealed frankly his religious scepticism to Hodgson who was ordained in 1812, but that did not dampen their friendship. Byron several times came to Hodgson's assistance with large loans, which were meant as gifts and treated so, when he himself was in financial straits. In all he gave Hodgson £1,500 to clear his father's debts so that he could marry Miss Tayler, a sister of Henry Drury's wife. Byron's friendship with Hodgson lasted through his years of fame but lapsed after he went abroad in 1816.

Elizabeth Pigot and her brother John lived with their mother, widow of John Hollis Pigot, a doctor of physic, just across the South-well green from Burgage Manor, where Mrs. Byron lived during her son's school and college days. The Pigots were Byron's closest friends in the town. When his mother's tantrums drove him out he escaped to the Pigots. Elizabeth, born in 1783, was the oldest of four children. Byron found he could be frank and genuine with her and did not have to play the suitor. He wrote her humorously of his friends and his exploits in Cambridge and London. She never imposed on his friendship and she retained memories and anecdotes of him which she shared with Moore when he was gathering material for his life of Byron.

INDEX OF PROPER NAMES

*Page numbers in italics indicate main references and
Biographical Sketches in the Appendix*

Dickens, Charles, *Pickwick Papers*, 197n

Dogherty, Dan, bout with Belcher, 162n

Drummond, Sir William, 254n

Drury, Benjamin Heath, *182 and n*, 183

Drury, Henry Joseph, and B. at Harrow, 41 and n, 42, 49, *144n*, 152; reconciles him to Butler, 145n; marriage, 144n, 173 and n, 245; at Montem, 247 and n

Drury, Dr. Joseph, 41n, 42n, 73–4; relations with B., 42 and n, 43, 49, 53, 56, 58; retirement, 53 and n, 54, 59, 62, 63

Drury, Mark, 49 and n, 50, 64n

Dubois, Edward, *190 and n*

Duff, Mary, marriage to Robert Cockburn, 116n

Dupont, General, defeat at Baylen, 221n

Dwyer, 247

Edleston, John ('The Cornelian'), 122 and n; object of B.'s *'pure* love and passion', *88n*, 110n, 116n, 118n, 124–5, 232n; appearance, 123; parting from B., 124; verses addressed to, 129n; accused of indecency, 256n

Eldon, John Scott, Lord Chancellor, 191 and n

Ellenborough, Lord, 139n

Ellice, Alexander, 209n

Ellice, Edward, *209nn*, 254

Erskine, Henry David, 121 and n

Erskine, Thomas, 121 and n

Evans, Mr., 42 and n, 49

Falkland, Capt., Charles John Cary, ninth Lord, *192 and n*, 195 and n

Falkner, Dr. T., 102 and n

Fanny, B.'s dog, 126 and n

Farrer, T., 73 and n

Fawcett, General Sir William, *47 and n*

Fielding, Henry, 13; *Tragedy of Tom Thumb*, 186, 208 and n

Fletcher, William, 43n, 161 and n, 163, 244, 249; unhappiness abroad, 10, 229–31, 235, 250; threat to send him home, 10, 244 and n, 249, 252; death of his father, 188; association with prostitutes, 203; Rushton, 203–4

Fox, Charles James, 67n, 113, 236n

Frederick Augustus, Duke of York, *197 and n*

Friese, German servant, 206 and n, 208

Fry, Elizabeth, 23

Gamba Ghiselli, Count Ruggiero, 17

Ganymede, 238

Gardel, 159n

Gell, Sir William, *238 and n*, 239

Geoffrey of Monmouth, 178

George, dragoman, 235n

George III, 113n, 236n

George IV (Prince Regent), 47n

Gibbon, Edward, 242

Gifford, William, 14, 174, 194, and n, 276

Giorgione, 94n

Glennie, Dr., 41 and nn

Glover, Richard, 113

Godolphin, Lord Francis, 60n

Goldsmith, Oliver, 2; *She Stoops to Conquer*, 94

Gordon, Lord Alexander, 130

Gordon, Charles David, 70 and n, 75

Gordon, David, of Abergeldie, 70n

Gordon, George, twelfth laird of Gight, 274

Gordon, Jane, Duchess of Gordon, 130 and n, 132

Gordon, Mr., wine merchant, 220

Graham, Sir B., 165

Grantley, Lord, 40n

Gray, May, *40 and n*

Gregson, Bob, pugilist, 162n, 182 and n

Grenville, William Wyndham Grenville, Lord, 62n, 67n, 113n, *186 and n*

Greville, Lady Charlotte, 19

Grey, Charles, second Lord, 209n

Grey de Ruthyn, Henry Edward, Lord, 46; Newstead, *44n*, 60, 163, 168; detested by B., 49–50, 54, 55, 59, 168n; marriage and death, 222 and n

Grimaldi, Joseph, 152 and n

Guiccioli, Teresa Gamba, Countess, 79n; no ear for B.'s style, 1; liaison with him, 8, 9, 20, 21; alleged abduction, 8; objects to *Don Juan*, 13

Gully, John, 162n, 182n

Hammersley, banker, 202, 205 and n, 214 and n, 233

Hanson family, 51n, 61, 275; country house (Farleigh), 64 and n, 72n, 76 and n

Hanson, Charles, 51n

Hanson, Hargreaves, s. of John, 43, 77n, 81 and n, 128 and n; at Harrow with B., 51n, 62; apprentice to his father, 64 and n; death, 64n

Hanson, Harriet, 51n, 107

Hanson, Capt. James, drowned in *Brazen*, *40 and n*

Hanson, John, 12, 40n, 49, 51, 275; solicitor of the stamp office, 62n, 113 and n; B.'s Court of Chancery allowance, 74n, 78n, 82n, 83, 90 and n, 128 and n; B.'s Rochdale property, 76 and n, 163, 181, 233–234; B.'s Cambridge expenses, 82, 83, 88, 91, 116, 119–20; excuses B.'s mother's behaviour, 85; B.'s mother's pension arrears, 89 and n; health, 107, 175; a mortgage on Newstead, 199 and n; B.'s will, 202 and n; sells B.'s Wymondham copyholds, 203n, 205 and n, 233; B.'s creditors, 256n

Hanson, Mrs. John, 51n

Hanson, Mary Anne, marries Earl of Portsmouth, 51n

Hanson, Newton, unpublished memoir of B., 51n

Hanson and Birch, 128 and n, 205n

Harcourt, General William (later Earl Harcourt), 46 and nn

Hardstaff, Newstead tenant, 183 and n

Harness, William, *154 and n*; favourite of B. at Harrow, 154, 155–6; Speech Day recitation, 166 and n

Hartington, William Spencer, Marquis of, 55 and n, 125 and n; sixth Duke of Devonshire, 55n, 125n, 139 and n

Headford, Marquis and Marchioness of, 132 and n

Henley, John, *Oratory Transactions*, 210 and n

Hero, priestess of Aphrodite, 237n

Hoare 'Pug', 109 and n

Hobhouse, Benjamin, M.P., 275

Hobhouse, John Cam (later first Baron Broughton de Gyfford), 4, 11, 16, 20, 104n, 121 and n, 241, 275–6; Cambridge Whig Club, 139n, 159–60; joint publication with B.,

141 and n, 239 and n, 248; dines at Annesley Hall, 173 and n; lines on Bowles, 188 and n; miscellany, 208, 210; B.'s swimming feats, 215n; in Cintra, 218n; to return to England, 239, 241, 245, 246, 253, 254; his reviews, 248, 253; *Imitations and Translations*, 141n, 239n, 241, 251, 255; *Journey Through Albania*, 276

Hodgson, Rev. Francis, 14–15, 88n, 178, 211–12, 276–7; marriage, 144n; indebtedness to B., 196n, 198, 276; *Lady Jane Grey*, 178n; *Sir Edgar, a Tale*, 246n; *Translations of Juvenal*, 191n, 276

Holderness, Mary Doublet, Countess, 273; Augusta's grandmother, 46n, 52n, 60n

Holland, Henry Fox, third Lord, 16, 157 and n

Homer, 109

Hoppner, R. B., 8

Horace, 145 and n

Houson, Anne, 94 and n, 104 and n, 126 and nn

Howard, Lady Caroline Isabella, 52 and n

Howard, Lady Elizabeth, 52n

Howard, the Hon. Frederick, 61 and n

Howard, Lady Gertrude, friendship with Augusta, 52 and n, 55, 61 and n, 66–7, 68

Hume, David, 14, 15

Hunt, James Henry Leigh, 10

Huntly, second Earl of, 273

Hussein Bey, 231 and n

Hutton, William, *The Battle of Bosworth Field*, 131 and n

Hyacinth and Apollo, 207 and n

Ibrahim Pasha, 226

Innes, Catherine (later Gordon), 274

Ipswich, Lord, 71 and n, 75

Jackson, John ('Gentleman'), 92n, *162 and n*, 169 and n, 170–1

James I, King of Scotland, 273–4

James II, Carnifex, 178

James, ? B.'s servant, 65 and n

Jeffrey, Francis, Lord Jeffrey, 3–4, 11, 193n; thought to have reviewed *Hours of Idleness*, 177n, 178n, 255n

Jeffreys, Judge George, 'Bloody Assizes', 178n
Jekyll, horse-dealer, 170, 171
Jervis, Sir John (later Earl St. Vincent), 220 and n, 244n
Johnson, Dr. Samuel, 53n, 111, 163 and n
João V, 218n
Jones, Rev. Thomas, 79 and n, 80, 100 and n
Josepha, Donna, gives B. a lock of hair, 219 and n
Junot, Andoche, 218n
Justinian, Emperor, 251
Juvenal, imitations by B. and Hobhouse, 141 and n; *Satires*, 194 and n

Keats, John B., 11
Kelham, William, 222n
Kemble, John Philip, 63n
Kemmis, James, 176 and n
King, money-lender, 89n
Kinnaird, Douglas James William, 4, 12, 139n, 274
Knight, Payne, 158

LaFayette, Marie-Joseph, marquis de, 16
Lamb, Lady Caroline (née Caroline Ponsonby), 4–5, 221n
Lauderdale, Lord 158
Laurie, Dr., and B.'s club foot, 41n
Lavender, Nottingham 'quack', 39n
Leacroft, Mr. and Mrs., 104–5, 106, 131n
Leacroft, Capt. John, 104 and n, 105–6, 127 and n
Leacroft, Julia, *51 and n*, 94n, 104 and n, 116
Leake, William Martin, 237; Resident at court of Ali Pasha, 227 *and n*
Leander, 237 and n, 242–3, 243–4, 250
Leigh, General Charles, 44n, 60n
his son's marriage to Augusta, 52 and n, 86
Leigh, Frances, 60n
Leigh, Col. George, 47n, 60, 180; marriage to Augusta, 44n, 165n, 273; Equerry to Prince of Wales, 165 and n
Leigh, Georgiana Augusta, 179 and n
Leinster, third Duke of, 125 and n
Le Sage, René, *Gil Blas*, 111 and n
Lewis, Matthew Gregory ('Monk'), 21

Litchfield, inn-keeper in Cambridge, 122 and n
Little, Thomas, *see* Moore, Thomas
Long, E. B., death of his son, 200 and n
Long, Edward Noel, 73 and n, 95 and n, 97n, 109 and n; in the Guards, 114 and n, 115nn, 118, 151, 200n; to dine at the Pantheon, 152 and n; death in the *St. George*, 200 and n
Long Henry, 119 and n, 151
Longman, Hurst, Rees and Orme, 132n, 141n
Lowe, Rev. Robert, 203 and n
Lucy (Lucinda), 187, *189 and n*, 232n; annuity, 189n, 191
Ludwig, John Frederick, of Ratisbon, 218n
Lyttelton, first (or second) Lord, 113
Lyttelton, George, first Baron, 146 and n
Lyttelton, Thomas, second Baron, 146 and n

Macdiarmid, John, *Lives of British Statesmen*, 141 and n
Mackenzie, Sir Alexander, *Voyages from Montreal . . .*, 256 and n
Mackenzie, Henry, 111 and n, 112, 113
Macri, Mrs. Tarsia, and daughters, 240 and n
Mahmout Pasha, 231 and n, 249–50, 254
Mahmud II, Sultan, 242 and n
Maitland, Sir Thomas, 239n
Maltby, Harriet, 127 and n
Malthus, Thomas Robert, 6
Mansel, William Lord, Master of Trinity, *81 and n*, 92 and n
Marat, Jean-Paul, 16
Marlowe, Christopher, *Tamburlaine*, 216n
Massingberd (née Waterhouse), Mrs. Elizabeth, *82 and n*, 122 and n; guarantor of B.'s loan, 87n, 93 and n, 166 and n, 183 and n
Massingberd, Capt. Thomas, R.N., 82n
Matthews, Charles Skinner, 81n
Mayfield, Mr., Birthday Ode to B., 188, 194
Mealey, Owen, 43 and n, 121 and n, 168 and n, 189
Medwin, Thomas, 1, 15
Mehmet III, Sultan, 250n

285

Melbourne, Lady (née Elizabeth Milbanke), 4–5, 6–7, 19
Melville, Henry Dundas, Viscount, 66 and n
Mercer-Elphinstone, Miss, 231n
Milbanke, Annabella (later Lady Byron), 7, 19; accepts B.'s proposal, 5; friendship with Augusta, 273
Mirabeau, Honoré-Gabriel, Comte de 16
Mitchell, Mr., saddler, 144 and n, 148–149
Mitford, Mary Russell, 154n
Mitford, William, *History of Greece*, 20–1
Molière, *L'Avare*, 52 and n
Montagu, Lady Mary Wortley, 189–190, 250 and n
Montesquieu, Baron, 'The Spirit of Laws', 148 and n
Moore, Sir John, 239n
Moore, Thomas, 14, 15, 158, 277; bowdlerizes B.'s letters, 4; on the Newstead ghost, 39n; influence on B., 103n; *The Poetical Works of the late Thomas Little*, 13; pseudonomous publication, 132n, 141 and n
Mortlock, Mr., ? Mayor of Cambridge, 92 and n
Mouctar Pasha, 231n
Murad III, Sultan, 250n
Murray, Joe, at Newstead, 138 and n, 176, 181, 189, 206; sent home to England, 221, 244
Murray, John, 142, 143, 248; literary coterie, 3; relationship with B., 4, 11, 12, 13; *Childe Harold*, 274

Naldi, Giuseppi, baritone, 195 and n
Napoleon, 77 and n, 224, 228
Norton, Miss, 40n

Oakes, General Sir Hildebrand, Commander in Malta, 224 and n, *239 and n*
O'Callaghan, George, 139n
O'Hare, Kate, adaptation of Fielding's *Tom Thumb*, 208n
Origo, Iris, 1
Ormonde, seventeenth Earl of, 125n
Osborne, Lady Mary, 60n
Osborne, Lord Sidney Godolphin, *45 and n*
Ossian, 130n, 132n, 163 and n

Oxford, Countess of (Jane Elizabeth Scott), 273

Palethorpe, tenant, 183 and n
Palmer, Rev. John, Professor of Arabic, 172 and n
Parker (née Byron), Charlotte Augusta, *39n 1*, 175n
Parker, Christopher, 39n, 175n
Parker, Margaret, 39n
Parker, Sir Peter, 39n 1, 175 and n
Parkyns, Fanny, 39n
Parkyns family, 39 and n, 149n, 196, 206 and n
Parkyns, George Augustus Henry Anne, second Baron Rancliffe, 39n
Parkyns, Mrs., *39 and n*
Pearce, Henry, 139n, 158 and n
Pearson, Dr., and B.'s health, 157, 158, 160
Pedro de Cevallos, Don, 193n
Perceval, Lady, possible identification, 185 and n
Perry, James, ed. *Morning Chronicle*, 190n
Petronius, *Satyricon*, 207 and n
Petty, Lord Henry (later Marquis of Lansdowne), 118 and n
Phillips, Thomas, 231n
Pigot family, 93 and nn, 94 and n, 125n, 136n
Pigot, Elizabeth Bridget, 88n, *93n*, 94 and nn, 125n, 203n; draws the Byron Arms, 50 and n; interest in Edleston, 124
Pigot, Henry, 51 and n, 136n
Pigot, John M.B., *93 and n*, 99, 100 and n, 136n; medical student in Edinburgh, 111n, 112n, 117 and n
Pigot, John Hollis, f. of above, 277
Pigot, Richard, 136n
Pillans, James, *191 and n*
Piozzi, Mrs., 53n
Pitt, William, 186
Ponsonby, Sarah, *125 and n*
Ponsonby, W., 139n
Pope, Alexander, 12, 13, 14, 134
Portland, William Henry Cavendish, third Duke of, 113n, 177 and n, 192 and n; B.'s Indian proposal, 179 and n; indebtedness to him, 201 and n, 202, 203

Portsmouth, Earl of, marriage to Miss Norton (1799), 40 and n; marriage to Mary Anne Hanson (1814), 51n
Poussin, Nicolas, 94
Pratt, Samuel Jackson, 163
Purvis, Admiral, 221
Pye, Henry James, *188 and n*

Quinn, George, 132n

Ridge, John, and *Hours of Idleness*, 125 and nn, 126n, 127, 129n, 130, 138; *Fugitive Pieces*, 96 and n, 97, 98, 125n; *Poems Original and Translated*, 137 and n, 144
Robespierre, Maximilien François de, 16
Roche, Eugenius, ed. *Monthly Literary Recreations*, 129n, 130n
Rodney, Admiral Lord, 244n
Rogers, 'Dummer', 39 and n
Rogers, Samuel, 6, 10
Romilly, Sir Samuel, 11
Rosel, Elizabeth and Gervase, 82n
Rousseau, Jean-Jacques, 13, 94n, 171 and n
Rushton, Robert, protegé of B., 187 and n, 194 and n, 202n, 222; Fletcher and, 203 and n; to go abroad with B., 204 and n, 206; sent home to England, 221–2, 244, 252
Rushton, Miss, 251 and n, 252
Rutland, Henry, fifth Duke of, K.G., 67n; marriage, 52n

St. Crispin, 194n
St. Paul, 148, 240
Salvo, Marquis de, 224 and n
Sanders, George, 197n, 206n, 243, 251
Sappho, 246n
Savage, B.'s Newfoundland dog, 120, 123n
Sawbridge, Col., lends B. money, 205 and n, 214n
Schultess-Young, Henry Schultes, *The Unpublished Letters of Lord Byron*, 26
Scott, Sir Walter, 2, 14, 20
'Lay of the Last Minstrel', 227
Sebright, John, 162n
Segatti, Marianna, 8
Shakespeare, William, 2, 4
B.'s Speech Day declamation, 69n,

166n; *II Henry IV*, 216nn; *King Lear*, 146 and n; *Macbeth*, 96, 182 and n, 241n; *Merry Wives of Windsor*, 216n; *Much Ado About Nothing*, 162 and n; *The Tempest*, 109
Sheldrake, T., and B.'s club foot, 41 and n, 43
Shelley, Percy Bysshe, 10, 11
Sheridan, Richard Brinsley, 19, 21, 22, 113
Sidmouth, Henry Addington, first Viscount, *186 and n*
Sinclair, George, 156 and n
Sinclair, Sir John, 156n
Smith, Abel (?), 122 and n
Smith, Mrs. Constance Spencer, love affair with B., *224 and n*
Smith, Sir H., 162 and n
Smollett, Tobias George, 13, 173
Smut, bulldog, 132
Socrates, 21, 148
Southey, Robert, 10, 11, 158; possible contributor to *Edinburgh Review*, 177 and n; *Thalaba*, 127n
Spencer, Georgiana Dorothy, 125n
Staël, Mme de, 9, 13; *Corinne*, 8
Stewart, Princess Annabella, 273
Stewart, Dugald, 214n
Strané, consul at Patras, 229, 230, 232, 233; in *Spider*, 229n
Strangford, Percy Clinton Smythe, Viscount, 137, 158
Swimmer (?), Dr., 51 and n

Tattersall, John Cecil, 65 and n., 109 and n; 'Davus' of 'Childish Recollections', 145 and n
Tavistock, Marquis of, 125 and n., 139n
Tayler, Ann Caroline, marriage to Henry Drury, 144n, 173n, 276
Tayler, Miss, sister of above, marriage to Francis Hodgson, 276
Thomas, money-lender, 205 and n
Tooke, Horne, 186n
Trevanions, the, 165n, 191
Trevanion, Sophia, marriage to Admiral Byron, 135n, 165 and n, 195n
Twiddie, Mr., possible contributor to *Monthly Mirror*, 150 and n
Tyrtaeus, 176 and n

Veli Pasha, *226 and n*, 231n
Vestris, Gaetano, 159n

287

Victor, Claude, Duc de Belluno, at Talavera, 217n, 221n
Virgil, 115, 118, 125 and n
Viscillie (Basili), 228 and n.
Voltaire, François Marie Arouet de, 14, 15

Wallace, Capt., 165 and n, 184 and n, 187
Ward, John William (later first Earl of Dudley and Ward), *214 and n*
Wardle, Col. Gwyllym, charges against Duke of York, *197 and n*
Waterhouse, Anne, 82n
Watson, Major, 172 and n
Webster, Lady Francis, 5, 6, 8, 10, 19, 171n
Webster, Sir Godfrey, 165
Webster, (Sir) James Wedderburn, 6, 10, *171 and n*
Wellesley, Sir Arthur (later Duke of Wellington), at Talavera, 217n, 221n
Westmorland, Lady (née Jane Saunders), *221 and n*
Westmorland, tenth Earl of, 221n
Whitaker, Mrs. 122 and n
Whitehead, William (gamekeeper), 149 and n

Whitehead, William, 161n
Wilkes, John, 161n
William, servant to Mrs. Byron, 43 and n
Windham, William ('Weathercock'), *186 and n*
Wingfield, John ('Alonzo'), *101 and n*, 109n, 119, 154, 176
Wolcot, John (Peter Pindar), 174n
Woodhouselee, Alexander Fraser Tytler, Lord, *112 and n*, 113
Wordsworth, William, 10, 14; B. reviews his *Poems*, 129 and n, 130
Wousky (dog), 94 and n
Wright, Walter Rodwell, 248 and n
Wylde and Co., 149n, 196n

Xenophon, *Retreat of the Ten Thousand*, 21
Xerxes, 115

York, Frederick Augustus, Duke of, 132
Young, Edward, 113; *The Revenge*, 63 and n, 170 and n

Zantachi, Andreas, 235 and n